THE LIVING WORD COMMENTARY
ON THE OLD TESTAMENT

Editor
John T. Willis

Associate Editor
David G. Jones

Psalms

Psalms

Anthony L. Ash
and
Clyde M. Miller

שְׁמַע יִשְׂרָאֵל יְהוָה
אֱלֹהֵינוּ יְהוָה אֶחָד׃

SWEET PUBLISHING COMPANY

Austin, Texas

LIBRARY OF CONGRESS CATALOG CARD NUMBER 79-67300

ISBN 0-8344-0114-2

PRINTED IN U.S.A.

Acknowledgment

This commentary is based on the text of the Revised Standard Version of the Bible, copyrighted 1946, 1952, 1971, and 1973 by the Division of Christian Education, National Council of Churches, and used by permission.

Writers in *The Living Word Commentary* series have been given freedom to develop their own understanding of the biblical text. As long as a fair statement is given to alternative interpretations, each writer has been permitted to state his own conclusions. Beyond the general editorial policies, the editors have sought no artificial uniformity, and differences are allowed free expression. A writer is responsible for his contribution alone, and the views expressed are not necessarily the views of the editors or publisher.

5 4 3 2 1

Contents

Abbreviations

AB	Anchor Bible
ASV	American Standard Version
BDB	F. Brown, S. R. Driver, and C. A. Briggs, *A Hebrew and English Lexicon of the Old Testament*. Oxford: Clarendon Press, 1957
KJV	King James Version
LXX	The Septuagint
MT	The Masoretic Text
NASB	New American Standard Bible
NEB	New English Bible
SBB	Soncino Books of the Bible
TOTC	Tyndale Old Testament Commentary

Preface

The joint authorship of a commentary entails both disadvantages and advantages. One of the disadvantages is the difficulty in consolidating the work of both authors. Ideally, we could have wished for constant mutual consultation. Unfortunately, we were separated by a distance of a thousand miles, and such contacts were severely limited. However, they were delightful when they did occur, and the authors discovered a most encouraging likeness of basic viewpoint and approach. Indeed, we are in general agreement, with no significant disagreement at all. The reader will, of course, notice variations in the way materials are handled in the two halves of the book. (The introduction and the commentary on Psalms 1–75 are by Ash, and the commentary on Psalms 76–150 is by Miller.) There may also be some overlapping in the discussions. These things seem inevitable. But any differences in method occur under the umbrella of a controlling unity of perspective. An advantage of joint authorship is that the reader is offered a diversity. He can note the work of both men and, hopefully, gain from each one something that might not have been gained from the other.

Everyone should write a commentary on Psalms. Though both authors had taught this material for some years previously, a richness has broken forth from the text under the discipline of learning in order to write. It is rewarding beyond expression to begin with the original text and work carefully, verse by verse, concept by concept, to the commentary form. So many things break into the mind in the process of research and prolonged reflection on these materials. Some are retained, and some are transient. Some can be expressed, and some defy capture in words. Yet all leave a deposit of enhanced appreciation and augmented faith with the student. Or so we have found in doing this work. We hope you will find it also, as you employ the fruit of our labors. May all be to God's glory.

I

Introduction

Anthony L. Ash

It has been said that somewhere in the Psalms can be found a reflection of virtually every religious experience known to man, and that the person familiar with the Psalter can find balm for every wound. This may not be strictly true, but it certainly reflects the high regard in which this material has been held over the centuries by those who have benefited from its richness. Here theology, worship, and daily living are blended. Poorer, indeed, is the individual who has not learned to drink from this source. It is hoped that these notes will open the pathway to the fountain of the Psalms for those who have not trodden it, and that it will make a familiar walk even more rewarding for those who have gone that way before.

POETRY OUTSIDE THE PSALTER

In Other Cultures

Considerable material has been discovered from various ancient Near Eastern cultures illustrating their use of poetry. It comes from the civilizations of the Tigris-Euphrates River Valley, from Egypt, and from pre-Israelite Canaan and Phoenicia. Much of it pre-dates the biblical psalms. When this material is compared with our Psalter, the similarities are apparent. There are likenesses of form and phraseology, as well as in the use of metaphorical and illustrative materials. There are also resemblances in religious concepts, for example, the praise of the supreme God, Creator of heaven and earth.

Since these materials are prior to the biblical psalms, there is wide agreement that the Hebrews borrowed forms of poetry that came to them from their world. That they also borrowed content from outside is not so generally conceded. Whether they did or not, the biblical poetry clearly reflects the uniqueness of Israel's faith, which was produced by Yahweh's covenant revelation of himself. Yahweh is above all gods and nature. There is constant reference to election and covenant. There is a grasp of the relation of the glory of the Creator and the glory of the Redeemer. The king has a lesser role in the biblical psalms and is nowhere considered divine. If "pagan" language was adopted, it was understood in a new way. It was purged of any conceptions that would contradict "the faith" and brought in line with Israel's religion.

In the Bible

Poetry in Israel was used in a broad variety of situations, as a consideration of the circumstances indicated by the various psalms will show. Thus it is to be expected that other parts of the OT would also contain materials similar in form to the Psalms. Some instances of this are found in Exodus 15:1-18; Deuteronomy 32:1-43; 1 Samuel 2:1-10; Isaiah 38:10-20; Jonah 2:3-10; and Habakkuk 3:2-19. Note particularily the laments of Jeremiah, in 11:18ff.; 15:15ff.; 17:12ff.; 18:18ff.; and 20:7ff.

A close examination of the materials outside the Psalter shows that some of the poems fit closely in the contexts in which they are found, while others seem to have a looser connection (i.e., not all the details "fit"). These latter cases suggest that upon occasion a psalm could be taken from an original setting and applied to another where it was felt appropriate (much as we do with Bible verses in some of our hymns). This may show that such poetic material was meant to be applied wherever it could be helpful. That would give it an enduring value, as it has indeed proved to have. One can imagine among the people a growing "fund" of poetry from which withdrawals could be made when the need arose.

This poetry has proved valuable as a comparative device against which to set the psalms in the Psalter, in regard to matters like style, historical context, modes of usage, etc.

In Israel, after the OT

The writing of poetry did not cease with the end of the OT period. Psalms are found in the intertestamental period (cf. the Psalms of Solomon), as well as in the NT (cf. Luke 1:46-55, 68-79).

Since the selections in the Psalter were not originally written for that collection, the question is raised as to why these 150 were chosen and not some of the others we have noted. No definite answer can be given, though it has been suggested that those omitted may already have been included as part of another work or, in some cases, may have been written too late for inclusion in some part of the Psalter. Yet it is interesting that Psalm 18 is also found in 2 Samuel 22.

HISTORY OF THE BOOK OF PSALMS

Collection

How, then, did the Psalter reach its present form? There seems no doubt that a number of smaller collections were brought together, though some psalms may have had a solitary history before inclusion in a grouping. Evidences of the earlier collections can be found in the headings (e. g., all those bearing the same name, as David or Asaph, or with a common occasion, as 120–134—Psalms of Ascents) and in the characteristic uses of the divine name (Pss. 1–41, 84–89, 91–150 prefer Yahweh, while 42–83 prefer Elohim). Psalm 72:20 speaks of an end of the psalms of David, indicating that this psalm may have concluded a collection (though other psalms of David occur later). There are doublets (14 with 53; 40:13-17 with 70:1-5; 108 and 57:7-11 with 60:5-12), suggesting these materials were found in separate collections, which those combining the collections were loathe to delete.

There are still questions to be answered. Why was the collection made? Certainly for worship. The Psalter has been called "the hymn book of the second temple." But many scholars insist that one should not so restrict the collectors' motives, for they may have intended to gather the poetry of the people for whatever beneficial purpose it might have served. Worship, after all, can occur on other than corporate occasions.

Why were there only 150 psalms included, and what is the rationale for the order in which they are found? Ingenious attempts have been made to answer these questions by attempting to analyze their use in some liturgical pattern, but nothing conclusive has been demonstrated. It does seem likely that Psalm 1 was deliberately chosen to open the collection. Perhaps Psalm 150 was consciously chosen to close it with a ringing orchestra of praise.

Why are the Psalms divided into five books (1–41; 42–72; 73–89; 90–106; 107–150)? The best suggestion is that this was a deliberate correspondence with the five books of the Law.

The collection was certainly complete by the third century B.C. when the LXX was translated. The collection was called by the Jews *tehillim* (songs of praise), but later with the LXX, the term Psalms was given to the book. Neither title is exactly appropriate to all the collection, but the latter has prevailed, albeit with some broadening of its meaning.

The Headings

Most psalms have a heading or superscription. Though some older translations numbered them as part of the text of the psalm, they actually form no part of the original writing. They can be divided into three classifications. (1) Some have to do with the form or performance of the psalm. These include such terms as "according to the Gittith," "according to the Hind of the Dawn," Maskil, Miktam, etc. The exact meaning of many of these terms is uncertain. For further information a good Bible dictionary or encyclopedia should be consulted. (2) Other psalms contain the names of various persons. (3) Finally, a few (3, 7, 18, 30, 34, 51, 52, 54, 56, 57, 59, 60, 63, and 142) have notes describing a historical situation from which the psalm is said to have come.

These headings were added to the psalms by Jewish scholars some time after they were written. We do not know if they were based on traditions or upon conclusions drawn from comparative studies of passages. If the former, we cannot assess the accuracy of the traditions. In some cases the contents of the psalms do not coincide with the headings (cf. Ps. 51:18f.), though it is possible that such difficulties may be due to a later editing. The ascription "to David" could mean "for David" or "belonging to David" (i. e., to a Davidic collection; the heading to Ps. 18 may be an exception), though certainly many psalms could have been by David himself. Though the superscriptions are not infallible, one can take them seriously and use them for guidance unless there is convincing evidence to lead to a different conclusion. However, since the evidence of the headings is characterized by some uncertainty, it is risky to use them as the major key to interpreting the psalms.

Original Purpose (Authorship and Date)

We have alluded to the reason for the collection of the psalms. We must now ask why they were originally written. To understand the answers to this much-debated question, and to prepare the way for later discussions of other matters, it is appropriate to review the history of psalm studies. According to one analysis, four stages can be discerned. The following descriptions will of necessity be somewhat general, so there could be variation within each.

The "traditional" approach. This perspective held the field until the advent of higher criticism in the last half of the nineteenth century and still finds its advocates today. The psalms were collected by Ezra for use in the second temple (after 515 B.C.). The headings were considered completely reliable, so that a psalm was interpreted in terms of its heading. This often involved connection with an episode in the OT historical books and an extensive interpretation of the psalm in light of those details. Further, since seventy-three psalms had Davidic headings, they were considered to be written by him. In addition to the guidance of the headings, the psalms were interpreted in terms of the NT. Psalms about the king were interpreted of Christ. Much in the Psalter was considered as predictive prophecy of the Christian period. Christian meanings were frequently found in the psalms, sometimes by the use of allegorical interpretation. The thrust of this method was to consider the uniqueness of each psalm, rather than any common elements that might bind psalms in like classifications.

The literary-critical approach. Due to the influence of B. Duhm and J. Wellhausen, psalm studies swung to the opposite extreme in the last half of the nineteenth century. Duhm and Wellhausen postulated a development of Israel's religion in which "natural" and "prophetic" stages were followed by a "priestly" period—to which the psalms belonged. The Psalter was dated very late, even, in some cases, into the second century B.C. Indeed, the psalms were not collected, but were written, then. Thus the headings were of no value in determining date, authorship, or historical circumstances of the psalms. What historical interpretation was given was in terms of the circumstances of these later centuries (fifth to second centuries B.C.). The royal psalms (since there were no more kings at that time) were sometimes applied to the Maccabean rulers (mid-second century B.C.). The psalms were no longer seen as messianic or predictive. Thus the relation to the NT in a prophetic sense was discarded. The common features in the psalms were considered a mark of stylized methods of composition.

The "form-critical" approach. Here we must deal with one of the most important figures in the history of psalm studies—Hermann Gunkel. Beginning about the turn of the twentieth century, Gunkel pioneered an approach which recognized and emphasized the common elements in the psalms, and which appropriated for study poetic material found elsewhere in the OT and the ancient Near East. His work centered in two foci—an analysis of the "types" into which the psalms fell and an attempt to discover the life situation from which each type arose. This assumed each type, or category, of psalms was derived from a given life situation in which it found its origin and initial use. Gunkel made an exhaustive analysis of the psalms in terms of language, structure, ideas, themes, etc., and found various types emerging. Then, from evidence within the psalms, and by comparison with similar materials within and without the Bible, he sought to discover whence each type originated. He concluded that the beginning point for the psalm types was the public worship of Israel, in its various facets. Israel did everything in songs. In the worship, word and act were combined. Some types retained this usage, while others were separated from their original context and came to be used by individuals as "spiritual songs." This development took place under prophetic influence. Psalms composed later (which comprised most of those in the Psalter), while retaining the earlier forms to a greater or lesser extent, were written for use outside the cultic context. These same psalms, however, with their inclusion in the Psalter, came to be used in worship, thus returning to the source whence they had sprung.

Psalms in which the individual's complaint were dominant used a form originally employed in worship ritual beseeching God's healing and forgiving mercy in times of sickness. In the developmental process, the forms came to be altered, and new forms emerged. One form, the wisdom poem, did not originate in the sanctuary worship.

Gunkel found five main psalm types and several subtypes. The main types were (1) hymns; (2) community laments; (3) individual thanks; (4) individual laments; and (5) royal psalms. Though Gunkel's analysis has subsequently been variously modified, the basic premise of type division has so commended itself that it remains as a given of virtually all subsequent psalm study. Later in this introduction we shall describe the psalm types more completely as preparation for the commentary proper.

This approach moved away from the importance of individual authors and the individual historical interpretations of the psalms. It also moved the psalms back much earlier in Israel's history than had been allowed by the literary-critical method, though generally not as early as David's time, as with the older traditional interpretation. Stress was now given to the elements shared by the psalms and to their place within the praise life of Israel.

The cultic approach. This perspective derived its chief impetus from Sigmund Mowinckel, a Norwegian scholar who had studied under Gunkel, and who built upon the foundation which the latter had laid. Operating with a stronger conviction of the continuing importance of the cult in Israel's life than had characterized Gunkel, Mowinckel maintained that nearly all the psalms originated and continued to be used in the cult. He disagreed with Gunkel regarding the development of spiritual songs.

Mowinckel's view led to his more intensive investigations of the nature of Israel's worship. This was not the easiest of tasks, since the material within the psalms and in the rest of the OT did not yield a great deal of evidence of specific worship contexts to which various psalms could be definitively connected.

Therefore, Mowinckel turned to extra-biblical materials for illumination. His most significant conclusion was to posit an annual autumn Enthronement Festival, at which, in a dramatic ritual, Yahweh was re-enthroned as king over the people. This concept has engendered much discussion, pro and con, and has led to other modified views which still retain the cultic emphasis. Artur Weiser, for example, suggests a Covenant Renewal Festival, held each autumn, in which there was an appropriate ritual, and for which many psalms were composed. H. J. Kraus argues for a Royal Zion Festival, held in Jerusalem on the first day of the Feast of Tabernacles, which celebrated God's choice of the Davidic dynasty and the selection of Jerusalem as the religious and political center of the nation.

Since the Enthronement Festival theory has influenced subsequent psalm studies, and since it relates to the question of the usage of many psalms, it seems pertinent to discuss it here. Mowinckel began with Psalms 47, 93, and 96–99, which Gunkel identified as coronation psalms. He argued that the expression "the Lord reigns" should be rendered "Yahweh has become king." This indicated, to him, a festival at which Yahweh was symbolically enthroned, and which celebrated his creative triumph over chaos (Gen. 1) as well as his military victories. In a procession in which God's presence was symbolized by the ark, he was acclaimed again by the people as the king, vindicating his elect, and making all things new. Operating with a parallel ceremony in Babylon (which he later indicated came to Israel through Canaanite channels), and with some late rabbinic materials, as well as with inductions from the biblical texts, Mowinckel drew over forty psalms into the orbit of his theory.

Those objecting to Mowinckel's thesis are disturbed by his assumptions regarding the interpretation of the phrase "the Lord reigns" because he seems to draw more from the OT than the evidence warrants, because he stresses parallels with a Babylonian festival, and because he uses late rabbinic sources to document earlier practices. Since there is no unequivocal evidence in the OT for an Enthronement Festival (which some think strange if it was so important), a number of reputable scholars have rejected Mowinckel's conjecture completely. Others have kept it as a working hypothesis, modifying it as they have felt the evidence demanded.

The effect of the cultic approach, like the form-critical, has been to diminish the importance of seeking for an author of a given psalm (though Mosinckel does seek to show that they were written by poets from the temple singers—so that worshipers could find psalms appropriate to their needs). It is generally granted by those with this perspective that many psalms can be earlier than the form critics allowed. Though the cultists would not affirm Davidic authorship of the psalms bearing his name, they would maintain that they could have come from his time.

In this commentary, it is recognized that many psalms

relate to the cultic life of Israel. However, rather than pressing the psalms into any cultic mold, each is allowed to speak for itself. If the content of the psalm implies acts of worship, that is noted. If not, the other emphases of the psalm are discussed. In this way it is hoped that the notes will be of abiding spiritual value, even with the coming and going of theories of their use in Israel's worship.

Further, the psalms are virtually impossible to date. In past years commentators have tried to date each psalm and to arrange them in chronological order. Examination of such works reveals that they are exercises in futility. In the rare cases when a psalm gives some internal indication of date, that is discussed here. Otherwise, concerns of dating and authorship are eschewed.

However, with regard to the authorship of the psalms, another line of evidence must be considered. Numerous psalms are quoted in the NT, and with six of them there is an ascription to David. Psalm 2:1-2 is quoted in a prayer to God, "who by the mouth of. . .David. . .didst say by the Holy Spirit" (Acts 4:24-25). Psalm 16:8-11 is quoted in Acts 2:25-28, with the formula "for David says." Romans 4:6ff. quotes Psalm 32:1-2 with the words, "So also David pronounces a blessing." Psalms 69:26 and 109:8 are cited in Acts 1:20, in which context Acts 1:16 says, "the scripture . . . which the Holy spirit spoke beforehand by the mouth of David." Finally, Psalm 110:1 is quoted in Mark 12:36 (parallel Matt. 22:43-44 and Luke 10:42) and is ascribed to David by Jesus (with Matthew and Mark mentioning his inspiration by the Holy Spirit). Traditionally this evidence has been considered decisive for Davidic authorship. Adherents of this view have felt that if the NT were in error in this regard, then it might as well be unreliable at any other place, including even important passages bearing on salvation. If the NT authors, and Jesus himself, proved to be liars, then the whole NT and Christian faith would be reduced to an uncertain shambles, they argue.

On the other side of the issue, many scholars argue that these NT references are simply reflecting the Jewish tradition that associated the Psalter as a whole with David, "the sweet singer of Israel." By this method, to say "David said" was to say material was from the Psalms, regardless of the true author. To refer to a book by its traditional title was not considered inaccurate or fraudulent, they argue. Many writings in antiquity were written pseudonymously (e.g., many books in the Apocrypha and Pseudepigrapha), and later references to those books used the authors' pen names with no sense of deception. Even in the Bible, Jude (vs. 14) refers to the prophecy of Enoch, which was certainly not from the Enoch of Genesis 4:21-24, but can be found in the pseudonymous Book of Enoch (1:9), dated in the third to first centuries B.C.

Each reader will need to make his own decision on these matters. If a psalm commends itself by content and by Jewish traditional ascription as being by David, so be it. On the other hand, one must be careful to allow for a first century use of tradition which was fully in accord with the customs of the times.

THE CONTENTS OF THE PSALTER

Text

Introduction. In the late 1930s Fleming James, in his *Thirty Psalmists*, delineated a number of reasons why the psalms are difficult to understand. These include:

> the absence in Hebrew of words giving the logical connection between sentences; the vagueness of the expressions used, so that one often cannot tell exactly what is meant; the way in which passion leads to exaggerated language whose literal significance can only be guessed at; the impossibility of knowing whether the Hebrew tenses refer to past, present, or future; the laconic brevity of style . . . the poor condition of the text.

In addition, there are Hebrew words (e.g., prepositions) that have such flexibility it is hard to know just how to translate them, and there are expressions susceptible to any of several legitimate translations. One should not become unduly pessimistic because of these observations.

Yet they expose problems of which the reader should be aware, and which can in part be resolved by an awareness of the material to be discussed below.

Poetic style and metre. Appreciation of the nature of Hebrew poetry was given its greatest impetus by the work of Bishop Robert Lowth of England (1753), who introduced to a wider public the idea of parallelism in Hebrew poetry. This involved the repetition of part or all of a thought in a second line, and even sometimes in a third. Various sorts of parallelism have been discerned in the Psalter (and other OT poetry). The commonest types are *synonymous* (the second line repeats the ideas of the first, in the same arrangement—cf. Pss. 2:2; 10:3, 7; 61:2); *antithetic* (the second line contains a contrast to the first—cf. Pss. 20:7-8; 32:10); *synthetic* (not necessarily a thought repetition, but yet a connection between the lines—cf. Pss. 3:4; 34:16; 96:1; 118:8, 22; 119:9, 13; 127:1; 135:16); and *climactic*, or *stairstep* (a part of the previous line is repeated with a further development—cf. Pss. 114:5; 136:21-22). In addition, other types of parallelism have been discovered by various students. An understanding of parallelism can often be helpful in interpreting a passage, especially where one member of the parallel would be otherwise difficult to understand.

Hebrew poetry is also characterized by a metric structure, the rhythm of which is difficult to reproduce in translation. Rather than the number of syllables in a verse, as in classic poetry, Hebrew poetry is characterized by the number of beats, or accents, per line. The rhythm most found is 3:3, but there are also frequent occurrences of 3:2, and, more rarely, 2:2. Though some of the older commentators would emend the text quite freely on metric considerations, the changes, even within one psalm, from one metric structure to another suggest that this method should be used only with great discretion.

Some psalms are acrostics, that is, successive lines or sections of the psalm begin with successive letters of the Hebrew alphabet. Psalms 9-10, 25, 34, 37, 111-112, 119, and 145 belong to this category. It has been conjectured that this device may have been a memory aid. Acrostics usually flow less freely, due to the restriction imposed by composing within an alphabetic scheme.

Emendations and translations. One who reads the psalms in Hebrew discovers a number of instances where the text is simply unintelligible. Reasons for this could be because we lack information about the meaning of the original text, or because our best manuscripts have a text which has not been accurately transmitted, or because the vowels (added by the Massoretes in the fifth to ninth centuries A.D.) confuse rather than clarify the meaning. It is sometimes possible to remedy these difficulties when there are two accounts, or doublets (e.g., Pss. 14 and 53; Ps. 18 and 2 Sam. 22; etc.). But in other cases, translators must resort to textual emendations, or changes, to obtain a sensible reading. This process is not done arbitrarily. Parallel passages are used for guidance, where available. Ancient translations (as the LXX, Aquila, Symmachus, Theodotion [all in Greek], Syriac, Jerome's Vulgate) or the Targums (Aramaic paraphrases of Scripture) are consulted for their possible witness to a better reading. Word usages in other parts of the OT may be compared. As a last resort, the translators may make what is felt to be a logical conjecture to obtain an understandable reading. Since this process contains a number of variables, different English translations of certain passages may vary widely. The RSV often footnotes passages where this process has occurred, though, as the commentary will show, this is not always the case.

Selah. This term, found often in the psalms, and even outside the Psalter (as in Hab. 3), has been much discussed. No consensus as to its meaning has been reached, but it is generally thought to be a musical sign, or a direction for the use of the psalm in worship.

The Forms of the Psalms

In discussing the form-critical approach to psalm interpretation (see above), we noted Gunkel's analysis of the psalms into types, and its importance. Over the years various modifications of Gunkel's types have taken place, for different reasons. But his main categories have stood. A consultation of commentaries and introductions on the Psalms shows varied modes of subdividing the types. Some psalms fall neatly into a clearly defined category, while others appear to combine aspects of literary types. A few psalms are hard to place in any category. The student should make his own determination of each psalm, noting (1) the central personage or personages in the psalm, and (2) the basic purpose the psalm unfolds for itself. Yet because there are broad divisions that encompass most of the Psalter which are useful for the student of this material, it is well to analyze the various psalm types.

Hymns. About forty psalms fall into this category. The hymn centers in the praise of God and is usually composed with an introduction (a call to praise), a main section (generally giving the grounds for praise), and a conclusion (re-echoing the introduction, and in some cases having a prayer or wish). It is hard to subdivide hymns on the basis of literary types. Therefore, some have suggested that a better classification would center on the subject matter, with the burden of the main section being decisive. Following this lead one would find the following subdivisions:

(1) Hymns celebrating God as Creator (Pss. 8, 19a, 29, 104)

(2) Hymns of sacred history (Pss. 78, 81, 105, 106, 111, 114, 135, 136)

(3) Hymns of the kingdom (Pss. 24, 47, 68, 75, 93, 95–100)

(4) Hymns of Zion (Pss. 46, 48, 76, 84, 87, 122, 137)

(5) Mixed hymns (Pss. 33, 103, 115, 133, 145–150)

From their nature, the use of the hymns in worship seems clear, though the exact worship occasion in each case may be harder to discern.

Individual laments (Pss. 3, 5–7, 13, 17, 22, 25, 26, 28, 35, 38, 39, 41, 42/43, 51, 54, 55, 57, 59, 61, 64, 69, 71, 86, 88, 102, 109, 120, 130, 140–143. Some would also include Pss. 4, 9/10, 31, 36, 56, 63, 70, 77, 83, 94, 108, 126).

Depending on how certain psalms are classified, laments of the individual and of the community comprise one-third or more of the Psalter. Individual laments are cries to God in time of trouble, begging relief. The difficulties faced range widely, including, among others, illness, slander, physical threat, severe apprehension, poverty, and persecution. The ultimate peril, expressed in many psalms, was death. Yet since the language of these psalms is laced with metaphor and perhaps poetic exaggeration, it is not always easy to discern a poet's exact historical circumstances. Indeed, if these psalms were written to be used by different individuals as felt appropriate, this might have been deliberate, since too concrete a historical locus might remove the psalms from general use.

Generally these psalms follow a pattern beginning with a call upon God to hear, followed by the lament, often in considerable detail. Next there is a specific petition for deliverance, with reasons why God should respond. Often these psalms include an expression of trust or thanks for God's concern and action, experienced or anticipated.

There are some special features of these laments which bear further discussion.

a. The certainty of hearing. Sometimes the author will express assurance that God hears and answers his prayer (cf. 3:7f.; 5:12; 6:8-10; 55:23; 63:9-11; 140:12). Additionally, some cases promise the fulfillment of a vow, which may be an animal sacrifice or a special expression of thanksgiving (Pss. 7:17; 13:6; 22:22-26; etc.). As the notes indicate, it is not always possible to know if these expressions are an anticipation by faith for the future or a reflection upon a past or present deliverance. Each psalm should be considered individually, and one's position will depend on the theory adopted regarding the circumstances of the psalm's origin and use.

b. The enemies. In the royal psalms and communal laments the enemies can be considered foreign foes. But most frequently enemies plague the individual. It is not always possible to determine, first, whether the enemies are responsible for the author's troubles or whether they use previous difficulties for their purposes. Second, it is difficult to know exactly who they are. Scholarship has often addressed itself to this problem, producing varied conjectures. Some consider them simply personal foes—envious slanderers of the author. Others see false accusers bringing the author before the judiciary because of a suspected sin (perhaps assumed because of the poet's illness). Mowinckel thought they were wicked sorcerers, leveling curses. Other suggestions have included political opponents, rich extortioners, robbers, or other dangerous criminals. One writer has divided the enemies into three general classes: (1) friends who had turned against the sufferer; (2) men who despised God and religion; and (3) those who were always the psalmist's foes and who used any occasion they could against him.

In unraveling this problem, there is probably no one theory that fits all cases. Again, the view taken depends on one's assumption as to why the psalm was written and how it was meant to be used. Each case can be examined separately, keeping in mind that the language used may often be stylized and characterized by poetic exaggeration.

c. Sinfulness and innocence. In some individual laments the author confesses himself a sinner (cf. in addition to the penitentials, below, Pss. 25:7; 39:3, 8, 11; 40:12; and 41:14). But in others he affirms his innocence (e.g., Pss. 7:3-5; 17:3-5; 18:20-24; 26:1-8, 11f.; 59:4). Some embrace both confessions in the same psalm (Ps. 32, cf. vs. 5 with vss. 10f.; Ps. 40, cf. vs. 12 with vss. 7-10; Ps. 41, cf. vs. 5 with vss. 7, 9; Ps. 51, cf. vss. 3 ff. with vs. 15; Ps. 69, cf. vs. 4 with vss. 11f.; Ps. 86, cf. vs. 5 with vs. 2; and Ps. 143, cf. vs. 2 with vss. 8-12). A number of these cases are discussed in the notes. Psalms which are exclusively one or the other are not as difficult to explain. But those with both elements have stimulated various resolutions. To the poets, these diverse statements were apparently not contradictory. The "innocence" words may well have been used to describe God's obedient people, who, blessed by his grace, could honestly admit and confess their sins. Those accepting the covenant seriously could practice this honesty, while the godless would have no such inclination.

d. Penitential psalms. These seven psalms (6, 32, 38, 51,

102, 130, 143) came to be designated by the medieval church as the penitentials, even though in some of them the expression of repentance is assumed by interpreters rather than explicitly stated in the text. The classic expression of this type psalm is doubtless Psalm 51.

e. Imprecations. Occasionally in laments, as well as in other types of psalms, we encounter curses against the psalmist's enemies. The strongest example may be Psalm 109:6-20, 27-29. Notable instances are found also in Psalms 58:5-10; 137:8f.; 139:19-22; and 143:2, to mention a few. Christian readers have wrestled with these passages, which have seemed to them so far from the spirit of Christ. Since Christians feel an evangelistic urge to call sinners to redemption, these curses on enemies perplex. But it should be recalled that the psalmists were not operating from the same perspective. Nor did the psalmists generally conceive of history as climaxing in a judgment in which all wrongs would be righted. To them there was an urgency that sought a here and now disposition of God's judgment. Thus, one factor to be remembered is that these writers, in most if not all cases, felt they spoke in harmony with God's nature, calling for his moral governance of the universe to assert itself. Not personal revenge, but vindication of the divine nature, was the impelling force behind these words. And, since the theme was so great, their feelings so strong, and the poetic vehicle so given to extravagant statement, the language of these curses was vivid indeed. Yet, as is often the case with such usages, one can catch the force of the spirit behind the words without needing to take them with absolute literalness.

If, recognizing these factors, we still find curses which seem to express personal vindictiveness, we may simply have to acknowledge our inability to explain all facets of this material. Since the psalmists are men speaking to God from their humanness, it may be tempting to say at times that "here one has gone too far" and extract the value in the words without caring for the complete mode of expression. We can appreciate their intense concern that right triumph and wrong be defeated (and so pray) without blessing those who destroy babies (Ps. 137:9).

Laments of the community (Pss. 12, 44, 60, 74, 79, 80, 83, 85, 90, 123, 125, 126, 129). These are similar in form to the individual laments, but depict a peril to the entire people (defeat, famine, etc.). They appeal to God's faithfulness toward his elect. They likely accompanied some corporate expression of lamentation, repentance, and petition. Though we have divided laments into individual and corporate, one should beware of too inflexible a demarcation, since the individual complaints may also have had corporate uses.

Psalms of thanksgiving (Individual, 30, 34, 40, 52, 66, 92, 116, 138; communal, 65, 67, 107, 118, 124). These psalms praise God in celebration of a deliverance accomplished on either the individual or communal level. They have the same elements as the laments, save that stronger light is thrown on gratitude for God's victorious grace, that is, "we suffered, he delivered, and we praise him." They were no doubt frequently expressive of acts of public worship, with sacrifices or special thanksgiving (cf. the discussion of certainty of hearing under individual laments).

Psalms of trust (Pss. 11, 16, 23, 27, 62, 63, 131). A greater attention to the poet's confidence in God has led some laments to change major focus and become psalms of trust. The problem is still within the psalm but has diminished to secondary importance.

Royal psalms (Pss. 2, 18, 20, 21, 45, 72, 89, 101, 110, 132, 144). These psalms are combined because of their similar subject matter—all center in the king. In literary type, they are diverse, having elements of lament, thanksgiving, hymn, etc. They come from the period of the monarchy and are written for various occasions in the life of the king (coronation, warfare, a wedding, etc.)—perhaps by court poets. Though each was no doubt composed for an occasion in the life of a specific monarch, they are now bereft of allusions allowing us to identify the king in question. This suggests that they came to be used for many (perhaps all) kings in Israel. They may have been composed with a vagueness which would allow reuse, or subsequent editing may have "generalized" the original for later use. Their language is idealized court language, perhaps involving what would be, for certain kings, overstatement. Yet, they speak of what the ruler should be. He is always important because of his relation to Yahweh and because, as God's vicegerent, he rules those chosen by the Lord.

The monarchy ended with the fall of Jerusalem in 586 B.C. but these psalms were preserved. This was because they centered basically in God's continuing relation to his people. This involved the hope for a better kingdom to come. Since the relationship continued, so did the psalms speaking of it. Many of the royal psalms, therefore, came to be understood of the messiah to come, who would bring God's time of fuller blessing. Thus, these psalms lay ready to hand for Jesus and the church and found their way, in a fulfilled sense, into the NT as the greatest of David's line assumed his throne as King of kings.

Wisdom psalms (Pss. 1, 14, 19b, 37, 49, 53, 58, 73, 91, 112, 119, 127, 128, 133, 139). These psalms, as a group, seem less closely attached to worship than any others. They probably arose in the lives and reflections of the people and were drawn later into a more specific worship context. Wisdom literature is found elsewhere in the OT and throughout the ancient Near East. It consists of two types: (1) pithy, bromidic sayings of a practical sort, about living; and (2) longer discussions of more perplexing "philosophical" questions. Within the Psalter both types can be found. Wisdom literature had its particular vocabulary (e.g., fear of Yahweh, instruction, proverbs, riddles, etc.). Some psalms were completely given to wisdom reflections, while others have it spotted amidst a larger context of other materials. These psalms centered, humanly, in the wise, pious man, either as the one advising, or as one who was extolled.

Other psalms. Virtually all the psalms have been included in one of the categories noted above. Again, it should be remembered that in some cases classification is difficult and that some psalms that are of mixed type have been put, for the sake of convenience, in classifications not entirely appropriate. After most psalms have been categorized, there remain a few that do not fit any larger grouping, and commentators handle them differently. The following grouping of the rest of the psalms, then, is suggestive, but not definitive. (For further remarks on these psalms, see the notes.)

> Psalms of innocence (Ps. 15)
> Liturgies
> > of judgment (Pss. 50, 82)
> > of praise for victory (Ps. 108)
> > of blessing (Pss. 121, 134)
> Doxology (Ps. 117)

The Use of the Psalms in the NT

Psalms, with Isaiah, is one of the OT books most quoted in the NT. Though numerous psalms are quoted, only a small number are used often. These include Psalms 2, 8, 16, 22, 34, 69, 110, and 118. These psalms are particularly cited in reference to Christ. An examination of the material in the NT leads to some interesting conclusions. The NT quotations usually follow the Greek translation of the OT, rather than the Hebrew. Thus there is sometimes quite a difference from the thought and wording of the Hebrew as we know it. Additionally, there are sometimes even differences from the Greek OT (LXX) as we know it. Psalms are usually quoted in the NT in reference to Christ on the basis of a key word (e.g., son in 2:7; son of man in 8:4, 6; Lord in 34:9). Even more striking is that the OT passages are often lifted from their original settings and "reinterpreted" in an entirely different sense in the NT. This means passages were understood in the early church in completely new ways.

We must now ask how we should understand this material. A point of view that has prevailed among some has been to take the NT perspective as the governing one, and, reading that back into the OT, to insist that the OT writers always meant what the NT writers said they did. But this overlooks an important beginning premise of OT study, that is, the OT must first be understood in terms of its own people and times. This means that certain psalms which the NT cites as fulfilled in Christ were yet not intended as predictive by the OT. For example, a fair reading of Psalm 22 through OT eyes must admit that verses 1, 7-8, and 16-18 were not trying to predict anything, but that the author was speaking of his own miseries. It is only in the gospels that these words, as applied to Christ, take on another meaning.

Thus, we understand the OT on at least two levels. First we see it through "Jewish" eyes, as a product of its own times. That is, we try to forget what we know as Christians and orient ourselves purely in terms of ancient Israel. But second, we read as those who believe that Christ fulfills the OT and who see it as a Christian book, given the church by its Lord. These two levels may bring us two different views, yet views which obviously touch at many points.

A key to this process is afforded by Luke 24:25-27, 44-48, where Jesus interpreted the OT (law, prophets, psalms) of himself, first to two men, and then to the complete apostolic company. We presume, then, that the early Christian use of the OT was by dominical authority. However strange such interpretations may be, they came, on this view, from the Lord himself. Accordingly, if the NT use of the OT does not suit our conditions of understanding, it is we who must change. Since all his dealings with man work to one end, God can, in his over-arching guidance of history, so arrange matters that this use and later reinterpretation of Scripture are what he intended from the beginning. All is done as he wills, and he unfolds the full meanings of his plans as centuries proceed. Although this is not the kind of prediction and fulfillment commonly used in arguments for the inspiration of the Bible, it is, in a far greater way, testimony to the infinitely wise planning of him who "sees the end from the beginning." One who understands what he reads, then, sees the great framework of God's call to man wrought out within Israel. Then that skeleton becomes a framework for the yet grander edifice of the completed revelation in Christ. Thus, scriptures that deal with the one are most appropriately used of the other, for all God's plan is a unity.

The Christian Use of the Psalter: A Personal Word from the Authors

The making of commentaries upon biblical books can easily produce the false impression that when words, outlines, theology, problems, etc., are discussed and understood, the task is done. Yet the psalms were not primarily written to be the subject matter for someone's commentary. They are statements of faith, produced under God's guidance. They have not found their mark until they have spoken meaningfully in terms of the faith of the reader. The prime concern, then and now, is the individual's confrontation with God.

Thus the reader will hopefully ask not only "What did it mean for them?" but "What does it mean for me?" His interest so stimulated, he will take the basic concepts of the Psalter and bring them to Christ. In the light of NT revelation, he will temper his grasp of the material and will then make it his own. His understanding of God's covenant with his people, for example, will no longer be just a here-and-now matter but will take on eternal dimensions by virtue of the resurrection hope. His laments will be calmed by the hope the risen Lord gives all Christians. The curses in the Psalms will retain their strong concern for God's moral sovereignty, though they will be mediated through the One who taught us to turn the other cheek. In the worship use of the Psalter by Christians, one will constantly ask, "How does faith in Christ appropriate this prayer and praise?"

To write only devotionally, ignoring the academic demands of background, word studies, theology, etc., is to be irresponsible to the OT. But to write only academically is to be irresponsible to the life of faith. We hope this commentary has avoided both dangers and will bless the reader both intellectually and spiritually.

Hints for Using the Commentary

Since the notes are based on the RSV text, other translations have been mentioned sparingly. The reader is encouraged, however, to read comparative translations, since they often are an interpretive aid.

Having the text well in mind will greatly enhance the reading of these comments. The authors have continually had the open text before them as they wrote, and it is only as readers do so also that maximum benefit can be realized. There are rewards that come from firsthand experience with the text that cannot be communicated in a commentary. As one reads imaginatively, with attention to word pictures and to the emotional tone of the writing, a rich appreciation for the material develops. Often as they have prepared these words, the authors have been thrilled by certain texts and the realities to which they witness. Yet such experiences cannot be put on the page. The best way the reader can know their power is by his own due attention to the Word, as these words are used to help him grasp its meaning.

Selected Bibliography

Commentaries and Notes on the Psalms

Anderson, A.A. "Psalms." *New Century Bible*. 2 vols. Greenwood, SC: Attic Press, 1972.

Barth, Marcus. *Introduction to Psalms*. New York: Charles Scribner's Sons, 1966.

Briggs, Charles Augustus and Emilie Grace. *A Critical and Exegetical Commentary on the Book of Psalms*. The International Critical Commentary. New York: Charles Scribner's Sons, 1906.

Buttenwieser, Moses. *The Psalms*. Chicago: University of Chicago Press, 1938.

Cohen, A. *The Psalms*. Soncino Books of the Bible. Edited by A. Cohen. London: Soncino Press, 1945.

Dahood, Mitchell. *Psalms I, II, and III*. The Anchor Bible. Edited by William Foxwell Albright and David Noel Freedman. 3 vols. Garden City, New York: Doubleday & Company, 1966.

Drijvers, Pius. *The Psalms, Their Structure and Meaning*. Herder and Herder, 1965.

Fleming, James. *Thirty Psalmists*. New York: Seabury Press, 1965.

Kidner, Derek. *Psalms 1–72 and 73–150. Tyndale Old Testament Commentaries*. Edited by D. J. Wiseman. 2 vols. London: Tyndale Press, 1973. (Printed in America by InterVarsity Press, 1975.)

Kirkpatrick, A. F. "The Book of Psalms." *Cambridge Bible for Schools and Colleges*. Reprint. London: Cambridge University Press, 1957.

Leslie, Elmer A. *The Psalms*. New York: Abingdon-Cokesbury Press, 1949.

Leupold, H. C. *Exposition of the Psalms*. Columbus, Ohio: Wartburg Press, 1959.

Lewis, C. S. *Reflections on the Psalms*. New York: Harcourt Brace Jovanovich, Inc., 1958.

Oesterley, W. O. E. *The Psalms*. London: S.P.C.K., 1953.

Rhodes, Arnold B. *The Book of Psalms*. The Layman's Bible Commentary, vol. 9. Edited by Balmer H. Kelley, et al. Richmond, Virginia: John Knox Press, 1960.

Weiser, Artur. *The Psalms*. The Old Testament Library. Edited by G. Ernest Wright, et al. Philadelphia: Westminster Press, 1962.

Willis, John T. *Insights From the Psalms*. The Way of Life Series, No. 131. Edited by J. D. Thomas. 3 vols. Abilene, Texas: Biblical Research Press, 1974.

Other Helps:

Archer, Gleason L., Jr. *A Survey of Old Testament Introduction*. Chicago: Moody Press, 1974.

Brown, Francis, S. R. Driver, and Charles A. Briggs, *A Hebrew and English Lexicon of the Old Testament*. Oxford: Clarendon Press, 1957.

Gunkel, Hermann. *The Psalms: A Form-Critical Introduction*. Translated by Thomas M. Horner. Philadelphia: Fortress Press, 1967.

Harrison, R. K. *Introduction to the Old Testament*. Grand Rapids, Michigan: William B. Eerdmans Publishing Company, 1971.

Kautzsch, E., and A. E. Cowley. *Gesenius' Hebrew Grammar*. Oxford: Clarendon Press, 1910.

Mowinckel, Sigmund. *The Psalms in Israel's Worship*. Translated by D. R. Ap-Thomas. 2 vols. Nashville: Abingdon Press, 1967.

II

Psalms 1–75

Anthony L. Ash

Psalm 1: The Righteous and the Wicked

This psalm may have been selected to open the Psalter because its "two ways" set forth the options with which the entire book is concerned. The style and teaching is that of the wisdom tradition, passing on teachings about the meaning of a life grounded in God, and observed by the wise (cf. Pss. 37, 49, 73, 112, 127, 128, 133).

Verses 1-3 deal with the blessedness of the righteous. He is characterized by abstention from evil (vs. 1) and delight in God's law (vs. 2). Then he is likened to a fruitful tree nourished by plenteous water (vs. 3). Verses 4 and 5 describe the wicked with a contrasting simile (chaff), then depict the sinner's lack of blessing. Finally, verse 6 makes a climactic statement about the relation of both to God.

The heart of the psalm is God's sovereignty and providence, as particularily expressed in verse 6. "Knows" means not simply "be aware of," since that would also be true of the wicked. Rather God "knows" the righteous with special concern that causes prosperity (vs. 3). Since God rules human destiny, to be wicked is to choose to perish (vs. 6). The man whom God "knows" is devoted to the law (vs. 2), is within the congregation of the righteous, where the wicked cannot stand (vs. 5), and is blessed (vs. 1). Thus, the entire psalm coheres in the truth expressed in the last verse. Either pursue the Lord's way, or follow the course of the wicked, which is no way at all, but like worthless chaff, wind scattered.

The blessedness of the righteous (vss. 1-3). [1] The Hebrew word for **blessed,** found thirty-three times in the OT, is always used of man, never of God. It can be rendered "happy," and here especially indicates how rewarding the life of the righteous is, in contrast to perishing **wicked** men. Here is to be found life's fulness.

The rest of the verse has a thrice-repeated formula. Each part, in addition to the negation, has a trio of terms which most authors consider to be in progressive parallelism. **Walks, stands,** and **sit** all indicate completed action and may imply increasing involvement with evil. **Counsel, way,** and **seat** amplify the same progress. Finally, the same pattern is in the terms with which the phrases close. **Wicked,** a term used chiefly in the wisdom literature, Ezekiel, and the Psalms, denotes one guilty of a particular charge, as opposed to the innocent. **Sinners** is a more comprehensive term, always used in the Psalms in an ethical sense, and referring basically to those who miss the mark. Indeed, in some OT passages it has this literal meaning (Job 5:24; Judg. 20:16). Here the mark missed was God's will. **Scoffers** is found often in Proverbs, but only here in the Psalms. A defiant and cynical freethinker, such a prideful person refuses instruction from God or man. He scoffs at the wise and righteous and becomes even God's opponent. This vividly contrasts with the lover of God's law depicted in the next verse. Thus, there is a beautifully constructed progression in the thought, delineating the life-style the **blessed** man avoids. The end of such activity, whatever its seeming promise, is emptiness.

[2] **Law,** or *torah*, means guidance or instruction and refers to the whole of God's revelation of his nature and will. **Meditates** is understood by some to imply reading aloud in a low voice, but it must surely imply as well reflection leading to application. The **delight,** then, is not simply in a piece of legislation but in applying it to one's life (cf. Pss. 19:7-13; 119). In effect, it is **delight** in God himself and in doing his will. **Lord** is the translation of the

covenant name of Israel's God, Yahweh (cf. Exod. 3:12-15; 6:3). The original meaning of the term is disputed, but its use always suggests the covenant. **[3]** As a **tree** flourishes, so the good man **prospers** (cf. Ps. 92:12; Ezek. 17:5-10; 19:10; and especially Jer. 17:5-8). The Hebrew word rendered **planted** actually means "transplanted," perhaps implying that the prosperity is due to God's action. The **streams of water** are likely irrigation channels. All circumstances favor the **tree** doing well what is natural to it—producing **fruit in season**. Fruitbearing is not a reward to a tree for goodness, but rather its natural function, when unimpeded by other factors. So here, prosperity is God's intention for a life, brought to pass by man's devotion to his will. It is the way man was made to be and contrasts with the life which, unnaturally, is driven away (vs. 4) or perishes (vs. 6). The prosperity is not simply a future reward, but the continuing quality of life.

The fate of the wicked (vss. 4-5). [4] With the simile of **chaff**, the psalm continues describing how reality works. Any course excluding God is doomed. Once each in the last three verses the word for **wicked** is used (as well as sinner in vs. 5). He is driven away, cannot stand in judgment, and perishes.

[5] Some see **judgment** as the final verdict of God, while others think of God's continuing assessment and rejection of the **wicked**. Though the psalmists see times when the **wicked** prosper (cf. 73:3-12), such a life must yet suffer divine disapproval and will fail, despite the illusory appearance of some immediate benefits. It is best to take the words here in the overall sense of a life which cannot stand God's inspection. **Congregation of the righteous** is likewise applied, by some, to the earthly assembly of the **righteous,** and by others, to the **congregation** which subsists after the resurrection. The last view reads "will not rise," rather than **will not stand,** and refers it to the resurrection. It is dubious, however, if such a concept is so clearly taught here. We prefer to believe the author speaks of exclusion from the worshiping community. The use of this expression in worship would announce the character of the **congrega-**

tion and affirm its disassociation from the **wicked**, who, even if present, do not really belong. By their very nature, they cannot.

Torah (law), **judgment**, and righteousness eventually became virtually synonymous terms referring to that which conformed to the nature and will of God. **Righteous** means to be what one should be, to respond appropriately to the norms set for one's situation in life. It is not just ethical purity, but the expected and appropriate response to God. The **righteous** do what God created them to do.

God knows (vs. 6). Knows and perish are the poles of this verse, of the entire psalm, and of all of life. To **know** implies special concern and has been translated by some as "watches over" or "preserves." Man's ultimate choice is existence or nonexistence. To reject the God-given guide (law) is to reject life and to refuse the only foundation upon which it is ultimately possible to stand. No light choice, this. The psalm deals with the elementals. It begins with happiness and ends with ruin. It cuts to the heart of the matter and challenges the reader at the entry to the Psalter to make clear his decision before entering. Live under God's care, or do not live at all.

Psalm 2: The Nations—Choice and Consequence

This psalm depicts the ways nations might choose, just as Psalm 1 showed the choices facing the individual. Acts 4:25 ascribes the psalm to David. Some argue that the NT language reflects a Jewish tendency to ascribe many psalms to David, though their exact authorship might not have been known. Others consider the passage in Acts an incontrovertible statement regarding authorship. Here there seems no compelling reason to deny Davidic authorship. Some say David never enjoyed the universal dominion over the nations which the psalm implies. But neither did any other Israelite monarch. The language is likely idealistic and thus could fit as well into David's time as any other. The psalm is based on God's promises to David and his descendants in 2 Samuel 7:11-16. Subsequent to David, it may have been customarily used at coronations.

In the ancient Near East, when a new monarch assumed his throne, vassal nations often used the disturbed circumstances to revolt. Such a bid for freedom, whether literal or only contemplated, may lie behind this psalm. It was incumbent upon the newly seated ruler to affirm his power, lest his empire be diminished by rebellion. Here, however, it is not the king's might but the mighty sovereignty of the Lord which is asserted.

Verses 1-3 describe the conspiracy of the nations and their rulers against the rule of the Lord and his anointed. Verses 4-6 contrast with this the power of God, whose intents will not be thwarted by the plottings of mere men. Verses 7-9 focus on God's appointment of his monarch, who will therefore be assured of power over the conspirators. Verses 10-12 appeal to all nations to serve the Lord, lest a terrible fate overtake them. The last line of the psalm is a blessing upon those trusting God (cf. 1:1). The king may well be the speaker in the entire psalm (cf. vss. 7-9).

Conspiracy of the nations (vss. 1-3). [1] The conspiracy and plotting amaze the writer, since he knows how futile they must be. The rest of the psalm explains the bewilderment of the first two verses. **Plot** translates the same Hebrew word as "mediate" in 1:2, though here with a bad connotation. [2] The **anointed**, or messiah, is the king. Anointing was an act of consecration, used both of objects (Exod. 29:36; 30:26; Lev. 8:10) and of people. Prophets, priests, and kings were all subject to the act (see 1 Kings 19:16; 1 Chron. 16:22; Exod. 28:41; Num. 3:3; 1 Sam. 10:1; 16:3; 1 Kings 1:39). The equivalent NT term is "Christ."

[3] **Bonds** and **cords** likely refer to the fastening of a yoke to an animal's neck and thus imply servitude.

The power of God (vss. 4-6). These verses show why the talk of the earlier verses ought not come to open rebellion. The section stresses God's choice of David and of Jerusalem. [4] This very dramatic verse forms a powerful contrast to the preceding. While men do their best to execute their plans, which to them seem so important and powerful, they are watched by a God who is so infinitely above them that he makes their schemes trivial. [5] The Lord speaks. It is a turning point of the psalm. His powerful word and action spell doom for his opponents. **Saying** at the end of the verse is interpolated by the translators to convey the sense of the quotation in the next verse.

[6] The opening **I** forms a strong contrast to the "Let us" of verse 3. Man's plans are futile next to God's power. **Zion** is Jerusalem. The **holy hill** was considered, in a special way, as the seat of the Lord's presence (cf. Pss. 3:5; 15:1; 43:3; 48:2; 99:9).

The king's commission (vss. 7-9). These verses record the commission and privilege of the king. Israel never literally had universal political dominion. However, parallel sources from the ancient Near East indicate such language was used in other cultures. It was used in the psalm, not because it was expected to find literal fulfillment, but because the God who called Israel is over all nations and events. Ultimately history will conform to his will, and righteousness will triumph. Even in hard times, Israel could know she was in rhythm with the true meaning of history's flow.

[7] The **decree** doubtless has reference to 2 Samuel 7:11-16. When Joash was crowned, he was given the "testimony" (2 Kings 11:12), which may have been the same as the **decree.** Thus a recitation of 2 Samuel 7 may have been part of the coronation ceremony. The king was declared God's **son,** that is, he was adopted. This extended the idea of Israel's becoming God's son when entering into covenant with God (Exod. 4:22-23). This reference to sonship is often cited in the NT of Jesus (Mark 1:11; 9:7 and parallels; Acts 13:33; Heb. 1:5; 5:5). [8] Dominion over the **nations** is not specifically mentioned in the promise in 2 Samuel 7 but is enunciated in Psalm 89:27. [9] **Break** implies a mace or implement of war. Some emend to "shepherd," in which case the **rod** might indicate a scepter. On the **potter's vessel,** see Jeremiah 19:11 and Isaiah 30:14. A nation so shattered would be beyond restoration, again emphasizing God's power.

'Serve the Lord' (vss. 10-12). The stress in this last section shifts from the king to God. The king is significant only as God's appointee. Here is the theological center of the psalm. **[10]** The universalistic note of verses 8-9 continues here. Not just the plotters (vss. 1-2), but all **rulers,** are admonished. **[11]** The choice is to **serve** or perish. In Hebrew the contrast is more impressive since the two words are pronounced basically the same and differ only in their initial consonant. The universal call to **serve** implies God's acceptance of the penitent wherever they might be found.

The literal translation of 11b, 12a seems to be "rejoice with trembling/kiss the *bar*." The passage in the Hebrew violates the metric arrangement and combines the ideas of rejoicing and **trembling** in a strange way. The RSV, assuming the Hebrew text was altered in transmission, follows a reading which moves the first two words in verse 12 to a position just before the last two in verse 11. Then, with slight changes in the letters, the present translation can be derived. **[12]** The word *bar* in verse 12 is the Aramaic word for "son." It would not likely be used here, especially since the Hebrew word for "son" has been used in verse 7. A vowel change would give the reading "cleanness" or "purity." Another suggestion is an alteration to "kiss the field." The RSV, by moving the words, combines *bar* with the word for rejoice, deriving the meaning "feet" and giving a meaning in harmony with the rest of the psalm. It is a difficult text. Ancient translations of the passage show there was always some confusion as to its exact meaning.

This psalm is frequently referred to in the NT. To the Christian, it is in Jesus that its truest and ultimate fulfillment is found.

Psalm 3: A Plea for Deliverance

According to the superscription, the flight from Absalom (2 Sam. 15–18) is the background for this psalm. But it nowhere mentions Absalom, which seems strange in view of David's great love for him (2 Sam. 18:33). There is no solid evidence either for or against Davidic authorship. If David is not the author, it is still possible that this individual lament comes from a king, faced with desperate problems (cf. the numerous foes, vs. 7, and the associated welfare of the people, vs. 8). Or some individual may have assumed the kingly position to illustrate his own problems.

The psalm begins with a complaint (vss. 1-2). Yet the author does not despair because he is sure of the Lord's provision for him (vss. 3-6). His reflection on the Lord's past care is the basis for his present prayer (vs. 7). He closes with renewed prayer, an affirmation of faith, and a blessing upon Israel (vss. 7-8).

The conceptual center of the psalm is help, or deliverance. The Hebrew word is found in vss. 2, 7 ("deliver"), and 8. Though his foes affirm that God will offer no help, they are wrong! He has been (and is) shield, glory, lifter of the head, answerer of prayer, sustainer, and giver of calm and courage (vss. 3-6). Thus, he will help again. The enemies who mocked his trust must face God's judgment (vs. 7). Thus, verse 8a is the heart of the psalm, from which all else derives significance. The poles around which the whole is built are the statements in verses 1b and 8a.

A complaint (vss. 1-2). [1] The threefold repetition of **many** stresses the author's plight (further amplified by "ten thousands" in vs. 6). They are described as **foes, rising against** him and denying that God will help him. **Foes** is general and often used in the Psalter (cf. 13:5; 27:2, 12; 44:11; 74:10). In the text they are also God's enemies.

[2] Though some think that the **many** were the writer's friends giving a counsel of despair, it is better to consider them the foes of verse 1. **Help** is a form of the central word of the psalm and can be rendered "salvation," "victory," or "deliverance." The reference may be to spiritual or to physical salvation (cf. Pss. 18:19; 60:11; 65:5-8; 69:14; 72:4; and 86:7). Usually in the OT the latter idea is in some way involved. We cannot know, however, the exact nature of the distress (unless we accept the superscription).

God's answer (vss. 3-6). [3] Things are not always what people propose. The picture of verse 2 was woefully inadequate. The opening **But thou** here offers defiant opposition to the doubt there expressed. God is both powerful and available. A rich past of divine provision assures the author in the present crisis. **Shield** is often used in the Psalter to describe God's help, in the figure of protection against attack (cf. 7:11; 18:3, 31, 36; 28:7; 33:20). This was a small **shield** of metal or leather, stretched over a wooden framework. **My glory** could either describe God, as the one in whom the writer gloried, or the author, as given and restored by God. The exact meaning of **lifter of my head is** not known, but it probably implies the elevation of one's fortunes in some way. [4] The verbs in this verse indicate incomplete action, showing prayers answered, but that the process continues. The author's faith rests upon a life of constant prayer. No wishful thinking, this, but a continuing reality giving present strength.

[5] The writer could **sleep** without apprehension, free of the anxiety which his foes supposed should have characterized him. Did not the fact he awakened after a night of rest, even when surrounded by foes, demonstrate God's care? Perhaps the psalm was written after such a night (some even suggest a night spent in the temple). [6] **Ten thousands** indicates hosts in battle array. There may be poetic exaggeration here. Yet whatever the size of the force, their might was nothing compared with that of the Lord.

'Arise, O Lord!' (vss. 7-8). [7] The first part of this verse seems to be an appeal, but there is disagreement over whether the second and third parts describe past action or elaborate the preceding prayer. Smiting **on the cheek** implies the humiliation of the enemy. Breaking **the teeth** may refer to a wild beast which is unable to ravage its prey. The language is striking and, though harsh, makes the point unforgettable. [8] This verse may be the summation of the whole psalm as used in the worship of the people. The writer asks for **deliverance (vs. 7),** and it is assured—for it comes from God. The second half of the verse is the consequence of the first. A literal reading of the verse is "to the Lord, deliverance. Unto your people, your blessing."

Psalm 4: An Appeal in Faith

This psalm has elements of lamentation, but trust in the Lord is the dominant motif. Psalms 3 and 4 are combined in some traditions (a morning hymn and an evening hymn, respectively), but the contents do not support a common authorship and occasion. Though some suggest the author may have been a king, high priest, or leader of the people, the words would be appropriate to any pious Israelite. It is possible the writer may have been falsely accused of a crime (vs. 2), to be resolved in a manner like that described in Deuteronomy 17:8, 13; 19:16-21.

The psalm begins with a threefold cry for help, punctuated by the writer's assurance based on past deliverance (vs. 1). Then the enemies are addressed; a description of their wrongs (vs. 2) is followed by a contrasting assurance of God's help (vs. 3). Next a series of imperatives admonish the opponents to repent (vss. 4-5). Then the attitude of the "many" is contrasted with the psalmist's joy in God (vss. 6-7). A closing affirmation sums up the central thought, beautifully illustrated by the peaceful slumber of one secure (vs. 8).

The psalm's basic message is that God insures safety (vss. 1, 8). Such security brings joy (vs. 7) and peace (vs. 8). Therefore the writer prays confidently (vss. 1, 3). Any threat from the enemies (vss. 2-3), consequently, can be overcome by the greatness of God, who calls for their repentance (vss. 4-5).

[1] Past blessings impel present pleas. **God of my right** may describe the righteousness of the writer (especially appropriate if he were faced with a false accusation), the vindication or salvation brought him by God, or both (God vindicates the writer's integrity). **Given room** is doubtless a military figure describing one hemmed in by enemies. God drives away the foe and "enlarges" the threatened one.

[2] Here is the center of the problem. The wrong is practiced by the (literally) sons of **men** (*bene 'ish*), an expression probably referring to men of rank, high degree, influence, or wealth (cf. Pss. 49:3; 62:10, where the same Hebrew expression has this significance). By contrast, another word for man (*'adham*) is used in the psalms to describe mankind in general. **Honor** is hard to define here. Does it imply some rank or dignity thus defamed? Was it his faith in God or his general reputation? Is a court case

implied? We cannot know. Also, one can only conjecture the specific content and context of **vain words** and **lies**.

[3] Of greater import is the writer's relation to God, assuming he is one of the **godly**. **Godly** (*chasidh*) can be rendered in both an active and a passive sense. The former indicates the writer's character, and the latter sees him as the recipient of God's covenant love (*chesedh*, the root of the present word). *Chasidh* occurs twenty-five times in the Psalms, but only infrequently in the rest of the OT. The poet's faith that God hears gives him confidence to call his enemies to repentance (vss. 4-5). He is concerned with those out of harmony with God's purposes.

[4] The opening part of this verse occurs in Ephesians 4:26. There, and in the Greek OT, the translation is "be angry." However, the Hebrew literally means "tremble" and may refer to the agitation caused by either wrath or fear. The RSV may have the sense right, or the psalmist's enemies may be called to tremble in dismay at God's blessing on the godly (vs. 3). At any rate, they are to keep their agitation within. This may parallel the second part of the verse commending nocturnal searchings of conscience (cf. 83:6; 149:5). Hopefully such introspection can lead to reformation. To **be silent** may imply cessation of the verbal transgressions depicted in verse 2. [5] **Right sacrifices** and **trust in the Lord** may follow the night's reflection. **Right sacrifices** may imply right ritual but more probably, in context, implies the **right** spirit (cf. 51:19). Outward rite depends on inward change. Since **sacrifices** indicate cultic activity, one wonders if the entire psalm presupposes formal worship experience.

Some see verses 4-5 as referring to the psalmist's followers, but this seems less satisfactory than the present interpretation. The view here sees an evangelistic concern motivating the writer.

[6] Are the **many** the writer's friends, or those suffering from a poor harvest (v. 7), or those discouraged for other reasons? Apparently they are the same foes addressed in verses 4, 5. Perhaps they had asked God amiss and thus received no good. They are now instructed in a proper

course to pursue to receive blessing. Their question, literally, is "who will cause us to see good?" God is asked to **lift up** (an unusual form of the Hebrew) his **light**—probably a reference to his favor (cf. 44:4; 51:11; 69:18). The petition seems patterned on the form of the high priest's blessing (Num. 6:24-26; cf. Pss. 67:2, 89:16). The **good** is God himself, as verses 7-8 indicate. Some translations alter this verse slightly to read "the light has fled," thus paralleling the last part with the first. This is smoother, but the text as it stands makes good sense. **[7]** A powerful contrast between sources of **joy** is given here. No wonder the psalmist speaks so victoriously. Contrast, too, the lying heart (vs. 2) with the joyful. **[8]** The psalmist indeed has the trust he commended in verse 5, and which results in **peace** as well as joy (vs. 7).

This psalm speaks of a splendid cluster of blessings which accrue to the life of trust. They are deliverance (vs. 1), assurance prayer is heard (vs. 1), God's favor (vs. 3), joy (vs. 7), peace (vs. 8), and safety (vs. 8). How much more fully the Christian rejoices in his appropriation of these same blessings though Christ.

Psalm 5: 'God, Give Heed!'

This psalm has five alternating sections. The first (vss. 1-3), third (vss. 7-8), and fifth (vss. 11-12) center in man's relation to God. The second (vss. 4-6) and fourth (vss. 9-10) deal with the writer's enemies. An opening threefold request (vss. 1-2) is followed by a twofold assurance of a hearing (vss. 3). Then seven descriptions of evil depict God's hatred of wickedness (vss. 4-6). The petition is renewed, with an acknowledgement of God's grace (vss. 7-8). Again the wicked are characterized, with petitions for their punishment (vss. 9-10). A call to rejoice in the God of righteousness and an affirmation of his blessings end the psalm (vss. 11-12). The ground and rationale of the entire psalm is the nature of God—who loves the righteous and hates the wicked.

The petition (vss. 1-3). [1-2] Three verbs imploring a divine hearing indicate the intensity of this petition. Also note the threefold **words, groaning,** and **cry. Groaning,** found elsewhere only in Psalm 39:3, may refer either to murmuring in sorrow or to an unspoken prayer. The psalms often depict **God** as **king** of Israel (10:16; 24:7, 8, 10; 29:10; 44:4). Other nations in the ancient world considered their deities as kings also. **[3]** From this verse some assume a connection of the psalm with the **morning sacrifice** (cf. 2 Kings 3:20; Amos 4:4). However, the verb **prepare** (set in order), though sometimes indicating sacrifice, could also mean to set one's cause in order. The word **sacrifice** is not in the Hebrew. "Watching" could imply an expected revelation (cf. Hab. 2:1), or a priestly oracle, or a favorable verdict from judges, if the writer had been accused with lying charges (vs. 6).

God hates the evil (vss. 4-6). [4] A vivid series of synonyms in verses 4-6 describe those who offend God's holiness. The nature of **God,** revealed in the same section, inspires the petitions of vss. 8 and 10. Notice the verbs describing God's reactions to evil here as well (see also vs. 10). **Sojourning** probably roots in the practice of hospitality. **Evil** cannot be accorded the status of a guest before God.

[5-6] The boaster, so important in his own eyes (cf. 73:3; 75:4), may not stand before God's. This could indicate God's refusal to accept his worship in the temple (cf. Josh. 24:1; 1 Sam. 10:19).

Lies (vs. 6) may refer to false testimony against the author. On **bloodthirsty** (literally "men of bloods"), see 26:9; 55:24; 59:3; and 139:19.

'I will enter thy house' (vss. 7-8). [7] The **worship** motif is resumed. The godly are admitted by God's grace. **Steadfast love** (*chesedh*) is a very important word. It is much like love, but it always implies the idea of the covenant, to which both parties, God and man, are committed. It is used of God's love, and of man's responsive love that does God's will. It implies a determined loyalty, not a vascillating emotion. **Fear** implies reverence and awe. Perhaps the writer's awe makes him aware that any approach to the Almighty must be by his abundant grace. **[8]** Having cleared his attitude, the author comes to the content of his prayer—that God's nature be vindicated before the enemies. God's **righteousness** could be his nature in itself, or as wrought out in salvation. It could also parallel **way** and indicate the proper behavior by the writer. God's word should be a deterrent, or lesson, to the **enemies**, which literally means "watchers" (i.e., with insidious intent). Straighten **the way** probably means being given ability to meet whatever problems life brings ("lead us not into temptation").

The wicked (vss. 9-10). [9] Here we return, in dramatic language, to the ideas of verses 4-6. **Heart** is literally "midst," probably referring to man's seat of thought. **Open sepulchre** clearly indicates the deadliness of their unreliable words. This verse is cited in Romans 3:13 in Paul's description of human wickedness.

[10] Evil reaches its limit, and if God is a holy God, wicked **counsels** must **fall**. So the poet prays. It is their rebellion that evokes these words. The focus is God's nature, not the writer's justification.

'Rejoice!' (vss. 11-12). [11] Now, personal problems are caught up in communal blessedness. Three verbs emphasize the **joy** of those trusting God. The rejoicing is due to God's blessing of the righteous (vs. 12), but, even more basically, because he is a God of holiness. All life receives unique significance from that fact. **Ever** (Heb. *'olam*, sometimes rendered "for ever"), basically means long duration and can refer to the past (ancient), to an indefinite futurity, to continuous existence, or to an indefinite, unending future. Thus it is not necessarily the same as the English "eternal." [12] The **shield** here is a large shield which protected almost the entire body (contrast 3:3). **Cover** is read by some as "crown."

Psalm 6: 'Rebuke Me Not'

This individual lament is the first of the seven penitential psalms (32, 38, 51, 102, 130, 143). The sufferings of the writer are unforgettably pictured. He begins by describing his affliction, which is related to the chastening wrath of

God. He prays for relief (vss. 1-3). He continues the plea, on the basis of God's steadfast love, in view of the threat of death (vss. 4-5). Then he elaborates his crisis in strongly emotional terms (vss. 6-7). In the last three verses (8-10), the mood changes. The writer has been heard, and his enemies are bidden to depart.

It is because of God's steadfast love (vs. 4) that the writer can pray confidently. The Lord will attend him in his extremity, with graciousness, healing (vs. 2), salvation, deliverance (vs. 4), and relief from enemies (vs. 8). In addition, the first verses doubtless imply serious wrong in the author's life. It must be expunged by repentance and by virtue of the Lord's grace before a resolution can come.

The troubled soul (vss. 1-3). [1] This is virtually identical to Psalm 38:1. Though this psalm does not specifically indicate the writer's repentance, surely his recognition of sin must lie behind these verses. Further, it must be on the ground of his penitence that he even feels confident to pray. Since in Israel difficulties were sometimes ascribed to the Lord's chastening (cf. Prov. 3:11; Jer. 10:24), one might see a prayer for help as an occasion for self-examination and repentence. Some psalmists plead their innocence (cf. 7:3-5, 8), but this author does not feel so confident. His bitter experience has worked for his spiritual betterment. He appeals from his frailty and humility to the divine compassion.

[2-3] **Bones** (vs. 2) and **soul** (vs. 3) may indicate physical and psychological grief, or they may be synonymous with I. If this is poetic language, no physical illness need be implied (but note the threat of death in vs. 5). He pleads for grace and healing, which may also involve a plea for forgiveness. Note the citation of this language in John 12:27. **How long** (cf. 13:1; 74:10; 79:5; etc.) expects God's answer but expresses frustration and perhaps doubt, because the response has been delayed. "I know you will act, Lord, but why not yet?" The formula is also found in Babylonian literature.

'Deliver me from death' (vss. 4-5). [4] See Psalms 90:13; 109:26. The writer now pleads, on the basis of God's **stead-**

fast love, expecting fulfillment of the promises made to God's people, as particularly applied to his own **life** (cf. 5:7). He is faced with the prospect of death (save my life, vs. 4; death, **Sheol**, vs. 5). Was this literal or poetic? No wonder he pleads so passionately. **[5]** God would lose a worshiper, but the author would lose the most precious of gifts—communion with God—should he be confined to **Sheol**. **Sheol** is probably related to the Hebrew verb meaning "to see," though the exact etymology is disputed. There is abundant biblical data to show the significance of the term. It was the place to which all the dead went— inescapable, dark (143:3), and silent (94:17). It was a place of weakness and helplessness (88:4), where fellowship with God was cut off. It seems to have been a shadowy existence which was almost no existence. Though not considered a place of punishment, to the pious Israelite it was terror indeed to be cut off from God's covenant presence. Yet the dead had no memory, so as to be aware of their deprivation. The fear of **death** bound the Israelite, for it meant the loss of all that mattered most. How much more meaningful this makes the victory over death which Christ insures.

The flood of tears (vss. 6-7). **[6]** Here one senses acutely the intensity of the author's suffering. **Every night** indicates long duration. **Flood** means, literally, "to make to swim." **Drench** means "cause to dissolve, or melt." (Cf. also Ps. 69:3; Jer. 45:3.) **[7]** The wasted **eye** may be physical affliction or poetic hyperbole. It is striking in either case (cf. 31:9). The **foes** (literally "vexers, harassers") are first mentioned here. Note also the terms "workers of evil" (vs. 8) and "enemies" (vs. 10). Their oppressions were doubtless part of the way the writer felt God's wrath (vs. 1). Were they responsible for his suffering, or were they using it as an occasion to taunt and mistreat him?

God hears (vss. 8-10). **[8]** Here anguish turns to triumph—a transition not uncommon in the laments (cf. 28:6ff.; 31:19ff., etc.). What precipitated it? Was it an inner assurance wrought by the psalmist's repentance? Was some worship experience understood as a reassurance from God (an oracle or a ritual promising salvation)? This seems to imply forgiveness and an end of troubles. Therefore, let the enemies **depart**. They can no longer prevail, so let them follow a wiser procedure. The assurance that the prayer is answered is stressed by a threefold statement in verses 8b and 9.

[9-10] The Lord has truly vindicated his steadfast love (vs. 4). God has **heard** and is still hearing. The fate of the **enemies** (vs. 10) contrasts sharply with the anxiety they had previously caused. "Troubled" (vs. 2) and "turns" (vs. 4) now describe the foes. Because God has turned, they must **turn back** and be shamed. Turning back (vs. 10) could imply defeat or some reversal of their fortunes. Perhaps the psalmist's vindication would humiliate those who had opposed him. Yet he does not gloat over the victory.

Psalm 7: God Judges Righteously

First Kings 8:31 speaks of an accused man coming before God at the temple, where divine justice would be administered for the guilty and righteous (cf. also Exod. 22:7-8; Num. 5:11-15; Deut. 17:8-9). This psalm may presuppose such a situation, either actually, or as a literary device to express the writer's experience. His key statement is "God is a righteous judge" (vs. 11).

The psalmist calls upon God to save him from lionlike enemies (vss. 1-2), because of his own righteousness (vss. 3-5, probably implying response to accusations against him). Then he petitions God to judge the enemies (vs. 6) and the "peoples" (vss. 7-8), as well as to establish the upright, because he is a righteous judge (vss. 9-11). The author, sure of God's response, depicts (vividly) the wicked receiving his due (caught in his own misdeeds—vss. 12-16). Therefore God is to be thanked and praised (vs. 17).

'Deliver me' (vss. 1-2). [1] Though we see a man in mortal terror, the psalm does not dwell on the danger but on the **God** who offers **refuge**, salvation, and deliverance. The writer's primary word is *trust in God*. Pursue can also be rendered "persecute," but the present translation most aptly fits the imagery of verse 2. **[2]** The ravaging animal is also found in Psalms 9:15; 31:4; 35:7-8; and 57:5. **Rend** (singular in the original) is translated as plural to make it agree with "pursuers" of verse 1. The second **me** of the verse is added by the translators for clarity.

'I am innocent' (vss. 3-5). **[3]** This indicates the writer's response to a false accusation. The Hebrew form implies a negative answer to the question. Such submission to God's verdict, if not sincere, would be blatant infidelity. Against lying opponents (cf. vs. 14), he sets God's judgment and his own righteousness (vs. 8). Note that this vow has three "if" clauses (vss. 3-4), followed by three consequence clauses. The last "if" clause and the first consequence clause each have two parts.

[4] For **plundered**, the original text has a word meaning "rescue, deliver." A transposition of letters within the word leads to the translation given. This makes the expression parallel to the first of the verse. **Without cause** can modify either the verb or the enmity. The RSV chooses the former, for a better paralleling with the first line. The psalmist probably contends that he has inflicted no **evil** for which an enemy can accuse him. This supports the suggestion that he was falsely accused. **[5]** Though he seeks (vs. 1) to escape his **enemy**, yet he calls down on himself just such a fate if he is guilty. He does not flinch from what he deserves. Note the progression from pursuing to overtaking to trampling to death. Also, three different words describe the author (**soul** here is the word usually translated "glory, honor").

The Lord judges (vss. 6-8). Here God is in his session as judge. **[6]** The psalmist includes a petition against his **enemies** (cf. also vss. 9, 14-16). **Arise, O Lord** is like the people's battle cry when setting forth with the ark (Num. 10:35; cf. Pss. 9:19; 17:13; 44:26; 102:13). **Anger** is holiness as it encounters sin. In contrast to verses 4-5, here is more than one enemy. Some argue the foes had a leader (verses 4-5) who spearheaded the false accusation. **My God** could as well be rendered "for me" (RSV note). In the former case (supported by the LXX), the word for God is plural (possibly the plural of majesty).

[7] This is an impressive call for God to judge. It may be based on a king's triumphant return from battle. **Take thy seat** literally means "return." The RSV reading involves a conjectural vowel change to fit the context more smoothly (cf. a similar reading in 9:5). [8] Note how often verses 8-11 use the terms **righteousness**, righteous, upright, and **integrity**. They contain a miniature theology of judgment. The author (returning to the ideas of vss. 3-5) does not fear coming before the righteous judge of the nations. Justice is one. His case is only a particular instance of a larger reality. He is not making an arrogant claim but rather is pleading "not guilty." (Cf. 9:7-8; 26:1; 35:24; 43:1; 82:3.)

The righteous judge (vss. 9-11). [9] God, who sees the inner man, is a source of confidence and terror. It cannot be determined whether the psalmist's expectations for the **wicked** and **righteous** are universal or are only in terms of his particular problem. **Minds and hearts** is literally "hearts and kidneys." "Hearts" (Hebrew) indicates the mind or intellect, and "kidneys" the seat of the emotions. God knows and judges both intellect and emotions. [10] This repeats, with a more personal touch, the thought of the last half of verse 9. This is made more forceful by the repetition of the word for **heart.** Line 1, literally translated, is "my shield over, or upon, God." Is **God** the shield bearer, or the **shield?** The latter seems more appropriate, since a shield bearer is a subservient position. [11] The thought of verse 10 is continued and amplified. The wicked is never safe from **indignation**, and the upright sustains hope even in apparent despair. Each **day** is lived in an equitable universe which vindicates right. The first part of this verse could also be translated "God judges the righteous."

The end of the wicked (vss. 12-16). These verses act as commentary on verse 11b. Verses 12 and 13, in the RSV, describe God's moving against the impenitent. Verses 14-16 see the sinner caught in his own devices. The point may be that evil, by nature, is self-destructive, and this constitutes God's judgment upon it. Or it may be that verses 14-16 anticipate God's special action in the case at hand.

[12] Some translations make the wicked **man** the subject

of verses 12-13, since **God** is not in the Hebrew. Thus, the **man** who **does not repent whets his sword**, etc. (cf. 11:2). Were this translation adopted, it would be unnecessary for the RSV to interpolate "wicked man" into verse 14 to change the subject. Yet the RSV does have a continuance of the theme of judgment from verse 11 through verse 16. **Bent** literally means "tread" and refers to the custom of bending a **bow** with the foot instead of the arm. **[13] Deadly weapons** literally means "weapons of death." **Fiery shafts** may be flaming **arrows** or a figure for the lightnings of God (18:14; Zech. 9:14).

[14] As noted above, the RSV interpolates **wicked man.** Some argue that the introductory **behold** suggests such a change of subject from the previous verse. After the initial exclamation, this verse has an interesting triad, in which each part is composed of a verb and object. The verbs, as translated in the RSV, indicate successive stages in the process of conception and birth. The last two verbs are used in this progression in Job 15:35; Isaiah 33:11; 59:4. However, the first verb means to "writhe, twist, travail" and so seems to fit the idea of giving birth, rather than conceiving. Thus the progression of the verbs is less clear in the Hebrew than in the RSV. In any case, the message is of complete and continued involvement in wrong.

[15-16] Evil's self-destructive nature is here seen "small and close." Two different words describe the **digging**, perhaps to make the doom of the digger seem more impressive. The reference may be to an animal trap, common in the psalms. **Violence** (vs. 16) implies the activities described in verse 2.

[17] The psalm closes with either a vow or a thanksgiving. If the latter, it is presumed that his request was granted. God of **righteousness** is a term drawing special significance from the language of the preceding verses. In a worship context this vow may have accompanied a sacrifice, though the language of the psalm itself gives no such indication. At the close of the psalm the writer, through his problems, finds an occasion to offer praise to God's glory. So should all life be lived.

Psalm 8: God's Glory, Man's Honor

This hymn celebrates the majesty of God as seen in his creation, of which man is the crown. After the introductory ascription of praise (vs. 1a), the author marvels at God's glory in the night sky (vss. 1b-3). This leads into a comparison with man, who, though so small (vs. 4), is yet the pinnacle of creation (vs. 5). Verses 6-8 offer exposition of the thesis of verse 5 in terms of man's grace-given dominion. The last verse repeats the eulogy with which the psalm began. Though over half the verses speak of man's role on earth, the psalm centers in God. Man's God-given sovereignty glorifies him who gave it.

The glory of God (vss. 1-2). [1] For the first time in the Psalter, an author associates himself with the elect community in addressing God, using God's covenant name (Yahweh—the first **Lord**), then reinforcing it by a more general term (the second **Lord**). Verses 1 and 9 bracket the more individual reflections of verses 2-8, which speak of man in general, not just as elect. The author overflows with the compelling witness of God's creation. As the heavens are universal, so should God's praise be. Comparison of translations will show a lack of unanimity in the rendering of verses 1b, 2. **Chanted** is based on an emendation of the Hebrew verb. The original seems to mean "give, set, or put," and is an imperative— "Set thy glory above." However, several ancient versions seem to support a declarative reading, which makes more sense, since God would not be asked to do what he has already done. Other suggested emendations of the verb include "praised" and "I will adore." Another possible reading is to put the comma at the end of verse 1 and then read verse 2 as a unit, without a comma after "infants."

[2] How is God's glory chanted by **babes and infants** (a thought found only here in the OT)? Are the **babes and infants** part of the heavenly court (a strained interpretation)? Or is the idea that God's power is shown even in small things? Or does this indicate the simple trust of a child (though dubiously ascribed to an infant)? More likely, in view of the context, the idea is that man, even in young childhood, is superior to other creatures and thus testifies to God's gift. Even this does not satisfy the praise implied in **by the mouth**, unless the expression is poetic. The **bulwark** may refer to the praise, or the heavens, or mankind. The last of verse 2 may indicate that any **enemy** of God or his people should be warned by contemplating the majesty of God as revealed through his creation. This verse is cited from the LXX in Matthew 21:16 (of children praising Jesus in the temple).

The honor of man (vss. 3-8). [3-4] Man's comparative smallness is counterpoint to the greatness given him by God (vss. 5-8). There is a double contrast—between **man** and **the heavens** and between man's smallness and his greatness. Like a skilled artisan, God has wrought his handiwork. How can he who has produced such marvels (modern astronomy increases our wonder) care for **man**? **Man** is driven to humility. **What** is the same Hebrew term as "how" (vs. 1)—a possible play on words giving added stress to the contrast of God's majesty and man's finitude. Yet God is mindful—exercises continuous care. **Son of man**, in the OT, often is a collective expression for mankind (cf. 17:4; 22:7; 36:74; and in the individual sense in 32:2; 84:6, 13). The LXX's rendering of this passage is cited in Hebrews 2:6-8, where it is applied to Jesus and his incarnation. Also compare a bitter twist in Job 7:17ff.

[5] The symphony of grace intensifies. In verses 6-8 it reaches its crescendo, so that one can scarcely avoid the refrain of verse 9. **God** (Elohim) can mean deity or can refer to superhuman beings generally (1 Sam. 28:13). Therefore the translation could be "gods," "divine beings," or "angels" (cf. 86:8; 95:3; 96:5; 132:6; 135:5). The latter is the rendering of the LXX, Vulgate, Targum, and Syriac. Translating **God** seems to contradict the distance from **God** previously depicted. Yet this may be a deliberate way of stressing the wonder of the divine blessing upon man: so small, yet raised so high! The expression must not be misunderstood as if man is slightly below deity on the ladder of being. His exaltation is in the area of sovereignty—which is in likeness to God's absolute rule. The gulf between man and **God**, over all, is still beyond comprehension. [6] Here begins an extended exploration of man's lordship over earth (a poetic form of Gen. 1:26-28), thus fortifying the poet's powerful affirmation. It says, in specific focus, that God created man in his image. This verse is cited in 1 Corinthians 15:26, of Christ. (Cf. also Eph. 1:22.) [7-8] Here the **all** is unfolded—both domestic and wild creatures. The one man has tamed, and the other he may tame or use.

[9] The refrain now has fuller significance to the reader, as he has been opened to the writer's mind and learns why he began the psalm with such praise. It is as if the author makes an affirmation of praise, then explains it, in order to draw the reader into like intensity of worship. In the use of this psalm in Jewish worship, this verse (with vs. 1) may have been sung in counterpoint to the rest of the text.

Psalm 9: Praise and Appeal

Psalms 9 and 10 contain elements of hymn, thanksgiving, and lament. They may have originally been one psalm. First, they are together in several ancient versions. Second, they seem to be part of a single acrostic scheme (other acrostics are 25, 34, 37, 111, 112, 119, 145). Yet its incompleteness may argue for the alteration of the text from some original form. Why else would the pattern be broken? Third, there is no title in Psalm 10. Since most psalms in this part of the Psalter have titles, it could be assumed the title of Psalm 9 covered both it and Psalm 10. Fourth, there are a number of linguistic similarities.

Yet the themes of the two differ. Psalm 9 is largely praise and thanks, while 10 is more lament and supplication. Psalm 9 is the utterance of an individual, while this emphasis virtually disappears in 10. Psalm 9 is primarily concerned with the enemies outside Israel, while 10 agonizes over those within. Still, they have common elements and may represent complementary materials combined into one psalm. Other psalms are also diverse (27, 40, 89). Both are concerned about enemies and God's saving acts.

Psalm 9 begins with praise, in connection with God's

mighty deeds (vss. 1, 2). Much of the rest of the psalm speaks of wonderful deeds (vss. 3-10, 12-13, 15-16, 17-20). In verses 3-4 the writer's enemies fall before God, the righteous Judge. Further discussion of God's victory over the nations, the wicked, and the enemy follows (vss. 5-6). God judges all with righteousness and equity (vss. 7-8). He is a stronghold for the oppressed and those who seek him (vss. 9-10). Thus all who dwell in Zion should praise him (vss. 11-12). There follows a plea for the Lord to be gracious, that he may be praised for his deliverance (vss. 13-14). Verses 15-17 further describe the doom of the nations. There is final reminder of God's care for the poor and needy (vs. 18), before a prayer for God to make the nations know their frailty (vss. 19-20).

Acrostics, because tied to an artificial literary plan, often suffer from a lack of unity. Though this does not flow as smoothly as some, the thought centers in the wonderful deeds of the Lord. This is based on the concept of God as a universal, righteous judge with the power to effect his judgments. Interpretations of Psalms 9 and 10 have described them as referring to past events, or to typical events, or as being eschatological.

[1-2] Five verbs in the first two verses express praise **to the Lord.** This, with verses 11 and 14, may indicate the psalm is for congregational use, telling of God's grace. Subsequent parts of the poem will indicate the reasons for the **thanks. Wonderful deeds** is used in Psalms to refer to creation, judgment, and redemption. The double verb in verse 2 intensifies the idea of exultation. **[3-4]** Apparently foes have threatened, but because of God's intervention (a wondrous deed), they are routed. Notice that the **enemies** here (also vss. 6, 13, 16) are equivalent to the nations (vss. 5, 15, 17, 19, 20) and therefore are foreign oppressors. "Stumble" and "perish" may imply God's characteristic action through history, rather than just a specific event in the author's past. Appeal to the continual action of God occurs throughout Psalms 9 and 10. If one has faith in God who redeems his people from wicked foes, panic is overcome.

[5] Verses 5 and 6 comment on verse 3. It is presumed

that the **nations** are in rebellion against God and are aggressors against Israel. Six verbs describe their judgment, whether past or anticipated, or the ultimate end of enemies of Israel. The emphasis is on God's decisive action. They are so obliterated that even their name no longer remains. **For ever and ever** translates two Hebrew words which are used for emphasis. [6] The last of the verse reads literally "their memory, they." The RSV gives an interpretive rendering. Other possibilities are suggested but involve altering the text. The present reading is legitimate and avoids interpolation or textual change.

[7-8] The thought of verse 4b is resumed, and a rationale for verses 5-6 given. The structure of the section is a majestic progressive parallelism. It is God's eternal dwelling, against the everlasting ruins of the enemy. Also contrasted are the wicked (vs. 5) and the righteous (vs. 8). All is given gravity by the threefold repetition of the concept "for ever" in verses 5-7. Verse 8 is cited in Acts 17:31, which speaks of Christ as judge.

[9-10] God's action as judge leads to the confidence which these verses express. The opening verb of verse 9 would literally be rendered "Let the Lord be," but most translators, with a slight change of vowels, read "The Lord is" or "was." The **stronghold** would be an inaccessible place which an aggressor could not successfully invade. On **oppressed**, see 10:18; on **times of trouble**, see 10:1.

[11] Verses 11 and 12 are a reprise of verses 1-2. Since reasons for praise have been explicated, what is more appropriate than a call to worship? Thus, the corporate use of the psalm becomes evident. Is this not also a call to evangelism, as the nations are informed of the lord's **deeds** (cf. vs. 1)? **Zion** indicates Jerusalem and, perhaps, the temple. But God's throne is also in heaven (see 11:4 for both ideas in one verse). [12] God is the subject of this verse. But is he the one seeking **blood** (as in Gen. 9:2; Ezek. 33:6), or does he remember (to judge) those who seek the **blood of the afflicted**? Both readings are possible. The first (RSV) better suits the parallel with verse 12b. Such a God is indeed a stronghold for those who are oppressed.

[13] After verses 5-12, the writer returns to his individual concerns. Aside from the mere mention of his enemies, here is the first explication of woes. Are they his alone, or does he speak as a representative of the entire people? I suffer is cognate in Hebrew to "afflicted" in the previous verse. Gates of death is likely part of the poetic imagery conveying his plight, rather than a literal statement about his health. But the severity of the calamity is clearly indicated. [14] Assuming his petition is heard, he utters an expression of hope which approaches a vow. He would be, not at death's gates, but at Zion's gates, rejoicing and retelling God's goodness. This might be a "sermon" or simply praise in a public place. How can the good news of God's deliverance not be publicized?

[15-16] The psalm now reconsiders the nations, as in verses 5-8. The enemies are caught in their own devices (pit, net). Perhaps this is due to the special action of God or to the fact that evil carries within it the seeds of its own downfall. All traps out of harmony with the intent of the universe catch their makers. The writer here speaks of completed action. Have the nations already fallen, or is he so sure of the Lord that he speaks as if they had? [17] The nations will die (depart to Sheol). This reaffirms verses 5-6.

[18] The needy (cf. vs. 12) may be those especially disadvantaged by the deprivations of the nations or may even be a synonym for Israel. God will not forget them (note the contrast with men who forget God in vs. 17).

[19-20] The writer returns to prayer (cf. vss. 13-14) for his faith to be vindicated and for the Lord to do as he has done. Let the nations be judged, be put in fear, and be required to see the real situation—they are but men. Men (Heb. 'enosh) implies creaturely weakness (cf. 10:18). Another translation of fear is "set them a teacher, master." This is the rendering of the LXX, Vulgate, and Syriac. The exact meaning of the Hebrew term is not clear.

Psalm 10: Against the Arrogant Wicked

This psalm may be outlined as follows: verses 1 and 2 call upon God to punish the wicked, who are described in colorful detail in verses 3-11; the petition resumes in verses 12-15, interspersed with amazement at what the wicked do and assurances they are not beyond God's judgment (as they had supposed); verses 16-18 express certainty that the Lord will procure justice. Because the Lord is king (vs. 16), vindication of the righteous is assured; the afflicted, fatherless, poor, innocent, hapless, meek, and oppressed can take hope; and the wicked will be broken. (See also the introduction to Psalm 9.)

The complaint (vs. 1-2). [1] The despair of this verse serves to set the later positive side of the psalm in stronger contrast. God does not always vindicate himself immediately, and this troubles the believer, more concerned with divine inaction than with the wrongs of the wicked. [2] A deliverance was noted in 9:3-4. That seemed to apply to the nations, while here the problem is with the **wicked** man within Israel. The latter part of the verse is reminiscent of 9:15. But it could be legitimately translated "they shall be caught" with **the poor** as subject. This would be closer to the thought of the first of the verse. **Schemes** literally means "thoughts" and seems to refer to the plans of the wicked.

Depiction of the wicked (vss. 3-11). [3] Renouncing **the Lord**, the **wicked** has deified his own **heart**. His boast may be that he makes no attempt to conceal his greed, or that he is prosperous without troubling about God. **Greedy for gain** is sometimes rendered "robber." **Curses** is the same as the word for blesses, but by an anomaly of language, it can sometimes have exactly opposite meanings. [4] This verse is difficult in Hebrew. The various translations agree, though, that **the wicked** believe **God** is not concerned with human affairs (cf. 14:1; 94:7). **Thoughts** is the same word as "schemes" (vs. 2). **There is no God** is literally "no God all his thoughts." God does not interpose, so why be concerned about divine interference?

[5] The real sting is that, though the wicked should not be expected to prosper, this man does. Because of this he concludes that God is unnecessary. If God were concerned, he would act to rebuke the wicked. The evil man's

outward success destroys his conscience. This, in turn, breeds further rebellion. Verses 5b-6 and 13 seem to be a commentary on verse 4. In a height of arrogance, the wicked **puffs** (probably contemptuously) at **his foes** (cf. Mal. 1:13). Verse 15 will show his folly. **[6]** His pride is so great he sees his security extended in time. Ironically, **I shall not be moved** is often the affirmation of the righteous (15:5; 16:8; 21:8; 62:3-7; 112:6). Verse 6b is rendered freely in the RSV, but the interpretation seems to be a good one.

[7] This powerful description of wickedness is employed in Paul's picture of human depravity in Romans 13:4. Five terms for human wickedness, all dealing with the power of speech, are used here. **Under his tongue** may refer to speech ready to be uttered or to his general character.

[8] Verses 8-11 employ the figures of an ambushing murderer, a lion, and a hunter. In the first image, **the innocent** are victims. Literal murder may have taken place, or the expression may be metaphorical. **[9]** The illustration changes within this verse from **a lion** to a hunter (since lions do not set nets). Perhaps a period after the first line would make the distinction more clearly. "Lurked" is used in both cases. This verse exhibits a linguistic climax, with the repetition of **lurks** and of **seize the poor.** Here we have **the poor,** and previously there have been the innocent and the hapless (vs. 8). Later we meet the fatherless (vs. 14), the meek (vs. 17), and the oppressed (vs. 18). These terms suggest a plea for social justice.

[10] This verse is somewhat obscure in the original. **Hapless** is the subject in the RSV, even though it is plural and the verbs are singular. Is the image here of a hunter, or has it returned to that of a lion (a net does not crush)? **By his might** literally means "by his mighty ones," which have been interpreted as the claws of the lion, or as ruffians in the employ of the persecutors (fitting neither the image of the lion nor of the hunter), or as a great number of persecutors. **[11]** The hapless concludes that **God** is unconcerned (contrast vss. 4, 6), echoing the prayer of verse 1. Or this may be the wicked speaking again. **[12]** The prayer is resumed from verse 1. **Forget not** contrasts with verse 11.

God is requested to lift his hand, often a symbol of royal authority (cf. vs. 16). Later he will bring it down to break the arm of the wicked (vs. 15). [13] Again the idea of verses 4 and 6 is repeated. New here is the psalmist's bewilderment at such a philosophy, for God will surely judge (verses 14ff.). Here, after the description of the wicked and the renewed prayer, the affirmation of faith is found which shows the futility of the wicked man's behavior. Contrast the bewilderment at God's "inaction" in verse 1. Now the bewilderment is over the wrongdoers.

[14-15] The opening (Hebrew "you see—even you") flashes forth as an unmistakable refutation of the spirit of verse 13b. Faith triumphs over appearances. God observes and is concerned. In verse 15 the prayer becomes more specific. A broken arm is powerless to harm others. The Hebrew of both these verses is difficult, and the RSV translates freely, since a literal translation is meaningless. Verse 15b seems a call to punish wickedness till it is entirely eradicated.

[16] Here is the center of the psalm. The theme of 9:7-8, 19-20 is resumed. Also, the focus now turns again to the nation, as in Psalm 9 (cf. vss. 5, 6, 15, 17). We cannot know how the enemies of the previous verses relate to the nations here. Perhaps there was collaboration between foreign oppressors and those who oppressed within.

When would the nations perish from the land? Is this past, future, or timeless? If past, it is impossible to know the time intended. If future, it must be fulfilled spiritually, unless one believes in a physical restoration of Israel, which Scripture does not teach. Perhaps this is a general affirmation of God's delivering might. The NT cites this verse in Revelation 11:15.

[17-18] The Hebrew makes it possible to consider God's hearing as an accomplished fact, upon the basis of which the subsequent actions of the verse were expected to take place. The meek has his desire, and the wicked man, for all his boasting, comes to nothing. The last clause of verse 18 is given an interpretive rendering in the RSV, since the literal Hebrew is somewhat abstruse. Man who is of the

earth probably means "mere man" as in 9:19-20. For those who have cried out in agony, there is glorious vindication. The nightmare will end.

Psalm 11: Refuge in the Lord

This is a psalm of trust in the sovereign God, who loves the righteous and hates the wicked. Its two parts depict two attitudes toward danger. In verses 1-3 the author, likely a leader among his people, is apparently threatened by danger. He is advised to flee. The reason he will not has been expressed in the opening words of the psalm, which are then explicated in verses 4-7. There he affirms his trust in God who oversees all and, assessing men, judges each. Faith, not flight, is the appropriate response to the danger.

Courage in danger (vss. 1-3). [1] The psalm opens with a resounding, even defiant, statement of faith. **In the Lord,** any danger can be faced! Flight can only be to God, though it involves remaining in the face of danger. The RSV, agreeing with several ancient versions, accepts a slight emendation of the Hebrew (a different word division and the addition of one letter) for its reading of the last line. It is more logical that the endangered man would be counseled to **flee** as a **bird** flies than that he would be called a **bird** (cf. RSV note). This advice may come from frightened counselors.

[2] Verses 2-3 may contain the reasons for the friend's counsel, as in the RSV, or the author's explanation that he needed to stay precisely because of the threat. The danger comes, treacherously, from **the dark,** so it would be difficult to defend against it. **The bow** was bent by placing the foot on one end, so **the string** could be fitted (cf. 7:13).

[3] Foundations may refer to fundamental principles of decency and order in society. If the enemies destroy them, chaos results. Or they may refer to a leader (perhaps the author), without whose guidance society would become anarchic. The last clause could be translated "what has the righteous done," either with the meaning that he had been powerless (hopelessness), or in bewilderment that he had incurred such opposition from the enemies. However, the RSV (though the verb describes completed action) gives a future interpretation. Do the advisors imply that the author can do nothing about the threat? If so, they are considering as a lost cause that which could be redeemed with trust in God.

The basis of courage (vss. 4-7). [4] God who dwells **in heaven** is also concerned with earth. To deny him would be denying his role as Surveyor and Assessor (vss. 5-7). The heavenly center of trust is infinitely higher than earthly mountains (cf. vs. 1). Yahweh makes all the difference. Note the progression, in the last line, from **behold** to **test.** **Eyelids,** obviously a parallel to **eyes,** perhaps signifies the squinting of the eyelids in close scrutiny. [5] Verses 5-7 advance on verse 4, describing the testing. **Test** indicates continuing action—it is God's characteristic demeanor. **Hates** indicates completed action—God always does so. Verses 5 and 6 indicate the result of the testing for the wicked, as verse 7 does for the righteous. [6] Notice the figures of speech here. There are **fire and brimstone** (cf. Gen. 19:24), as well as **wind** (the scorching sirocco from the desert?). The **cup** refers to their lot, under God's judgment (cf. 16:5; 75:9). The wicked cast down the foundation, so God casts down **fire! Coals** in the Hebrew literally means "bird traps." The RSV accepts a slight emendation (with one ancient version), which by reversing the last two letters of the word, obtains **coals.** This more appropriately unites with the idea of fire and brimstone.

[7] Note how the psalm has centered in **the Lord,** with the mention of his name in verses 1, 4, 5, and 7. Here the contrast between the wicked and righteous draws to its climax. To see God's **face** is the ultimate blessing. Probably he refers to that sense of divine fellowship which is granted the saints. It is not a literal vision but a continuing experience, in which God's reality becomes clearer to one who lives the life that reflects his nature. The nature of the psalm indicates that **righteous deeds** are those done by men, rather than by God. The psalm closes with an affirmation of stability, founded on ultimate reality. This foundation cannot really be destroyed by the wicked (vs. 3), so the faith of the author is vindicated.

Psalm 12: Help Against the Ungodly

In a society fraught with corruption, this writer trusts God for strength. The psalm emphasizes the power of speech. Wrongdoers function by misuse of the tongue, but God responds with the assurance that his words are pure. Verses 1-4 contain a plea for help, with an increasingly specific description of the corruption of society. The second main section, verse 5, is an oracle in prophetic style, assuring those troubled that God will respond. The third section, verse 6, extols the promises of God. The psalm ends, in verses 7-8, renewing the prayer and restating the problem.

'Help, Lord' (vss. 1-4). [1] It is a time of moral desolation, when no one seems concerned to do God's will. The author may have been especially sensitive because he was a leader of the people. Others think the problem may have been corrupt leadership. "Kindness"and "faithfulness" are possible alternative translations for **godly** and **faithful**. That still does not relieve the intensity of the author's dire depiction of society. (On **godly**, see Ps. 4:3.) [2] The tongue is no longer for sharing, but for snaring. Lying, flattery (literally, smooth lips), and hypocrisy have been characterized as empty talk, smooth talk, and double talk. **Lies** means emptiness (24:4; 41:7; 144:8, 11); and elsewhere in Scripture, it indicates insincerity (Ps. 41:6; Hos. 10:4) and irresponsibility (Exod. 20:7). **To his neighbor** can also be rendered "with" his neighbor, implying collusion in lying. **Double heart** (literally "with heart and heart") indicates a person with two minds, suiting his character to the occasion with no regard for truth or personal integrity. The form of the verb translated **speak** indicates a custom or habit.

[3-4] Boasting is added to the catalog. These are probably the people making life hard for the pious, so the writer prays for the cessation of such activity. In verse 4 the description peaks. The evildoers' speech was their means of success. So proud were they in their schemes, they acknowledged no **Lord**. Such presumption suggests another Babel. Another possible translation of line one is "to our tongues we give might."

God will arise (vs. 5). The form here is like a prophetic oracle in which a spokesman speaks with the Lord's words, setting them against the words of the wicked (vs. 4). **The poor and needy** may be the godly and faithful of verse 1, or those who complain that there are no righteous people to insure justice in society, that is, leadership has broken down. This specific reference to the nature of their difficulty indicates social oppression, likely as a result of the wrongs detailed in verses 2-4. In worship, these words would likely be a priest's response to the congregational recitation of verses 1-4. **Safety** is from the same root as "help" in verse 1. The last line means, literally, "he will puff at him, it." Of many suggested translations, the RSV offers as satisfactory a rendering as can be found.

God's promises (verse 6). This verse expresses a general truth, here applied in a specific context. Perhaps in the use of the psalm in worship it offered a congregational "amen" to the oracle of verse 5. **Promises** literally means "words," stressing the purity of God's words in contrast to those of men (vss. 2-4). Some suggest other translations of **furnace**—a word that occurs only here in the Hebrew Bible. **On the ground** may refer to the refined silver pouring out near **the ground,** or to the **furnace** as built **on the ground,** or to the refining apparatus as being a crucible of clay (earth). Some also suggest emending the Hebrew word translated **ground** to "gold" and putting a comma after **furnace,** thus connecting "gold" with the next line. **Silver**—in some periods more valuable than gold, particularly in its purest forms—is the image for the purity of God's words. Their utter truthfulness, and therefore dependability, is welcome respite to the man weary of the deceptive words of his fellow men. **Seven times** apparently indicates great purity.

'Protect us, Lord' (vss. 7-8). [7] The prayer is resumed, petitioning the safety of the needy. **This generation** doubtless refers to those described in verse 2-4. The RSV translates both verbs as imperatives, though they might legitimately be rendered as future indicatives ("you will **protect** . . . you will **guard**"). [8] One might expect, in psalms such as this, a closing statement of trust, or perhaps a vow, rather than a reprise of the problem, as here. Perhaps this indicates that prayers have been uttered, and that God has promised response, but the corruption remains. The writer may be affirming that it no longer terrifies him, now that he trusts God more fully. Or perhaps he reiterates the problem to emphasize the seriousness of the matter that God will resolve. Is the psalm promising to change ills in society or just to give the needy security to subsist in the situation? Perhaps both are involved, though the second is not indicated as explicitly as the first. **Prowl** implies walking about openly. The exaltation of **vileness** may suggest that wickedness characterizes those in authority. For the problem to be removed, the leaders of society must change.

Psalm 13: A Davidic Lament

This is an excellent example of an individual lament. In verses 1-2 the writer laments the seeming absence of God and his own incessant inner anguish. Verses 3-4 contain a prayer for God to consider, answer, and lighten his eyes, lest he face death and the taunting mockery of enemies. The tone changes in verses 5-6 to trust, joy, and singing, because of God's steadfast love, salvation, and bountiful blessing. These realities express the central thought of the psalm.

'How long, Lord?' (vss. 1-2). [1] The fourfold **how long** of verses 1-2 sets forth the complaint sharply. If God cares, why has he not responded? Yet **how long** contains the hope that there will be divine action, in spite of present appearances. This expression is also found in certain ancient Babylonian laments. **For ever** could mean "utterly" or "continually." [2] The author turns from contemplating God's absence to look within himself. His daily burden is wearing him down. Though **bear pain** makes sense in the context, and only involves a change of one letter from the Hebrew, the original reading (RSV note) could be understood as referring to the writer's psychological plans for dealing with his problem. Some argue that the original Hebrew word can be rendered "agony," making the change in the RSV unnecessary. Exaltation of the **enemy** is further elucidated in verse 4.

The petition (vss. 3-4). [3] A progressive, threefold request begins the poet's prayer. The threat **of death** (final separation from God) would be the grim culmination of the forsakenness already noted (vs. 1). **Consider** is the antithesis of "hide" (vs. 1). "Quit looking away, and look here!" **Death** is often conceived under the figure of **sleep** (76:6; 90:5). Darkening the **eyes** symbolizes sickness and sorrow (6:7; 38:10; Lam. 5:17), and lightening the eyes the revival of physical strength and moral energy (1 Sam. 14:27, 29; Prov. 29:13; Ezra 9:8). Perhaps he is asking for faith in the fullest, to deal with the problem. Note the blessings in verses 5-6. This prayer, and the singing of verse 6, likely indicate the cultic use of this psalm.

[4] Mockery by enemies would reflect on God, he whom the author trusted, if it implied their denial that God would aid him. Did they pose a death threat (vs. 3), or was the idea that any increased misfortune seemed to favor their cause? To be **shaken** usually pictures misfortune in general (cf. 38:16, and contrast 10:6; 16:8, etc.).

Expression of faith (vss. 5-6). [5] The tone changes from lament to trust. The form of the Hebrew word translated **trusted** indicates completed action. Has he always **trusted** God or is this the condition to which he comes in connection with the prayer? Such trust may be the faith for which the petition "lighten my eyes" yearned. **Salvation** is doubtless cessation of his particular misery and of enemy opposition.

[6] Verses 5-6 are one in Hebrew. This verse is a pinnacle of exaltation, out of the depths of despondency. How different are "forget" and "hide" (vs. 1) from **dealt bountifully** (completed action), which may refer to God's customary action in the past or to his answer of the writer's prayer in the present, or may be the strong affirmation that he would act, described as if the deed were already done (cf. 116:7; 119:17; 142:1). Singing is the inevitable expression of the soul's joyful gratitude to God.

Psalms 14 and 53: The State of the Wicked

How did Psalms 14 and 53, nearly identical, both come to be included in the Psalter? They may originally have been parts of separate collections, which, when incorporated in our present book, were allowed to stand because of some differences between them. Or the author of one psalm may have consciously adapted the text of the other to a new situation. Stylistically, this psalm comes nearer the wisdom type than any other.

Verses 1-3 describe the miserable state of society. God searches to find wise men and fails in his quest (but cf. vs. 5). Verses 4-6 show the futility of such wickedness (in unknowledgeable and frightening opposition to God). Verse 7 is a wish-prayer for God's deliverance, anticipating exultation when it comes.

Psalm 53:5, if the original Hebrew be retained (see discussion), focuses more on the judgment of the wicked than does 14:5. Thus 14:5 stresses that God is with the righteous, while 53:5 stresses the doom of the wicked. These are two sides of the same reality, and are the centers of the two psalms. The following discussion applies to both psalms, unless otherwise noted.

'None do good' (vss. 1-3). [1] The foolishness is not a theoretical (philosophical) atheism, but a practical unbelief, which is impudent and unaware of **God**. Fools ignore **God** in their moral decisions. They would probably not even trouble themselves to deny him. Essentially, they are their own gods. The Hebrew word for **fool** is *nabhal* (1 Sam. 25:25; cf. Isa. 32:6), which, though singular, refers to a class, since it is used with plural verbs. It describes an aggressive perversity. Some argue (on the basis of similarity in language to Gen. 6:1ff.) that verses 1-3 picture pre-flood humanity, as typifying human depravity whenever and wherever found. This is a deeply disturbing picture of much of mankind. Yet it overstates for effect, since eight righteous people survived the flood, and since the psalmist would not consider himself a fool. For **abominable deeds** (14:1), 53:1 has the even stronger "abominable iniquity".

[2] God observes **from heaven** (cf. 2:4), seeking men of wisdom (cf. Gen. 11:5; 18:21). Some think all mankind is here considered, while others think it is Israel (cf. Paul's use in the former sense in Rom. 3:10-13). We cannot say which is correct. The Hebrew word for Lord in 14:2 is Yahweh, but in 53:2 it is Elohim. However, Psalm 53 is in a section of the Psalter that consistently uses Elohim for God. [3] Divine investigation discovers straying (Ps. 14), falling away (Ps. 53), corruption (Ps. 14), and depravity (Ps. 53). The last two terms (the same Hebrew word, despite the difference in the RSV) come from a word which in other literature can mean "to become sour." Some Greek manuscripts insert Romans 3:13-18 after verse 3 here, under the influence of the NT. The material was obviously not in the original Hebrew.

The error of the wicked (vss. 4-6). [4] The writer, in his amazement, seems almost to appeal to the fools to recognize the utter absurdity of their conduct. Those that **eat** God's people as **bread** might be foreign oppressors or corrupt leaders within Israel. Relative to the latter, some suggest a degenerate priesthood, eating sacrificial offerings. However, the metaphor probably indicates those who do evil as easily as they would eat bread. We think the writer of Psalm 14 refers to leaders within Israel, but Psalm 53 may offer a different perspective (see below). **My people** seems equivalent to the "righteous" and "poor" (vss. 5-6).

[14:5-6; 53:5] These verses picture the result of God's looking and the real nature of things. Some say **there** implies a cultic episode, but it could as easily mean that wherever evil is found, judgment comes. **Terror** is likely produced by their realization they are defeated by the Almighty. They learn how costly ignoring him has been. Note that 14:5 is future, while 53:5a is present. Verse 6 refers to **the poor** for the first time in Psalm 14. Their **plans** may be their trust in **the Lord**, which the wicked attempt to frustrate but which God vindicates. Here we find the greatest divergence between Psalms 14 and 53. Psalm 53:5 adds **such as has not been** (literally, "not was afraid"). Other possible translations could indicate that, despite lack of previous fear or reason for it, calamity comes to the wicked nevertheless.

With the exception of **righteous** (14:5), which is not paralleled in Psalm 53, the Hebrew words of these passages are remarkably similar, leading to the supposition there is a literary relationship between them. Could a manuscript of one have been blurred, or incomplete, and the other be an attempt to reproduce the text? More likely, perhaps, is the possibility that one was adapted from the other to fit a different situation, with an effort made to use words as close to the original as possible. "Him who encamps against you" (RSV note *e* to 53:5) is an emendation making Psalm 53 more congruent with Psalm 14. But the Hebrew, paraphrased as "your besieger," is possible and would imply some military assault that God would thwart. "You will put to shame" (RSV note *f* to 53:5) is a possible reading; with a slight change in a verb ending, this could become "you will put him to shame." This would imply, again, defeat of a foe. The change in the RSV is more in harmony with Psalm 14. Perhaps Psalm 53 is describing a foreign threat, and the already familiar Psalm 14 was adapted to a new situation. Or perhaps the military terms are metaphorical descriptions of a personal enemy.

A prayer (14:7; 53:6). This prayer for deliverance has a liturgical flavor and seems to place the psalm in a worship context. It may have been a later addition. The concern here seems national, whereas Psalm 14, and the RSV of Psalm 53 have seemed personal. Psalms 14 and 53 have different forms of the same word for **deliverance**. In Psalm 53 it is plural, implying "saving acts." Here deliverance comes from **Zion**, whereas in verse 2 it was from heaven. The verse is cited in Romans 11:26-27.

Psalm 15: Who Dwells with God

Psalms 15 and 24 both have to do with entry into the place of worship. Psalm 15 opens by inquiring about the character requisite for a man who would sojourn in God's tent and dwell on his holy hill. There follows the response (vss. 2-5b), in which are set forth ten (eleven?) requirements. It concludes (vs. 5c) with a summary statement, which gives the heart of the psalm.

Israel may have followed the ancient Near Eastern custom of informing worshipers of the cultic requirements to be met for admission to the temple. However, this psalm is not speaking of cultic actions, but of social responsibilities. It may have sprung originally from a cultic background, but was later used in an ethical sense (cf. especially Isa. 33:14-16; also Jer. 7:1ff; Ezek. 18:5-9; Mic. 6:6-8). This response-seeking form (vs. 1) may also relate to seeking God's answer through a minister of the sanctuary (see 2 Sam. 21:1; Hag. 2:11ff.; Zech. 7:1-2; Mal. 2:5-7).

These have been called the ten commandments for the true worshiper (if vs. 4ab is taken as one requirement, rather than two) on the assumption that there is a deliberate parallel with the Ten Commandments. Their nature, however, is different from the first four of the original Ten. These obligations do not make a complete list.

The question (vs. 1). The **tent** has been related to the tabernacle (2 Sam. 6:17) and to the temple (Pss. 27:5-6; 61:5). More important is the crucial concept of fellowship with Yahweh, in which one enjoys his protection.

The response (vss. 2-5). [2] The answer in verses 2-5b was probably given in worship by a priest. The validity of the cult is affected by the quality of the life. The ideas here will be elaborated more specifically in verses 3-5b. **Blamelessly** means "sound, innocent, having integrity," and refers to one loyal to the will of Yahweh. **Truth** means faithfulness or reliability (a quality of life). This verse speaks of attitudes and intents (**from his heart**). [3] These moral demands of verses 3b-5 are not all parallel. Note the strong emphasis on social ethics. **Slander with his tongue** is difficult in the Hebrew, but perhaps indicates the behavior of one who goes around gathering and repeating tales to discredit others. **Takes up a reproach** may mean to utter reproach, or to rake up otherwise unnoticed evidence, or to add reproach to the burden of a neighbor.

[4] A **reprobate** is one who is rejected. **Despised** may mean that the man of integrity declares that he stands

opposed to the **reprobate**. Compare the same verb used of God's "despising" wrong in 22:25; 51:19; etc. This first part could also be translated "who is small in his own eyes, of no account." Though it does not contrast with the next line, it does change the spirit of a clause which some find objectionable. Line 3 describes an integrity which may even turn out to one's advantage. Proverbs 6:1-5 indicates similar instances where a man can beg release from an obligation and try to find another resolution. But in both cases the man still acts honorably. Another suggested translation, "swears to his friend," involves only a slight change in the Hebrew.

[5] In Israel loans were made in cases of need. Israelites were not to profit from a brother's misfortune. Their wealth was to benefit the needy. A fellow Israelite was not to be charged **interest**, though it could be taken from a foreigner (Exod. 22:25; Lev. 25:37; Deut. 23:20; Neh. 5:7; Prov. 28:8). When interest was taken, rates were exorbitant. Here the usual distinction between Israelite and foreigner is not made. Is the implication that all men were to be treated with impartiality? Bribery was especially odious when it deprived **innocent** people of their rights. The man of integrity resists such temptations, for to him people are more important than wealth. (On bribery, cf. Exod. 23:8; Deut. 10:17; 16:19; 27:25; etc.) The man described in verses 2-5b **shall never be moved**. His life is anchored in ultimate reality. He has learned the real values of life. **Never** fortifies the point. The life of integrity is eternally justified.

Some say verse 5c was a later addition, giving the psalm a broader sense than the purely cultic. Whether this is the case or not, this line admirably completes the sentiment of the whole.

Psalm 16: 'Thou Are My Lord'

This psalm is a magnificent affirmation of trust in the Lord from one whose life is passionately grounded in him. The text itself gives little clue as to its authorship. The ascription to David in the heading is also reflected in Acts

2:29. (Cf. the discussion of Davidic authorship in the introduction to this commentary.)

In verses 1-2 the writer states the foundation of his life.
Next he contrasts his attitudes toward the saints and those
worshiping other gods (vss. 3-4). Verses 5-11, by a series of
descriptions, repeatedly affirms his God-centered existence. Here is the deepest source of life's meaning, security, and satisfaction. The frequent use of terms expressing
delight in Yahweh has led one writer to say the psalm is
"flooded with dancing sunlight." God is to the author "portion" and "goodly heritage" (vss. 5-6), cup (vs. 5), counselor (vs. 7), sure foundation and security (vss. 8-9), source
of joy (vss. 9-11), protector from death (vs. 10), guide (vs.
11), and source of complete satisfaction (vs. 11). No wonder he says, "I have no good apart from thee" (vs. 2).

God the refuge (vss. 1-2). [1] If the author was experiencing trouble, the rest of the psalm is singularly silent
about it. Perhaps his words simply ask for God's customary preservation to be continued. There he always finds his
refuge, whatever the options. [2] Here is a powerful statement of a life philosophy. How few can truly make it!
Every genuine good is implicit within God. **I say** of the
RSV is "you say" in the Hebrew. The RSV is based on a
slight change in the vowels and agrees with several ancient
versions. If the Hebrew be kept, a subject must be supplied for the verb (e.g., the man's soul). The last line (see
the RSV note) is difficult to translate satisfactorily. A
change of one letter in the Hebrew produces "my good is
all upon you." Even without the change, the RSV yields as
good a sense as could be expected.

Saints and idolators (vss. 3-4). [3] Relationship with God
determines relationships to people. This author appreciates
the fellowship of those who serve God. **As for the saints**
could also be taken as another direct object of the verb
"say" in verses 2 (i.e., "say to the saints that they were
noble"). **Saints** is often used of persons set apart in some
particular way. Though its early usages did not necessarily
indicate piety, it seems to do so here (cf. vs. 10). However,
some commentators have felt the word indicates heathen

gods (cf. the NEB), in agreement with verse 4. This is possible since, in the Psalms, the term is used more often of heavenly than of earthly beings. However, all the ancient versions indicate **saints** in the sense of men, and the writer may add **in the land** to indicate that this was his meaning. Translational difficulties also appear in connection with the word for **the noble** (cf. the modern versions). The RSV seems to follow some ancient versions in omitting the prefix "and" from the word.

[4] This is the only statement of its sort in the psalm. Was the writer concerned with the worship of heathen deities, or was this a device to show that fulness of life is possible only through Yahweh, and alternate paths produce multiplied **sorrows? God,** not in the original, is interpolated by the RSV to complete the thought. Since the verb **choose** usually means "hasten," some would omit **god** and render "those who hurry backward" (i.e., apostates). However, this does not fit the rest of the verse as well. **Sorrows** are multiplied, because apart from Yahweh there is no real and ultimate good. Various explanations have been offered for **libations of blood** (human sacrifice; actual blood offered; sacrifices with blood-stained hands; detestable libations; or Jewish apostasy). The general idea is clear. **Names** could refer to the gods or to the worshipers. The former is more likely.

'God is my portion' (vss. 5-11). [5-6] A series of images shows what God is and does. **Chosen portion** refers to one's allotted share—language frequently describing the Levitical inheritance (Num. 18:20; Deut. 10:9; 18:1; Josh. 13:14). Thus, some maintain that the author was a Levite. But in a broader sense God is the portion of all Israel (Pss. 73:26; 119:57; 142:5; Jer. 10:16). **Cup** is a figure for one's situation in life. **Holdest** may indicate both apportioning and upholding. God both grants and sustains his blessings. **Lines** were used to measure property. Like a lover of the land describing a most favored and desirable spot, so this author delights in God.

[7] Blessing **the Lord** (cf. 26:12; 34:2; etc.) includes acknowledging his being with deepest gratitude (he is

counselor). The **counsel** is probably the path of life (vs. 11). The poet's nocturnal reflection drives sleep from him. Perhaps the experience involved prayer. This meditative exercise (if such it is) increases his understanding. The Hebrew word rendered **night,** is plural, and may mean "in the dark night" or "every night." **Heart** is literally "kidneys," the seat of emotion or reflection. **[8]** Here is the "practice of God's presence." His discipline (**I keep**) grounds his life securely. God, on the **right hand**, is always near to help. The RSV adds **he**, which the sense seems to demand. Another reading could be "from his right hand I shall not be moved." Verses 8-11 are cited from the LXX and reinterpreted in Acts 2:24-28, where Peter applies the language to the resurrected Christ.

[9] Here is the result of his walk with God. Even when thinking of death (vs. 10), he is overwhelmed with optimism. **Heart, soul**, and **body** are a strong way of indicating the total person. **Soul** (usually translated "glory") conveys the idea of the noblest part of the inner man. **Dwells secure** indicates resting securely in the Lord's land. **Secure** became "in hope" in the LXX, from which Acts 2:26 quotes, applying the language to Jesus' corpse in the tomb.

[10] Here a strong faith is expressed—one to which death has lost its dreadful importance. Not even that barrier disturbs one who finds security in Yahweh. He may feel that God will let him live to a good old age. But since death (**Sheol, Pit**) was popularly conceived as taking one away from God's presence, this writer's triumphant response denies that anything can sever his relation to the Lord. In Acts 2, Peter, quoting the LXX, applies this verse to Jesus' resurrection. **Pit** has the same consonants as the word for "corruption" (the LXX translation), which lends itself to Peter's argument (see also Acts 13:35). However Peter may have been guided by God in applying this text, the psalmist is not teaching resurrection here. That concept is only faintly taught in the OT, and that at a later period. On **godly one**, see 4:3. Acts 2:27 applies the term to Christ.

[11] The "refugee" of verse 1 is rich beyond imagination (unbounded **joy** and limitless **pleasures**). Here climaxes the

contrast between life with God and life without him. The
path of life is how one must live in order to experience life
in the fulness that God intended. **Forevermore** means as
long as life lasts. Though the author is probably not depicting everlasting life in the NT sense, he rises to a height of
faith which trembles on the brink of that exalted reality.
Further revelation through Jesus Christ would give content
to what this poet apprehended dimly.

Psalm 17: A Plea for Vindication

This psalm is a lament, with a strong affirmation of innocence, perhaps from one falsely accused (cf. Deut. 17:8-11;
1 Kings 8:31). Despite numerous suggestions, there is
hardly sufficient evidence to deduce the author's exact situation. Verses 1-2 are an innocent man's cry for vindication.
There follows a further declaration of innocence (vss. 3-5).
Verses 6-9 are a renewal of prayer, especially for relief from
enemies. The enemies are described in verses 10-12, and
then the prayer again taken up in verses 13-14. The last
verse is a final expression of confidence.

'Attend to my cry!' (vss. 1-2). [1] An urgent threefold
entreaty opens the prayer. **Just cause** could either modify
Lord (O righteous **Lord**) or **cry** (as in the RSV). **Cry** can be
understood as a piercing shriek. On the author's innocence,
see the introduction to this volume. [2] The writer rests
not only on his righteousness (vs. 1), but also on the just
Judge of all. The Lord can be addressed confidently by the
man of integrity. **Vindication** (often translated "judgment")
here indicates a saving, not a condemning, verdict. He
asks that any human decision reflect God's justice. **Right** in
the psalms often implies equity in government (cf. 9:8).

Declaration of innocence (vss. 3-5). [3] The author offers
his life to God's scrutiny (vss. 3-5, cf. 7:3-5), for above all
else he desires a right relationship with him. **By night** may
suggest that even quiet nocturnal meditations show devotion to God. Some even conjecture here a night vigil in the
sanctuary (cf. 16:7; 63:5-6; 77:2-6; 119:62). The last line has
the psalm's second affirmation of integrity in speech. Was
this in response to specific charges against the author (cf.

also vs. 5)? **[4]** From words he turns to acts, and gives the source of his strength—God's **word!** God's revelation implies grace, so the poet is not suggesting his merit alone is his ground for pleading. Violence elsewhere indicates robbery or murder. **[5]** Continuing the imagery of "ways" of verse 4, the writer describes his conduct positively, with solid footing in well-defined **paths.** Consequently, confident prayer comes from such a firm footing.

The plea renewed (vss. 6-9). [6] Now, his innocence declared, the psalmist resumes his petition—at first with general (vs. 6), and then specific (vss. 7, 8, and especially 9) requests. **God** will **answer! [7]** This verse, only six words in Hebrew, is not easily translated. The key is God's **steadfast love,** upon which the author stands, beyond his personal integrity. Yet that integrity is a prelude to claiming such **love. Wondrously show** is a difficult term, with various translational possibilities. **Their** is added by the RSV to show that the **refuge,** not the **adversaries,** is at God's **right hand.** Another possibility is "*with* thy right hand."

[8] The preceding request is beautifully amplified, claiming the intimacy of God's protection. **Apple of the eye** (literally "the pupil, daughter of the eye") refers to that which is most precious and to be guarded with utmost care (cf. Deut. 32:10; Prov. 7:2; Zech. 2:8). **Shadow of thy wings** may suggest the watchful care of a mother bird, or the wings of the cherubim above the ark, or even the wings of the Egyptian solar disc protecting the king. The first interpretation seems preferable.

[9] The writer's problem is now stated more specifically. The imagery may indicate a besieged city, an ambush (cf. vs. 12), or a chase and capture. The term **surround** suggests the seriousness of the plight. **Deadly** is the word usually translated "life, soul," or sometimes "appetite." The idea may be that their enmity resides deep within them, and they are therefore the more dangerous.

The enemy (vss. 10-12). [10] Verses 9-12 contrast impressively with the author's previous affirmations of innocence (vss. 1-5). Here are men inwardly insensitive. **Heart** (literally, "fat") is a physical attribute describing a psychological reality. This is characteristic of Hebrew, with its dearth of psychological terms. The RSV adds **to pity** to aid in interpretation. The Hebrew reads simply "their hearts they close." **Arrogantly** emphasizes the pomposity and presumptuousness of their utterances.

[11-12] Verse 11 is most difficult in the original. The RSV has accepted an altered text. The Hebrew of line 1 reads literally "our goings now they surround us." "Our goings" is emended to **they track me. To cast** is also from an emended text (literally, "to bend down"). The RSV adds **me** after **cast** to improve the sense. In verse 11 the image progressively shows one pursued by wild beasts. This fits well with verse 12, where, in terrifying imagery, the writer exposes his fears. Setting the **eyes** likely indicates attention given to accomplishing their designs. **Young lion** is the psalm's first reference to the enemies in the singular.

'Deliver my life!' (vss. 13-14). [13] For the first time the author calls for the destruction of his enemies, with a progressive series of imperatives. **Overthrow** means, literally, "cause to bow down in death." God is pictured as a formidable warrior, who will surely defeat his enemies.

[14] This difficult verse could refer to a curse or to a blessing. The language sounds like a blessing, but the RSV translates it as a curse. If verse 14 forms an antithesis to verse 15 (the RSV adds "as for" in vs. 15), a curse is called for. Despite the unlikely language, this seems the most sensible interpretation; yet it still leaves serious problems in translation, which can be noted by comparing modern versions. **World** simply refers to this age. The meaning may be men who find it, rather than God, their ultimate concern. **Stored up** sometimes refers to treasure, but not always. If taken in a good sense here, the author admits that the wicked have material blessings (though not that blessing delineated in vs. 15). Taken in the bad sense, it would be God's punishment for them and for their children. The same options relate to the interpretation of **more than enough**, or another reading might be "they shall have **more than enough children**" indicating abundant progeny. But they still lack fellowship with God. Over all, this verse in

the RSV refers to God's judgment afflicting the wicked so severely that even his descendants face it, as it were. Though not removing all problems, this seems to make the passage most intelligible.

'I shall behold thy face' (vs. 15). Here the real prosperity of the author appears. If the children of the wicked have more than enough, the writer's satisfaction is even greater (vss. 14 and 15 use the same Hebrew verb). How will he **behold** God's face? Perhaps he refers to an inner spiritual blessing or to a visionary experience. He may not have a clear concept himself, but an overwhelming faith that his relationship to God will somehow bear its reward. **When I awake** may have some literal sense, or it might refer to the "morning" of God's answer after a night of anxious sleep. However we understand the final verse, it offers a powerful and thrilling statement of the central reality of the author's life.

Psalm 18: The Lord, the Rock

The theme of this psalm is found in verse 50, "great triumphs he gives to his king." Whatever the original circumstance, the psalm has been broadened to general dimensions, perhaps to be used for state and cultic occasions. It is virtually identical to 2 Samuel 22, where it is ascribed to David. This is not impossible, though reference to the temple in verse 6 may tell against it. The author is clearly a king.

This vigorous, energetic psalm moves through diverse elements, all centering in God's victory given to the king. Verses 1-6 are thanks for God's answer to prayer in distress. Verses 7-19 depict God's mighty coming to set the king, delivered, in a broad place. Verses 20-30 describe the righteousness of the author, leading to deliverance, in consonance with God's character. Verses 31-42 depict the preparation and successful prosecution of the battle; verses 43-45 show the aftermath of victory; and verses 46-50 are a final ascription of praise to the Lord.

Trust in God's aid (vss. 1-6). [1-2] This hymn-like beginning sets the tone for the rest of the psalm, which will detail the basis of the author's **love**. The beloved God is also the terrible foe (vss. 7-19)—an interesting counterpoint. Nine terms, many used elsewhere in the Psalms, impressively picture what God means to the writer. This extended series strikes us with the power of the writer's feeling. Two Hebrew words for **rock** are used, the first indicating a crag. **Horn** (i.e., strength) probably derives from the horn of an animal. Less likely is the idea of refuge found at the horns of the altar. **[3]** To such a God confident prayer is made. **Praised** represents the root from which the term "hallelujah" comes. The **enemies** here are not precisely identified. A fuller description will come in verses 37-45. **Call** and **saved** both indicate incomplete action—they are ongoing realities.

[4-5] (Cf. 116:3.) Four images depict the extremity of the peril. **Death**, alternately described as **perdition** and **Sheol**, even if symbolic, shows the severity of the plight. This is the ultimate desperation. "The scene has a titanic scale." Some suggest exodus imagery here (cf. vs. 15). **Cords** may also mean "pains" or "sorrow." **Torrents** suggests being swept away helplessly. The word **perdition** is a translation of the Hebrew term *beliya'al*, which is variously understood. The central idea seems to be destruction and ruin (cf. 41:9, "deadly," and 101:3, "base"). **Snares** suggests a hunter. **[6]** Prayer is again central (as in vs. 3). The verbs in Hebrew represent incomplete action, perhaps continual. Whether the **temple** is earthly or heavenly, the point is the appeal to **God**, the only hope in such straits.

The Mighty Deliverer (vss. 7-19). These verses, read with imagination, are truly awe-inspiring in their dramatic and colorful description of God's power (though his *form* is nowhere described). One is reminded of storm and earthquake, and perhaps the exodus (cf. vs. 15). **[7]** When God comes, even **earth** and **mountains** are unsteady. The impact of line 1 in Hebrew is intensified by an assonance of the words. "Reel" elsewhere describes tossing waters, or a reeling inebriate. **He was angry** is literally "it burned to him." **[8-9]** The God of the storm pours forth his wrath. God's consuming **fire** is often mentioned in the OT (cf.

Exod. 15:7; Deut. 4:24; 32:22; Ps. 97:3). **Fire** and **coals** may symbolize lightning. The storm is a way of depicting God's fierce anger. God descends in **darkness**—perhaps a dark canopy of clouds, enshrouding the earth (cf. 97:2; Exod. 20:21; Deut. 4:11). **Bowed** may mean "spread apart."

[10-11] **Cherubim** are winged creatures, upon whom the Lord rides (80:1; 99:1). They may personify the storm cloud or the wind (paralleling line 2, cf. 68:33; 104:3; Isa. 19:1; and see also Ps. 68:4). Ezekiel 1:4ff. presents a similar scene. The last line of verse 11 is difficult (literally, "darkness of waters cloud masses of thin clouds"), but may picture a great storm cloud heavily laden with **water**.

[12-14] These verses depict thunder, lightning, and hail, breaking from the gloom of the cloudy darkness. **Coals** suggests lightning (cf. vs. 8). Another possible reading is "his cloud passed before him, (as well as) hailstones." **Thunder** (vs. 13) probably symbolizes God's voice (though with no specific message here—cf. 29:3; 104:7). The last line of verse 13 duplicates the last of verse 12. Since 2 Samuel 22:14 and the LXX omit it, it may have been a copyist's mistaken duplication. In verse 14, storm and warrior images are intermingled. **Arrows** may represent lightning or even thunder (cf. 77:17; Hab. 3:11). **Scattered** could refer to enemies or to the dispersal of the **arrows**.

[15] This language is reminiscent of the exodus (cf. Exod. 15:8; Pss. 104:7; 106:9), which would imply both God's judgment and his saving grace. The last line, depicting a mighty wind, implies divine wrath. Verses 7-15 skillfully associate dynamic natural phenomena with the unleashed power of God in behalf of the praying king.

[16] Verses 16-19 depict the explicit deliverance. The poet exults that the majesty has been for his sake. The exodus symbolism continues, with the **waters** suggesting his present foes. **Drew** is used (besides 2 Sam. 22:17) only in Exod. 2:10, which describes Moses being drawn from the water. [17-18] How ineffectual were **strong** and **mighty** foes compared with the stormy force of verses 7-15! **Stay** (vs. 18) suggests a support or staff, offering stability in shaky circumstances. Here is yet another way the poet

extols God's aid (cf. vss. 1, 2). [19] The climax is deliverance into freedom—a broad place. The cords and snares (vss. 4-5) have been burst. God's delight in the author becomes the theme of verses 20-30.

God rewards the righteous (vss. 20-30). This passage is based on deuteronomic theology. Verses 21-23 comment on verse 20, and then verse 24 gives a reprise of verse 20.

[20] The king knows both the quality of his own life (righteous, clean) and God's grace. He is not speaking pridefully but is affirming his appropriate covenant response to God. Had the monarch been wicked, the psalm would not have been written. [21-24] His life was constantly determined by God's intents. The blamelessness that God demanded had to do with observance of the law (Deut. 18:13; Ps. 15:2).

[25-26] In the first three statements there is a correspondence between the human attribute and the verb describing the divine response. But the fourth case is not so. One would not ascribe crookedness to God. **Perverse** has the basic meaning of twisting. God appears perverse because of his judgment upon the **crooked** and because he leaves the sinner to the perversity of his character. Yet Matthew 5:43-48 adds another paragraph to the story. [27] This is the first corporate note in the psalm. Some take the word translated **humble** to mean, rather, "poor, needy," seeing God as championing the underdog. But **humble** seems more appropriate in contrast to the **haughty.** There may be a hint here of the king-people relationship, since the character of the nation takes its cue from that of the monarch.

[28] Several additional images continue the picture begun in verses 1-2, and amplify reasons why God is loved. The light/**lamp** symbol depicts the contrast between life and prosperity on one hand, and disaster, disgrace, and death on the other. [29] The word for **crush** could also be translated "run"—that is, either run up to the enemy (fearlessness) or run after him (speed of pursuit). A protective **wall** is no barrier to the enthusiastic warrior. Here is a foretaste of the triumph of verses 31-45. [30] This verse sums up the present section with a reaffirmation of God's

perfection (cf. Deut. 32:4). The writer's experience has confirmed what he affirms. **Promise proves true** is literally "word is refined." His word has stood the test, as pure metal purged of dross.

The king's victory (vss. 31-45). This section shows the king routing his enemies—in God's strength. **[31] God** (Eloah) is a more general term. **Lord** is Yahweh. Who is God, if he is not? Though pagan deities were sometimes called **rock** (cf. Deut. 32:4, 31), this denies that such is a reality. Those following them are left without ultimate aid.

[32] Safe is the same word as "perfect" in verse 30. **God** produces what he is. God prepares his king, wrapping him with **strength** (elaborated in vss. 33-36). **[33]** The **hind** was sure footed and could move swiftly. If wars were fought mostly on foot, the image is particularily apt. **Set secure is** literally "cause to stand," perhaps indicating holding one's ground in battle.

[34] God outfits the warrior. On line one, see 144:1. The Hebrew of line two is difficult. Another suggested translation is "make my arms a bow of bronze." Bows were actually bent with the foot, not the arm. Since bows would not be **bronze,** suggested interpretations include a wooden bow, strengthened with metal, or bronze-tipped arrows; or that this is a figure emphasizing fulness of the preparation (i.e., as if he could literally bend a bronze bow with his arm). **[35-36]** Gentleness (RSV note) is probably a better translation than **help.** Some keep this idea and refer it to a virtue given the king. But gentleness seems to be a strange preparation for war. Some see here the Hebrew verb "answer"—i.e., "thy answer (to prayer) **made me great.**" The RSV seems to give a generalizing interpretation. **Feet** in verse 36 is an unusual term. The idea is of ample standing room and unobstructed movement (cf. vss. 19, 33).

[37] Verses 37-45 describe the rout. The verbs are vivid. The **enemies** (except in vss. 43-45) are never specifically identified. Their end will be decisive and complete. **Consumed** means "finished." **[38-40]** Turning the **backs** may refer to headlong flight. It could also indicate the victor putting his foot on the enemy's neck, though that implies a finished conflict, while the next verses see it as continuing.

[41] In desperation, the adversaries petition Yahweh, unusual for foreigners (vss. 43-45), but not unparalleled (1 Sam. 5:12; Jon. 1:14; 3:8ff.). Contrast the psalmist's answered cries (vss. 3, 6).

[42] This verse climaxes the battle scene. The victory is devastating! **Mire** is usually trodden down, not **cast out** (cf. Isa. 10:6; Mic. 7:10; Zech. 10:5). [43] Verses 43-45 show the king ruling a universal empire (or, less likely, rebels within Israel). These verses are probably a hopeful idealization of the future glory of the kingdom, though they may be spurred by an actual victory. [44-45] Those not slain come **cringing**. These may be envoys coming with flattery. They feel their fortresses are inadequate. **Lost heart** is literally "sink, drop down exhausted." The subjugation is complete. The foes have no more spirit to resist!

Praise for the victory (vss. 46-50). [46] What could conclude the psalm more appropriately than this triumphant emotional cry? He **lives!** How splendidly this has been demonstrated! [47-48] **Vengeance** in the hands of men can be mean and vindictive, but this is God's perfect and righteous judgment, which must be wrought (cf. 94:1; Ezek. 25:14, 17). [49] The king vows worldwide praise. He would magnify his sense of gratitude. Romans 15:9 cites this to show that Christ came for Gentiles as well as Jews. Though the NT refers to salvation of **the nations**, that does not appear to be the central point here. [50] At last the writer is identified as the **king** (1 Sam. 7:15f.; Ps. 89:20, 29, 34, etc.). **Great** could either modify **triumphs** or **his king**. The meaning is probably not substantially different. **Steadfast love** will always be reliable. The psalm prepares us for the larger NT messianic concept.

Psalm 19: The Works and Word of God

We meet here a remarkable sensitivity to God's world and word. Verses 1-6 extol God through his creation; verses 7-14 through his law, and one man's rich spiritual apprehension of it. The two parts differ markedly in subject matter and style. Yet they have a unifying God-centeredness. It is interesting that the sun and justice were often associated in the Near East, as in this psalm. There is a beautiful likeness between the approaches of the two parts. Many, therefore, contend that the psalm was an original unity. Those taking the opposite view either argue that verses 1-6 sounded too pagan, and so a pious editor added verses 7-14, or that a psalm of praise for the law was later prefixed by a nature psalm.

Creation tells of God (vss. 1-6). **[1]** To this man of faith **the heavens** were particularly impressive. Unimaginably vast, fraught with mystery, magnificent, stretching the mind to new limits, they call man beyond them to their Maker. On **firmament,** compare Genesis 1:6 and Job 37:18.

[2] Verses 2-4 offer a bold paradox. Words which are not words produce knowledge for him who listens in faith. **Day to day** and **night to night** may suggest an ongoing witness or may emphasize the individuality of each, passing its fragment or nuance of the whole to the next. It is delightfully stable, yet ever fresh, revelation. And to God is the glory, as the poet listens to the heavenly communiques.

[3-4b] There is no spoken sermon nor oracle. But they are there, a proclamation of the One who so stationed the heavens. "In reason's ear they all rejoice." The heavenly message is universal. He is no local God, but encompasses the heavens and **earth.** Perhaps the poet is wishing that men everywhere would "hear" the heavens as he does. The RSV note refers to a measuring line. Perhaps the idea is that since the heavens measure all the earth, so no place is unreached by their message. But the RSV (in agreement with the LXX and Jerome) chooses to read **voice,** which assumes a slightly different Hebrew text. Other suggestions include "call," "cry," and "law."

[4c-5] **The sun** becomes the focus of verses 4c-6 (cf. 148:3). Since some cultures deified the sun, this may be a polemic against such, for the sun is only part of God's creation. The **tent** may signify night. The groom is either going to his wedding or **leaving** his quarters after the wedding night, both joyous occasions. The strength, beauty, and freshness suggested here are gifts from God. **[6]** As in verse 4, universal dominion is stressed here. As with the sun, so **nothing** is **hid** from the sun's Creator.

The perfect word (vss. 7-14). [7] The divine name (used but once) in verses 1-6 was El. In verses 7-14, Yahweh is used seven times. In verses 7-10 **the law** is described, and in verses 11-14 its effect on the poet's life is indicated. Verses 7-10 use six synonyms for the law (cf. Ps. 119, which uses eight), describe four benefits to the faithful, and note eight attributes of the law (nine, if we include "enduring" of vs. 9). Verses 7-9 demonstrate in detail why the law offers the author such delight (vs. 10). The characteristics of the law are ultimately those of God. We cannot always discern the exact correspondence between the term used for the law and the accompanying characteristic, if indeed any were intended. **Reviving** has the basic idea of returning or bringing back. **Sure** means reliable or dependable. **Simple** comes from a word indicating one open to guidance.

[8] **Right** means equitable or just. **The precepts** also produce joy (cf. vs. 5). **Pure** can imply brightness or brilliance and is a term used to describe the sun in Song of Solomon 6:10 (cf. vss. 4c-6). **Enlightening the eyes** probably refers to a quickened understanding. [9] The parallel structure of verses 7-8 breaks down here. **Righteous** represents a verb, not an adjective, in the Hebrew of this verse. **Fear is** not used elsewhere as a synonym for the law. It puts more emphasis on human response than do the other terms (cf. Prov. 1:7). Some would emend to "word" for a better parallel. **For ever** indicates satisfaction of the human craving for the changeless. **True** is cognate to "sure" (vs. 7) and denotes the perfectly just and dependable. Another suggestion for the last line is "they are vindicated together," emphasizing human reaction more than the law's nature.

[10] Such a law is a joy. Its blessings to the inner man are valued beyond wealth and beyond the choicest sensual delicacy.

[11] The truth of which the poet speaks is not a mere generality; it has been vindicated through his own experience. **Warned** may mean illumined. **Reward**, or "conse-

quence," is defined in verses 7-9, 12-13. For the poet no reward is greater than inner purity and peace with God.

[12] Verses 12-13 focus on both secret and presumptuous sins. Provision was made in the law for unwitting sins (Num. 15:27-36). Are **hidden faults** here those unnoticed because so characteristic of one; or lesser sins that might easily escape notice; or those of ignorance or inadvertence? The prayer seems to imply that one attains increased insight by considering the law, leading to repentance and clearing (acquittal). Yet there is no enslavement here to morbid fears about undiscovered transgressions.

[13] **Presumptuous sins** are proud and deliberate (cf. Num. 15:30). The assumption is that the law offers strength. The poet would be God's servant, not sin's. Perhaps he is saying he needs God's help to keep the law, without clearly understanding how the process would work. The psalm indicates that the more the law is imbibed and understood, the easier it is to keep. The last line is a splendid statement of his summum bonum. [14] The benediction asks for God to accept the psalmist's prayer, and his whole life. He exposes word and thought and asks God to make him what God wants. Thus, total vulnerability produces complete security.

Psalm 20: Prayer and Praise

A king, apprehensive before battle, invokes God's aid. He receives intercessions and assurances, perhaps accompanied by the offering of sacrifice (vs. 3, and cf. 1 Sam. 13:8-15a). This psalm mates with Ps. 21, which expresses thanks for the victory given. Verses 1-5 of the present psalm pray that God will give victory to his king. A response assuring such a triumph occurs in verses 6-8. Verse 9 is a repetition of the prayer.

Blessings invoked (vss. 1-5). [1] Verses 1-5 may be sung by a group (cf. vs. 5) or by a priest addressing the monarch. The peril is of great importance to the congregation, for the king's destiny profoundly affects theirs. The **name** may stress God's covenant relation with his people (cf. vss. 5, 7). No foe enjoys such security. **Protect** implies being set on high, away from danger. **[2]** **Sanctuary** is literally "holy place." It was there that attention was particularly focused on God. The idea may be that **help** comes because God's people praise and serve him.

[3] Though these were possibly the king's devotions of days gone by, they are more likely **sacrifices** offered in connection with the occasion of the psalm. The **sacrifices** and the covenant they imply offer assurance the prayer will be heard. **Offerings** were probably cereal and oil, while **burnt sacrifices** were animals entirely consumed at the altar. **Regard with favor** means literally "may he find fat."

[4-5] **Heart's desire** and **plans** are synonyms for **victory** and the strategy to achieve it. In verse 5 the subject changes to **we**, indicating that a chorus speaks. Their security and happiness are personally invested in this wish. The Hebrew word for **victory** comes from the same root as the word meaning salvation. The word also occurs in verses 6 (help, victory) and 9 (victory). **Banners** (cf. Num. 1:52; 2:2ff.; Song of Sol. 6:4, 10) is enigmatic. Some, with the ancient versions, would transpose two letters of the Hebrew to get "we shall be magnified."

God will give victory (vss. 6-9). **[6]** Now the mood changes. The first person singular is employed, and there is a strong assurance of victory. If the king speaks, perhaps some act within the worship context augmented his faith. Since the king would probably not refer to himself in the third person, however, perhaps a priest, or even a prophet, speaks. Had reassuring news just come from the battlefield? Did God give some sign? Or is this simply an intensification of faith under the impetus of corporate prayer? With **holy heaven**, compare "sanctuary" in verse 2 (cf. also 11:4; 18:16).

[7-8] **Some . . . some . . . we** and **they . . . we** sharply depict contrasting centers of faith. **Horses** and **chariots** were dreaded enemy apparatus, but not nearly so awesome or effective as **God**. The Hebrew word translated **boast** literally means "mention" and is strengthened by the translators, though is would seem reasonably so. On **name**, see verses 1, 5. Note the antithesis, in verse 8, between the

last two verbs and the first two. **[9] Answer** (vss. 1, 9)
brackets the psalm, as it moves from trouble through
prayer to **victory**. God save **the king**—and consequently the
nation! The Hebrew reading (RSV note) is difficult because
the tenor of the psalm indicates that the author is requesting a divine **answer**. The LXX, on which the RSV is based,
involves a change in one letter of the verb for **answer**.

Psalm 21: An Exaltation of God

This psalm depicts God's aid to the king, in response to
his prayers. Psalm 20 was a king's prayer before battle,
while Psalm 21 is often considered a king's thanks after
victory (cf. especially vss. 8-12). Yet there is no dominant
note of thanks in the psalm, despite verse 2. There are no
concrete references to a particular victory. Verses 8-12 indicate incomplete, likely future, action (as in the RSV). This
leads some scholars to couple Psalms 21 with 20 as two
pre-battle psalms. Other interpretations see this as a coronation psalm (see vs. 3), or as celebrating a royal birthday
(vs. 4). The evidence that is provided by the psalm itself
seems inadequate for a positive determination of its specific
occasion.

The psalm centers in God's multifaceted blessings
brought to the king's aid. Verses 1-7 praise God for
answering the king's prayer and bestowing his varied benefits. Verses 8-12 depict the victories the Lord gives the
monarch. Verse 13 is a final exclamation of praise.

Blessings given the king (vss. 1-7). [1] Verses 1-6 elaborate the theme of God's loving kindness (vs. 7). **The king is**
significant only as God's viceroy. **Strength** and **help** surely
refer to verse 2, but also have a broader scope, as the
entire psalm shows. Note the intensity of the joy God's aid
releases. **[2-3] Heart's desire** suggests Psalm 20:4, though
the Hebrew terminology is different there. Verse 3 seems to
refer to the blessing of kingship, with its concomitant
blessing for the people whose ruler is thus favored. If the
context implies deliverance from a particular disaster, its
nature is not further clarified. If verse 3 indicates a coronation ceremony, it may have been the occasion for the

psalm, or this language may simply be a way of stressing that the king is God's monarch.

[4] **Life**, glory, splendor, majesty, and joy are among the "goodly blessings" bestowed by God. **Life** could mean preservation in battle, but more likely indicates general prosperity or longevity (cf. "Long live the king!"; 1 Sam. 10:24; Ps. 72:15; etc.)—life under divine favor. On **for ever,** see 5:11. [5-6] These attributes are first and primarily God's. The king, without God, is nothing. **Most blessed** literally means "blessings," that is, many of them. Verse 6 could also be translated to indicate the king procuring blessing for the people. [7] Here is the reason for all the preceding. God offers his covenant love, but **the king** is so blessed because he **trusts.** The ruler's faith would be an example, and thus a blessing, to the people. This verse leaves the form of direct address which has characterized verses 1-6 and may reflect a liturgical change to a different speaker.

Blessings promised the king (vss. 8-12). [8] Verses 8-12, addressed to the king, seem idealized projections, rather than references to a specific conflict. **Find** may mean discovering and opposing, or find while in battle pursuit.

[9-10] Note how the Lord's **wrath** and the king's are linked here. The image is of fuel burned in a furnace and might symbolize a city burned by its conquerors. The picture produces awe at God's judgment. Vassal treaties in the ancient Near East commonly featured destruction of the enemy's **children,** to prevent future retaliation. The destruction is complete. [11-12] Not even their plots will succeed. Strategy, no matter how carefully wrought, would be useless against the Lord's king. The Hebrew of verse 12 is awkward. The foes are demoralized and flee as they face a barrage of arrows.

'Be exalted' (vs. 13). This concluding **praise** appropriately climaxes the preceding depiction. God has been and will be **exalted.** His strength mandates man to **praise.**

Psalm 22: 'Why Hast Thou Forsaken Me?'

Because of Jesus' cry (Mark 15:34; Matt. 27:46), taken

from verse 1, Christian attention has set particular focus on this poem. It is one of the most moving descriptions of suffering in the Psalms, but also one of the most elevating, as the sufferer's search is at length rewarded. The author's devastating agony, increased by the presence of vicious foes, is made almost unbearable because God seems far away, despite constant pleadings for aid.

The psalm, though vivid, is so general, that no particular illness or distressful situation can be identified. Fact is difficult to distinguish from imagery. Many consider this an individual lament, perhaps "enriched" by a broader use of language. Other see here the ideal righteous man in suffering. Some also suggest a national interpretation—the sufferer is idealized Israel—though the number of individual features seems to forbid this. Finally, the older view, based on NT usage, sees the psalm as a prediction of the Christ. Rather than viewing it as a prediction, it is better to say that an OT sufferer spoke in language that would later appropriately describe the Messiah. Jesus' use of the language may have implied his faith that the agony was not the end of the story (note vss. 22-31). This intense and vivid language is employed in the NT to describe the Lord's sufferings (cf. vs. 7 with Mark 15:29; Matt. 27:39; vs. 8 with Matt. 27:43; Luke 23:35-36; vs. 18 with Mark 15:24; Matt. 27:35; Luke 23:34; John 19:24). Care must be exercised in taking parts of the psalm not cited in the NT to be predictive of the Lord (as is sometimes done in the case of vs. 17).

The opening two verses are a prayer, followed, in verses 3-5, by a reminiscence of God's goodness to the nation in past days. Verses 6-8 are a lamentation, after which the author notes his past experience with God and renews his prayer (vss. 9-11). In verses 12-18 the lament is again taken up, with a final plea in verses 19-21. The last part of the psalm, verses 22-31, celebrates the poet's deliverance, with a mighty call to praise the Lord.

A cry of anguish (vss. 1-2). [1] Has **God** no compassion for sufferers? It is from the pain, terror, and bewilderment of such a fear that the startling **forsaken** comes (cf. Isa.

49:14). Yet faith still carries the problem to God, whom the poet does not abandon despite his feelings. This dilemma, perplexing and painful as it is, occurs often in the laments, and in life. Notice the recurrence of **far** in verses 11 and 19. The expression binds the lament together. **Groaning** is a word used elsewhere of a lion's roaring (Isa. 5:29). **[2]** Relief has not failed for lack of fervent petition. **Day and night** the tears continue, without respite. The impact of these words is powerful.

God's goodness (vss. 3-5). [3] This verse begins an alternation between personal references (vss. 1-2, 6-8, 12-18) and references to God (vss. 3-5, 9-11, 19-21), which occupy the first two-thirds of this psalm. Verses 3-5 look to God's help in the nation's past. Hopefully the future will be as days gone by. The writer does not blame God, nor is he cynical; he is hurt and bewildered. **[4-5]** God's throne is the hearts and praise of the people, for he delivered **them** (cf. 2 Sam. 6:2; 2 Kings 19:15; Pss. 80:2; 99:1). The author would share in such praise—as one delivered. Why has God changed (as it seems)? **Trusted** occurs three times in verses 4-5. **Disappointed** (literally "put to shame") may imply his shame because his situation seems the reverse of that of his forefathers.

The scorn of men (vss. 6-8). [6] The sufferer returns to his own problems, stressing another element—the scorn of **men. Worm** (cf. Isa. 41:14; Job 25:6) is probably his own estimate, though the enemies may so malign him. It is utter humiliation (cf. Isa. 49:7; 51:7; 52:14; 53:3).

[7] Make mouths, here only in the OT, is an expression of scorn, though its exact nature is unknown. Head wagging, another such gesture, is mentioned also in Job 16:4; Pss. 64:8; 109:25; and Lam. 2:15. Jesus would experience the same treatment in circumstances that would enlighten the darkness surrounding the grief of all sufferers.

[8] This charge, some believe, reflects the view of those who think the author falsely claimed to trust God. If he had genuinely trusted, God would have delivered him. Therefore, his hypocrisy opens him to spite. It is also possible that the taunters are irreligious people taking any chance to revile believers. **Committed**, in Hebrew, is imperative (i.e., commit!) and might be an encouragement from, say, a priest. But this reading is awkward, grammatically, in relation to the rest of the verse. The RSV, therefore, translates in harmony with the ancient versions, and adds **his cause**. Matthew 27:43 quotes this form.

The prayer renewed (vss. 9-11). These verses again speak of God, with attention on the author's past. The concluding request, in verse 11, which is the first petition in the psalm, is especially pathetic. Why can the past not become the present? If the psalmist had been accused by mockers of irreligion and hypocrisy, he now refutes that charge by referring to his life thrust. Verse 10 emphasizes his life long devotion (cf. "my God" with vs. 1).

'Poured out like water' (vss. 12-18). [12-13] The author returns to his present condition. This psalm frequently uses animal imagery (cf. vss. 6, 16, 20-21). **Bulls** would trample and gore, and lions (vs. 13) rend and devour. These violent figures intensify the description of his agony. There seems no escape. **Bashan** was known for its cattle (Num. 32:1ff.; Deut. 32:14; Amos 4:1). [14] Verses 14-18 (except vs. 16) describe severe physical distress. They may refer to the writer's physical manifestations of extreme fear and anxiety, but more likely are vivid poetic pictures of an illness. We do not know its nature, nor if the language is literal or symbolic. But the description is unforgettable. The second line says literally "all my bones have been separated from each other"—almost too painful to read. [15] The pathetic picture continues, climaxed here by the threat of **death**. This was God's work (**thou dost**). If it implies judgment for wrongdoing, there is no other reference to it in the psalm. Indeed, the writer has affirmed the opposite (vs. 10). Probably in his view of God, all things must be attributed to divine sovereignty. He who gave life can take it. What cannot be comprehended is accepted by faith. A **potsherd** is a fragment of broken pottery.

[16] Now a pack of wild **dogs** (a well-known phenomenon in oriental cities) symbolizes the threats of his mockers. They fly at his **hands and feet**. The Hebrew of the last

line reads "like a lion my hands and feet" (RSV note). Some suggest lion-like dogs, but it would be unlikely for one animal image to elaborate another. The RSV **pierced** follows the LXX, which is based on a slightly emended Hebrew text. Other suggested solutions raise more problems than they resolve. **[17-18]** He depicts himself as severely emaciated (cf. Job 33:21; Ps. 102:5). He is watched with malicious anticipation. Perhaps the watchers are like robbers waiting to capitalize on his condition, or like those who await his death and their subsequent enrichment. They may be greedy heirs caring more for selfish gain than for exhibiting compassion. The words of verse 18 are appropriated in the NT to describe the division of Jesus' **garments** (see the introduction to this psalm).

'Deliver my soul' (vss. 19-21). Here is an impassioned climax of petition, repeating the dog (vs. 6), lion (vs. 13), and oxen (vs. 12) images. **[19]** The opening **But thou** contrasts God, his **help**, with his opponents of verses 16-18.

[20] My life means literally "my only one" (RSV note)—a unique and priceless possession. The RSV offers an interpretive translation, which, though it may clarify the sense, is less interesting than the original language. It is a grim thought to consider a **dog** destroying one's most precious possession! **[21]** The RSV follows the versions in translating **my soul.** "You answered me" (RSV note) would be a strange statement to conclude such an unmitigated lament. Yet some suggest the literal reading anticipates the totally changed mood of verses 22ff. Others suggest a change in the Hebrew vowels to obtain "thou hast humbled me." But this would depart from both the Hebrew and the versions.

A hymn of praise (vss. 22-31). [22] The mood now changes drastically to **praise,** thanks, and vows. The writer proclaims God's deliverance and invites a great host to join him. Explanations for the change suggest a liturgical event (between vss. 21 and 22) symbolizing divine response to the previous agony; or a renewal of faith in divine deliverance not yet a reality, triggered by the catharsis of verses 1-21; or a resolution of the problem. This verse is quoted in Hebrews 2:12, as a word of Christ.

[23-24] This impassioned preacher issues to Israel a threefold call to **praise, glorify,** and **stand in awe,** stamped with his own hard won "amen." Verse 24, experientially, is the center of verses 22-31. The God who was far off (vss. 1, 11, 19) is no longer **hid!** This is a word of joy, but also of hope for other sufferers. the **afflicted** reader can take heart, for he will **not** (ultimately) be **despised!**

[25-26] In the assembly of the people, **vows** made in time of trouble are now fulfilled (cf. Lev. 7:16). This apparently involved providing a meal (cf. 2 Sam. 6:17-19), in which **the afflicted** shared. These may have been fellow sufferers, or those who symbolically partook of the affliction of the writer. If we read "poor" (RSV note), this could be an act of charity. Whatever the case, the occasion is to God's glory. The last line of verse 26 may be a blessing pronounced by the host upon his guests. May they be delivered, as he has. **[27-28]** The God whose deliverance the author had so joyfully experienced is universal sovereign, envisioned as receiving world-wide worship (cf. Pss. 2:8; 67:7; 72:8; 96:7; 98:3). Could any less response be appropriate for a God who had so marvelously delivered him? **Him** (vs. 27) is attested by the ancient versions and involves only the change of a single letter from the Hebrew "thee" (RSV note).

[29] The psalmist enlists a mighty chorus in praise. To the great congregation (vs. 25), those who seek God (vs. 26), the ends of the earth, and the families of the nations (vs. 27), are added **the proud** and those **who go down to the dust,** and subsequently, generations to come are asked to join (vss. 30-31). "They have eaten" (RSV note) is a reading some would keep, associating it with the idea of verse 25. The RSV has conjectured a slight change, separating the Hebrew into two separate shorter words, and changing the vowels slightly. The Hebrew word translated **proud** means literally "fat," that is, the rich and prosperous. Opinions differ as to the exact sense to give the term. **Those who go down to the dust** may be the dead, though this would be a bold figure, since usually in psalms the dead do not praise God (cf. Ps. 115:17). More likely these are the afflicted and dying—like the author himself. Thus the text calls upon both high and lowly to praise.

[30-31] The good news passes from generation to generation, likely implying a cultic repetition of the mighty acts of God. **He has wrought it** (deliverance?) is a fine contrast to the aloneness of verse 1. **Coming** in verse 30 actually takes a verb from the first of verse 31 and uses it to modify the last of verse 30. This seems to catch the thought of the Hebrew better than a slavishly literal translation.

Psalm 23: 'The Lord Is My Shepherd'

This writer asserts his supreme confidence in God's care, employing the images of shepherding (vss. 1-4) and hospitality (vss. 5-6). A few sholars see a third image—guide—in verses 3b-4. The idea of trust in familiar yet perilous circumstances, coupled with the beauty of the language, has made these words speak powerfully to the human heart. The author makes no demands of God, nor does he complain. But he is overwhelmed by God's continuing care in the face of every threat.

The Good Shepherd (vss. 1-4). [1] Provision and protection were the two functions of the **shepherd.** God is often so designated (Pss. 74:1; 77:20; 78:52; and especially Isa. 40:11). In most occurrences the flock is the nation, leading some to assume this is a communal psalm. But the personal usage is found (cf. Gen. 48:15). The OT references impel one's mind forward to the Good Shepherd—Jesus. **I shall not want** indicates incomplete action (past, present, future). This is the nature of the God in whom the author's confidence resides. [2] The shepherd, as does God, acts for his flock's sake—yet ultimately for his own sake. **Green pastures** (with water and rest) were not always easily found in arid Palestine. The Hebrew word translated **green** means literally "of grass." The Hebrew word translated **beside** could perhaps be better rendered "unto." **Still waters** suggests an untroubled pool. The Hebrew probably indicates a place where the sheep rest (RSV note), perhaps a well or fountain, rather than the more popularly conceived stream.

[3] The author's "life" (RSV note) is revived and his

vitality restored. He can go on with renewed energy. Some
see in verses 3b-4 the image of a guide, since there are no
references to sheep. Others argue that this complicates the
imagery, and retain the figure of the preceding verses.
"Right paths" (RSV note) would be more appropriate for
sheep, which are not morally responsible creatures. But for
a man "right paths" and **paths of righteousness** could be the
same, and the psalm may play on this concept. **Paths** (from
a word indicating a track, as of a wagon) refers to one's
course of life. The guidance, and all human endeavor, is **for
his name's sake.** For what other reason does man live, and
God act? **[4]** Here is a new dimension of God's care—
protection. Note the intimacy which now addresses God in
the second person. The choice between **shadow of death**
and "deep darkness" (RSV note) involves a difference in
the vowels of the Hebrew term (cf. the same word in Pss.
44:19; 107:10; Job 3:5; Isa. 9:2). Scholars are divided on
the better reading, though in either case the image indicates an extremely dangerous position (with perhaps
threatening death), through which one passes unalarmed.
The **rod** was used for defense and the **staff** for aid in walking. Some think these refer to a shepherd's crook.

God's hospitality (vss. 5-6). [5] Now Yahweh is a host.
The focus is no longer on survival, but triumph (though it
is debated whether gloating over enemies is implied by line
one). God's message to the foes is "leave my friend alone!"
In oriental custom, a host obligated himself to protect his
guest. Anointing (literally "make fat, grease") was a mark
of hospitality. The last line literally means "my cup saturation," showing how well the guest's needs were provided.

[6] Rather than enemies and danger, the poet now experiences a beneficient pursuer. His expectation is for continued blessings. The last line may imply worship, or it may
be a general expression of security and joy (cf. Pss. 5:4;
15:1; 27:4; 61:4; 84:4).

Note the variant translations in the footnotes. The RSV
points these out especially in this psalm, since the usages
hallowed by time have led to some misconceptions which
the original language does not warrant (as with **for ever**).

Psalm 24: Entering the Holy Place

This is a hymn associated with entrance to God's holy place, either the city, or the temple, or perhaps both (vss. 1-6 the former, and vss. 7-10 the latter). Despite disagreement, the most common view is that the latter section refers to the ark of the covenant, which symbolizes the Lord. Suggested uses of the psalm have included the Enthronement Festival (see Introduction), the Feast of Tabernacles, and the New Year Festival, but no definite conclusion is possible. The first two verses depict Yahweh as Creator and Ruler. In verses 3-6 attention is directed to him who would ascend and worship God. The last three verses describe the entry of the King of glory.

'The earth is the Lord's' (vss. 1-2). These verses may have been sung by worshipers approaching the gates, or may simply set the psalm into the most impressive background. The importance of the occasion involving the psalm could scarcely be greater, since it involves the Creator God. He brings order out of chaos, an idea found in various ancient Near Eastern creation accounts.

[2] Founding of **the earth upon the seas** is a concept occurring also in Genesis 1:9; Deuteronomy 33:13; and Psalm 136:6. **Rivers,** if used in parallel, may refer to the currents of the sea.

The acceptable worshiper (vss. 3-6). These verses are similar to entrance liturgies in Psalms 15 and 100, and Isaiah 33:14-16. They may have been sung outside the gate, or verse 3 may have been sung, inviting the responsive verses 4-6 from within. The text seems to imply some kind of antiphonal performance. [3] Ascent to the **holy place** (temple) is highest privilege, but a privilege in which the demand for ethical integrity is implicit (vs. 4).

[4] These four qualities stress right motives and freedom from disreputable action for those who would praise the God of all creation. Though **what is false** could refer to idolatry, it more likely indicates dishonesty in dealings with other people.

[5] The all-powerful Creator is not remote, but active. **Blessing, vindication,** and **salvation** probably indicate the

covenant goodness of **God** wrought in many ways. **Vindication** is the word sometimes rendered "righteousness." It is the appropriate response of God to his worshipers.

[6] This verse sums up the section. The Hebrew (RSV note) has been emended on the basis of the ancient versions, since one would not seek "the face of Jacob." Other suggestions retain the Hebrew reading but have the sense of the RSV text.

The king's entry (vss. 7-10). [7] The psalm here changes subject. The worshipers ask entrance for **the King of glory.** This seems to be the climactic moment, for which the previous verses prepared. What is entering that is identified with Yahweh, the king (cf. 5:2; 10:16; 29:10; etc.)? The most common view is that it is the ark of the covenant. Some say the psalm was composed for the ark's initial passage to Jerusalem (1 Kings 6:23-28). But the temple **gates** were not yet constructed. Others assume a regularly recurring ceremony, ritually repeating the initial circumstance, but there is no clear OT evidence for such. Other suppositions regarding cultic circumstances for which this psalm was appropriate flounder for lack of verification. **Lift up** could include the idea "exalt yourselves," appropriate for such an auspicious occasion. The word translated **ancient** could also be rendered "everlasting." Perhaps the term was used because the doors bounded the abode of the Eternal One. **Heads** were the lintels of the gates.

[8-9] Verse 7, spoken from without, is answered in line one, eliciting a further response in lines two and three. Military imagery now depicts the glory of Yahweh, the war **king** (cf. Exod. 15:3). Verse 9 repeats verse 7 (with slight changes), making the reality more impressive by repetition.

[10] The interchange continues, repeating the initial inquiry. The Hebrew adds a word to verse 7, best seen if we translate "**Who is** he, **this king of glory**?" This focuses attention more clearly on **the Lord.** The reply of lines two and three begins, in Hebrew, with "he"—a measured and impressive response. "He, and none other!" **Hosts** may imply an army or indicate the heavenly bodies. The latter would appropriately complement verses 1-2.

Psalm 25: Prayer for God's Help

This psalm is an incomplete acrostic. Despite some jerkiness in the flow, the following sections can be distinguished. Verses 1-7 are in lamentation form, praying for God's help against enemies, for teaching, and for forgiveness. Verses 8-15 (except vs. 11) are in wisdom form, extolling the Lord as teacher and noting the blessings of the man so taught. Verses 16-22 return to lament and prayer, with requests for relief, protection and forgiveness. The last verse broadens the psalm to the entire nation.

The author's faith centers in God's steadfast love (cf. vss. 10, 15). Though his problem seems unresolved, his faith utters the laments in hope (cf. "wait" in vss. 3, 5, 21). He is troubled by enemies, but also by his own wrongs. To him God is a protector, but also, importantly, a teacher. The acrostic style, plus the general (though intense) language, lead some to conjecture that the psalm was written to be employed by any person who might find it appropriate for his approach to God (yet cf. vss. 7, 15, 16, 19). The comments will, nonetheless, occasionally assume the problems of a particular individual.

'In thee I trust' (vss. 1-7). **[1]** A twofold affirmation of trust in verses 1-2a precedes a twofold personal plea in verse 2bc, which is broadened in verse 3. Trust is a keynote of the whole psalm, never lost despite all anguish.

[2] Shame and exultation of enemies might be occasioned by the author's sin (cf. vss. 7, 11, 18). It may have been interpreted as a mark that God had forsaken him, or it may have been a cause of public humiliation. This verse breaks the acrostic arrangement slightly, since the second word (not the first) begins with the appropriate letter of the alphabet. Some suggest the first word in Hebrew (**O my God**) should go with verse 1, thus remedying the problem.

[3] This is almost an exhortation in prayer form. **Wantonly**, from a word meaning "in vain, without effect," might possibly be read "treacherous" without accomplishing anything." **[4]** God as teacher is a theme repeated in verses 8-10, 12-14. The request for instruction perhaps asks fuller understanding and guidance. The author may feel his sins and inadequacies are partially responsible for his problems. Real trust is always open to teaching and growth.

[5] Truth is basically faithfulness and refers to God's nature as revealed in the covenant. This attribute, producing **salvation**, emboldens the prayer and enlightens the waiting.

[6] Mercy and **steadfast love** probably amplify "truth" and "salvation" of verse 5. God's past blessings, revealing his nature, can still be expected. **[7]** In his introspection, even his youthful folly is recalled (unless he writes as a young man). He does not plead his merit as cause for cleansing. It is God's **steadfast love** (cf. vs. 6) and **goodness** upon which he relies.

The great Teacher (8-15). [8] Verses 8-14 employ a hymnic style. The description of God as **good, upright**, and an instructor of **sinners** is appropriate to the poet's own situation (vss. 4, 7). God is seen as more eager to *instruct* **sinners** than to judge them. The Hebrew words translated **instructs** and **law** (torah) come from the same root.

[9] Way suggests the paths of verse 4, with reference to the author, and is used in verse 8 with reference to sinners. Probably the writer considers himself as the **humble** man, who is a sinner (vs. 7), yet who desires to keep God's covenant (vs. 10). **[10] Paths of the Lord** (cf. vs. 4) probably refers to God's nature and his expectations for man. **Steadfast love** (vss. 6, 7) and **faithfulness** (truth, vs. 5) are both blessings and an awesome challenge.

[11] Verses 8-15 are interrupted by a brief petition, perhaps triggered by the author's consideration of God's requirements. Again divine grace is the ground of his plea. The Hebrew reads "and pardon." The RSV omits "and," since it makes an incomplete thought. **[12-13]** The author stresses his point by a question. "Fear" is profound respect for and submission to God. Note the recurrence of **way** (cf. vss. 4, 8-10). Instruction is probably the same as in verses 4-5. **Prosperity** is literally "good." The Hebrew word translated **abide** (vs. 13) can be rendered "lodge," suggesting the figure of good as the locale to which one comes for the night. The second line of verse 13 recalls the land promise of Genesis 17:8 (cf. Pss. 37:9, 11, 29; 44:3) and may represent all the good God gives.

[14] The basic idea of **friendship** is of intimates (i.e., those in council). The subject matter of the "conference" is the **covenant**. **Makes known** is probably the granting of further revelation and insight (perhaps in part forgiveness and deliverance). The covenant relation can be ignored or be deepened, depending on individual response. The last line may also be translated "his covenant is to give them knowledge," which would change the meaning of the verse.

[15] Since he has affirmed his trust in God, it is to be expected that the author would express confidence that God would deliver him. In this assurance he returns to hopeful lamentation (vss. 16-21).

Prayer for relief (vss. 16-22). [16-17] Verses 16-18, with six petitions, return to prayer with new intensity. He again pleads God's grace (cf. vss. 7, 11). Was his loneliness caused by friends who ignored him because they thought him forsaken by God? If so, what an ironic contrast with verse 14. The difference between the RSV text of verse 17 and the note depends upon the interpretation of one verb.

[18] Here is the final plea for forgiveness (cf. vss. 7, 11). We still do not know the exact relation between his **sins** and his suffering, save that removal of the former seems an essential prerequisite to relief of the latter. Otherwise, the request to **consider affliction** and **forgive sins** would be strange, indeed.

[19] He again calls upon God to **consider** (as in vs. 18). There are **foes** (resuming the plea of vs. 2) who are **many**, and who act with **violent hatred** (perhaps implying the lengths to which they would go). Intense opposition spurs urgent prayer. [20-21] Do **integrity** and **uprightness** describe the Lord or the psalmist? In the latter case, they might indicate an honest determination to do right. Or he might be asking that these virtues be granted him, assuming strength of character to be the best defense and preserver of his life while awaiting final deliverance from his foes. On **wait**, see verses 3, 5. [22] This verse goes beyond the acrostic scheme and uses a different divine name (Elohim). It was probably added by the original author, or a

later editor, to make the psalm more appropriate for use in worship.

Psalm 26: A Personal Vindication

Though often classified as an individual lament (cf. vss. 1, 9, 11), this lacks the detail and fervor of other lamentations. It has also been considered a psalm of innocence or a psalm seeking God's protection. The author is unknown, though suggestions have included a Levite (cf. vss. 6-8, 12); a worshiper at the temple gates (cf. Pss. 15, 24); an accused person, coming to the temple for vindication (cf. vss. 4-5 with 1 Kings 8:31-32; Exod. 22:7-11; Num. 5:11-31); or one who has taken refuge in the temple.

The author opens with a cry for vindication, pleading integrity and trust in God (vs. 1) and offering his life to God's view (vs. 2). The ground of his life is God's steadfast love (vs. 3). In verses 4-5 he disclaims affiliation with evil men and then makes a positive assertion of innocence and praise, expressed in cultic terms (vss. 6-7). An affirmation of love for God's house (vs. 8) precedes the prayer, in verses 9-10, that he not be swept away with evil men. The psalm closes with a reaffirmation of integrity, a renewed plea, and a statement of praise to God (vss. 11-12). The writer sees God as the giver of covenant love (vs. 3), which love carries its demands for personal integrity—that is, covenant demands responsibility.

'Prove me, O Lord' (vss. 1-3). [1] An appeal on the basis of one's innocence is not unusual in the OT (cf. 7:8; 35:24; etc.). The writer may have had particular charges leveled against him. He is not self-righteous, but submissive. The entire thrust of the psalm is that of need, requiring prayer, not of spiritual sufficiency due to his goodness. The Hebrew word rendered **vindicate** is the word elsewhere translated "judge." The psalmist may be asking God to acknowledge his righteous character. **Walked** refers to manner of life. **Integrity** is wholeness, implying sincerity. **Without wavering** can be rendered as in the RSV, but one could also translate "I will not waver," as a result of trust. This might better suit the Hebrew, but it perhaps does not fit the context as smoothly.

[2] He offers himself for divine scrutiny, using three verbs to indicate the intensity of the desire. **Test** is a word used of refining metals. He asks to be evaluated, as metal is, for its purity. **Heart** and **mind** (literally, kidneys and heart), probably refers to his emotions and intellect. Though unstated, it may be presumed that he also wishes any wrong to be purged away. [3] God's **steadfast love** is the ground of the prayer. God will always be true to the covenant promises he has given to his people, and they in turn must give him covenant loyalty. "In thy faithfulness" (RSV note), if adopted, would parallel **thy steadfast love** in line one, and would emphasize the utter reliability of God's promises.

A disclaimer (vss. 4-5). [4] Do these verses imply any charges against the writer? **False men** were those of empty speech, worthless. **Dissemblers** were those who conceal, in this case probably their faults, in order to deceive. Integrity calls for honest dealings. [5] Contrast **hate** with love in verse 8. **Hate** was not personal, but a reflection of God's abhorrence of wrong. **Company** (Heb. *qahal*) contrasts with the great congregation (*qehalim*) in verse 12.

Innocence asserted (vss. 6-7). [6] There is insufficient evidence to connect this ceremony with any known ritual described in the OT (cf. Pss. 51:7; 73:13). Some suggest a ritual of purification (cf. Deut. 21:6; Matt. 27:24), and others a ritual declaration of good faith. He may even mean he does in spirit what the priest does, ritually, in his washings (cf. Exod. 30:17-21). Whatever the actual experience, the general import of the statement is clear. On the march around the **altar**, see Psalms 27:6; 42:4; 68:24; 118:27; 1 Samuel 16:11; 30:16. God's goodness and man's participation in it lead to public thanks and proclamation of God's actions. Does he have in mind all God's marvelous **deeds** (vs. 7) or those that particularily relate to his own needs? See the blessing in verse 12.

An appeal (vss. 8-10). [8] Attention now switches to the temple. This verse affirms **love** for God in a roundabout way. Was the **place where the glory dwells** the entire temple, or the Most Holy Place, or the Shekinah, or even the ark (cf. Exod. 33:18-20; 1 Sam. 4:21-22; Exod. 16:10; Ps. 78:61)? **[9]** Here is the lament. The author seems to fear moral condemnation, perhaps even a premature death, along with the sinners. The Hebrew expression translated **bloodthirsty men** means literally "men of bloods."

[10] These, we may be sure, are **men** who would be excluded from the temple. Such types were doubtless the source of the writer's troubles. **Devices** indicates they deliberately plan and execute crime. The **bribes** were either given or taken by the wicked. Either would be reprehensible. In the latter case, we might suppose them to be men of some authority or leadership.

Plea and praise (vss. 11-12). **[11]** In antithesis to the horrible men just described, the writer returns to his earlier affirmations of innocence. He grants that he is inadequate to the needs of his life and must rely upon God. In verse 1, **walk** indicated completed action (probably what he had done) while here it indicates incomplete action (what he will do, customarily, because of his life intentions.

[12] The first half of the verse indicates his manner of life, and the latter his vow/intention. **Level ground** may refer to the temple court (cf. vs. 8), or it may mean he has sure footing. **Level** translates the Hebrew word elsewhere rendered "upright." **Great congregation** renders a plural Hebrew word, and **great** is added to indicate the assembly of God's people. The writer wishes all men to know of the Lord's magnificence and loving concern. This exultant note, in contrast with verse 1, shows how marvelously the psalm has taken us from concern to triumph.

Psalm 27: An Appeal Made in Faith

The first six verses of this psalm express jubilant trust in God before terrifying opposition. Verses 7-14 contain an individual lament, laboring under opposition greater than the first section depicts, and therefore is less exhilarated. Diversity of the sections has led to debate about the unity of the psalm. Those arguing for two independent compositions, here joined, point to differences in tone; to the fact that trust usually follows, rather than precedes, lament; and to the fact that both parts are self-contained (vss. 1-6 address God in the third person, and vss. 7-14 in the second). Those arguing for unity point to a concern for enemies in both parts (vss. 2-3, 6, 11, 12); and to affirmations of faith in verses 7-14. Some think a lament is preceded and followed by trust (vss. 1-6, 13-14), while others think the author rises to faith, then succumbs (temporarily) to despair, as humans usually do.

Trust in the mighty God (vss. 1-6). [1] The author stands upon his past experience with God. He is delivered from anxiety and apprehension. On **light,** see 13:3; 18:28; 44:3; 89:15; Isaiah 10:17; 60:19-20. On "refuge" (RSV note), see 31:4; 37:39. Two different words refer to **fear.** The second conveys more the idea of dread.

[2] The Hebrew word translated **assail** means literally "draw near." **Uttering slanders** is an interpretive translation, based on parallel usages in Daniel 3:8 and 6:24, where "eat up" (RSV note) means "denounce, slander" (cf. usages in Pss. 14:4; 17:12; Jer. 30:16; 50:7). The writer hopes God will change his situation. **Stumble and fall** both describe complete action, either past, or, as in the RSV, a sure expectation for the future. God being what he is, this must be the inevitable fate of the wicked.

[3] Here is a powerful expression of peace of mind. Not even **war,** with its untold horrors (the Hebrew may indicate a particular battle), can terrify. Those who had known the horrors of conflict could deeply appreciate the poet's words.

[4] In this beautiful statement, the author declares his life's consuming concern. The language may indicate a temple functionary, or one who chooses to express his devotion as if he were (cf. 17:15; 23:6). **The beauty of the Lord** has been understood as joy in worship, or as a life lived in his service, or as God's graciousness. Does the author inquire to know more of God and his service, or does he seek an oracle? Certainly the general meaning is that he would wish constant divine direction for his life.

[5-6] The images of God's help are resumed (cf. vs. 1). Note the exuberance of the praise. As one **set upon a rock,** he is above the danger. The Hebrew phrase rendered **sacrifices with shouts of joy** means literally "sacrifices of shouts of joy," which has a slightly different meaning. The RSV apparently did not wish to equate shouts with **sacrifices.**

A lament in faith (vss. 7-14). The mood changes to lament, yet even here there is faith, though not as joyfully as in verses 1-6. **[7]** The affirmations of verses 1-6 are put to the test in a concrete situation: **when I cry.**

[8] The quoted command **seek ye** [plural] **my face** may not refer to any particular passage, since in essence it occurs throughout the OT (cf. Exod. 23:17; Deut. 4:24; Ps. 50:15; Jer. 29:12-13). The author does as God commands (vs. 8b). In Hebrew the second line of this verse comes first, followed by the last four words of line one. **Thou hast said** (vs. 8a) has been added as an explanation by the translators. Other suggestions for rendering this section have also been made.

[9] The petition is so intense that it is repeated with four verbs here, before the expression of faith in verse 10. If it is part of the intensity of the poetry, **anger** may indicate God's response to wrongdoing on the writer's part. Yet there is no other reference in the psalm to wrongs repented of or to be forgiven. The poet appeals on the basis of his past experience with God. These words are the preface, making the author's subsequent prayer and affirmation of faith stand out more vividly. **[10]** There is beauty and considerable emotional power in the announcement that God's love transcends the intimacy of parental care (cf. Ps. 103:13; Isa. 49:15). No human can care as much as God does. Even one who is parentally forsaken is not alone. We do not know if this was the writer's literal situation (as some suggest) or just a strong poetic expression.

[11] This is the first reference to **enemies** in this part of the psalm. **A level path** could be an upright path. The author may feel a life of rectitude is his best security and defense. The enemy would find no cause against him (vs. 12). Or he may simply be asking wisdom to know the safe thing to do in his situation. [12] Finally the poet unveils his specific apprehension. It is anguish enough to suffer for wrongdoing, but worse to be the victim of lying and misrepresentation. The Hebrew word rendered **will** is usually translated "soul" or "life," but it might also be rendered "greed," indicating greedy men satisfying their desires by violence.

[13] Confidence again breaks to the front. He who waits for God will not be vanquished. This writer will **see** God and his help while he lives (perhaps indicating he has no physical ailment). The opening word in the Hebrew ("if not, unless, except that") is omitted in the RSV. Though it does create a strong contrast between the problem of verse 12 and the faith of verse 13, it seems to leave the verse grammatically incomplete. A corresponding word is not found in the ancient versions, and many scholars consider it spurious. [14] Lamentation, subdued by confidence, must now develop patience. There is a time of waiting till God acts. The author may be exhorting himself (the verbs are singular), or another (a priest?) may be offering encouragement in worship. The psalm ends as it began, with trust—but trust tried by difficult times.

Psalm 28: From Petition to Praise

Here is an individual lament which moves into a song of thanks and praise. The specific threat is difficult to discern, but involves fear of being swept away with the wicked (vss. 3-5). Verse 2 hints at a worship context, and verse 6 may be the poet's response to reassurance given him within the experience. Some suggest, from the closing two verses and the reference to the anointed, that this is a royal utterance. Others feel verses 8-9 were later additions to adapt the psalm to congregational use. Verses 1-5 are a cry for vindication. Verses 6-7 are the thankful response of the author to God's gracious concern. The last two verses are a prayer for God's blessings on his people.

A call to God (vss. 1-5). [1] The writer struggles to escape the silence of God. Though he petitions deliverance, his faith is early affirmed with **my rock** (cf. vss. 7-8). **Pit is**

frequently a metaphor for death and is often equivalent to Sheol (Job 7:9; Pss. 30:3; 88:6; 143:7; etc.). Going **down to the Pit** may be equivalent to being taken off with the wicked (vs. 3) who do not regard God (vs. 5) and are subject to requital (vs. 4). Is it that he only fears death, and that the evil will suffer a premature death? Or does the term have moral implications—not simply "spare me death," but "spare me the wicked man's death"? Death was the symbol of the ultimate punishment of wrongdoers.

[2] The author calls aloud for **help**, probably due to pressures caused by the wicked (why else the imprecation of vs. 4?). Sacrifice may have accompanied the prayer. **Supplication** is mentioned again in verse 6, but there it has been heard. This, in miniature, depicts the movement of the psalm. **Hands** could be lifted either toward heaven (1 Kings 8:22) or the temple (1 Kings 8:35). **Most holy sanctuary** (cf. note) is no doubt the Most Holy Place (cf. 1 Kings 6:5-31; 8:6ff., 30). [3] The wicked were likely the cause of the lament. Had false charges been lodged against the psalmist? The fact that he distinguishes himself from such people obliquely affirms his innocence. Their duplicity is evident from the conflict between their public well-wishing and their inner mischief-planning.

[4] The author calls for requital. May the punishment fit the crime. This is no personal vendetta, but a plea for justice and integrity in society. Should not every man be called to face his **deeds**? Can God judge otherwise?

[5] This verse is a bridge from the entreaty to the affirmation of verses 6-9. So God's universe operates for those who ignore God's **works** (note the frequency of this and synonymous terms in vss. 4-5). These **works** could be creation or redemption.

God hears (vss. 6-9). [6] This verse marks the change from petition to praise. The imperative (hear) becomes a perfect (**heard**). Divine response engenders gratitude. What has changed the writer's thrust? Was it a liturgical act, or redemption from his untenable situation, or is he anticipating a deliverance so sure he speaks of it as accomplished fact? [7-8] The **song** (vs. 7) may imply praise in the congregation. Verses 8-9 could be its text. In verse 8 the psalm moves from the individual to the **people** and their king. Though this verse is awkward to translate, the RSV does as good a job as any. **His people** is an interpretive translation of the Hebrew expression meaning "to them," and is based on the ancient versions. **Saving** is plural, perhaps indicating the great and numerous acts of God (cf. vs. 5). **His anointed** is the king, with whom the fortunes of the people rise and fall. [9] The psalm concludes with a congregational petition. Is a specific national problem behind the request, or is it general? Note the beautiful picture of the **shepherd** with which the psalm closes (cf. Isa. 40:11).

Psalm 29: The Song of Thunders

Here is an unforgettable hymn, sometimes called the seven thunders of God because of the sevenfold repetition of "the voice of the Lord." The awesome storm points to the majesty of its Creator and Controller. Appropriately, the setting of the psalm is the heavenly throne scene (vss. 1-2, 10-11). If composed for worship, the psalm may have been connected with the coming of the seasonal rains. Because of various similarities, it is thought that the author may have adapted and rewritten, in terms of Israel's faith, an ancient Phoenician hymn praising Baal Hadad, the weather god.

In form, the psalm is characterized by a strong parallelism. Verses 1-2 contain a call to worship, addressed to the "heavenly beings." Verses 3-9 move to earth, describing the progress of the storm in its various manifestations. Verses 10-11 take us above the storm to the Lord's throne.

'Worship the Lord' (vss. 1-2). These verses are very similar to 96:7-9. [1] They open with a call to worship—made impressive by the threefold recurrence of the phrase **ascribe to the Lord,** and the tight-knit parallelism reinforcing the point. Reasons for this invitation follow in verses 3-10. "Sons of gods" (cf. RSV note) in some Ugaritic texts were minor deities. Perhaps the psalm adopts a purged form of this expression to refer to angelic or other celestial **beings** (cf. Job 38:7; Pss. 82:6; 89:6; 103:20f; 148:1-2; and the heavenly court in Job 1). It is also possible that the reference is to powerful nobles. The former meaning elevates the praise and suggests Yahweh's greatness is such that man cannot praise him adequately. Thus, men are always summoned to a task which is beyond them.

[2] The Hebrew phrase translated **holy array** means literally "in the splendor of holiness" (cf. Pss. 96:9; 110:3, RSV note). The expression can either refer to holy garments (cf. Aaron in Exod. 28:2) or to God's holiness, in which case the thought would be to worship God for the splendor of his holiness. Understanding the former interpretation would depend on the meaning of "sons of gods" in verse 1. Both ideas emphasize the exalted experience of the worship of such a God.

The voice of the Lord (vss. 3-9). [3] The tight parallelism continues, and one begins to hear **the voice of the Lord** with its majestic cadence. **The voice** is thunder. The sea was probably the Mediterranean. Note the repetition of **glory** from verses 1 and 2. Many scholars believe that the description of a storm has mythical associations—also suggesting the power of Yahweh in bringing order out of chaos. [4-5] The sonorous rhythm continues, with the booming thunder (cf. Ps. 93:4). The idea may be that the Lord's **voice** is power itself and **majesty** itself. The storm smashes inland, hurling itself against the mountains and shattering **the cedars**—proverbial for strength and durability. **Lebanon** is the principal mountain range of Syria.

[6-7] Though the RSV indicates that the mountains **skip as a calf,** the original text could be interpreted of the cedars as well. The imagery is, in either case, audacious. Perhaps an earthquake is implied, also. These mountains are considered the abode of pagan gods, over whom Yahweh thus displays his superiority. **Sirion** is probably Mount Hermon (see Deut. 3:9). Lightning (vs. 7) **flashes forth** (literally "divides, cleaves") like licking flames. It, too, is the voice of Yahweh. [8] **Kadesh** is usually assumed to be in the south (cf. Num. 20:1), yet because of the Syrian emphasis of the previous verses, some have suggested a location in the Syrian desert on the River Orontes. The earth gyrates from

the stormy violence. Again, some commentators suggest an accompanying earthquake. A variant suggestion is that the animals and/or vegetation of the **wilderness** tremble (in fear).

[9] The RSV makes a slight vowel change from the Hebrew word meaning "hinds" (RSV note) to the word meaning **oaks**, to preserve the parallelism. The note, if adopted, sees the females stimulated to bear by a sudden change in barometric pressure. However, this seems a strange way to emphasize the greatness of the storm. The last line returns to the praise of verses 1-2. One should glorify the God who is Lord of such powerful natural displays. This line joins the earthly and heavenly praises (cf. vs. 1, unless **temple** here refers, again, to heaven). Men join in declaring that which nature has so powerfully proclaimed—God's **glory**.

God enthroned (vss. 10-11). [10] Far above the turmoil and destruction, Yahweh is **enthroned**. This is why the poet has been concerned about the storm. This vision of God, which the heavenly beings enjoyed, is now given to men, with power, because God's might has been seen in the storm. The perspective of this verse naturally leads to the strength and peace of the next. **Flood** (used elsewhere in the Bible only of the deluge of Noah's day) refers to torrents of rain here. The word may suggest both the judgment and salvation motifs of the Noah story.

[11] The RSV renders this verse a prayer, but it could also be translated as a simple future. The storm exhibits **strength**, and the God above and controlling it shows **peace**. One faces life with strength, but it rises above anxiety by confidence in the One who is the perfect Peace beyond all turmoil.

Psalm 30: The Lord, the Helper

This psalm, though used in corporate worship (vss. 4-5), arose from an individual thanksgiving. The author, once secure (vs. 6), suffered severe reversal (vs. 7). In his fear (vss. 2-3), he cried to God. Because God answered, the poet responds with praise and thanks (vss. 1-5, 11f.). Verses 1-3 contain the poet's thanks and a review of his prayer and deliverance. In verses 4-5, he calls the congregation to praise, and to affirm God's favor. Verses 6-10 rehearse the psalmist's adversity and his prayer for help. The last two verses describe the joy of rescue and offer concluding thanks.

Deliverance (vss. 1-3). These verses describe God's deliverance in five ways. **[1-2]** The man who has been **drawn up** (presumably from the Pit, vss. 3, 9) lifts God up (**extol**). Praise is the essential note of the psalm. The **foes** are mentioned only here, and in insufficient detail to afford much insight (did they interpret his suffering as God's judgment upon him—cf. 38:16?). The appeal for healing (vs. 2) could possibly imply illness, even threatening death. **[3]** The death described here may be a poetic parallel to illness. **Sheol** and **the Pit** may symbolize weakness, anguish, sickness, or any human condition that seems to lead to death, rather than life (i.e., a moribund condition of existence). The second line parallels the first, though the footnote indicates that he was kept from even going **down to the Pit**. The difference is a change of one letter in the Hebrew verb, and scholars differ as to which is the better reading.

Praise for relief (vss. 4-5). **[4]** The author summons God's people to join the praise (vss. 4-5). He would have all recognize the great truth (vs. 5) implied in his own deliverance. Faith cries out in jubilation, inviting others to enter blessedness. On **saints**, see Psalm 4:3. The Hebrew word translated **name** literally means "remembrance" and is not the usual term for "name." God's name brings to remembrance all he is and does. The two terms are often used in parallelism (cf. Exod. 3:15; Job 18:17; Ps. 135:15).

[5] The great lesson expressed so beautifully here is the transience of adversity and grief. Behind the frowning face, God is revealed as loving (cf. Isa. 54:7-8). His wrath then, must have, with fuller understanding, a healing and constructive intent (though this thought is not developed in the psalm). This marvelous insight is a mighty incentive to trust and perseverance. The first half of the verse states a general principle which the last half illustrates. **Weeping** is personified as a traveler, lodging during **the night**. Another traveler, **joy**, is close behind and will soon set up a more permanent dwelling. One survives **the night** (literally "evening") in expectation of the day.

The poet's adversity (vss. 6-10). [6] The author had become proudly confident in his blessedness and had lost his prime focus on the Giver of all gifts (cf. Deut. 8:11-20). **Prosperity** (only here in the OT) means quietness, ease, peace, security. **[7]** For some reason (perhaps the psalmist's pride) God's **face** was hidden, and the psalmist was dismayed. The reversal was probably the illness of verses 2-3. He was led to self-scrutiny and prayer (though no specific confession of sin is noted). The Hebrew phrase rendered **strong mountain** literally means "my strong mountain." The RSV follows a slight emendation.

[8] Cried and **make supplication** both indicate incomplete action, perhaps showing the intensity and persistence of the prayers. The content of the cry and supplication is given in the next two verses. **[9-10]** He would glorify God, but cannot as a dead man. The covenant **faithfulness** does not extend there. He may be saying that to **praise** fully he must be restored (he does not mention praising God in his affliction). Or he may be penitently reflecting on the danger to his life from an arrogant and self-confident attitude. This would better fit the sense of **profit**, which is often used of unjust gain. The Hebrew term translated **my death** means literally "my blood." In verse 10 he gives his straightforward appeal for God's grace.

Joy in deliverance (vss. 11-12). [11] The exuberance of verses 1-5 returns. The psalmist's change is described by two images (a transition from **mourning** to **dancing**; and a change of garments). No doubt his external circumstances were improved, but the emphasis is on his inner reaction to God's gracious answer. **[12]** The man who was self-sufficient (vs. 6) now praises. The psalm might be called a message to the self-centered. He understands that he was delivered in order that he might **praise**. **My** is added by the RSV. The Hebrew word rendered **soul** here literally means "glory" (as in 16:9 and elsewhere).

Psalm 31: 'Be Thou a Rock'

This psalm is loosely constructed. The author indicates that he suffers terribly (vss. 9-13) from enemies (vss. 7-8), upon whom he calls a curse (vss. 17-18), as he cries for succor (vss. 1-4, 15-17). His deep trust in God's steadfast love (vss. 7, 16) leads to exultant praise and a calling upon others to place confidence in Yahweh (vss. 19-24). Some see here two separate psalms, since the problem resolved in verses 7-8 breaks out even more intensely in verses 9-18. Those arguing for unity feel the second part is simply another stanza repeating and expanding the first (cf. Ps. 35).

The petition (vss. 1-4). [1-2] Verses 1-3a, with minor variations, are also found in Psalm 71:1-3. In a rapid-fire, petitionary series the author pleads for God's intervention, relying for his hope on the divine **righteousness** (i.e., his faithfulness to the covenant). In verse 2 he asks God to be to him what he knows God is (**rock** and **fortress**. The Hebrew word translated **strong** means literally "for a house." The language intensifies the word for **fortress**.

[3-4] Having asked for refuge, deliverance, rescue, and salvation, the poet now requests guidance. **For thy name's sake** recognizes that God's nature is to deliver (cf. his righteousness, vs. 1). Verse 4 is the first reference in this psalm to the poet's enemies.

God's steadfast love (vss. 5-8). [5] Here petition changes to trust. **Hast redeemed** describes completed action, which could mean the author has been delivered (safe in the fortress or refuge, vss. 1-3), or that he anticipates a security so sure that he can write as if it were already accomplished. **Faithful** emphasizes the absolute reliability of **God**. Where could any security be found, if not there? These words were used in death by the Lord (Lk. 23:46) and by Stephen (Acts 7:59). In their extremity they relied upon the ultimate security. The message is powerful.

[6] Idolatry is mentioned only this once in the psalm. Perhaps his foes were idolaters, or the contrast may have been to emphasize the author's **trust**. The Hebrew expression translated **vain idols** literally means "vanity of lies" (cf. Jer. 8:19). One author calls them "beings without being," who can only arouse false hope. The RSV prefers **thou hatest**, which is found in several ancient versions, to **I hate** of the Hebrew (RSV note), though the latter renders good sense. **[7-8]** The author now uses the covenant term par excellence—**steadfast love**. In it he will **rejoice** (does he suggest cultic activity?) because of his deliverance—either accomplished or anticipated beyond doubt. He is like a man once cramped by his enemies, but now set free **in a broad place** (vs. 8).

'**My strength fails**' (vss. 9-13). **[9]** Despite the faith expressed in verses 7-8, the poet's petition for help continues as the second part of the psalm begins. This appeal is followed by a prolonged lamentation describing his situation (vss. 10-13). The wasting of the eye may refer to physical emaciation or to copious tears (cf. Ps. 6:7). Even if symbolic, the picture is striking. The Hebrew word translated **body** literally means "belly." **[10]** The author describes a devastating wretchedness, using four expressions. The Hebrew word translated **fails** literally means "stumble," as a once strong man begins to stagger. The word rendered **misery** represents only a slight change from the word for "iniquity" (RSV note). If the MT were kept, it would be the psalm's only reference to the author's transgressions. Lack of supporting evidence has no doubt led the RSV translators to prefer the alternative.

[11] Another powerful, fourfold description shows the author's extreme loneliness and rejection (cf. Pss. 79:4; 89:42; 109:25; Isa. 53:1-3). Why does he have aversion to **neighbors** and **acquaintances**? One can only guess. Perhaps he was physically repulsive from some illness. Or they may have thought his troubles were a judgment from God, making him one to be avoided. Perhaps they feared that his enemies might attach them also. The language could even be a symbolic description of the author's inner feelings about his situation. The translation **horror** is based on a conjectural emendation and gives a more sensible reading than "exceedingly," which appears in the MT (see RSV note). Other conjectures have also been suggested.

[12] Now this tale of woe describes him as forgotten like a buried corpse or as unimportant and useless as a **broken pot.** [13] This sorrowful section concludes with a reference to surrounding plotters who torment him (cf. Jer. 20:10). Perhaps they plot false charges (cf. vs. 18). Their death plans paint a picture of absolute horror.

'I trust in thee' (vss. 14-18). [14] The power of his **trust** shines brightly because it has been set against the dark background of verses 10-13. A prayer for vindication follows. Verses 15-18 resume the petitions for help. [15] The declaration of faith continues. **Times** probably refers to one's fortunes—that is, one's whole life (cf. "years" in verse 10). [16] He appeals to God's **steadfast love** (cf. vss. 7, 21). The shining of God's **face** contrasts with the hostility of the enemies. The request is for favor and grace. Verse 17a repeats the prayer of verse 1. [17b-18] Rather let **the wicked be** shamed—thus begins the only imprecation in the psalm. The speech is harsher here than in the psalm as a whole. The Hebrew word translated **dumbfounded** means literally "they shall be silent." Not only are they consigned to death, but speechlessly so, with all opposition, arrogance, **lying,** and **contempt** driven from them.

God's goodness (vss. 19-24). The mood of the psalm changes again, and the remainder reflects deliverance. Verses 19-20 speak of God's care for those who fear him. Verses 21-22 are the author's corresponding personal experience. Verses 23-24 call upon all saints to trustfully wait for the Lord. The section is richly flavored by a sense of gratitude.

[19-20] An interval may be supposed between verses 18 and 19, in which God had responded by granting **refuge** (note the emphasis on refuge and shelter in these verses). There is now no apprehension from **plots** (cf. vs. 13) and **strife of tongues** (false accusations?). [21] The exuberant praise continues. The **city** under siege (or perhaps a "strong city" is probably not an historical reference, but a figure of speech. God's **steadfast love,** to which previous appeal was made (vss. 7, 16), is wonderfully manifest.

[22] **Alarm** and a sense of isolation from God had been

part of his affliction. **Alarm** doubtless indicates a highly distracted emotional state. The author, who had felt his distance from God (cf. RSV note), now affirms that his perspective was illusory and offers his experience to others with similar misgivings. The whole psalm shows the author relying on what he believes to be true about God, not just on what he feels. [23-24] The psalm closes with a reprise and a call to **love**, strength, and **courage**. The author turns preacher for the sake of others who can benefit from his experience. The one who was lonely tells the **saints to love** a God who is sure. He will finally requite (abundantly) the haughty, but even for those who suffer till their enemies are judged, there is strength.

Psalm 32: The Blessings of Penitence

This is the second of the seven penitential psalms (6, 32, 38, 51, 102, 130, 143). It insightfully depicts the inner movement from sin and agony to repentance and joy. It also becomes (implicitly) a psalm of thanks for deliverance and a psalm of instruction. It was likely prepared for worship (cf. vs. 11), perhaps for some public occasion dealing with purification and forgiveness.

Formally, the psalm is composed of pairs of verses, except for verse 5. Verses 1 and 2 are the blessing on the forgiven man. Verses 3 and 4 depict the poet's unforgiven and suffering state. Verse 5 is the turning point, as he confesses his sin. Verses 6-11 are composed of exhortations to others to trust God when in trouble (vss. 6-7), to be malleable to instruction (vss. 8-9), and to experience the joy of divine beneficence (vss. 10-11).

[1-2] Before rehearsing his spiritual pilgrimage, this teacher states the conclusion of his journey. Happy are those who have reached this destination—forgiveness. His words are a sigh of relief and a shout of joy. With a rich, threefold emphasis he speaks of wrongdoing and deliverance. **Transgression** stresses rebellion against the divine will. The Hebrew word rendered **forgiven** literally means "borne away" (also vs. 5). The term translated **iniquity** can stress wrong (Isa. 43:24; Jer. 11:10), guilt (Exod. 34:7),

and/or punishment (Gen. 4:13). Perhaps the idea of guilt is predominant here; the same word is rendered "iniquity" and "guilt" in verse 5.

Verses 1-2a are quoted in Romans 4:7-8 to support Paul's discussion of justification by faith. Verse 2b changes to a positive virtue, sincerity, which is intrinsic to the writer's experience, as described in verse 5, and the prelude to recovery. He blesses as one who has has escaped from the snares of **deceit**. The author knows blessedness in his healing and consequent happiness (vss. 5, 7).

Sufferings of the impenitent (vss. 3-4). [3] Because of his refusal to confess **sin**, the poet suffered terribly. His colorful description may be meant literally or figuratively. If the latter, this by no means lessens the extremity of the case. The first line says, literally, "when I was silent my bones wore out." The RSV gives an interpretive translation, assuming (because of vs. 5) that it was his **sin** he refused to acknowledge. The Hebrew word rendered **groaning** could be translated "roaring." This deeply moving struggle (mental/physical) may have been the result of his failure to confess, or it may describe the situation leading to a self-examination in which **sin** was discovered and confessed.

[4] Incessantly he felt God's blows. The difficult last line literally means something like "my juice/sap/moisture was changed by the heat of summer." The word for "juice" occurs in this sense only here in the OT, though in Num. 11:8 it refers to the taste of manna. The RSV understands it to mean one's vitality. The author suffered as one dehydrated with intense fever (as though exposed to a blazing **summer** sun).

Confession of sin (vs. 5). Truth won out, confession was made (obviously with repentance), and healing followed. This verse is a burst of light in a darkened place. Reality is turned around—grief becomes joy (cf. Prov. 28:13; 1 John 1:8-9). As in verses 1-2, a threefold literary scheme is employed, using the same words for **sin** here as there. **Iniquity** and **guilt** translate the same Hebrew term. The second line of the verse is awkward in Hebrew, but the RSV has rendered it very sensibly.

Exhortation to trust God (vss. 6-11). The author exhorts for the remainder of the psalm. He has prayed meaningfully and bids others do likewise. **[6]** The translation **at a time of distress** depends on the conflation of two Hebrew words and a consonantal change. Many expositors, however, accept the MT as it stands ("at a time of finding only"; see RSV note) and try to make sense of it. Thus they explain it as a time for finding grace, or a time of acceptance, or a time of finding God in worship, or even a time of being found by God (arguing from Isa. 55:6). **Great waters** would be a stormy deluge. The prayerful penitent will not be swept away.

[7] The exhortation to pray is interrupted by a threefold personal affirmation, which makes it even more powerful. The verse enlarges the security indicated in verse 6. "Shouts of" is omitted in the RSV (cf. note), because the word is rare, and because of the possibility that it was a mistaken recopying of the last three letters of the preceding Hebrew term. Yet the reading could make sense, especially if public worship were presumed. **[8]** Like a wisdom teacher the psalmist proceeds. Since "you" in **you should go** is singular, some suppose that God, or his designate, here addresses the author, who in turn speaks to the group in verse 9, where "be not" is literally "you (plural) be not." The **eye** may be the eye of the human exhorter or God's assurance that nothing is hidden from him.

[9] The strong language here seems rather uncomplimentary to those addressed, but its strength may reflect the author's feeling that he had been like a beast. Only when forced to it by suffering did he "come round," like a senseless beast driven to a destination. He would spare others that mode of help. Let them serve God willingly. The last line is somewhat obscure, and some see it as a assurance of protection (e.g., then nothing can approach **you**—i.e., to harm). The NEB omits it entirely.

[10-11] The contrast of the entire psalm is summed in verses 10-11. The psalmist has experienced both—**pangs** and **steadfast love.** A life of trust, righteousness, and uprightness is abundantly joyous (note again the threefold expression). The covenant produces such a possibility. How stark the contrast between verses 3-4 and 11. Who should want to choose the former over the latter?

Psalm 33: 'Rejoice in the Lord'

This is a call to God's people to praise the Lord. The initial invitation (vss. 1-3) is followed, in verses 4-19, by a depiction of God as Creator, Sovereign, Judge, and Savior. The hymn concludes with a reiterated statement of trust and a petition for continued blessing (vss. 20-23). The psalm seems undeniably intended for corporate worship. The occasion may have been an annual festival recounting creation and salvation traditions or a deliverance from a threatened national peril.

This is the only psalm from 3 to 41 lacking David's name in the superscription. Further, there is a remarkable closeness between verse 1 and Psalm 32:11, which could indicate a deliberately consecutive arrangement of the two.

Call to praise (vss. 1-3). [1] Here is an exuberant, fivefold call to **praise**, addressed to the people of the covenant (**righteous** and **upright**). On instrumental praise, see Psalm 150. **[2]** The Hebrew word translated **praise** in verse 2 could also be rendered "give thanks." **[3] A new song** (vs. 3; cf. Pss. 40:3; 96:1; 98:1; 144:9; 149:1; Isa. 42:10) may refer to the present psalm, or to a special composition, or to a new way to speak of ancient truths. Whatever the meaning, it suggests the continual freshness and challenge of being God's people. The possibilities of praise are inexhaustible. **On the strings** does not occur in the Hebrew text; it is an explanatory addition of the RSV. **Loud shouts**, showing the enthusiasm of the worship, may be the song itself, or adjunct praise.

God is worthy of praise (vss. 4-19). [4-5] This section extols **the Lord** with four propositions. They offer reasons for praise, and give general faith statements upon which the rest of the psalm is built. In his **word** and **work** God is absolutely consistent and dependable (the idea of **faithfulness**) in fulfilling his covenant promises. All other attributes are received because of his **steadfast love**. Perhaps a particular manifestation of covenant grace calls forth this hymn. The **steadfast love** is worldwide. God's people are never away from his goodness. [6] Verses 6-9 speak of creation, expanding on the "word" and "work" mentioned in verse 4. The Hebrew word here rendered **breath** is the word rendered "spirit" in Genesis 1:2. The **host** of heaven here is probably the heavenly bodies.

[7] God controls the mighty seas (cf. Job 38:8-11, 22). The translation **bottle** represents a slight change from the MT, in conformity with the ancient versions. The Hebrew word in the MT means "heap" (the same word is used of the piling up of the waters at the exodus). God impounds vast **sea** as simply as a skin flask would be filled. Some think of the clouds as the bottles. **The waters** are stored till needed. [8-9] Verse 8 gives an exhortation before a crisp restatement of the creative power in verse 9. What more abundant reason could there be for **all** creatures to **fear** God? The Hebrew of verse 9 is even more pointed than the English: "The divine word! and the creation stands forth like obedient troops!"

[10] Verses 10-19 discuss God and **the nations**. He who initiates history also acts in it, so that even national rebellion is futile. Some suppose that this implies plans against Israel, but the rest of the psalm lends no supporting evidence for this view. [11] History is truly understood only from God's perspective. Note how his **counsel** and **thoughts** contrast with man's (vs. 10). His counsel **stands**, as he caused creation to stand (vs. 9). [12] Israel, most **blessed**, is at the center of the divine concerns (cf. Deut. 33:29; Ps. 144:15). This is the practical conclusion of the previous discussion, and the reason why exuberant praise is appropriate (vss. 1-3). [13-15] God's power calls for human responsibility—a thought repeated frequently in verses 13-19. The section might be entitled "the eye of the Lord." He has perfect knowledge, so"mind how you act." Yet he acts out of love for his people (vss. 18-19). Note the impressive repetition of **all**—four times in verses 13-15, representing two different Hebrew words. Verse 15 indicates that he who sees also made what he sees. How could the

contents of any heart be hidden from its Maker? Thus any response but obedience is futile (cf. vs. 10). This transcendent reality leads naturally to the implied call for trust in verses 16-17.

[16-17] Real greatness (note the threefold use of the adjective form) lies not where men might suppose. The mighty force, drawn up in battle array, learns it is inferior in power to those who trust God. God is the center of ultimate strength—let man not rest on false hopes, whether in battle or elsewhere. On horses, see Isaiah 31:1 and Ezekiel 17:15. The Hebrew word translated **might** (vs. 17) is essentially the same word that is rendered **army** in verse 16. **Might** could refer either to the **king** or to the **horse**, but the overall difference is insignificant. **[18-19]** Here is the effective conclusion of the psalm to this point. God's delivering power comes to bear upon those **who fear him** and **hope in his steadfast love.** He who sees all will know beyond doubt who truly fears him. So he is to be praised (vss. 1-3), trusted, and called upon (vss. 21-22). In verse 19 the danger changes from military opposition to hunger and **death.** These foes are probably representative of all threats. **Death** no doubt refers to a catastrophic experience, since all expect natural death. Even when all human help seems futile, one can expect deliverance from the Creator and Sustainer.

'We wait for the Lord' (vss. 20-22). These verses move to a corporate concern. Israel places her confidence in God. How appropriate it is, in the light of what the psalm has disclosed! Hope, trust, obedience, joy, and patience all meet here. Further acts of God for his people may be anticipated. **[22] Hope** is grounded as firmly as possible (cf. vs. 18). Beneath all is God's **steadfast love** (cf. vss. 5, 18), without which his greatness would not be accessible to Israel. They, therefore, have a vision, revelation, and expectation not shared by others. Upon this glorious forecast the psalm ends, but the relationship continues.

Psalm 34: Blessing the Lord

This is a thanksgiving psalm from an author who generalizes upon his personal deliverance. "I sought the Lord" (vs. 4) may imply a cultic setting. The psalm is an acrostic and is thus less cohesive than the typical non-acrostic psalm. There seems to be an arrangement of the verses in pairs.

The author, with a rich variety of language, celebrates God's care for those who love him and describes the opposite fate of the evil. Verses 1-3 contain personal praise, enlarged to a general call for others to join. Verses 4-10 speak of the writer's petition and God's answer (vss. 4-6), leading to a broader exhortation to "taste and see" and "fear" the Lord (vss. 7-10). Verses 11-22 continue the exhortation in didactic style, interspersing the blessing of such service with references to the fate of the unrighteous (vss. 16, 21).

Notable are the several references to the good man, who, though afflicted, is yet not finally defeated. Instead, he is blessed.

"Abimelech," in the superscription, is inaccurate. The episode in 1 Samuel 21:11-15 concerned Achish.

Praise the Lord (vss. 1-3). [1-2] In a noble expression of purity (vs. 1), the poet states his resolution to spend his whole life praising God. As one **afflicted**, but delivered (vss. 6, 9, 18-19), his boast offers encouragement to other sufferers to trust **the Lord**. In God anxiety can be resolved. His boasting actually implies deep humility, since the author has realized his own inadequacies, and thus trusts God for his strength. **[3]** The afflicted, and perhaps a larger group, are called to share in praise. The specific reason for the psalmist's invitation is yet to be given (though God's very nature is more than ample justification for such an invitation).

The Lord is good (vss. 4-10). [4] Note the ways salvation and deliverance are described in verses 4-10. In verse 4 the author gives his personal reason for praise. Seeking the Lord may refer to a visit to the sanctuary. **Fears** indicates terror or dread (Ps. 31:13; Prov. 10:24; Isa. 66:4), and contrasts with the fear of the Lord extolled in verses 7, 9, and 11 (which is a different word and means reverence). Deliverance could have come through provision of either a modification of external circumstances or the provision of inner resources to deal with apprehension. The rest of the psalm does not offer sufficient data to decide. **[5]** This verse could also be translated as a declarative statement. **Radiant** is a strong word and appears elsewhere only in Isaiah 60:5. There it describes a mother's joy at the return of children long regarded lost. Perhaps there is also the idea of the person being transformed by the glory of God's salvation. The statement is especially touching if it describes the "afflicted" (vs. 2). The reading **your** represents a minor change from the MT based on several ancient versions.

[6-7] **Poor man** may describe the author or a similar, perhaps typical, individual. The case is offered as proof that God cares for his people. In verse 7 the psalm generalizes and commends the faith previously described (vss. 1-6). One can experience security as if firmly ensconced amidst a ring of mighty protectors. **Angel of the Lord** may be synonymous with God, but note Psalms 35:5-6; 91:11, as well as Exodus 23:23; Joshua 5:14; Daniel 10:13, 21; 12:1. **[8]** This is an unusual call to personal verification. The Hebrew word translated **taste** may mean "perceive" or "judge," as in Proverbs 31:18. With such a refuge available, why should a man remain undefended?

[9] Absence of **want** could refer to inner resources, or it might be an affirmation that eventually God always provides his people's needs. Nonetheless, various psalms of lamentation reflect a keen feeling of the absence of desired blessings (cf. especially Ps. 88). The present psalm is an expression of covenant theology (cf. Deut. 28). On **saints,** see Psalm 4:3. **Fear** (reverence) is seen in verse 11 as the subject of instruction. **[10]** Here **want** (cf. vs. 1) is depicted in terms of **hunger,** indicating that material necessities will be provided to the saint. **The young** of the predators are less well cared for than the afflicted (vs. 2) and poor (**vs. 6**). This theme is elaborated in verses 12-14. Since some versions read "rich," instead of **lions,** it has been suggested that **lions** may be a symbol for the rich. The resultant concept is impressive, though not entirely convincing.

Wise counsel (vss. 11-22). Here the author adopts the wisdom style, detailing the Lord's attitude toward the righteous (vss. 12-15, 17-20, 22) and evildoers (vss. 16, 21), and their consequent advantages and disadvantages. **[11]** On verse 11, see Proverbs 1:7. **[12]** The way of **life** and **good days** is detailed in verses 13-14. On **life**, see Psalms 16:11; 30:3. The **good** a person enjoys depends on the good a person does. **Enjoy good** is literally "see good" (cf. "taste and see" in vs. 8). How wrong are those who seek these blessings anywhere except in God! Verses 12-16a are quoted in 1 Peter 3:10-12. **[13]** The previous general exhortations are now applied specifically (cf. Prov. 4:24; 13:3; 21:23; Pss. 15:3; 24:4).

[14] This advice advocates a whole way of life (cf. Ps. 37:27). Do not speak or practice **evil.** Take another direction. **Seek** the well-being (**peace**—Heb. *shalom*) of others.

[15-16] Now the thought turns to times of trouble. For **the righteous** there are deliverance (vs. 17) and good things (vs. 12). **Evildoers,** by contrast, become as if they had never existed. To make the contrast stronger, the RSV reads **against** for a Hebrew preposition which does not generally express contrast. Note the stress on **the righteous** in verses 15-22, especially verses 15, 17, 19, 21 (but see the comments on vs. 17). On verse 15, see John 9:31.

[17] This verse parallels, and further develops, the thought of verse 15. The RSV adds the phrase **when the righteous** on the basis of several ancient versions (the Hebrew has only "They cry"). This makes the contrast with the evil man of verse 16 clearer. Some Jewish scholars have held that this verse refers instead to evil men who repented. Note the similarity of this verse to verses 6, 19.

[18] The theme of affliction and deliverance continues. **A crushed spirit** would imply humility. **[19]** There is a great division between those whom God accepts and rejects. The entire psalm has noted this, and verses 19-22 sum it up. What if deliverance never seems to come in this life? Does verse 19b imply a hope beyond death? Some scholars think so, and see here a strong faith looking for deliverance after death, should it not come in this life (cf. 49:15).

[20] **Bones** means one's essential life. "Broken bones" is an expression used of disease (Ps. 51:8; Isa. 38:13) and oppression (Mic. 3:3). See also Psalms 22:14, 17; 31:10. John 19:36 uses this language of Jesus. [21] Verses 21-22 offer the final antithesis of the psalm. **The wicked** man is caught in his own trap (**evil**), either in the inevitable course of events or by God's special design. He is **condemned**— that is, made to bear his guilt. [22] By contrast those taking **refuge** in Yahweh will not be condemned. This clear, black/white contrast is typical of the wisdom style. Redemption and condemnation sum up the thought of the entire psalm. The Christian finds the last verse full of meaning because of Christ.

Psalm 35: Prayer for Rescue

This writer has been mocked, plotted against, and threatened by those whom he once treated lovingly. He has suffered evil for good. Now he prays both for deliverance (and vindication) and judgment on his enemies. Each of the three units of this psalm (vss. 1-10, 11-18, 19-28) contains lament, petition, and a final vow. The psalmist prays hopefully but is frustrated because divine help is delayed. Verses 1-10 describe threats to his life and possessions. Verses 11-18 chronicle the opposition from those whom he had helped. False accusations against him occupy verses ·19-28. His most optimistic point comes at the close of the psalm.

'Rise for my help!' (vss. 1-10). [1] God is petitioned as a warrior bidden to the author's defense. The Hebrew word translated **contend**, often used in legal contexts, could also mean "plead my case." The poet considers his cause to be God's cause. He will later describe his character to us, as well as his distress. [2-3] The imagery becomes more specific. The **buckler** was a large shield which might cover the entire body, in contrast to the small **shield**. **Javelin** presents a textual problem. The Hebrew word seems to mean "shut" or "close," which is not a sensible reading. Various alternatives have been conjectured ("battle axe," "socket," "clasp of blade"). "Javelin" is obtained by changing one letter of the Hebrew. In the latter part of verse 3 the poet asks for reassurance, as well as defense.

[4] Foes **seek** the writer's **life** and **devise evil against** him (cf. also vss. 7-8, 11-12, 15-17, 19-21, 24-26). He wishes for them **shame** (disappointed expectations? defeat?), **dishonor**, repulsion, and confusion. This is not personal vindictiveness, since God's reputation is at stake. Men who oppose his righteous servant should expect dire consequences. This verse is almost identical with Psalms 40:14 and 70:2 (Pss. 70 and 40:13-17 are virtually the same).

[5-6] **Wind**-driven **chaff** symbolizes the decisive rout of the enemies for which the author prays (cf. Pss. 1:4; 83:13; Isa. 17:13). The curse assumes a nightmarish quality, as the figure changes to envision the enemy in terrified flight. To be pursued is frightening; to flee an **angel** unimaginably so. Added to this is the desperation of essential blindness (**dark**) and a lack of sure footing (**slippery**)!

[7] This verse justifies the curse. The opposition is unjust, that is, **without cause** (cf. yss. 12-16, 19-20). It is also secretive, as is a **net** or **a pit**. The RSV footnote points out a slight shift in the Hebrew text. The first line, in Hebrew, has two objects and the second none. An exchange of two consecutive words solves the problem and makes the verse intelligible. [8] May the man who sets a trap to **ensnare** an unsuspecting animal be caught **unawares**. May evil repay itself with **ruin**. This conveys the idea of poetic justice. The RSV has altered the Hebrew verb of line two, which is third singular, into third plural. The sense is not changed, and the verse reads more smoothly.

[9-10] These verses contain a vow concluding this section, following the pattern usual in such laments. He no doubt vows public praise. Verse 10 explains why his pleas had been so impassioned. He was weaker than his foe. But God was stronger! **Weak** can also imply a spirit toward God, and the second usage likely includes that nuance. God's strength works in weakness. **My bones** is a vivid way of saying "myself." **Despoils** often implies the depredation of a robber, and may do so here.

Unreturned friendship (vss. 11-18). [11] The second

cycle (vss. 11-18) adds detail to the first. The tone of these verses is less vindictive and fiery, and more reflective, pained, and melancholy. This repetitive form is unusual, and reminds one of consecutive stanzas of a hymn which build upon one another. The writer may be facing untrue accusations and be frustrated because he is called to account for crimes of which he knows nothing. [12] The burden is made heavier because his enemies return **evil for good** (cf. Pss. 38:20; 109:5). He suffers both from opposition and accompanying mockers (vss. 15-16). Consequently, he is **forlorn** (a word which carries the basic idea of bereavement).

[13] He graphically describes the good he had done his betrayers. They seem to be people whom he did not know well (vs. 15), making his intense concern even more impressive testimony to his goodness. Sickness was sometimes interpreted as God's judgment upon a sufferer, and the pious would regard such a person with distaste. But our author has reacted with compassion, not aversion. The last line is obscure in Hebrew (RSV note). Some say the meaning is that the prayer returned answered; others, that the author now asks that his prayer for such people will be unanswered; still others, that the expression depicts the intensity of the author's concern—it weighs upon his heart. The RSV adds **head** and considers it to be a reference to the posture of prayer, as in 1 Kings 18:42. "Bowed down" in verse 14 seems to support this, unless that is describing a mourning posture.

[14] With masterful climactic description, the writer elaborates his grief in the most intimate way (from **friend to brother to mother**). This makes the enmity seem increasingly odious. Further, he affirms that he cares for their sickness as deeply as for his mother's death. Even allowing for poetic exaggeration, the picture is unforgettable. **Mourning** is from a Hebrew word meaning "to be dark"—perhaps referring to the dark garb of mourners, or, according to some, to their dark state of mind.

[15] Now circumstances are reversed, and his extreme sensitivity is answered with the vilest opposition. **Stum-

bling, indicating calamity, adds a new dimension to the poet's description. To **stumbling** is added mockers, and to that the frustration of unfair and callous opposition. The Hebrew expression rendered **gathered in glee** means literally "they rejoiced and they gathered." He is **slandered** by concerted effort. **Cripples** may represent a different group than that in the first two lines, since it is hard to think he would have such intense concern (vss. 13-14) for those he **knew not.** However, one could translate "cripples gathered and I did not know it." **Cripples** is a problem word. The RSV assumes that the basic meaning is "those who have been smitten." The basic meaning of the word translated "slander" is "tear, rend." **Without ceasing** literally means "and were not silent." It was a continuous persecution.

[16] Various attempts to retain the Hebrew text (RSV note) suggest that the enemies mocked to please the rich and receive food; or that they played the role of mockers to entertain others by their slanderous humor; or that some magical curse is indicated. The RSV (with the LXX) prefers to change one letter in order to obtain the reading given. The last of the verse indicates the raging intensity of the enemies (cf. Ps. 37:12; Acts 7:54). [17-18] The second section of the psalm concludes with renewed petition and vow. For the first time the writer betrays some impatience because God has not acted (cf. vs. 22). **Lions** have been referred to elsewhere as an image for enemies (Ps. 22:21). The Hebrew word translated **life** here means literally "my only one (my darling)," an unusual expression. The vow of verse 18 (cf. vss. 9-10) indicates the setting of the psalm to be public worship.

False accusations (vss. 19-28). The third section resumes a description of the unwarranted hostility. [19] The Hebrew phrase translated **wrongfully my foes** could also be rendered "treacherous (lying) foes." **Winking** indicates a malicious collusion (cf. Prov. 6:13; 10:10). This verse is cited in John 15:25, where it is applied to opposition to Jesus.

[20-21] Rather than the usual desire for the **peace** or well-being (Heb. *shalom*) of another, the enemies have

abandoned fellow-concern. **Quiet in the land** (only here in the OT) again indicates the inoffensive innocence of the sufferer. In verse 21, the RSV seems to indicate false accusations boldly made (on **open wide their mouths,** cf. Isa. 57:4). The enemies claim to have seen the poet's imagined wrong. Or they could be claiming to see his fall (in which case the open mouth would refer to gloating).

[22] Verses 22-27 contain a prayer for vindication, leading to the psalmist's concluding vow. In contrast to what his enemies "saw" (vs. 21), God has **seen,** knows the truth, and will deal justly. This may indicate that verse 21 refers to false accusation, rather than the writer's fall.

[23-25] Verse 23 begins a long series of requests, some of which are shockingly strong. **Bestir** and **awake** almost imply an indolent and unconcerned deity. Though he probably did not mean that, the writer had no hesitation to express the strength of his request. It was time that God responded (cf. "how long" of vs. 17)! He pleads his **right,** but without boasting, for it is based on God's **righteousness** (vs. 24). He is willing to be judged (vindicated) on that basis. On **rejoice** (vs. 24), see verses 15, 19. Whatever wrong the foes intended, thwart them (vs. 25)! The Hebrew expression rendered **Aha, we have our heart's desire** is literally "Aha, our desire."

[26] He prays for the defeat of his foes, so that they might know the appropriate consequences of their wrong (**shame, confusion, dishonor**) rather than the joy and pride they had heretofore experienced. In addition to its similarity to verse 4, this and the following two verses closely resemble Psalms 40:14-16 and 70:2-4. [27] He turns to a broader **joy** experienced by good men (**who desire his vindication**). He is confident that his prayer will be answered, occasioning such joy. God **delights in the welfare** (Heb. *shalom*) of his servant, though the enemies reject it (vs. 20, "peace"). Perhaps this general joy indicates that the writer was a person of some prominence or leadership. [28] He adds his **praise** to that of others (vs. 27). God's **righteousness** is the poet's vindication of verse 27 (both translate the same original term). The covenant binds the ideas in one.

The psalm closes on a high note. The deliverance may yet be future, but it is seen as sure and inspires continual praise. To achieve such faith may be an even greater victory than the actual cessation of adversity.

Psalm 36: The Wicked Versus Steadfast Love

Verses 1-4 of this psalm describe the wicked in wisdom form but with overtones of lamentation. There follow three paragraphs, each opening with reference to God's steadfast love and going on to describe God's character (vss. 5-12). The greatness of his steadfast love (vss. 5-6) is for man's benefit (vss. 7-9). Therefore the poet prays for that love to bless his own life, especially in deliverance from the wicked (vss. 10-12).

Despite the diversity of form in this psalm, the request for faith in verses 10-12 ties it together by including concepts from the preceding sections. The unity of the psalm can be argued on this basis, though it may combine originally independent elements.

The deceitful wicked (vss. 1-4). [1] The first line employs the formula generally describing a divine oracle to a prophet, except that here **transgression speaks** (as a god) from **deep** within (rather than from without, as God would). The **wicked**, with no **fear** [i.e., dread] **of God, is a** practical atheist (cf. Pss. 10:4; 14:1). This verse, appropriately, is used as part of a mosaic of passages depicting human depravity in Romans 3:18.

The translation **his heart** is based on the ancient versions. The Hebrew reads "my heart." The suffixes for "my" and "his" could be easily confused by a copyist, and the versions are obviously more sensible.

[2] This text, especially the last part, is ambiguous enough that any translation must be tentative. As rendered here, we learn that the "inspiration" of the inner evil has warped the wicked man's view of God. Not only is God not feared, but he is believed to be either unconcerned about **iniquity** or impotent to deal with it. **[3]** The evil man's "message" is **mischief and deceit**. Though at one time he may have had a sense of wisdom and **good**, it is now gone. Why **act** prudently, when he has no apprehension about being called to account? **[4]** Words, actions, and now **plots** are seen as the issue of the transgressor's spirit. He plans nefarious schemes at night, which he can accomplish in the morning (cf. Mic. 2:1). He has no revulsion for **evil**. Yet once he might have known the power of a God-fearing life.

The loving God (vss. 5-12). **[5]** Now, in impressive contrast to verses 1-4, the character of God is extolled. We see the difference between the outlook of a wicked man and one with his mind centered on God. Verses 5-6 present four attributes of God, which are related to four aspects of nature. **Steadfast love** is God's covenant love to Israel. It is immeasurable, as is his **faithfulness** (dependability). Some think the writer composed these words as he stood on a spot where he could view sky, sea, and mountains. This verse is virtually the same as Psalms 57:10 and 108:4.

[6] God's **righteousness, like the mountains of God** (or perhaps the *mighty* mountains, is stable, enduring, and absolutely dependable. The author may have thought of peaks like Mount Hermon, which would appear the most stable of earth's topographic features. His **judgments, like the deep,** are inexhaustible, vast, even mysterious. The last line states the natural consequence of the premises given before. All things exist by God's continuing gracious subsidy (cf. Ps. 104:27-30).

[7] Here God's **steadfast love is** intimate and personal, producing joy because of the safety he affords. The people appropriate the magnificence shown in verses 5-6. Once again life in God's love contrasts markedly with the spirit of the one described in verses 1-4. Some feel that this verse, with the general term for **God** (Elohim) and the expression **children of men,** may show a universal concern. Others argue that the language of the next verse shows these words are appropriate only to Israel.

[8] God's grace is extended from refuge (vs. 7) to food and **drink** (vs. 8) to life and light (vs. 9). **Thy house** could be the temple, or just a general reference to God as a host. The words **feast** (literally "to be saturated") and **abundance**

("fatness") bespeak his generous provision. The Hebrew word translated **delights** is from a term that suggests Eden. This oblique reference to the Genesis story may suggest that God's rich graciousness is as it was at the beginning.

[9] For the first time the poet used the personal **we** (for self and community). There is no other way to live, and man's enlightenment (joy, purity, insight?) depends upon God. Here is a powerful personal affirmation regarding the Source of all that is worthwhile. (On **fountain**, cf. Jer. 2:13; 17:13; Prov. 10:11; etc.) **[10]** The last stanza (vss. 10-12) petitions God's continued **love** in deliverance and in judgment of the wicked. Again the crucial need for the continuance of God's **steadfast love** is obvious from the way it has been discussed previously. How could that kind of love do anything but respond to the **upright** knowers of God?

[11] Here **the wicked** of verses 1-4 seem to be presented as the author's enemies. **Foot of arrogance** may refer to a military leader humiliating a defeated opponent by placing a foot on his throat. He prays that he not be separated from God by evil men, so that he becomes like an aimless wanderer. **[12]** The final vision is of God's victory and the irrevocable fall of **evildoers**. The Hebrew verbs describe the act as complete. Indeed, things are not as they seemed in verses 1-4. Ultimate reality often reverses temporal appearances. Faith reaches beyond the latter to the former.

Psalm 37: The Righteous Will Be Vindicated

This psalm is an acrostic, in which a series of proverb-like cameos (perhaps in part derived from popular sayings) are strung together in the wisdom style. The author was an old man reflecting upon God's dealings with the wicked and the righteous.

Though it is difficult to outline the psalm, it does have a unity of concept—the inevitability of God's justice, blessing the righteous (vss. 3-6, 9, 11, 16-19, 21-26, 28-31, 33-34, 37, 39-40) and punishing the wicked (vss. 2, 9-10, 13, 15, 17, 20-22, 28, 36, 38). There seems to be no logical progression from theme to theme, but a rich interweaving, with repetition, further elaboration, and new suggestion, until finally an overall tapestry with a dominant pattern appears complete.

Theoretically, covenant theology undergirds the psalm (cf. Deut. 28). However, not all psalmists are as convinced as this one (cf. Pss. 44, 73; but note vs. 7, "him who prospers").

[1] This warning is against anxiety, fed by envy over **wrongdoers**. Perhaps they seemed to do well, so that justice appeared to tarry (cf. Ps. 73:2-3). The psalm continually counters this worry by references to the destinies of the righteous and **wicked**, giving this opening command substantial support. On **fret**, see verses 7-8; the Hebrew term means literally "heat in vexation." This verse is virtually repeated in Proverbs 24:19. [2] Evil is short-lived, and its end can be seen by one who waits in faith (vs. 3, and cf. vss. 20, 34). That which is discordant with reality cannot abide.

[3] Verses 3-7 center on **the Lord** (**trust**, take delight, commit, be still, wait patiently, fret not). Such behavior will yield **security**, desires of the heart, vindication, and justice. All four verbs in the Hebrew text of this verse are imperative. The RSV changes the last two to indicatives and interpolates **so**. If the imperative sense were retained, the verse could be seen as an exhortation to claim possession of **the land**—perhaps inappropriate if they already dwelt there. The idea of possessing **the land** recurs in verses 9, 11, 22, 29, and 34, so the dropping of the imperative here may be to make this verse harmonious with the others. The Hebrew expression rendered **enjoy security** could also be translated "feed on faithfulness/trust," emphasizing, as does the RSV, the immutability of God's promised care.

[4] This verse will be amplified in the next couplet, while the entire psalm could explicate **the desires of your heart**. It is only as the self is centered **in the Lord**, however, that these desires are fulfilled. **Delight in** Yahweh leads to delight in prosperity (vs. 11). [5] Here is a further call to **trust**, antithetical to fretting. The Hebrew word translated **commit** means literally "roll."

[6-7] Verse 6 climaxes the thought of verses 3-6. On **vindication** like the sun, see Isaiah 58:10. Such a man need not fear darkness. Verse 7 resumes the message of verse 1a, and counsels patience. The matter is in God's hands (vs. 5). But waiting is not easy when matters seem to be going the wrong way.

[8] Anger is another element of anxiety. Is this anger directed against the wicked, or against God because he has not acted? Whatever its nature, it should be subdued by a proper understanding of God's working. **[9]** That the **wicked** will be **cut off** is also noted in verses 22, 28, 34, and 38. As in the Conquest, it is God's people to whom **the land** belongs. The antithesis in this verse is further developed in the next two verses. **[10-11]** Here is the essence of the psalm, calling for the patient waiting for God's retributive and rewarding action. **The meek** (vs. 11) are those who wait. On **delight**, see verse 4. The Hebrew word rendered **prosperity** means literally "peace" (cf. "security" in vs. 4). Matthew 5:3 quotes this verse from the LXX.

[12-13] From this point nearly every remaining verse in the psalm mentions **the righteous** or **the wicked**. From contemplating the mind of the righteous man, we now see his external problems, and understand why he was fretful and angry (cf. vs. 32). But God has the last word. Who can be dismayed by that at which God **laughs** (cf. Ps. 2:4)? **His day** is undoubtedly God's sure judgment. **Wicked** (vs. 13) is added in the RSV for clarification; the Hebrew reads "at him."

[14-15] Verse 14 elaborates verse 12, adding further causes for anxiety (poverty, need). But, ironically, **the wicked** fall by their own evil (cf. Pss. 7:14-16; 9:15).

[16-17] Poverty is not such a disadvantage for one who has God's security. Also the entire psalm testifies to even better expectations. Verse 17 gives the reason for the encouragement of verse 16 (cf. vss. 2, 9, 10, 12, and the connection with the preceding couplet at vs. 15). Righteousness will be supported, for Yahweh's power cannot be broken. **[18]** The wicked awaits a day of judgment (vs. 13), but God **knows** [i.e., blesses] **the days of the blameless**. The

heritage (of the land) will extend to his posterity, since God controls history. Contrast **for ever** with the cutting off of the wicked (vss. 9, 22, 37-38).

[19] **Evil times** and **famine** have their terror taken from them (cf. vs. 25). These may be generalized expressions rather than references to specific events in the writer's experience. [20] The transience of **the wicked** is illustrated by the figures of a glorious field and **smoke.** Those living in Palestine would appreciate the stark contrast between the lushness of spring and the scorched countryside of summer. **Vanish** is repeated to intensify the idea.

[21] This verse takes up the idea of verse 16, and is explained by verse 22. Israel was to be a lending, not a borrowing people (Deut. 15:6; 28:12, 44), for the borrower was viewed as slave to the lender (Prov. 22:7). **The wicked** does not repay because of dishonesty or inability. The lot of the insolvent debtor was hard (Neh. 5:4-5; Isa. 50:1; Amos 2:6; 8:6). **The righteous** man, who enjoys God's blessings, can afford to be **generous** (cf. vs. 26). But woe unto him should he grow selfish. The verb for **pay back** has this meaning only here in the psalms. The basic sense is to "make whole" or "restore." The Hebrew word rendered **peace** comes from the same root.

[22] These thoughts recur throughout the psalm. **By the Lord** is an interpretive clarification of the Hebrew "by him." This avoids the implication that the righteous man does the blessing or cursing. [23-24] This couplet uses the image of a man walking with the support of **the Lord.** The statement about a man's **steps** being **from the Lord** means that he lives uprightly, not that he has some providential guidance. Verse 23 could also be translated "From the Lord the steps of a man are established, and (in) his way he delights." Further, the last of verse 23 could as legitimately indicate man's delight in God's **way.** Any translation must be tentative. Verse 24 depicts one who has stumbled (possibly from adversity) being pulled to his feet. Ruin is averted by the same hand which had steadied him before he fell. Does the entire figure indicate that man is really not able to walk by himself?

[25-26] The well-known words of verse 25 celebrate God's goodness to his people from a lifetime of experience. If the rule has seeming exceptions (cf. Job), this man has never known of them. The good man's prosperity is closely related to his generosity. **Lending** would be without interest (Exod. 22:25). He apparently influences his posterity to show the same generosity, and therefore the family continues to be **a blessing**. There may be hidden here a significant lesson about the good effects of teaching children to have loving concern for others.

[27-28a] The author appropriately returns to the instructions of verses 3-8, in view of the blessings of righteousness. Verse 27 seems to indicate the blessedness of the good man's descendants. All rests upon God's absolute dependability (verse 28a). [28b-29] The RSV breaks verse 28 because of the unusual length of the Hebrew text. Since this makes the translation awkward, the words **the righteous** (which are not found in the Hebrew) are added for smoothness. **For ever** picks up the thought of verses 27-28a. Note the contrast of **children** between verses 28 and 26. Are **the children of the wicked** punished for the wrongs of the parents, or are there to be no progeny; or do they adopt the wickedness of their parents; or is the expression simply strong symbolism?

[30-31] Four characteristics of **the righteous** man are given here. **Wisdom** was grounded in the fear of the Lord (cf. Prov. 1:7; 10:31-32). A man is righteous because God's **law is in his heart** (vs. 31). On **steps**, see verses 23-24.

[32-33] On the evil intent of **the wicked**, see verses 12, 14. Some think these verses imply preferring charges in court (cf. 1 Kings 21:8ff.; and vs. 33, here). God thwarts such intentions, whatever they might hope to accomplish. The Hebrew word here translated **power** means literally "hand." [34] Therefore be patient, for anxiety and potential condemnation will be displaced by inheritance (cf. vs. 9). The last line is an assurance that God's justice will be done, and is therefore not a matter of gloating.

[35-36] The doom of the **wicked** is further amplified by the figure of **a cedar of Lebanon**. Verse 32 spoke of the

threat from the wicked, verse 34 of his destruction, and verse 36 punctuates verse 34. The footnote to verse 35 in the RSV indicates that the translation is based on the LXX, since the Hebrew is obscure. **Overbearing** translates a Hebrew word elsewhere rendered "depraved" or "ruthless" (Pss. 54:3; 86:14). The word **towering** represents a Hebrew word which means "spreading out." The word translated **cedar** means a native tree; **Lebanon** does not occur in the Hebrew text. The sense is that one seemingly strong will be destroyed. Upon further observation no trace can be located. It is no slight thing for a tree or the **wicked** to disappear (cf. vs. 10). Note the change at the beginning of verse 36, which is based on the versions.

[37-38] Here previous ideas are reiterated, with emphasis on **the posterity** (the word could mean "future" or "latter end") of good and evil (cf. vss. 25-26, 28). Childlessness was tantamount to annihilation in the Hebrew way of thinking.

[39-40] The psalm appropriately closes by ascribing all to Yahweh. Verse 40 elaborates the last part of verse 39. Note the many words for salvation in these two verses, especially the repetition of **delivers** in verse 40. The movement of the psalm can clearly be seen by comparing the calm trust of verse 40 with the fretful anxiety of verse 1.

Psalm 38: Complaint and Confession

This is the third penitential psalm (note Pss. 6, 32). The author complains of pathetic physical distress, forsakenness, opposition from enemies, and the injustice of being repaid evil for good. The impact of his progressive description strikes the reader as with a series of blows. The language is similar to that found often in other psalms, perhaps indicating the author uses stylized language to express himself—though no less intensely by doing so. Though he confesses sin (vss. 3-5, 18), we cannot determine the exact connection between his wrongdoing and his suffering (God's rebuke, vss. 1-2).

The psalm begins and ends (vss. 1, 21-22) with a plea to God for relief, fellowship, and salvation. The author's physical distress is described in verses 2-10, his forsakenness in verse 11, and his opposition from enemies in verses 12-20. The psalm closes with the externals of the problem unresolved, but implying the writer has settled the issue into trustful waiting.

'**Rebuke me not**' (vs. 1). After this verse, the author's prayer does not resume until verses 16, 21-22. He does not protest an unfairness in God's **anger** and **wrath**, but wishes it tempered. He no doubt feels he is being chastened for transgression (cf. vs. 3, where divine indignation is apparently viewed as a response to his sin). This verse is virtually identical to Psalm 6:1.

The psalmist's distress (vss. 2-10). [2] The author begins to describe vividly his situation. His was no light burden. (On arrow wounds as a metaphor for divine judgment, cf. Deut. 32:33; Job 6:4; 16:12-13; Lam. 3:12-13.) God's **hand** may indicate a more continuous judging presence (cf. Pss. 32:4; 39:10). **Sunk** and **come down** are from the same Hebrew verb, uniting the verse more completely than is apparent in English translation. [3] His own wrongs are indicated by the words **sin**, iniquities, and foolishness in verses 3-5. **No soundness** may describe desperate illness. The Hebrew phrase translated **no health** means literally "no peace" or "no well-being." Whatever his previous spiritual condition, we might suppose that his illness drove him to a more intense recognition of his need for God. As C. S. Lewis says, "Pain is God's megaphone to rouse a deaf world." (Cf. this and the following verses with Isa. 1:6.)

[4] His **iniquities** (possibly *punishment* for iniquities) **have gone over** his **head**, perhaps like a flood (cf. Pss. 18:4-5; 69:2, 14-15; 124:4-5). The last line employs a forceful repetition in Hebrew—literally, "heavy, they are heavy."

[5] This verse is almost repulsive (but inescapable) in its imagery. **Wounds** may be either literal or figurative. On **grow foul** (literally "a stink"), compare the literal (Exod. 16:24) and symbolic usages (1 Sam. 27:12) elsewhere. "Festering" (rotting, cf. Isa. 34:4; Zech. 14:12) can symbolize pining away. [6-7] With unmitigated intensity the writer continues. He moves about as a mourner (the root

idea implies one wearing black; cf. Pss. 35:14; 42:9). **Burning** (vs. 7) may indicate fever or inflammation (cf. Job 30:30). Verses 7b is identical to verse 3a.

[8] **Spent** conveys the idea of one who is feeble or numbed. He is like a man with body broken and energies depleted; he can only **groan** (perhaps, as one scholar suggests, like a beast in pain). [9-11] He opens his inner self to God (vs. 9), as if to affirm that the **Lord** he knows will not abide the continuance of such suffering. Verse 10 returns to the picture of physical affliction. Brightening or dimming of the eye represents one's situation in general—good or bad (cf. 1 Sam. 14:29; Pss. 6:7; 13:3; 31:9; Job 17:7). Verse 11 adds forsakenness. **Plague** sometimes describes leprosy (Lev. 13:3), but is also used more generally. It may be either literal or symbolic here. **Afar** is an interpretive addition of the RSV.

Enemies pursue (vss. 12-20). [12] Now a new element of distress is added—enemies. They are secretive, devious, and unwavering in their **treachery.** Were they trying to capitalize on his other suffering, or were they the cause of it? Could they have been any of his former friends (vs. 11)? They seem so intent on enmity that they have little regard for integrity in their relations to him. They are mentioned again in verses 16, 19-20. [13-14] Like a **deaf** and **dumb man,** the author attempts to ignore the opposition (save for this psalm). Some say this was because he was enervated, but that seems counter to the entire psalm's expression. Others suggest that silence came from his awareness of sin. If so, he waits in trust (vss. 15-16), confident that the resolution of the problem is with God. He can therefore rise above rebuking.

[15-16] Because he trusts, he is not fretful or defensive. Only let his confidence be vindicated, so wicked men will not take advantage of his situation. **Boast** (literally "they make great") might also be rendered "triumph over."

[17] But deliverance has not come yet, as his situation testifies. The first line literally means "for I to limping/stumbling am established/ready," and the RSV gives an interpretive translation. The description continues the fig-

ure of verse 16b. He seems to say he cannot endure his
pain much longer. [18] The confession returns to the theme
of verses 3-5. Does he consider confession as the key to
healing, or is it something that was always a part of his
obedient supplication to God? The former view would imply a time when he was impenitent, and therefore anxious
and concerned. But the latter seems more plausible in this
context, though the present verse may be a "reminder" to
God, urging divine response.

[19] The enemies are **mighty** and **many**. Their opposition
is **without cause**, and **wrongfully** engaged in. "Living" (RSV
note) could be conjecturally translated "the enemies of my
life" or "my enemies flourish." However, the RSV, to preserve the parallel with **wrongfully**, and with verse 20, and
on the analogy of Psalm 35:19, has changed one letter of
the text to arrive at **without cause**. [20] **Evil for good**, because so unfair, is a hard burden to bear (cf. Pss. 35:3-5;
109:3-5). Though he has confessed sin, the author was not
abandoned to it. The foes, apparently, were not capitalizing
on his wrongdoing, but on his misfortune. He had treated
them well.

Petition resumed (vss. 21-22). His agony fully portrayed,
the author resumes his prayer (cf. vss. 1, 16) with a threefold petition. The helpless author, completely exposed,
awaits the divine comradeship and salvation. Let not the
absence of **God** add to loneliness already experienced! This
language combines the pathos of "how long" with the stir-
ring "I trust" and delineates the tension in which life must
often be lived.

Psalm 39: Trust in Time of Trial

Deeply troubled about his sin and about his relation to
God, this author expresses his feelings in strong language.
Yet his outward circumstances are not clearly delineated.
He was in anguish, perhaps near death (vs. 13), troubled
by the wicked, and aware of God's judgment upon him for
his sins. Yet, penitent, he pleads for God to remove his
agony. Beyond this he seeks understanding of his state. His
faith, amidst such perplexity, shows that trust can survive

even in the context of melancholy, for he has yet no relief from his trouble, and no hope of life after death.

Verses 1-3a speak of the mental turmoil and psychological explosion caused by the poet's distress. Verses 4-6, a prayer, puzzle about the brevity and seeming futility of life. Verses 7-11 are a statement of faith, confession of sin, and prayer for deliverance from "God's stroke." Verses 12-13 are a pathetic final appeal for a time of gladness before life's end.

Dire distress (vss. 1-3). [1] The writer tried to remain silent **in** the **presence** of **the wicked**, lest in speaking he might sin. He may have feared that **the wicked** would use his suffering as a case against God (cf. vs. 9; Ps. 10:4). Or perhaps he did not wish to offer them opportunity to ridicule a faith that complained under duress. Or he may have been avoiding the pronouncement of a curse upon the wicked. Whatever the motive, he was torn within. **Bridle** is a word used only here in the OT. The Hebrew reads "I will keep for my mouth a bridle"—an interesting description. [2] The Hebrew of this verse begins with three consecutive words (be **dumb** and **silent,** hold **peace**) stressing the poet's attempts to contain himself. But it was useless, for the inner storm raged more furiously. Perhaps his external problems were also intensifying. Though **to no avail** (literally, "from good") might be rendered other ways, the RSV has caught the basic meaning. The last line means literally "my sorrow was stirred/troubled." [3] The third and fourth expressions intensify the picture of his worsening inner storm. Like smouldering coals which finally burst into flame, he **spoke** at last. If the following words are his outburst, they are in prayer form. On the other hand, if he had broken out into complaint, the remaining verses may be a later reaction to it—that is, a subsequent meditation by which the author attempts to resolve his agony through prayer.

The brevity of life (vss. 4-6). [4] Since his few **days** seem dominated by suffering, he wishes some insight (to **know** as God knows) so he may learn to enjoy them (vs. 13). He seeks a way to deal with feelings of futility, but he also hopes for deliverance (vs. 8). He cries for some rationale by which his view of **life** can be made tenable. Though he trusts God (especially vs. 7), this trust awaits a more specific resolution. **[5]** Though seeming to answer his own question, the author is actually strengthening his point about life's brevity with a series of arresting illustrations (cf. Job 7). A handbreadth is about three inches (four fingers) wide. The RSV adds **a few,** since the Hebrew means simply handbreadths. **Nothing** refers to life's brevity, not to its valuelessness. **Mere breath** (also vss. 6, 11) is a favorite word in Ecclesiastes, where it is translated "vanity."

[6] With a disheartening repetition of **surely** (three times in vss. 5-6), life's brevity is presented. The Hebrew word rendered **nought** is the word translated "mere breath" in verses 5 and 11. Rather than giving an exhortation to others, the author seems to beg a deliverance from God that will make brief life meaningful. Is he speaking pessimistically or realistically? In either case, he is speaking to God, and here is the power of the psalm. Prayer sometimes must emanate from depression, moving into confusion, but bastioned by trust.

Prayer for healing (vss. 7-13). [7] Though perplexed, he has nowhere to turn but to God. This verse gives one of the great devotional statements of the OT, like a light from a dark place. **[8]** Here is his first reference to his **transgressions** (cf. also vs. 11), but their relation to his suffering (and to his silence—vss. 1-2, 9) is unclear. Does he believe forgiveness would resolve his other problems, or at least make them endurable? **Fool** translates the Hebrew *nabhal* (cf. 14:1), a strong word. Was **the scorn** for a trust which seemed to go without vindication, in which case deliverance would resolve the problem? Or was it directed at tragic circumstances in the poet's life, which might be altered by God's deliverance from transgression? (Cf. Pss. 22:8; 31:11; 38:16.)

[9] If this and verse 2 refer to the same silence, the author now offers further explanation for his reticence to speak. He did not wish to blame God. Having burst out with complaint and prayer (vss. 3-8), he returns to the condition of the first two verses, his feelings vented.

[10] He is desperate, feeling unable to go on much longer. **Stroke** is a translation of the same Hebrew word represented by "plague" in 38:11, but we cannot know the exact distress. "Hostility" (RSV note) represents a word found only here in the OT. The RSV chooses to render it **by blows.** [11] **Mere breath** (cf. vs. 5) is now associated with God's chastisement **for sin.** Thus it appears that life's difficulties result from his religious failures. But he has repented and the agony should stop. Line two, though problematical, shows the intensity of his grief. All that is **dear to him** has been consumed, as **a moth** would destroy clothes, tapestries, etc. Was **what is dear** his possessions, physical health, reputation, or the like, or was he forced from less important items to consider the basic realities of life?

[12] The psalm's final sob begs a brief respite before death, in a threefold petition. He seems to plead for divine sympathy for his weeping. He likens himself to an alien (**passing guest**) residing in a land not his own, and to **a sojourner,** like the patriarchs. [13] The psalm closes with a forlorn wail. The spectre of death hovers forebodingly, and the poet longs for God's judgment to be lifted (**look away**) so that a bit of **gladness** may enlighten his remaining days (cf. Job 7:19; 14:6). This melancholy ending could leave the reader most depressed (cf. a more severe example in Ps. 88), but is countered by the author's faith as he throws himself upon God. Trust in such a situation preaches a powerful sermon, which is made even more powerful to the Christian by Christ's resurrection.

Psalm 40: A New Song

The most unusual thing about this psalm is its structure. Though psalms usually begin with complaint, and then move, if such is their message, to thanks, this one reverses the order. Thanks (vss. 1-10) is followed by lament (vss. 11-17). Therefore some feel that two originally separate sections were put together, with verses 11-12 (or just vs. 12) as transitional. They point out the virtual identity of verses 13-17 with Psalm 70 and with parts of Psalm 35, arguing that the section had an originally independent existence. Yet there are resemblances between the two sections. The order could be explained as the poet's wavering between assurance and petition, or as due to a gratitude so strong that he reverses the normal order to give prominence to the thanks, or as a recurrence of a problem once thought solved. Or the original author could even have added the last part later, under changed circumstances.

Verses 1-3 reflect on God's glorious deliverance of his patient servant, leading to a blessing (vs. 4), extolling of God (vs. 5), a statement of personal commitment (vss. 6-8), and public proclamation of God's salvation (vss. 9-10). This thanksgiving is followed by a prayer for God's steadfast love (vs. 11) in the face of innumerable evils (vs. 12). Verses 13-17 contain a renewed plea for help and judgment on the poet's enemies, punctuated by an expostulation on the joy of salvation (vs. 16).

Thanksgiving for deliverance (vss. 1-11). [1] The author plunges at once into thanks and praise, recalling his trouble and the time spent in yearning for relief. The Hebrew expression rendered **waited patiently is** literally "waiting, I waited." Some suggest that this means persistent waiting. But the main point is that God **inclined and heard.** How many forfeit God's blessings because they lack this writer's perseverance? [2] Two images indicate disaster, and two safety. "Pit of tumult" (RSV note) suggests a difficult concept, so the RSV emends the Hebrew to obtain **desolate pit. Pit** sometimes symbolizes death, though not necessarily. His distress was also like struggling in mire (cf. Ps. 69:2; Jer. 38:6). But the great trust is God's deliverance—safety on **a rock,** with solid footing and security. The contrast between states is strongly put.

[3] Praise, heard by others, creates within them **trust in the Lord.** The **new song** of deliverance supplants the "old" song of complaint. References to **our God** and to **many** seem to imply public praise. [4] **Trust** is contrasted to pride and idolatry. Do these rival trusts reflect problems in the psalmist's own past, or is he reflecting upon his

society? **False gods** (literally "lies") is an interpretive translation. The proclamation of verses 4-5 may fulfil a vow the author promised to accomplish upon his deliverance.

[5] The poet expands to a marvelous ascription of greatness to Yahweh for his **deeds** and **thoughts**. The first part of line one could also be translated "great things you have done." **Compare** is from a verb meaning "to set in order." Nothing, when thus displayed, comes close to Yahweh—certainly not any other "deity" (cf. Pss. 89:6; 92:5; 104:24; 139:18; and Isa. 40:18). The last line could be rendered "they are mighty—beyond telling!" How this theme has overwhelmed the author; he is transported by it!

[6] The central movement of verses 6-8 seems to suggest an obedience which, rather than opposing the cult, seems to want to go beyond it to the ultimate expression of gratitude—with his whole self, in all of life. Ritual, after all, can by hypocritically practiced (cf. Pss. 50:8-13; 51:16; Amos 5:21-24; Hos. 6:6; Isa. 1:11; Mic. 6:6-8). Verses 3, 5, 9-10 do show his involvement in congregational and cultic activities. The wealth of sacrificial language (four words) is to emphasize his resolution. "Not this, nor this, nor this . . . , but this." The RSV gives the interpretive translation **ears thou hast dug for me** (cf. note), which does not involve emending the Hebrew, and which no doubt catches the essence of the original. That is, "you have given me ears so I can hear and obey!" What else, ultimately, are ears for?

[7-8] It is best to interpret the perplexing details of these verses in terms of one who delights to do God's will, beyond the ritual requirements. **Roll** would equal **thy will and thy law**. He sees himself as fulfilling what **it is written in** scripture that a man should be. Thus **I said** may be a dramatic way of showing his response, when learning of God's requirements. What **God** desires delights him (the Hebrew verb is the same in both cases; cf. vs. 14). Verses 6-9 are quoted from the LXX in Hebrews 10:5-9, where the point is made that Christ has abolished the offerings of the law to establish the offering of the body of Christ. Thus Hebrews speaks of Jesus' obedience.

[9] Good **news** demands proclamation. It is rooted in personal receipt of God's blessing. The "new song" (vs. 3) is brought to worship. The message offers hope to all (**deliverance** is again accomplished!) and thus binds the community of faith more closely together. [10] Here, as if unable to contain himself, the author overflows with a wealth of terms describing divine mercies (**saving help, faithfulness** (two words), **salvation, steadfast love**). These the writer freely declared.

'**Preserve me!**' (vss. 11-17). [11] He asks for the continued outpouring of the divine mercies of verse 10. **Withhold** is the same word as that translated "restrain" in verse 9. Verse 11 repeats two of the rich terms from verse 10 and adds **mercy**. Here begins the first prayer in the psalm. Though its theology and language are close to verse 10, the prayer seems to be as yet unanswered. This blends well with the following lament. There is disagreement over whether the verse belongs with verses 1-10 or with verses 12-17. It is unusual for thanks to precede lament, as here, though the writer may be recalling previous distress in verses 12-17, against the background of his gratitude for God's answer (vss. 1-10).

[12] Now the poet depicts his woeful, overwhelmed situation. **Encompassed** may imply being surrounded as by flood waters. He is **overtaken**, as by a pursuing nemesis. **My heart fails** may refer to a loss of courage. Here, for the only time, he acknowledge his **iniquities**. This verse is a shocking change from verses 1-11. Though verses 13-17 are a prayer for deliverance, they do not (except possibly vs. 14) come near the graphic depiction of problems we find here. If the psalm is a unity, the author's sins may be "the pit" and "miry bog" of verse 2. Perhaps he describes how at one point, being totally without personal resources, he had desperately thrown himself upon God. Others, arguing that we have two originally independent psalms, see this as a linking verse, drawing together emphases of the preceding and following sections.

[13] The rest of this psalm is nearly identical to Psalm 70 and parts of Psalm 35. This may indicate that we have here

oft-used liturgical language, employed by this author for his own purposes. We feel his urgent need for relief (cf. Pss. 22:19; 38:22; 71:12; 141:1). Psalm 70:1 uses the general word "God" instead of **Lord**. **Be pleased** is not in the Hebrew, though the RSV includes it in the translation.

[14] Psalm 70:2 omits **altogether** and **to snatch away**, but is otherwise identical. Psalm 35:4 also omits **altogether**, reverses **put to confusion** and **to snatch away**, and instead of **desire** has a verb which means "devise." See also Psalm 35:26. Here is his first reference to foes. Rather than desiring their total destruction, he would have them dishonored, as a defeated army. [15] This verse is identical to Psalm 70:3, except for the first Hebrew word (though they are rendered the same in English). See also Psalm 35:21, 25. **Appalled** can mean "to be desolate" or "stunned." May those who gloat see their wrong for the abomination it is.

[16] Differences between this verse and Psalm 70:4 are minor, the most marked being the uses of the divine names. See also Psalm 35:27. The author turns again to positive praise (cf. vss. 3, 9-10), probably describing public worship. The outcome—indeed, the goal—of **salvation** is to praise the one who wrought it. There is no deeper cause for joy in human experience than reception of God's blessings. It fosters continual respect. [17] He contrasts his state and need with God's strength and concern. Psalm 70:5 has different divine names than this verse and also has "hasten to me" for **takes thought for me**. The former parallels **do not tarry**, but seems less patient (cf. vs. 1) than this psalm. The writer is not yet rescued, but he is sure that help will come.

Psalm 41: The Lord Sustains

The core of this psalm seems to be the lament and prayer in verses 4-10, which describe an illness aggravated because of enemies (cf. especially vs. 9). Attached to this are the wisdom-type introduction of verses 1-3 and the thanksgiving of verses 11-12. The author has either experienced deliverance before writing or is so sure it will come that he speaks of it as certain. Some scholars feel verses 1-3 and

4-10 do not describe the same person. But this is very unlikely, since the sections have so many congruences.

The great realization of the author is that God is gracious. Appeals to him are heeded, and moral instruction can be grounded on his goodness.

The gracious Lord (vss. 1-3). [1] If he who **considers the poor** (or "weak," RSV note) is the author himself, he experienced suffering before knowing blessedness (vss. 4-9). But, his ordeal past, the author commends compassion, despite his temporary adversity. In view of verses 5-9, his foes are certainly not blessed! The blessedness of verses 2-3 is described differently from verses 11-12, but this may be due to a different perspective. If so, verses 1-3 are the conclusion reached by the author as a consequence of all his experiences (cf. Ps. 11:1).

[2] Verses 2-3 enumerate six facets of this blessedness. Though the RSV takes the Hebrew verbs here to be declarative presents, they also could be rendered as futures or imperatives. **Keeps alive** reflects the fear of death often found in the laments. The RSV supplies **called.** The passage could also be rendered "he is made blessed." **Will** renders the Hebrew word which often is translated "soul" or "life." Note that the last line changes back to the third person. The ancient versions have the third person throughout. [3] Verses 5-10, where the author further describes his **illness**, should be compared with the present. The last line is translated interpretively by the RSV, since the meaning of the Hebrew (cf. RSV note) is obscure. Perhaps the idea is that one's **illness** is changed into health.

Plea for healing (vss. 4-10). [4] Now the lament begins. The author opens (vs. 4) and ends (vs. 10) with an appeal for God's grace. He confesses transgression, and one may assume an implied prayer for forgiveness. He only mentions his sins this once and does not refer to his misfortune as a divine punishment for wrongdoing. Is his confession simply a standard part of prayer for help, or is the connection between the iniquity and distress deeper than the psalm indicates? Here the first option seems preferable. Any request for deliverance might appropriately include such a statement. Contrast "integrity" in verse 12. **Me**, in line two, represents the Hebrew word for "my soul." The same word is translated "will" in verse 2.

[5] The antagonism of **enemies** continues through verse 10, but we cannot assess their exact relation to his illness, except that they take advantage of it and intensify his agony. He would become well so he might deal with them (vs. 10). Contrast his words to God (vs. 4) with the enemy's words about him. **Of me in malice** (literally "evil to me") is also subject to other interpretations. On the **name** (memory, influence) perishing, see 2 Samuel 18:18; Psalms 9:6; 109:13.

[6] He describes a disillusioning experience which began as a promise of sympathy for a sick man and ended in betrayal. Memory of this may have triggered the opening statement of the psalm. Imagine visiting a sick man with such malignant intent! The gossip was at least the contents of verses 8-9, if not more. Were there any enemy speculations about sins which had led to his illness? Were they spreading untruths based upon misuses of their observations? **[7]** Added to hypocrisy are whispering and the hopeful assumption that **the worst** is true of the sufferer. The word translated **imagine** could be rendered "devise," giving an even stronger meaning.

[8] We overhear a fragment of their speech as they revel in his misfortune. His situation is grave. He **has a deadly thing**, literally "a thing of Belial" (cf. Ps.18:4). Could this have been some sin, or a particular illness? Some even suggest that he had been cursed or put under a magic spell. Whatever his enemies mean, we must remember that their interpretive comments are not necessarily true. The RSV adds **they say** (not in the Hebrew text) to clarify the nature of the statement.

[9] The bitterest element is now added (cf. Ps. 55:12-14). Among the betrayers is one formerly a **trusted friend**, a sharer in **bread**. One of the closest human bonds has been violated. The Hebrew phrase translated a **bosom friend** means literally a "man of my peace," that is, one pledged to my well-being. **Lifted his heel** translates the Hebrew for "made great a heel." This implies violence (trampling, kicking, tripping?), whether literal or figurative. This verse is applied to Judas in John 13:18 and is also echoed in Mark 14:18; Matthew 26:23; and Luke 22:21.

[10] May God reverse the intention of his enemies (contrast **raise** with "not rise" in vs. 8). The Hebrew verb translated **requite** contains the same consonants as the Hebrew noun rendered "bosom friend" (vs. 9). Perhaps a play on words was intended. The motive for his petition seems somewhat ignoble. Yet he may have wished his recovery to be requital, or he may have identified his purposes with God's judgment on their evil.

'Thou hast upheld me' (vss. 11-13). [11] Verses 11-12 resume the emphasis of verses 1-3 and apply to the poet himself the confidence expressed there. Deliverance has come, or is sure of coming. The enemy has not vanquished him. The Hebrew verb translated **triumphed** means literally "shout in triumph." How can this assurance be reconciled with the fact he had sinned? He had confessed his sin. Who can God assist aside from those who have sinned? There are no other kinds of people.

[12] He appeals, then, to his **integrity**, despite verse 4. He had the **integrity** for honest introspection and faith in God. He made no attempt to delude himself or others. Thus, he joyously participates in God's **presence** for as long as he lives (the probable meaning of **for ever**). Contrast this with verse 5. The sufferer, begging grace, finds himself at last in that presence from which all blessings emanate.

[13] Since it is basically the same as the doxologies ending each section of the Psalter (72:18-20; 89:52; 106:48), this verse is considered to be separate from the psalm proper. It closes Book I of the Psalter. Its use elsewhere (1 Kings 1:48; Neh. 9:5; Luke 1:68) indicates it was a much-employed liturgical formula. The double **amen** also seems to imply the strong endorsement with which material of some substance (as a book of psalms) would be concluded. But even if the verse were used orally in worship, it may also have been employed as a conclusion for the psalm itself.

Psalms 42–43: 'Why Are You Cast Down?'

Though Psalms 42 and 43 are numbered separately, there is a general consensus that they are actually a single psalm. Beside the thrice-repeated refrain in 42:5, 11, and 43:5, parts of 42:9 and 43:2 are virtually identical. The meter, thought, language, and problems are the same. Further, Psalm 43 is the only one (except Ps. 71) in this section of the Psalter (Pss. 42–72) without a heading, which probably indicates that it was not intended to stand separately. Assuming this unity, then, the problem is to explain why the psalm was divided. Though we cannot know for sure, it may have been related to its use in worship.

The text vibrates between complaint and optimistic trust in God. The refrain divides the text neatly into the units 42:1-5, 6-11, and 43:1-5. Though complaint is continually present, the psalm seems to grow progressively more positive and hopeful as it moves along. The author seems to be in the north (Ps. 42:4, 6), unable to travel to Jerusalem for the Jewish festivals. He fervently wishes God to make the pilgrimage possible again (Ps. 43:3-4). It is problematic whether he was hindered by illness, since there are no clear references to affliction (but note Ps. 42:7). But there is no doubt of the anguish imposed by his skeptical foes (Ps. 42:3, 9-10; 43:1-2). Scholars have conjectured that the author was a soldier away from Jerusalem on a military campaign, or a temple singer exiled in the north, or an Israelite under foreign oppression and unable to travel. Each of these has something to commend it, but there is inadequate evidence to reach a conclusive position.

Thirsting for God (vss. 1-3). [1] The land suffers from drought, and a thirsty animal seeks eagerly for water. The hart's yearning becomes a powerful figure of the longing for God experienced by this writer. He feels he is isolated from the yearned-for sustenance. [2] Though some suppose the psalmist does not know that **God** is found in all places, it is preferable to think he longs for a particular experience— feast-time in Jerusalem. Otherwise, why would he expect God to hear a prayer uttered away from Jerusalem? This yearning for God thus includes the joys of God's community and the cult. Public worship is, for him, a burning necessity. The term **living God** may be intended to complete the parallel with the continually flowing stream sought by the hart. Others think it may contrast with false gods to whom his enemies gave allegiance (cf. vss. 3, 10; 43:1-2). Compare "God of my life" in verse 8.

The reading **Behold** is based on a slight emendation of the MT, where the Hebrew means "appear before."

[3] Perhaps the reference to a diet of **tears** indicates that his distress was as persistent as the need for **food**, or else that his grief took away his appetite. Further, he is being taunted (cf. vs. 10) **continually** (literally "all the day"). Did the scorn imply that **God** was powerless, or unconcerned, or non-existent? Or was the author assumed to be godless because God had not delivered him? For such a God-centered man, this mockery was an excruciating inner torment. The opposition he experienced may have inspired the writing of the psalm. The **where** of the foes led to the "when" (vs. 2) of the writer.

Memories of God (vss. 4-11). [4] Amidst his anguish he sweetens his lot by remembering the good days gone by, for which he hopes again. It was an exuberant time, and his description helps us understand the strong feelings of verses 1-3. **Went** and **led** signify incomplete action in Hebrew and could be understood as wishes rather than reminiscences. Or they could indicate continuous action in the past, and, hopefully, in the future, as well. **Led them** is the translation adopted for a very difficult phrase in Hebrew. Some suggest emending the Hebrew to "Majestic One," as in the ancient versions. The RSV seems to imply that the poet was a leader of the people. A change in the vowels of the Hebrew word here rendered **multitude** would yield "booth" or "tabernacle," which is what most versions suggest. Then the reference would be specifically to the annual Feast of Booths.

[5] Verse 5 is a refrain that divides the psalm (cf. also vs. 11 and Ps. 43:5). Here are reflection, lament, and **hope**, made dramatically effective by the device of the man addressing his own **soul**. This formula expresses the tension

of the whole psalm. There is reason to groan, but there is greater reason for joy. He cannot find deliverance by simply grieving. Grief must yield to positive faith which assaults his troubles. The Hebrew word translated **disquieted** is from the same root as that rendered "multitude" in verse 4, perhaps drawing attention to the contrast between that joy and the despair in this verse. A probable copyist's error has produced a slight difference between **my help** and **my God** here and in verse 11 and Psalm 43:5. The RSV emends and translates all three passages in the same way. **Help** is plural in Hebrew and perhaps denotes many saving acts of the Lord in which the author has shared and hopes to share again. Notice that the first three words of verse 6 properly belong with verse 5.

[6] Being **cast down** seems to be countered by the remembrance of God, presumably of his steadfast love (vs. 8). Recall the memory in verse 4. **Hermon** is a mountain in extreme northern Palestine. It is supposed that **Mount Mizar** was in the same area. The word means "little" or "insignificant." **The land of Jordan**, then, may well indicate the sources of the Jordan river. These locales probably tell us where the author dwelt—too far from Jerusalem! He must transcend the distance by faith. [7] Aesthetically, it is attractive to think the poet contemplated a waterfall and thought of **waves and billows** thundering upon him as did the waters in nature. In the Bible the **deep** and the waters are often considered potentially destructive (cf. Gen. 1:32; Pss. 18:4; 69:1-2; Jon. 2:3, 6). This expression also may be interpreted figuratively; then it may be based on myths of overwhelming waters (perhaps the water of the underworld). They are *God's* **waves** in either case. The divine hand is behind the calamities, but more importantly, God also offers steadfast love (vs. 8).

[8] In contrast to his tears (vs. 3), the psalmist now celebrates God's **steadfast love** and **song**. Since he turns again to despair in verses 9-10, some scholars suggest that the present verse is more a recollection of past blessings and an expression of hope for the future than a description of his present state. The vascillation is strange but true to

human experience. This is the only verse where **Lord** (Yahweh) is the name used of God. Everywhere else in the psalm, some form of the divine name El is employed.

[9] The author's remembrance (vss. 4, 6), stands in contrast to his complaint of God's forgetfulness. Yet even this is not hopeless, for **God** is still his rock. The depression expressed in this verse continues until verse 11 affords another glimpse of brightness. Most of this verse from **why hast** onward is virtually identical with Psalm 43:2. **[10]** The repeated **taunt** (cf. vs. 3) is likened to **a deadly wound**. Though the Hebrew word rendered **deadly wound** is unclear (suggested interpretations include "slay," "crush," or "death stroke"), the image is inescapable. His is an agonizing situation. Perhaps the enemy's question was made especially bitter because the author had been wondering the same thing himself. **[11]** The refrain from verse 5 is here repeated.

Appeal to God (43:1-5). [1] Enemies are still on his mind (cf. Ps. 42:9-10). Three verbs convey his prayer—**vindicate, defend** (**cause** translates a cognate word in Hebrew), and **deliver. Ungodly** could indicate those not in covenant relation with God. This, plus the word used for **people** (*goy*, often meaning "Gentiles") leads some to suspect non-Jewish foes. However, this is not a necessary conclusion. The word translated **men** is actually singular in Hebrew, i.e., "a man"), so some scholars think a particular foe stood out from the others. On the other hand, the singular is sometimes used in a collective sense, and the RSV has so interpreted "a man" here. **[2]** The last three-fourths of this verse is virtually identical with Psalm 42:9. The first line is also similar (**refuge** equals "rock"). The psalm becomes more optimistic from here to its end.

[3] In verses 3-4 the psalmist pleads that he be enabled to return again to Jerusalem for the festivals. This implies resolution of the poet's hindering problems. His foes would no longer have ground for taunts. **Light** is a figure for guidance (Pss. 4:6; 36:9; 44:3; 89:15) and was one means by which Israel had been led in the wilderness (Exod. 13:21). **Truth** indicates God's absolute faithfulness and reliability.

Thus, the prayer grounds itself in a conviction about God's provident nature. [4] The thought of verse 3 continues, with an amplified description of the author's **praise**. This anticipation has the quality of a vow, and it vibrates with joy. A literal translation of the second line might be "to God of the joy of my rejoicing." Note, in retrospect, all the ways that this poet has described God (cf. 42:1, 2, 4, 5, 7, 8, 9; 43:1, 3, 4). For all his lament and depression, his is a powerful faith! [5] The refrain is repeated a third time. We presume the stress is now more on **hope** than on despair.

Psalm 44: A Bewildered Prayer

After a terrible national defeat, a spokesman for Israel pours out bewilderment and prayer to God. Why has a God who led them victoriously in the past now changed? Such might have been expected had they sinned, but their fidelity to God has continued unabated. Suggested dates for this psalm run from Hezekiah's reign to as late as the Maccabean age. However, no date can be definitely determined. Quite possibly the psalm accompanied some liturgical occasion expressing national concern.

Verses 1-8 review the happy past under Yahweh's blessings. Verses 9-16 describe the miserable present—the people are defeated, shattered, taunted. Verses 17-22 are a profession of innocence, which acknowledge God's justice in punishing the wicked. Verses 23-26 are an impassioned closing prayer. Despite God's shocking departure from his nature as the nation has known it, they continue to trust him. Adversity leads to renewed appeal.

Blessings recalled (vss. 1-8). [1] Knowledge of past victories has been passed on from the **fathers**. This shows the importance of the preservation and transmission (usually oral) of tradition in Israel (cf. Exod. 13:14-16; Deut. 6:20-25; Josh. 4:6-7; Ps. 78:3). Present and future were understood in terms of those traditions (as in this psalm).

[2] The deeds of verse 1 are elaborated. The conquest of Canaan is described by a double contrast between the dispossessed **nations** and Israel. The first of the verse is emphatic in Hebrew—"you, your hand"—stressing God's

power in history. This introduces the note of grace more fully affirmed in verse 3, but also sharpens the perplexity expressed in verses 9-10. **Planting** is a term used often of God's setting Israel in Canaan (Exod. 15:17; 2 Sam. 7:10; Ps. 80:8).

[3] God's **delight** was due to his grace, not to the people's merit. Battles, heroes, and victories all came because of divine power (**right hand, arm,** and **light**). **Light** symbolizes favor and help (cf. Pss. 4:6; 89:15; and Prov. 16:15). Israel, then, had the highest incentive to gratitude, trust, and humility.

[4-5] Verses 4-8 assert the personal faith of the author and the community. The psalm moves from its usual plural (the nation) to occasional singular usages (vss. 4, 6, 15-16), as the personal earnestness of the poet, a spokesman and leader of the nation, breaks through. This is no detached historian's view of the past, but that of one who acknowledges **God** as his **king.** The RSV (vs. 4) has avoided the imperative sense of the original Hebrew, and follows the ancient versions. They do not have the petition begin until verse 23. **Push** and **tread** (vs. 5) may imply the actions of a wild ox in its power. The Hebrew term rendered **assailants** literally means "those who are against us."

[6-8] The previous themes are reiterated in verses 6-7. Verse 8 amplifies the attitude of the people. It likely indicates some sort of public worship. **Boast** implies the idea of praise, rather than bragging. The people have not given up faith. They have a substantial past on which to build. But everything written to this point will be put in shocking perspective by the next paragraph.

Sufferings endured (vss. 9-16). [9] Like a rapid series of shocking blows, the staccato description of the present woes (vss. 9-16) staggers the reader. The psalm is turned inside out. In asking why, one is brought into the perplexed heart of the writer and the nation. **Cast off, abased,** and deserted, they have lost a battle, and, their faith dazed, seek an explanation. Has the past lied to them? Have they misread God's nature? [10-11] Routed, despoiled, slaughtered, **scattered**—so continues the mournful litany.

Each new ingredient heightens the questions burdening the author. The word translated **slaughter** actually means "food"; a different Hebrew word is used in verse 22.

[12] Even worse, Israel, once God's delight (vs. 3), is now **sold** (like a sheep or slave?), and for a pittance. There was not even any haggling over her value.

[13-14] The dominant note of verses 13-16 is the disgrace that all this has brought upon the people. The theme is repeated with a number of words (**taunt, derision, scorn, byword, laughingstock,** shame, reviling). It is a problem of reputation. Those once victorious are now brought low. **Byword** (vs. 14) translates the Hebrew word elsewhere rendered "proverb," indicating that their downfall was spoken of as commonly and surely as a proverb. **Laughingstock** (vs. 14) is a translation which assumes the shaking of the head in ridiculing laughter (cf. RSV note). [15-16] Nor can the problem be put aside. The poet feels the nation's plight with especial keenness, as a personal, continued **disgrace.** The last line of verse 15 is literally "shame of my face covers me," as if he were so humiliated that he dreaded appearing before others. Verse 16 uses four words to describe the opponents and further explains the emotions of verse 15.

Innocence maintained (vss. 17-21). [17-19] Here is the real core of the agony. Wicked people would deserve such judgment, but the writer affirms that neither in attitude nor in action has Israel done wrong. Nor is there any reason to suppose that he was lying in affirming their innocence. The whole structure of covenant theology, based on God's nature, and confirmed by past history, seems shattered. **Jackals** (vs. 19) would inhabit a desert place, perhaps even the ruins of a destroyed city. The people have been devastated and seemingly abandoned. The Hebrew term rendered **deep darkness** is literally "shadow of death." The RSV translates a variant form of the original Hebrew term (cf. Ps. 23:4).

[20-21] They could not forget the Lord, nor pray (**spread hands**) to another without his knowledge. This affirms the author's integrity, for he would not dare lie about the

innocence of the people to such a deity. Perhaps the poet also believes God's knowledge offers a resolution of the problem. If God **knows**, will he not act appropriately? Our understanding of the meaning here depends on how we interpret verse 22.

'**Rouse thyself!**' (vss. 22-23). [22] **For thy sake** (literally "unto you") is an expression crucial to understanding the psalm. The author may mean only that God has caused the circumstances. But Romans 8:36 uses the verse of those suffering for Christ's sake who see a redemptive value in their experience. Could the author here be breaking through to such a concept? Does he see, for the first time in the psalm, that the national agonies have a divine purpose in them? Can the poet understand that God may bring a suffering upon men that is seemingly without reason? If so, then this is perhaps the most significant verse in the psalm. Yet such an interpretation is problematic. Since the remaining verses are a striking prayer for succor, it seems probable that this verse also expresses complaint, rather than a deeper explanation of the tragedy. If they have been defeated because of their faith, they are now eager for their faith to stir God to bless them.

[23] The psalm concludes with an explosively emotional cry for help. This frank call for a dramatic reversal of God's actions stuns Christian ears. Imagine rebuking the Almighty, asserting that it is time that he rise from his slumber (cf. Pss. 7:6; 78:65; and contrast 121:4)! This strong anthropomorphic language undeniably shows the depth of the national concern. Because of Christ's message about the power of suffering, Christians have learned, in pain, to pray, "Thy will be done." They understand that greater victories may come through circumstances that appear for the moment to be defeats.

[24-25] The impassioned verbs continue. God has slept, cast the people off, hidden his **face** (contrast vs. 4), and forgotten. Verse 25 may show the result of this, echoing the humiliation already depicted in verses 13-16. However, some scholars interpret the passage in terms of worshipers begging divine aid through intense supplication.

[26] A final appeal is directed to the center of Israel's faith—God's **steadfast love**. Despite all, God will vindicate his covenant love. The bewilderment has not been removed, but faith shines gloriously. They still maintain that God loves. Yet they may have great truths to learn about this love before a resolution comes. Perhaps only in Christ is such truth exposed to men. But those who read this lament can find inspiration to persist in God's cause, whatever the circumstances.

Psalm 45: A Nuptial Song

This psalm celebrates a king's wedding and may even have been used in the ceremony. Whatever the original occasion (Solomon, Jehu, and Jehoram are conjectured grooms), quite possibly it came to be used repeatedly in Israel's royal nuptials. Though some suggest a cultic use of the psalm, this seems a strained possibility. Later the psalm was interpreted messianically, and still later allegorically. The former step seems natural (cf. vs. 6), but the latter is quite dubious as an interpretive mode for the psalm.

After a scribal introduction (vs. 1), the king is heroically described as handsome and eloquent (vs. 2), a mighty warrior (vss. 3-5), a paragon of just sovereignty (vss. 4, 6, 7), possessor of an eternal throne (vs. 6), specially blessed by God (vs. 7), and magnificently prepared for the wedding (vss. 8-9). In verse 9 the bride is introduced. She is advised and promised blessing in her new role (vss. 10-13a). Her wedding procession is beautifully pictured in verses 13b-15. Finally a blessing (vs. 16-17), including a divine oracle (vs. 17), is bestowed upon the pair.

The psalm's greater emphasis, behind the immediate festivities, is upon the Lord, from whom the couple's blessedness comes, and to whom their lives are given (especially vss. 2, 6, 7, 17).

To the king (vss. 1-9). [1] The author uses his arts to celebrate an auspicious occasion. His **theme** (literally "word") bubbles forth. The word translated **verses** literally means "doings." The last line may describe the author as a **scribe**, or only **like** one (as in the RSV). His **tongue**

has the nimbleness, or expertise, of the scribal pen.

[2] Verses 2-9 flatter the king. Perhaps some kingly groom was this marvelous (cf. Judg. 8:18; 1 Sam. 9:2; 10:23; 16:12; 2 Sam. 14:25; 1 Kings 1:6), but it is more likely that the scribe uses poetic exaggeration. The king is handsome and a good speaker. These were probably ways of speaking of the blessedness of the kingly office, rather than reasons why God blessed the king. There would be a perpetual beneficence (cf. 2 Sam. 7:16).

[3] Verses 3-5 picture an invincible warrior preparing to go on a noble crusade. God would so bless him. Here was a man to be admired and followed. If he were marrying a foreign princess (cf. vss. 11-12), it would be politically appropriate to thus extol him. The RSV adds **in** to the Hebrew to make it clear that **glory and majesty** describe the king. [4] Sword girt, the king rides into battle for the noblest of causes—**truth** and **right**. This redounds to his, and God's glory. **Truth** is faithfulness or fidelity. The idea seems to be that warfare has its limits, and wanton bloodshed and aggression are ruled out. Some think "meekness" (RSV note) does not fit with the last line of the verse, and so emend to the alternate reading. Others feel "meekness" could describe even a warrior, and they would read "truth, meekness, and righteousness" (which also involves emendation). [5] The second and third phrases of this verse occur in reverse order in the Hebrew text, and **fall** could conceivably be the verb with **arrows**, rather than with **peoples.** However, the RSV seems to make better sense.

[6] This verse contains the main interpretive difficulty of the psalm, since "God" ('*elohim*—RSV **divine**) is used apparently to modify **throne.** It seems strange to use the word in this sense, and various explanations are offered. The basic idea is doubtless that the king is divinely ordained and his "throne" is eternal. The RSV text and notes indicate the possibilities. The context (cf. vs. 7b) would indicate that the king is in mind here. Virtually all the ancient versions agree with the RSV. Other OT uses of Elohim do refer to men or to beings less than God (cf. Exod. 7:1; 22:8-9; 1 Sam. 28:13; Zech. 12:8).

The reading in the RSV note could indicate that the monarch in Israel was deified—and some scholars maintain this in arguing for an Israelite pattern of divine kingship. But no other passage unequivocally supports such a view, and the position raises serious problems. This verse offers a striking concept of kingship, but one reference does not justify a major departure from the general OT conception. Hebrews 1:8 applies this and the next verses to the deity of the Son in his superiority to angels, but we should not assume this is what the author of the psalm had in mind when he wrote.

[7] The first line is the strongest compliment yet. The groom is a fine specimen morally, as well as militarily. Is the king **anointed** because of his character, or is he just an admirable example of what a king should be? Perhaps the one for whom these words were originally composed was a person of such sterling qualities. But no doubt in subsequent uses these words may have been poetic desire rather than factual description. Anointing here takes on a special meaning due to the excellence of the monarch. **Oil of gladness** may refer to the king's coronation, but could also refer to anointing for the wedding (cf. Isa. 61:3), paralleling verse 8. [8] The king's garments are fragrantly perfumed. The RSV adds **are all fragrant** to indicate the lovely scent of **myrrh, aloes, and cassia.** Perhaps the spices were in the anointing oil. (Cf. Song of Sol. 3:6; 4:14; etc.) **Ivory palaces** and **stringed instruments** complement the description. The former probably refers to ivory inlays.

To the queen (vss. 9-15). [9] Now we meet **the queen,** and for the first time the psalm clearly indicates a wedding. **Daughters of kings** are thought by most to be the king's harem—a strange note in our modern conceptions of wedding! This would indicate a marriage made to seal a political alliance. **Gold of Ophir** was apparently especially noted, though little is known of **Ophir** (Job 28:16; Isa. 13:12; and cf. 1 Kings 9:27-28). The **right hand** was the place of honor.

[10-11] Verses 10-13a offer counsel to the bride, telling her to invest her life in her mate—a situation not without its rewards. We do not know by whom they were spoken in the ceremony (a court official or priest?). No doubt they reflect wedding conditions previously agreed upon. Duty was placed even above her **people** and her **father's house**. These could be simply her kinsfolk, but if she were a Tyrian princess the implications were further reaching. Foreign wives could be a baleful influence, as Solomon and Ahab learned. Thus, such exhortation could have deeper religious significance. **Desire your beauty** may refer to the consummation of the marriage. **Bow** is a strong and unusual term. Some would suggest a slight emendation, connecting it with "the people of Tyre" of verse 12. But this would imply a stronger subjugation of the Tyrians than the RSV indicates. It seems better to leave the text as it is.

[12] The RSV note indicates the textual problems in verses 12-15. "Daughter of Tyre" (cf. note) is translated so as to refer not to the queen but to the nation (cf. daughter of Babylon, Ps. 137:8; daughter of Zion, Ps. 9:14). It would seem unusual for the bride to be described as giving a gift. Perhaps the bride was from **Tyre, or Tyre** may be mentioned as typical of neighboring nations paying honor at such an auspicious occasion. Though the RSV completes the sentence of verse 12b with verse 13a, it would be possible to read as the note indicates. There are also other suggested translations. The meaning is not significantly altered in any case.

[13] We envision the wedding procession (vss. 13b-15) from the bride's **chamber** (literally "within"). She is beautifully clothed, as befits a **princess** (literally "daughter of a king") marrying a monarch. [14-15] The bride's procession is a joyful occasion. The author further describes her attire and the procession. Though in verse 9 she was already at the king's right hand, that was probably prospective advice. The **virgin companions** may have been childhood friends (which is the basic meaning of the word translated **escort**), but we do not know the express reason virgins were part of the ceremony. The Hebrew term translated **in her train** means literally "those brought to you" (RSV note). It is assumed that the two phrases are equivalent,

though it is a strange mode of expression.

The benediction (vss. 16-17). **[16]** The last two verses are addressed to the king, not to the queen (as might be supposed from the immediately preceding context), since the pronouns are masculine. These words might have been part of the ceremony, blessing the union. Their posterity will be distinguished. **[17]** The Hebrew text especially emphasizes the continuing blessing and fame of this union—a wedding significant far beyond normal expectations. This verse is in the form of a divine oracle, crowning the psalm with God's promise.

Psalm 46: 'God Is Our Refuge'

This magnificent psalm speaks of a faith which surmounts threats of cataclysmic natural upheavals (vss. 1-3), raging of nations (vss. 4-7), and martial activity (vss. 8-11). The central focus is found in verses 4-7, which verses 1-3 elaborate symbolically, and verses 8-11 generalize and extend to universal dimensions. From an unknown circumstance the author rises to the ultimate and final victory of God and his exaltation in all the earth. The specific cultic situation of the psalm cannot be definitely determined from its contents.

'We will not fear' (vss. 1-3). **[1]** Here is the confidence against which the turmoil of subsequent verses is set. **God is refuge** (sure defense), **strength** (dynamic aid), and **help.** The Hebrew phrase rendered **very present** literally means "making himself found exceedingly" (cf. RSV note). **In trouble, God** is accessible, and his aid is enough for any situation. This verse inspired Luther's moving hymn, "A Mighty Fortress."

[2] The cataclysmic catastrophes of verses 2-3 are interpreted in various ways. Some see the primeval chaos from which God ordered the creation. Others see the world catastrophe which was to precede the Messianic Age (assuming such a concept was then current in Israel). A third position, and the simplest, is that an earthquake (perhaps the author had experienced one) is pictured. In any case, the stable **earth** has become insecure. All sources of strength and security are ripped away till only the ultimate remains. Yet the poet is unafraid, for he trusts God. If he is not safe there, no safety can be found, and all is indeed chaos. [3] The description of the natural violence continues. Imaginative reading here will show the terror of the author's vision, and thus the greatness of his faith. Since verses 7 and 11 offer an identical refrain following the second and third stanzas of this psalm, the same words may originally have been found after verse 3. If so, they probably dropped out in transmission.

God helps his people (vss. 4-7). [4] The focus now turns to the threat of opposing nations (vss. 4-7), centering in God's care for Jerusalem. In contrast to the turbulent water of verse 3 we now find gladdening watercourses (the RSV adds **There is** for clarity). **River** is probably in apposition to "God" (vs. 5). Actually no river flowed through **the city** of Jerusalem. The image probably indicates great blessing (cf. Gen. 2:10-14; Isa. 33:21; Ezek. 47:1-12; Joel 3:18; Zech. 14:8; Rev. 22:1-2). One can imagine the power of such a picture to people in a semi-arid land where drought was a real danger. [5] The symbol of verse 4 now takes form. The presence of **God** is the significant factor. The Hebrew word rendered **moved** here is the same as that rendered "shake" in verse 2 and "totter" in verse 6. One can almost derive the theology of the psalm from this word. **Right early** (literally "to the face of the morning") implies divine deliverance as day begins, perhaps after a night of anxious concern (cf. Exod. 14:27; 1 Sam. 11:9).

[6] As the psalm progresses, danger is emphasized less, and security more. The might of **nations** is nothing against the mighty power of the divine word. The Hebrew word translated **rage** is the same as that rendered "roar" in verse 3. [7] This refrain (also in verse 11) is the central thought of the psalm—a mighty shout of victory. Yahweh is **Lord of hosts** (earthly armies—1 Sam. 17:45, or heavenly hosts— 1 Kings 22:19?), mighty enough to vanquish any foe. He is also Jacob's **God. Refuge,** a different word in Hebrew from that used in verse 1, implies an inaccessible height.

'Be still and know . . . ' (vss. 8-11). [8] Verses 8-10

depict God's power as totally overwhelming any threat and bringing the peace of his reign. How is this section (and therefore the entire psalm) to be interpreted? If historical, the language is too vague to pinpoint an occasion. Or does the writer have in mind an eschatological vision of God's final victory and peaceable kingdom? Again, some suppose the text implies cultic activity in which God's exaltation is recognized and celebrated. However the psalm be interpreted, the faith of the author shines clear.

Desolations probably refers to the end of whatever usurps God's authority or would thwart his peaceful design. The first line of this verse is found also, with slight changes, in Psalm 66:5.

[9] The opening statement is elucidated by three concrete descriptions, regarding **the bow, spear, and chariots.** Men fight to impose their will, but God imposes his to end fighting. All battle fields, strewn with shattered and burned implements, offer mute testimony to Yahweh's universal sway. **Chariots** is from a term that means "carts." One vowel change in Hebrew would give "shields," and some modern versions have adopted this emendation.

[10] This psalm, powerful in concept and expression, climaxes with a divine word. It is an overwhelming call to response, uttered within Israel but to be heard by all. Let the opposing forces bow before him lest they be desolated. Let Israel rejoice and be confirmed in her faith. This is the final reality of history, and for it all human intercourse exists. As used in worship, this may have been the triumphant assertion given by a priest at the climatic moment in the liturgy. [11] The refrain is repeated, more meaningfully after verses 8-10. It is a response to God's self-revelation in verse 10.

Psalm 47: The Reign of God

The center of this psalm is the kingship of Yahweh (cf. Pss. 95–97; 99; and 46:10), celebrated in worship (vss. 1, 5-7). Beyond this, interpretations vary from historical to eschatological to cultic (cf. the discussion of Ps. 46:8). The latter view is most popular. Some see here the annual

Enthronement Festival, but see the discussion in the introduction for problems with this view. Others suggest a festive acknowledgment of Yahweh's kingship, though not as an enthronement ceremony. God's promise to David of eternal dominion and the establishment of Jerusalem as the seat of Israel's religion are elements in the background of this psalm.

Some would divide the psalm into two parts: verses 1-5 and 6-9, beginning each section with a call to worship. The presence of "Selah," however, suggests a division into three parts: verses 1-4, 5-7, and 8-9.

God the great king (vss. 1-4). [1] Reasons for this exuberant call to praise are explained in verses 2-4 and 8-9. Such displays accompanied coronations in Israel (1 Sam. 10:24; 2 Sam. 15:10; 2 Kings 9:13; 11:12). The immediate praise was in Israel's cultus, but they believed **all peoples** should, and eventually would, praise with them.

[2] God is above **all** earthly sovereigns and deities who would claim kingship (cf. Pss. 95:3; 97:9; 99:2). This summons is justified in verses 3-4. **Terrible** has the sense of "awe inspiring." Yet because of the covenant Israel could praise him with joy (vs. 1).

[3-4] These verses seem to refer to the conquest of Canaan, or even to victories beyond those in Israel's history. **Heritage** (vs. 4) is often used of Canaan (Deut. 4:21, 38; Jer. 3:19; etc.). The land was **the pride of** the people—indicating their grateful approval of God's grace (**he loves,** vs. 4). The universal king rules all, but one people he gives particular blessing! For their sake he controls the fortunes of **nations** for weal or woe.

'Sing praises!' (vss. 5-7). [5] The import of the phrase **God has gone up** is central to the psalm's interpretation. Historical interpreters see God's return after having come to aid his people. Cultic interpreters suggest cultic activity in celebration of God's action—perhaps a procession with the ark (cf. Pss. 24:7-10; 68:25-28). They note that the **trumpet** was sounded in connection with the New Year (Lev. 23:24; Num. 29:1; 2 Sam. 6:15) and with the coronation of the king (1 Kings 1:39). Others see God's victory

over all nations at the end of the age. It is possible, as
Weiser suggests, that all three views were present in one
ceremony. But any reconstruction of the actual circumstances must be speculative.

[6-7] Here previous ideas are reemphasized in the ecstatic cry of people caught up in praise. Note the fivefold
imperative. Verse 6 adds **with a psalm**. The Hebrew term
(cf. RSV note) is *maskil* (cf. the headings of Pss. 32, 42,
etc.). The Hebrew root from which the word comes may
mean "make wise or prudent," which would suggest that
the *maskil* is a teaching psalm. But that is not the case with
most psalms so headed. Other possibilities emphasize the
skill with which the psalm was written, or its beauty, or its
efficacious spiritual influence.

God on the throne (vss. 8-9). [8] These verses amplify
the universalism of the psalm. The **throne** of God is at
times upon the ark (Ps. 99:1; Jer. 3:16-17) and at times in
heaven (Isa. 66:1). **God** has reigned, and will. The cult may
reemphasize the fact. But the gathering of the nations (vs.
9) must express a hope for what is yet to be. [9] The idea
that all men will be part of the chosen **people** was a daring
one, but was implicit in the promise to **Abraham** (Gen.
12:1-3). Will the rulers (symbolized as **shields**, cf. Ps. 89:18)
come willingly, or by constraint? The lack of martial language implies the former. This vision of the unity of man
centers in the glory of God, as the concluding line reminds
us. The reader cannot but concur—God **is highly exalted!**

Psalm 48: God Defends Zion

This psalm centers in Zion, significant because she testifies to God's glory. She is safe from hostile forces because
of him. This deliverance may refer to some historical circumstance, or may be a picture of God's great victory in
the end time, or may refer to God's continued protection of
the people. Though the circumstances for which the psalm
was composed are not known, suggestions include a celebration after some great deliverance, or a cultic ceremony
which involved encircling and surveying the city, or a feast
of covenant renewal.

In verses 1-3 the psalmist praises God, Zion's defense.
Verses 4-8 describe the onslaught of foes, who are completely routed, presumably by Yahweh. Verses 9-11 reflect
further upon God, especially his steadfast love leading to
universal praise. Verses 12-14 counsel a survey of the city,
as a monument to God's everlasting care, which is to be
proclaimed to coming generations.

Zion made a citadel (vss. 1-3). [1] Great is the Lord is the
psalm's center. Because of him, Jerusalem is significant.
Here deliverance of **the city** is the particular impetus to
praise. The RSV puts the last clause of this verse with
verse 2 to give it a subject and for metrical reasons.

[2] The natural beauty of **Zion** would not surpass that of
other Palestinian mountains. But it is was specially endued
because God dwelt there, and thus took on special glory
through the eyes of faith. **Joy of all the earth** may be a
poetic exaggeration, or it may express Israel's hope that in
coming times all nations would join in praising Yahweh.

Zion was not literally **in the far north** for a Palestinian
writer. Thus the reference may have theological significance. One suggestion is that in mythology the gods of
Babylon and Canaan were said to assemble in the far north
(cf. a reflection of this in Isa. 14:13). The psalmist counters
by saying that Yahweh really reigns there, that is, he is
King, and not the pagan deities. Another view contrasts
Yahweh with kings reigning in the far north (cf. Ezek. 38:6,
15; 39:2). They are also called "great king" (2 Kings 18:19,
28), but only Yahweh can be truly so styled. In either case,
the overall concern is the exaltation of the Lord. **[3]** The
premise stated here is elaborated in verses 4-8. It is not her
military prowess that makes the city safe, but the Lord.
The Hebrew term translated **sure defense** means literally
"high tower."

Opposing kings panic (vss. 4-8). [4] Verses 4-7 employ a
rapid fire series of verbs, presenting in the original a more
vivid scene than the English captures. They show the dis-
integration of an organized aggressor league of kings.

[5-6] Verse 5 in Hebrew has only six words, four of
which are verbs. The RSV adds **as soon as,** which may

produce clarity but reduces the impact of the original. **It** apparently refers to whatever way God chose to defend his people. What a contrast between the force pictures in verse 4 and verses 5-6! The mighty force is routed, shaking and agonizing like **a woman** in birth pains.

[7] Tarshish was probably in Spain. **The ships** were apparently of the largest sort, shattered by a violent **wind** off the land (cf. Ezek. 27:26). Was their cargo armaments, so that even the supply sources of the defeated army were destroyed? Some suggest ships symbolize defiance of God. But the exact significance of these words remains something of a mystery. They show God's power, but why here in this way? **[8]** If the reference is to the worshiping community, what had they **seen** that confirmed what they **heard**? Perhaps the entire aspect of the city and the cult so impressed them (particularly if they were pilgrims). Some specific part of the ceremonies may have had great impact (e.g., a recitation of God's saving works, vindicated by present blessedness).

God's love is known (vss. 9-11). [9] In the temple, at worship, thoughts focus as nowhere else on God's covenant mercies, past, present, and future. **[10-11]** God's universal acknowledgment is again noted, as in verse 2. His victories make his name known, and therefore praised. Verse 11 shows why the joy of verse 2 is appropriate. **Judgments** (vs. 11) were likely the victories of verses 4-7. **Daughters of Judah** is an unusual way of referring to the people.

Consider Zion's safety (vss. 12-14). These verses suggest a walking tour of the city, not to glory in strong fortifications but in God who is the city's real defense.

[12-13] Israel reflects on what is sure, to know its deeper meaning. She sees behind physical phenomena. The walking tour may refer to some cultic act, or to a pilgrim jaunt, or even to a mental survey. In either case, the meaning is the same. The psalmist bids the message be passed on through the generations. God's bond with his people is to be perpetuated. **[14]** The final **for ever** represents a slight emendation, supported by many manuscripts, from the literal "unto dying, death." Some take the literal sense to indicate that God gives victory over death. But if so, a new thought is introduced at the very end of the psalm, which seems unlikely.

Psalm 49: The Folly of Riches

This psalm discusses the futility of placing ultimate trust in wealth, in view of inevitable death. Death is the final defeat of false trust, but it is also the point at which trust in God is most powerfully vindicated (vs. 15). The author may be a poor man who shares his wisdom with other poor in this proverb set to music (vss. 3-4.)

Verses 1-4 introduce the poet's wisdom. Verses 5-9 affirm that wealthy persecutors are not to be feared, since they cannot avoid death. Neither wealth, lands, nor pomp keep them from dying like beasts (vss. 10-12). Verses 13-15 depict the poet's hope that God will ransom him from Sheol—the psalm's high point. Verses 16-20 reiterate that the rich keep none of their treasure in the grave and are therefore not to be feared.

Solving the riddle (vss. 1-4). [1] The psalmist deals with a universal problem, so he calls for a wide hearing. **World is** a word which indicates passage of time, and probably refers to those who live where all is transient. **[2]** The contrasting states of **low, high, rich,** and **poor** will be the burden of the psalm. Each group has things it must learn. **Low** and **high** both translate the Hebrew expression "sons of man," but with a different word for man in each case. The repetition would be strange unless the author had in mind some distinction. The RSV infers that it is between common people and those of station, as in Psalm 62:9. However, the meanings "low" and "high" do not inhere in the Hebrew words, so there are disagreements about the correct translation of the text.

[3] This claim is not arrogant, but is a considered conclusion based upon observation of life **(meditation). Understanding** here no doubt means the practical conclusion of the mental process. Such a statement is intended to arrest the hearer's serious attention. **[4]** The poet will be open to the sagacity of the past. **Riddle,** or dark saying, probably means a perplexing problem—with which the psalm deals. Some see **music** as a device to assist insight (cf. 1 Sam. 10:5; 2 Kings 3:15), but it is better to think of a musical presentation of the author's answer (though no other OT texts refer to instruction being accomplished by **music**). Thus, this bit of understanding is made more impressive by its musical form. This may also imply continued use of the psalm in worship.

No self-ransom (vss. 5-9). [5] The problem is now introduced. **Why fear the trouble** generated by wealthy, powerful **persecutors**, when things are not really what they seem? The Hebrew phrase translated **iniquity of my persecutors** means literally "iniquity at my heels." Some suggest the author is confessing his own iniquity, but verse 6 supports the interpretation of the RSV. [6] Money is (apparently) power, and such force directed against oneself with malicious intent is terrifying. This opposition opens the question of God and **wealth**, which is to be illumined throughout the psalm. Perhaps here is also the implication that these **men** have obtained their **wealth** through wickedness (cf. Pss. 62:10; 73:12).

[7] Wealth cannot insure indefinite prolongation **of life**. In the OT a **ransom** could be paid for certain missteps (cf. Exod. 21:30), but even there some things were beyond **ransom** (Num. 35:31). How much more so could one not buy more time, showing the folly of one whose primary investment was in insecure material things. The RSV has made some slight emendations in the first line to obtain a translation compatible with the context (cf. note).

[8-9] God cannot be persuaded, no matter how immense **the ransom**, to relinquish control of man's physical nature. Why, then, fear the monied, who, finally, are impotent? If the footnote to verse 8 is retained, the reference is to mankind or to the rich in general. Verse 9 completes the thought of verses 7-8. **The Pit** is death.

The certainty of death (vss. 10-12). [10] Whereas verses 7-9 stressed the impossibility of ransoming oneself, verses 10-12 emphasize the universal sureness of death, and the consequent worthlessness of wealth as currency then.

Though the psalm extols wisdom, **the wise** also dies. But he has deeper resources than lost wealth (cf. vs. 15). **Stupid** indicates one who feels himself above criticism, and who hates to receive it (cf. Prov. 12:1).

[11] The rich presume that their land holdings offer unshakeable security but will discover that their only permanent home is **their graves**—which would not even be a possession! Attempts to make sense of "inward thoughts" (RSV note) suggest the idea that they inwardly supposed that their **lands** would continue forever. This is not impossible, but such an interpretation seems strained. The reading **graves** is based on a transposition of two Hebrew letters to agree with the ancient versions. [12] Neither wealth, lands, nor **pomp** keep man from dying like the beasts (cf. Eccles. 3:19). These words, here and in verse 20, form a refrain. For this reason they are seen as a key to the psalm. They have an air of curt finality, driving home what has been said elsewhere.

God ransoms from Sheol (vss. 13-15). [13] Verse 13 seems to sum up the preceding part of the psalm. The arrogance of **those** whom men might be prone to fear (vss. 5-6) is built on sand. On **foolish confidence**, see verse 10. The reading **the end of those** involves a change of one letter from the Hebrew (cf. note). The Hebrew word rendered **portion** literally means "mouth," and some understand this to mean "sayings," that is, they **are pleased** with their own talk. [14] This verse, in the RSV, is an unforgettable picture of **Death**, shepherding the once mighty into his realm (cf. Jer. 9:21). However, the verse is fraught with translation problems, and most commentators despair of obtaining a sure rendering. **Straight . . . descend** is a reading based on a few textual changes which are not unreasonable. However, some would keep the footnote reading, interpreting **in the morning** as an ultimate divine blessing on the upright which the evil do not share. This assumes that verse 15 speaks of trans-earthly reward and punishment. Yet even if verse 15 implies blessing after **death**, one might still prefer the RSV text over the footnote.

[15] This verse focuses the positive hope of the author.

He is confident that **God will ransom** him, in contrast to those of verses 7-8. Surely the author does not expect to live for ever (though escape from **Sheol**, i.e., long life, may be a symbol for good life). Nor does he expect any reversal of the financial fortunes of himself and the wealthy. It seems probable that he (perhaps echoing Gen. 5:24) makes a logical, but daring, thrust of faith into the unknown. Without knowing how, he affirms that God's care will go beyond present existence (cf. Pss. 16:10; 73:24), though we must not see here more of a concept of an afterlife than the text warrants. The NT takes up these fragmentary rays of light and brings them into the steady beam shined upon humanity by the Christ. One man is happy with his wealth while he lives, but then comes death. Another, somehow, will have prolonged happiness, death notwithstanding.

Do not fear the rich (vss. 16-20). [16-17] Verses 16-20 return to the reassurance that the wealthy should not be feared (vs. 5), for their situation is transient (vss. 10-11). These last five verses may be instruction to a wider audience. The tragedy is that wealthy persons must irretrievably lose the very thing that was most important to them. Theirs is, really, life without hope. On the translation "wealth" (RSV note), see Genesis 31:1; Isaiah 10:3; 66:12; Nahum 2:9.

[18-19] The rich man counts himself **happy** (literally "blesses his soul"), but if he assumes such a state will never end, that confidence will be destroyed by death. Nothing permanent is gained by his efforts. **Generation of his fathers** is a synonym for death. No **light** (well-being) penetrates that gloomy realm. The RSV makes some minor changes of person in these verses, which make for a smoother reading without affecting the sense.

[20] The refrain of verse 12 is repeated. **Abide** is a reading that follows the ancient versions. The Hebrew verb (differing from vs. 12) is "understanding." The difference may be significant, since in verses 14-15 the author has unveiled the great contrast in lives upon which true happiness depends. Thus, not only will the rich fail to **abide** (vs. 12), but they also fail to understand the nature of reality.

Psalm 50: A Summons from God

God calls his people into judgment, both as plaintiff and judge. As in the Ten Commandments, the psalm deals first with obligations to God (vss. 7-15), and then with man to man relations (vss. 6-21). With prophet-like mandates the psalm challenges worshipers to serve God. Most of it (vss. 5, 7-23) is in the form of a divine oracle, possibly proclaimed by a cultic prophet, or by a priest.

The psalm opens impressively, describing the awesome coming of the Lord to judge! (vss. 1-6). The divine word challenges the people to go beyond ritual and sacrifice in serving God with thanksgiving and humility, based on a correct grasp of the divine-human relationship (vss. 7-15). Then the social sins of the wicked are described, with eight bursts. God's previous silence has come to an end (vss. 16-21). The psalm closes with a call to repentance, and a promise of blessing (vss. 22-23).

'Our God comes' (vss. 1-6). **[1]** This psalm explodes upon the reader with a magnificent summons. Three divine appellations open it, and two others are used in verses 14 and 22 (Heb. *'eloah*). Verses 1-6 depict God's mighty coming in language reminiscent of Sinai. The **summons** to the earth probably includes only Israel, since they are those whom the poem addresses, unless the nations are called as witnesses. **[2]** The reference to **Zion** and the sacrificial language of later verses imply that the psalm relates to worship in Jerusalem. **Zion** derives her **beauty** from God's choice of her and/or his presence there (cf. Lam. 2:15; Ps. 48:2). Not nature, but supernature, draws this beautiful praise from the author. Other peoples likewise extolled their central city (cf. Ezek. 27:3). **Shines forth** no doubt refers to the declaration of God's will.

[3] With howling wind, furious storm, and flashing lightning (fire? cf. Ps. 97:3-4) **God comes** (cf. Exod. 19:16-17; Job 38:1; Ps. 18:8). **He does not keep silence,** though he once did (vs. 21a), and Israel misinterpreted. A variant reading, "Come, and let him **not keep silence,**" would indicate that Israel calls for his word, though it would be stern and judging. **[4]** That voice which is heard from sunrise to sunset rings now **to the heavens,** calling the covenant people into judgment. This judgment will occupy the remainder of the psalm. There will be no mistaking the evidence, for heaven and earth, witness to all, and in all time, are summoned, and the judge is the perfectly righteous one (vs. 6). It was not unusual in the ancient Near East for natural forces and entities to be called as witness to confront people with their broken promises.

[5] Verse 5 is the climax of this section — the voice of Yahweh for which the reader has been prepared. This verse prepares the way for later discussion of the sacrifices God does and does not want. It may be a serious reference to covenant origins (cf. Exod. 24:5-8), or an ironic one to those who sacrifice, supposing what they do is enough when it is not. **Faithful ones** may be the pious who also stand in judgment against the unrighteous. Or if it refers to Israel in general, it might better be translated, in light of subsequent verses, as "my covenant people," since they were not pictured as faithful. [6] God's role as **judge** is reaffirmed, declared by **the heavens** (cf. vs. 4), and thus impossible to avoid.

The arraignment (vss. 7-15). [7] The rest of the psalm is God's arraignment against the nation. The sacrificial cultus is generously patronized (vss. 8-13), but it is not enough. On **hear,** see Deuteronomy 6:4-5. [8-9] Their wrong was not the neglect of ritual. That may have been their first concern when they considered their relation to God. But their view was superficial. God will no longer **accept** what they offer. The question "Why was properly observed ritual rejected?" whets the reader's curiosity for the further message of the psalm.

[10] Man can supply no divine need by returning to God what is God's own. No animal is entirely a man's, just because it is in his flock or herd. That would ignore the reality of ownership and be a man-centered view. Therefore God refuses sacrfice here, because the wrong assumption of man's relation to God lies behind it. God supplies man's need, as man, in humility, must acknowledge. The last line is awkward in the original, and some modify it to

obtain the meaning "thousands of beasts."

[11] The thought of verse 10 is extended. **Air,** as in the ancient versions, is more logical here than "mountains" (RSV note). The Hebrew phrase rendered **all that moves** is unclear, and various translations have been suggested.

[12-13] Since Israel's view of God certainly did not conceive of him as devouring sacrifice, it is probable that this is an ironical statement. God creates needs in his creatures, and then creates sustenance for those needs. In denying this, Israel was like those who actually thought they fed the gods. He is not the kind of deity the primitives imagined, nor is he the sort those whom he is judging imagine. [14] Having disposed of the false view, the divine word unveils the Lord's desire, climaxing the discussion to this point. Three terse statements deal with **thanksgiving,** vow paying, and prayer, which involve humility, acknowledgment of creaturely status, and trust.

If actual animal **sacrifice** were meant, then a new spirit behind ritual must emerge. But compare the footnote and verse 23, which center on a frame of mind and its expression in life. Were **vows** sacrifices, voluntarily offered, which demonstrated the spirit Yahweh wanted? Or was the use metaphorical for a heartfelt discharging of covenant responsibilities (cf. Pss. 22:25-26; 56:12)? [15] Prayer would show their recognition that they could not **deliver** themselves from **trouble.** Such confidence in God would find its response, and they would subsequently **glorify** him. Though the ritual of verses 8-13 failed in its purpose, the attitude of these verses would rectify the failure.

Judgment against the wicked (vss. 16-23). [16] Now attention turns to social justice. Serious attention to covenant obligations should lead to social concern, not to wicked behavior.. Why **recite** laws they did not intend to keep? After a reference to religious duties appropriately observed, a series of explanatory charges follows (vss. 17-20). Therefore God will judge, breaking his silence (vss. 21-22). (Since the first line breaks the meter of the psalm, some consider it an editorial gloss.) [17] A series of eight charges is brought in verses 17-20. Man refuses disci-

pline, showing a proud spirit totally contrary to covenant demands (cf. Jer. 17:23). The **words** of God may be recited, but they are thrown back useless. The succeeding verses may define **words,** and if so, they are essentially the seventh through the ninth of the Ten Commandments.

[18] Though God condemns thievery (eighth commandment) and adultery (seventh commandment), the wicked man condones them, or even participates. The Hebrew expression translated **keep company** means literally "with your portion." [19] Sins of the **tongue** violate the ninth commandment. **Give free reign** freely translates the verb which means "send." **Frames** is from a verb which means "bind together," either indicating deliberate scheming, or that the wicked harnesses deceit for his intents.

[20] Their monstrousness is seen in the betrayal even of brothers. **Sit** may imply deliberate scheming, or indicate a formal accusation, or suggest continuous opposition. Imagine people such as those described in verses 17-20 pretending the piety of verse 16.

[21] They have misinterpreted God's longsuffering for acquiescence and made a god in their own image. Thus, each half of this psalm exposes a false view of God. Because of such transgressions, God shatters the silence (vs. 3) and breaks through to judge. **But now** is added in the RSV for clarity. The Hebrew term rendered **lay the charge** means literally "set in order." [22] This is how **God** really is. Those who persist in their delusions about him will be rent—as if torn and ravaged by a wild beast. The doom will be inevitable and inescapable. [23] A final word calls for the proper spirit. Just as in verse 14, **thanksgiving** may have reference to an attitude or to thank offerings. Some consider the first line a summing up of verses 1-15 and the last two a summing up of verses 16-22. The second line literally means "sets a way," and invites an interpretive translation (as in the RSV) to make good sense.

The psalm indicates clearly that blessing demands responsibility. It warns those who, ignorant of the Governor of the universe, would build their lives around their own limited concepts and desires.

Psalm 51: 'Cleanse Me from My Sin'

This is the zenith of the penitential psalms (6, 32, 38, 102, 130, 143). There may be no more impassioned or beautiful prayer for forgiveness and renewal in the Bible than here. The poet's wrongdoing has overwhelmed him. His remorse and his plea are intense. There are multiplied uses of the imperative, as well as tremendous stress on the personal relation to God which he wished fully restored. The honesty of the psalm is at times painful.

The superscription, and popular piety, say David was the author (cf. 2 Sam. 11–12). The wording seems amazingly appropriate to this view. But verses 18-19 seem to conflict with it (see discussion there). Whoever prepared the psalm may have had David in mind and have written what David might have said, to be used by others caught in like circumstances. Some feel the psalm was written for or by a king.

An opening cry for mercy (vss. 1-2) is followed by the poet's expression of the enormity of his sin (vss. 3-5). The plea continues in verses 6-12, with increasing emphasis on the inner change the author knows he needs. In verses 13-17 the writer, anticipating deliverance, vows to praise God and tell others of his grace. Verses 18-19 ask God's blessing on the rebuilding of the wall of Jerusalem, so he can be praised appropriately by offering animal sacrifices.

Confession of sin (vss. 1-5). [1] The intense language here indicates that the psalm, to be appreciated, must be read with the emotions as well as the intellect. A man dominated by the sense of his wrongdoing comes to **God** as a beggar, asking that to which he can claim no intrinsic right. He rests his case squarely on God's nature. Even if intellectually convinced that one request would elicit God's forgiveness, he is so overwhelmed by his wrong that he pleads repeatedly. The Hebrew term translated **have mercy** means literally "be gracious." The second Hebrew word rendered **mercy** literally means "womb," implying a parent's tender care for a child. **Blot out** (also vs. 9) could describe the cancellation of a debt, wiping away of defilement, or removing a record from a book.

[2] The strength of the poet's feeling is indicated by **thoroughly**. In the OT **cleanse** (cf. also vss. 7, 10) may be used in a physical, ceremonial, or moral sense. No doubt the last two ideas predominate here. **Iniquity** can convey the basic ideas of crookedness (Jer. 11:10), guilt (Exod. 34:7), or punishment (Gen. 4:13). Here the poet seems more concerned with his sinful character than merely with wrong acts. **Sin** (cf. also vss. 3, 4, 5, 9, 13) indicates missing the mark.

[3] Having acknowledged and entreated God's grace in verses 1-2, he now confesses in verses 3-5 his wrong with greater passion. His conscience unceasingly accuses him, and we sense his agony.

[4] Sin is sin because God is God, and all wrongdoing is most importantly against him. The poet is not denying that other people have been hurt by his misdeeds, but is poetically expressing the matter in its ultimate dimensions. If there were no moral governor of the universe, by what standard would one determine that wrong had been done to others? **Sentence** and **judgment** may be God's disapproval expressed in his total covenant with Israel, or else in the life experiences of the poet himself. The "criminal" recognizes that his fate is due him. God has acted appropriately. Part of this verse is quoted from the LXX in Romans 3:4, where Paul stresses the faithfulness of God ("Let God be true"). [5] With bold poetic exaggeration, the poet describes the depth of his corruption by speaking as if the fatal flaw had been his from conception. He is not trying to excuse himself by advancing some concept of universal, hereditary depravity. Rather he is engaging in further self-abnegation. He takes full responsibility. It is inadmissable to base some doctrine of the nature of man on this touching bit of poetry. See Isaiah 6:5.

Plea for purging (vss. 6-12). [6] The first line of verse 6 states a promise, to which the author returns at intervals in later verses. **Truth** is fidelity to God. The spirit within man must be converted. The author exposes his lack of insight (**wisdom**) and power (vss. 10-11) to God's operation. **Secret heart** (literally "what is closed up") parallels the first line of the verse, though other translations have been suggested. The Hebrew imperfect verb form in verses 6b-8 can be translated either as future or imperative. The RSV sees fit, in a psalm full of imperatives, to pursue the same pattern here. However, the actual Hebrew imperative does not resume until verse 9. Are these verses the author's faith, or his plea?

[7] The Hebrew verb rendered **purge** is from the same root as that rendered "sin" in verses 2-3, but this form means to "de-sin." **Hyssop** refers to small branches used to gather and sprinkle water or blood (cf. the Passover, Exod. 12:22; on cleansing, see Lev. 14:51). The poet likely speaks metaphorically. On **snow,** see Isaiah 1:18. [8] He prays to know again the **joy** that his wrongdoing had taken from him. Transgression severs one from God, the source of real **joy** (cf. vs. 12). The psalmist may speak of his inner perspective or of joy in religious observance. **Bones** seem to symbolize the entire person (cf. Pss. 6:2; 35:10). Some see here physical illness, though the rest of the psalm offers no corroboration. **Broken** (also vs. 17) may be the depression resulting from his wrong or some specific adversity from God (cf. vs. 4).

The RSV footnote "make hear" (with joy) could anticipate a word of forgiveness or the happy participation in life and worship. The text of the RSV is due to an emendation based on the Syriac. [9] The text returns to the imperative. **Hide** usually refers to God's withdrawal from the sinner (cf. vss. 10-11), so the present usage is unusual.

[10] Verses 10-12 stress inward change (note the **spirit** in each verse). The approach requests a new outlook and power so the author will no longer vascillate, but be steadfast. This idea, though found in the prophets (Jer. 32:39; Ezek. 36:26), is rare in the psalms. **Create** (used in Gen. 1) and **new** indicate the strength of his need and his trust in God.

[11] He wants purity (vs. 10), joy (vs. 12), and the continued blessings of God's **presence.** Not to be **cast** off presupposes forgiveness and strength. There was no concept in the OT of the third person of the Godhead, which

to the Jew would seem to compromise monotheism. References to the **spirit** of God are generally to his power—here shown in its ability to create holiness ("God, make me holy"; cf. Ps. 143:10; Isa. 63:10). **[12]** Salvation would include a new outlook. **A willing spirit** is probably a free and generous disposition to serve Yahweh, which he feels he cannot create by his own efforts. This would be the antidote to becoming involved again in the wrongs of which he here repents.

Promises and petitions (vss. 13-17). **[13]** With this vow the psalm takes a new turn. Verses 13-17 alternate vow and continued petition. Such a great deliverance would demand proclamation, rooting in the author's personal experience of God. **Return** (vs. 13) and "restore" (vs. 12) are the same verb, strengthening this point. The RSV adds **then** for clarity. **[14]** He cannot speak to others until his problem is resolved. The Hebrew word translated **bloodguiltiness** literally means "bloods." Some take it to mean "death" (RSV note; cf. Ps. 30:9)—perhaps an illness (cf. vs. 8) or a threat from opponents. But there is no other reference in the psalm to the fear of death. The idea of **deliverance** from moral stain comports well with the ideas of the rest of the psalm. **Deliverance** is the word elsewhere translated "righteousness." God's righteousness is the basis of the sinner's deliverance.

[15] This is the last individual plea in the psalm. The verb here could also be translated as a future, as with verses 6b-8. He cannot even **praise** fully except by God's help. **[16]** Such praise (vs. 14) would be worth more than all ritual, because of the spirit prompting it (cf. vs. 17). No atoning sacrifices were indicated in the OT for sins like adultery and murder. If this was the author's wrong, then his need was penitence. Such passages appear often in the prophets (cf. Amos 5:21-24; Isa. 1:10-17; Mic. 6:6-8), condemning sacrificial activity unaccompanied by inward dedication to God. The grossest hypocrite could go through the ritual. But it would be unacceptable without a change of heart. Presumably God would accept the **sacrifice** offered by the person described in verse 17. **[17]** The man whose bones were broken sees a **broken spirit** as **the sacrifice acceptable.** All arrogance has been wrung from the writer, who in the first verse threw himself on God's mercy. Only the **broken heart** is big enough for God to dwell in. Thus, **sacrifice** is driven inward to the altar of man's **heart. Sacrifice acceptable to God** is the RSV's interpretation of a Hebrew expression which means literally "sacrifices of God." The RSV footnote accepts a slightly different form of the Hebrew word for sacrifice.

Regarding Zion (vss. 18-19). **[18]** We are now contemplating **Jerusalem** and the cultic activities there. There is an intense concern for national renewal. How does this relate to what has gone before? Does the poet parallel the nation's situation with his own? Or does his joy in deliverance now embrace the entire people? The temple was not built until after David's death, nor were the walls rebuilt until the fifth century B.C., countering the popular conception of Davidic authorship of the psalm. If verses 18-19 are part of the original, then the entire psalm was written after 586 B.C. and before **the walls** were rebuilt (Neh. 12:43). However, many scholars believe verses 1-17 are earlier, and that verses 18-19 were a later interpolation, added to counter the seeming anti-cultic sacrificial spirit of verses 15-16, and to make the psalm more appropriate for public worship. This could be the case, but if the interpretation given above for verse 16 is correct, why did the persons adding these verses misunderstand it? Perhaps they were apprehensive about how the passage would be taken in public worship, though not convinced it was really antisacrificial.

[19] It would seem that God cannot be praised aright until the city is rebuilt, just as in verses 1-17 he cannot be praised aright until a life is rebuilt. The psalm joins similar concerns. **Right sacrifices** (literally "sacrifices of righteousness") may be those commanded by God, or perhaps those offered in the right spirit (cf. vs. 17). It is not possible to know the exact distinction between **burnt offerings** and **whole burnt offerings.** The second term is rare.

Psalm 52: The Folly of Wickedness

The people, troubled by an avaricious man who has laid aside human concerns, describe (or pray for) God's response to the situation. The description does not seem to fit Doeg (cf. the superscription with 1 Sam. 22:9-10). Verses 1-4 describe the boastful "mighty man," implying that the future will demonstrate the futility of this course. In verse 5-7 this expectation is fulfilled, to the delight of the righteous. In verse 8 the author states his own attitude, which forms a sharp contrast to that of the mighty man. He knows the true source of security. Therefore he thanks God and vows to proclaim his name before the godly (vs. 9).

'Why do you boast?' (vss. 1-4). [1] In the second line the RSV reverses two words, and emends each slightly, in order to obtain its reading. However, the unchanged Hebrew could be read "God's kindness is (for) all the day," or even "God is merciful," putting all the day with verse 2. The latter would offer a counterpoint to the boaster. [2] This evil is carefully premeditated and effectively pursued. **Destruction** and **treachery** are the results. As a sharpened **razor** would be the most effective, so their crafty words were calculated for maximum response (cf. Pss. 55:21; 57:4; and 64:3).

[3] The man so acts because his heart is committed to **evil.** His unscrupulous methods lead the psalmist to define his outlook as repudiation of **good** for **evil. Lying** might imply false or slanderous charges. The Hebrew word rendered **truth** here is the word often translated righteousness. [4] **Devour** depicts greed. Evil would swallow, while love would give. **Deceitful** is used elsewhere of false weights and balances (Mic. 6:11; Amos 8:5) and of ill-gotten gain (Jer. 5:27). The evil man was probably trying to disguise his intents from the unsuspecting.

God and the righteous respond (vss. 5-9). [5] The words **but god** mark a decisive about-face in this psalm. The boaster must face the judgment described in verses 5-7. This is why his boasting is useless (vs. 1). The verbs indicate the forceful and decisive nature of God's action. It will be **for ever**, with no hope of restoration. **Tent** and **land,** symbols of security, will not be adequate to alleviate his wrath. Contrast the security of verse 8. **[6]** Though the OT condemns malicious joy (Prov. 24:17; cf. Job 31:29), we can understand the exultation caused by the reversal of a vexing situation. These words indicate delight in God's moral governance of the world, rather than personal vindictiveness. Indeed, such a psalm as this may have been a call to the wicked to repent, as he sees his insecurity.

[7] Here is the insightful cry of the delivered man. The Hebrew word translated **man** has the same consonants as "mighty man" in verse 1, which is perhaps a deliberate device to heighten the contrast in the psalm. The RSV emends slightly in harmony with some ancient versions. If the reading of the Hebrew text (RSV note) were adopted, the "destruction" would be that which the evil **man** brought on others. But this was a means to *obtain* **riches,** not his **refuge** itself. **[8]** The author's faith and confidence contrast remarkably with verses 1-4. God's **steadfast love** grounds his life (cf. the note to vs. 1, where the same Hebrew word is rendered "kindness") and forms the conceptual center of the psalm. An **olive tree** was valuable, and the greenness implies particular prosperity. **House of God** may poetically describe the best place one could be, or it may imply the use of this psalm in temple worship. Whether or not olive trees actually grew in the temple cannot be definitely ascertained.

[9] The poet closes with thanks and a vow. **For ever** means as long as he should live, perhaps indicating he expects God's justice to function always (contrast vs. 5). The vow of proclamation apparently implies worship. The Hebrew term rendered **the godly** means literally "your godly," showing the covenant relation. "Wait for" (RSV note), if read, would imply waiting on God to accomplish the judgment described in verses 5-7. If this reading were correct, the entire psalm would be anticipatory, rather than accomplished.

(Psalm 53 is discussed in connection with Psalm 14.)

Psalm 54: Prayer for Deliverance

Though we cannot know definitely, this may be a writer falsely accused, who sought vindication at the sanctuary (cf. 1 Kings 8:31-32). He opens with an appeal for salvation and vindication (vss. 1-2). His problem was occasioned by insolent and ruthless men, who sought his life (vs. 3). Yet God would help and uphold his people and punish the wicked (vss. 4-5). Therefore the author gratefully responds to this deliverance (vss. 6-7).

[1-2] The author, confident of his rightness, addresses **God**. God's **name** symbolizes his total being. References to the **name** here and in verse 6 bracket the psalm, and show its movement from the appeal to thanksgiving. The Hebrew word translated **vindicate** means literally "judge," here with the sense of finding in one's favor, perhaps implying a court procedure. Verse 2 underscores the fervency of the request. [3] Here is the cause of the lament. "Strangers" (RSV note) is usually used of non-Israelites (except Isa. 1:4). It could be read, but the implication that sinners are within Israel, and the parallelism of the verse, argue for **insolent**, which is found in some ancient versions, and represents a change of only one letter in the Hebrew term. These men who ignore **God** and glorify self are terrible foes. (This verse is substantially repeated in Psalm 86:14.) [4] **Behold**, in contrast to verse 3, introduces the author's trust. The translation **upholder** is based on several ancient versions. The RSV note, if read, would see **God** as behind all who uphold, as the source of their power. Secure in such assistance, the writer is sure his trauma will be resolved. [5] The center of the psalm is God's **faithfulness**, referring to his steadfastness, and thus to his very nature. Therefore, right must be vindicated and wrong punished. **Enemies** (literally "watchers") implies those who watch with insidious intent.

[6] Grace begets response from an overflowing heart. **Freewill** offerings are those made voluntarily (cf. Exod. 35:29; 36:3), usually in connection with the great festivals (2 Chron. 35:8; Deut. 16:10; Ezra 3:5). Note that this verse uses the divine name Yahweh (**Lord**) in contrast to the rest

of the psalm. [7] Here is the consequence of the affirmations of verses 4-5. This may refer to deliverance from the **trouble** previously outlined in the psalm, or to past deliverances giving hope in the present instance, or to expected deliverances spoken of as if already accomplished. In any reading, the note of surety sounds clearly.

The RSV adds **in triumph**. The Hebrew says literally "my enemies my eye sees." If these words were omitted, the verse would sound less harsh. Yet this is probably not personal vindication, but an affirmation of how things must work in a world ruled by a God of faithfulness.

Psalm 55: A Plea for Deliverance

This psalm abounds in masterful imagery. The author and date are unknown. Whoever the author was, he was terribly affected by the depredations of his enemies. It may reflect his state of mind that the psalm moves jerkily, though consistently, through its course.

Verses 1-8, after the call upon God to hear (vss. 1-2), describe the problem, particularly in terms of the author's reaction to it. So overpowering is the experience that he yearns to escape (vss. 6-8). Verses 9-11 call for God to destroy the plans of the wicked and describe the crimes they have wrought in the city. Then we are told that a leader of the wicked was once the writer's close friend, and a pious man (vss. 12-14) before the prayer for judgment is resumed (vss. 15, 16-19). After a reprise describing the former companion (vss. 20-21), the psalm concludes with encouragement, punctuated by the author's statement of commitment (vss. 22-23).

The psalmist's plight (vss. 1-8). **[1-2]** A repeated entreaty begs God's attention and response. In verse 2 the author begins to describe his problem, particularly in terms of his emotional reaction. **Overcome** indicates restlessness. **Trouble** emphasizes murmuring or complaint (another translation could be "I am restless with my complaint"). **Distraught** elsewhere describes the confusion of a demoralized army. The RSV combines the last verb of verse 2 with verse 3, so that the first line of verse 3 will have a complete thought.

[3] **The noise** (literally "voice") **of the enemy** could be slander, insults, threats, false charges, or the like. **Oppression** (only here in the OT) may imply pressure of some sort. The trouble will continue because of the **enmity** cherished **against** the author. This verse refers to the enemies both in the singular and the plural. Perhaps the poet was troubled by a particular individual from the larger group of the wicked (cf. vss. 12-15, 20-21).

[4] Nightmare-like experiences torment the author (vss. 4-5). **Anguish** translates a Hebrew verb with the basic meaning of whirling or writhing about. The Hebrew word rendered **terrors** is cognate to the Hebrew word for **death**, doubly stressing the idea. There could be no greater consternation than fear **of death** (even if this is a figure).

[5] Words could hardly describe a more distraught condition than this threefold reference to **fear, trembling**, and overwhelming **horror**. He was inundated by the experience—out of control beneath it. We are carried to the very limits of emotional panic.

[6-7] Despite his wish to flee, the author must stay and responsibly face his agony. He counters the nightmare experience with prayer, and in so doing offers guidance to any believer faced with the "flee or pray" dilemma. Yet prayer may involve continued suffering and great trust, until resolution comes. **Lodge** (vs. 7) changes the bird metaphor to that of a traveler. [8] The figure changes again. Now a storm must be faced, rather than avoided. This verse may be a poetic description of the violence and strife of verse 9.

The petition (vss. 9-11). [9] The prayer of verses 1-2 now resumes, with the specific request—**destroy** them. The poet's concern widens to **the city** (Jerusalem?). In it he sees **violence, strife** (vs. 9), mischief, trouble (vs. 10), ruin, oppression, and fraud (vs. 11). Some see these seven personified as grim foes going about the various locales. Thus, all activity would fall under their devastating influence. It is a frightening picture. It is thus essential that God intervene!

A variant translation of line one could be "destroy and confuse their tongues," that is, "render communication impossible." The reference may root in the divine action at Babel (Gen. 11:2-5). May God thwart human wickedness as effectively here as he did there!

[10] Look on the walls—the dread foes are there! **Day and night they** patrol. Perhaps this figure is drawn from the observed presence of wicked men at all these places in the city, as if it were said of an individual, "There goes trouble." The Hebrew word rendered **mischief** here is the same word translated "trouble" in verse 3. Here it indicates grievousness. [11] **Oppression** and **fraud** would operate most successfully in the **market place**. The seven spectres shown in these verses constitute one of the most dramatic pictures imaginable of a desperate situation.

The enemy's identity (vss. 12-15). [12-13] With verse 12 we are prepared for a surprise. The situation is one from which he cannot **hide**—thus, the wish of verses 6-8 cannot be fulfilled. In verse 13 the exposure comes—the problem is with an erstwhile **friend.** The author uses a threefold description to show how intimate the two had been. The Hebrew term translated **my equal** means literally "according to my valuation," that is, valued as I am. Perhaps the two shared a like rank in public life. **Familiar friend** is from the passive form of the Hebrew verb "to know," which the OT uses of the very closest of relationships. [14] The marvelous past experiences of the poet and his friend make the present even more bitter. They had a closeness intensified by their mutual religious consecration. It must have been bewildering that so religious a person could have become a betrayer. One does not wonder that Christians later came to apply these words to Judas.

[15] This section ends with a powerful curse upon the former comrade and others, perhaps uttered to counter one issued against the psalmist. (Cf. the fate of Korah, Num. 16:33.) The Hebrew word rendered **death** here is difficult. It occurs only here in the OT, but is similar to the word for "desolations" (cf. note). The RSV divides the Hebrew word to obtain the textual reading. The second footnote in

the verse is not an impossible reading. The RSV text involves a variant meaning of a term, and some transpositions of letters in certain words. Though not supported by any of the ancient versions, it does give a better reading, without going beyond principles of emendation often used to clarify OT passages.

The Lord will save (vss. 16-19). [16] The prayer now moves to a request for salvation (vss. 16-18). The psalmist has great faith that the horror will be ameliorated. Trust, not escapism, wins the day. [17-18] **Evening, morning,** and **noon** may have set times for petition, or may show the intense fervency of the poet. The Hebrew word translated **safety** (vs. 18) literally means "peace" (*shalom*). **Against me** could also be rendered "with me." If so, we are not told whom these allies might be. Some suggest, with no support from within the psalm, angelic hosts.

[19] This verse is a fit conclusion to the section, but unfortunately it is very difficult to translate, as witnessed by the various attempts in ancient and modern versions. There are several problems, the most significant of which is that indicated by the footnote, which gives the literal Hebrew reading. Various suggestions have been made, usually either indicating the impenitence of the wicked, or the judgment they will face. The RSV preserves the tenor of the passage, on any interpretation, and has the advantage of agreeing with "violated his covenant" of the next verse.

The deceitful friend (vss. 20-21). [20] The theme of the false friend (the RSV adds **my companion** for clarity) is reintroduced. Others beside the psalmist have suffered—**friends,** too. The Hebrew word translated **friends** comes from the same root as that rendered "peace," that is, those at peace with one. The context would be considerably illumined if we knew the nature of the ruptured covenant, but we do not. The Hebrew word translated **violated** literally means "profaned." [21] Finally, another painful facet of the betrayal of friendship is noted. He who was guilty practiced hypocritical and deceitful flattery, described here with marvelous imagery. Perhaps the sting of the author's pain was because he had been so long deceived before learning the truth. Beneath the facade of peace was the raging of **war** (cf. the peace/war antithesis here with the word for friends in vs. 20).

The resolution (vss. 22-23). [22] The psalm closes with words of encouragement and exhortation. The poet may be encouraging others, or this may be a word from an officiant in worship. This is the way the problem must be resolved, which is what the author is doing. The truly stable life is one that can follow this advice, even in times of extreme distress. **Burden,** as the note observes, refers to one's lot or fortune. Whatever life brings, trust it to God. The person who does, though perhaps suffering for a time, cannot ultimately **be moved**—any more than God himself can be moved.

[23] **God** can be trusted, because he will vindicate his nature. **Cast down** returns to the petition of verse 15. The poet, who felt himself threatened by death (vs. 4), recognizes that death is the lot of the wicked. **The lowest pit** is probably a figure for dire judgment. Long or short life is used in the psalms as a figure of blessing and punishment, the good life and the bad, God's blessing and disfavor. It is sad that this must be the author's final word regarding his once intimate friend. But **God** must be trusted at all costs. Nothing should destroy that.

Psalm 56: 'Put My Tears in Thy Bottle'

These words alternate between descriptions of suffering because of foes and expressions of trust, with the latter predominating. We do not know if the author has been delivered, or yet expects to be. The latter seems more likely.

Verses 1-4 describe the trampling and fighting of his enemies (vss. 1-2), countered by the author's trust in God (vss. 3-4). Verses 5-7 further describe enemy activity, with a call for God to recompense them. The author finds great comfort in knowing that God is aware of his agony (vs. 8), and therefore reaffirms his faith with renewed vigor (vss. 9-11). Verses 12-13 speak of his response (vows, thanks) when God delivers him, and celebrate his happy state under divine blessing. The psalm's inclination to repetition is most obvious in the refrain of verses 4, 10-11.

The enemy's oppression (vss. 1-4). [1-2] The author repetitively describes the oppression **enemies** have brought him. He has been trampled and fought against (the Hebrew word rendered **foemen** in vs. 1 is from the same root as that translated **fight** in vs. 2). The opposition is continued—**all day**. **Proudly** is a neutral word drawing its meaning from its context. Though sometimes it applies to God (Most High, Mic. 6:8; Ps. 92:8), there is no doubt that the negative sense is correct here.

[3] But the defeat is only apparent. The author has a greater resource than his foes, so fear is overridden by **trust**. Any outer problem is countered by this inner reaction. The first line means literally "(in the) day (when) I fear." (Cf. the day he calls upon God, in vs. 9.) **[4]** These words are found in a fuller form in verses 10-11 (some think vs. 4 was originally identical to vs. 10 but has become abbreviated and corrupted in transmission). See also Psalms 118:6 and the quotation in Hebrews 13:6. Is the **word** of **God** an oracle, or a promise of salvation, or the law? (Cf. Pss. 1:2; 19:7-14; 119.) How can **flesh** harm that which **God** protects? One who has inner security can endure the most adverse external circumstances.

'Recompense them' (vss. 5-7). [5-6] The author again notes the continued and unrelenting opposition of the enemies (cf. vs. 2). Perhaps like hunters they act in concert, lurking (or hiding) and watching, with **evil** intent, for their chance to kill. The death threat could be literal, or it could be a figurative description of other dangers. **[7]** As the helpless prey, the author pleads for justice, so that the hunters may become the hunted. The reading **recompense** is based on a change of one letter in the Hebrew verb, since "deliver" (note) seems contrary to the thought of the passage. This is a cry for God's moral governance of life to be wrought, not for personal vengeance. A man must reap what he sows. **Peoples** is probably a general term for the enemies.

God's care for the sufferer (vss. 8-11). [8] The writer

takes great comfort that God knows his sufferings. The exact import of **tossings** is unclear, but it implies his agita- tions (some think in penitence). The terms rendered **kept count** and **book** are from the same Hebrew root. The **bottle** would have been one made of skin. (On God's book, cf. Ps. 40:7; Dan. 7:10; Mal. 3:16.)

[9-11] The two possible translations of verse 9 (cf. note) indicate either a general observation or a specific hope because of God's care. Verses 10-11 are virtually the same as verse 4. The repetition of the refrain draws increased meaning from verses 5-9.

Deliverance (vss. 12-13). [12] **Vows** and **thank offerings** are consequent upon deliverance (cf. Pss. 22:26; 50:14, 23). The first line means literally "unto me, O God, your vows," so that the RSV is a free translation. **Thank offerings** may be sacrifices (Lev. 7:12) or songs of gratitude (Ps. 26:7). [13] The **death-life** polarity is again indicated, as in verse 6. **Light** is to live as God intended, illumined by his presence and blessings. The author's great and final idea is to **walk before God.** How can he go wrong? His faith speaks to us across the centuries. (Cf. Ps. 116:8.)

Psalm 57: In the Midst of Lions

This psalm is similar to Psalm 56, as the opening "Be merciful" (vs. 1), the repeated refrain (vss. 5,11), and the reference to trampling (vs. 3) show. Verses 7-11 are virtu- ally identical to Psalm 108:1-5, leading some to think the psalm may have been compiled from various previously existing elements. But this thesis lacks adequate support. Other repetitions (besides the refrain) occur within verses (1, 3, 7-9) and between verses (3, 10). The form of the psalm is lamentation (vss. 1-6) and thanks (vss. 7-11). A strong note of trust resounds throughout.

Verses 1-3 contain the cry for mercy, colored by trust in God. Verses 4 and 6 describe peril, with an intervening refrain of praise (vs. 5). Verses 7-10 contain an exuberant paean of praise and thanks for God's steadfast love and faithfulness. The refrain concludes the whole (vs. 11).

Plea for mercy (vss. 1-3). [1] The opening plea for divine mercy comes from one who knows that **God** is a **refuge**. The first **take refuge** refers to complete action, and the second to incomplete, implying both past and continuing experience. On **shadow of the wings**, see the discussion at Psalm 17:8. **God** is a place of safety away from the ravages to which the author would otherwise be exposed—a most reassuring thought.

[2] **His purpose** is not in the Hebrew. The verb is without an object. Various other meanings have been suggested for the clause. The Greek and Latin versions suggest "who deals bountifully with me," perhaps meaning "to perform all that needs to be performed for me." Whatever the translation, the verse expresses assurance that **God** will do the right and best thing. In that the poet can rest secure. His case is being well handled. [3] This is the first reference to the author's foes. Salvation is due to twin messengers—**steadfast love and faithfulness**. These terms refer to God's covenant loyalty and absolute dependability. On trampling, see Psalm 56:1.

Enemy plots (vss. 4-6). [4] The mixed metaphor of **lions** and the military show how precarious his situation was. Deliverance would seem hopeless, were it not for God. The translation **greedily devour** is derived by a change of one letter in the Hebrew of the footnote reading. However, many scholars believe the text can be a legitimate translation of the original term, without the necessity of emendation. [5] The refrain pictures the God who will deliver. He is a universal sovereign, with irresistible power. God's **glory** may be his acts of deliverance, convincing men that he is who he is. Praise such as this challenges the mind of man even beyond its limits in grasping the reality of God and his goodness.

[6] The first three lines of this verse give the psalm's final description of the author's situation. The alternation between faith and complaint in verses 3-6 seems to say—there is distress but also relief. As verses 2-3 answer the problem of verse 1, and verse 5 answers verse 4, so verses 7-11 answer verse 6. Though **bowed down** could indicate the falling of one whose feet were caught in a net, we

prefer to believe it is a metaphor for the inner depression of one who knows men are out to snare him. In the last line a marvelous change occurs. God has acted, and the wicked are caught in their own trap (cf. Esth. 7:10).

Thanks for deliverance (vss. 7-11). **[7]** Verses 7-11 are essentially identical to Psalm 108:1-5. The literary history of this relationship is not known, but it is not surprising that there would be such repetitions in the praise of the people. On a lesser scale there is much of it in the Psalter. Note the forcefulness of the repetitiousness in verses 7-10. We have here a joyous and surging song of praise, with the reason for verses 7-9 being given in verse 10. Such joy is appropriate to one fully aware of God's protection in dire peril. **My heart is steadfast** could depict the poet's trust, or perhaps his singleminded resolution to praise God for his help. He is not lost to uncertainty because of the difficulties that he faces.

[8] He is so eager to praise that he rouses before **dawn** and calls the musicians to join in his joyful exercise—a marvelous display of the exuberance of a life lost in a sense of God's blessing, and bursting to express it. Perhaps the preceding night was filled with struggle that finally broke through into trust. The Hebrew word rendered **soul** literally means "my glory" (as in Pss. 7:5; 16:9; 30:12). **[9-10]** The author is so lost in God's glory that he would have it proclaimed to every human, for he is a God of all the earth (vss. 5, 11). The message is that God's **steadfast love** and **faithfulness** (cf. vs. 3) are as high as **the heavens.** These are the foundations of Israel, and of the author's life. They are as broad and as high as man can conceive. (Cf. Eph. 3:18-19; Ps. 36:5; and the NT citation in Rom. 15:9.) **[11]** The refrain of verse 5 is repeated, with minor changes.

Psalm 58: *God Against His Enemies*

The center of this psalm is the fact that Yahweh is judge, as triumphantly stated in verse 11. He is called to act against the "gods" (cf. the discussion at vs. 1). The psalm uses some of the more remarkable and daring imagery within the Psalter. At the same time, a number of passages are extremely difficult to translate.

The psalm opens (vss. 1-2) with an indictment against the gods, not only for their failure to judge rightly, but for being wicked themselves. Just how wicked they are is depicted in verses 3-5. Consequently a devastating sevenfold curse is called upon them (vss. 6-9). The last two verses express the assurance that God's moral purposes will be worked out and the joy that God is thus vindicated.

The straying wicked (vss. 1-5). [1] The depiction of unrighteousness begins with two questions. Several suggested translations have been offered for **gods** (cf. note), depending on the vowels given the Hebrew word: (1) as an adverb emphasizing more strongly the preceding **indeed**; (2) "in silence"; (3) "band" or "congregation"—an Aramaic form; or (4) gods or angels. With the last, most commonly adopted view, the question is whether earthly rulers or pagan deities is meant. The word is often used to describe earthly rulers (Exod. 15:15; 2 Kings 24:15; Job 41:25; Ezek. 17:13; 32:21), and nothing within the psalm contradicts this view. The other possibility (gods, angels) assumes a picture of God amidst a council of the gods pronouncing judgment on them. This strong polemic against pagan deities does not necessarily imply that the author believed in their existence. Psalm 82, with its unquestionable reference to the council of the gods, supports this view, even though a different divine name is used there. The concept was a part of Israelite thought and could conceivably be in this psalm as well. On either position the psalm inveighs against injustice and unrighteousness, either within Israelite leadership ("lords") or among pagans (as in the RSV). In the latter case, we might suppose that Israel was being oppressed by neighboring peoples.

[2] The gods/lords were corrupt both in attitude and action. If the meaning of verse 1 is "gods," surely the onus here falls on the national leaders of the countries worshiping those deities. **Deal out** implies scales and balances. Instead of a just measure, people received **violence**.

[3] Whether **the wicked** are the gods/lords of verse 1 or

leading men among the adherents of the gods, still human transgressors are considered. They are so evil, it seems as if they had been born to it (cf. Ps. 51:5). This is literally impossible, and those who use this verse to argue for infant depravity surely miss the author's poetic point.

[4-5] A deadly viper which cannot be charmed will surely poison its victim. The picture is of an evil person so intent on his machinations that he cannot be dissuaded. The Hebrew word rendered **venom** is the same word for wrath. Other uses of the word for **serpent** show a cobra's characteristics (Deut. 32:33; Job 20:14, 16; Ps. 91:13; Isa. 11:8). **Deaf** is not a scientific statement, but indicates one not amenable to control. The Hebrew word translated **enchanter** means literally "one charming charms." The root meaning of the word is "trying, binding," perhaps implying the binding power of spells. (Cf. Eccles. 10:11; Jer. 8:17; Ecclus. 12:13.)

Curses on the wicked (vss. 6-9). [6] Verses 6-9 contain a sevenfold curse upon the wicked (cf. Num. 5:21-31; Deut. 27:14-26). Now it is **lions**, not serpents. **Break** and **tear out** are violent words, often used of breaking down walls. The judgment is decisive. A toothless lion cannot continue its aggressive marauding. [7] The second line, translated literally, means something like "he shall tread (aim) his arrow(s) like the ones (that) are cut off (wither?)." The RSV's construction of this difficult passage is one with which most modern versions offer substantial agreement. The point is well established by parallels in the psalm, so this line is not crucial.

[8] Not only should the threatening power be destroyed, let it be as if it **never** existed. **The snail** leaves a trial of **slime** after it has crawled away, leading to the illusion that it has **dissolved**. Some would translate the Hebrew word rendered **snail** as "wax" or "worm." Others would translate "miscarriage" and thus parallel the lines of this verse (cf. Job 3:16; Eccles. 6:3). [9] This verse is difficult to translate successfully, and various emendations have been suggested. The RSV conveys the idea of a fire coming quickly, probably indicating a hasty doom for the wicked

before they can bring their plans to fruition. The Hebrew word rendered **green** means literally "living," and **ablaze** is literally "in wrath" (from a root meaning "to burn"). The RSV renders the terms in antithesis. **Sweep away** implies a storm wind.

God will judge (vss. 10-11). **[10]** The time must come when evil can no longer be tolerated. Despite forms of expression unattractive to Christians, there is a strong moral sense pervading these words—a sense necessary for the preservation of society. The joy is because God is vindicated, not because men are punished. **[11]** It is Israel's **God who judges,** and if verse 1 referred to pagan gods, this climaxes the presentation of his supremacy over them. The faith of the covenant people is thereby justified. **Who judges** is plural in the original. Perhaps the word **God** (a plural) was used by pagans in the sense of many gods. Now it is taken from them, and, still plural, applied to the one God of Israel, Yahweh (vs. 6).

Psalm 59: An Innocent Sufferer

At some points the words of this psalm sound like the lament of an individual (vss. 1-4) and at others like a national complaint (vss. 4-5, 8, 10, 13). Perhaps an individual expresses his problems as typical ones against the larger background of oppression of the nation by foreigners. There is a double refrain within the psalm, appearing first in verses 9, 17ab (vss. 10 and 17c are similar), and then in verses 7 and 14.

Verses 1-4a open with a cry for deliverance, describing the enemies and the writer's innocence. Then comes a cry for judgment on the treacherous nations (vss. 4b, 5), described as a pack of dogs (vss. 6-7). The author trusts God's superiority, and is sure his prayer will be answered (vss. 8-10). A curse is leveled against the foes in verses 11-13, to the end that God will be glorified. Verses 14-15 return to the imagery of verses 6-7. Verses 16-17 conclude with an effusive vow of praise to God for his might, steadfast love, and protection.

'Deliver me' (vss. 1-4a). **[1-2]** A fourfold petition opens the psalm, using four terms to depict the author's opponents. The Hebrew word rendered **protect**, cognate to the word translated "fortress" (vss. 9, 16-17), implies setting the besieged one beyond the reach of his attackers. This is no clash of personal interests, but a call to God to demonstrate his moral sovereignty in a particular case. **Bloodthirsty** (literally "men of bloods") may indicate an actual murder threat or else may be a figure for men so unscrupulous that not even human life is sacred to them.

[3-4a] The author is helpless, like a man fearful of an ambush or of wild beasts lurking along his path. The Hebrew word translated **fierce** literally means "strong." Yet the author is an innocent man, unjustly opposed (cf. 1 Sam. 20:1; 24:11 with the superscription of this psalm). If the foes sought any pretext for their actions, a false charge might have been involved, though if national problems were involved, such would not have been the case. Perhaps the author expresses his anguish as typical of that felt by his countrymen before a foreign enemy.

The division in the middle of verse 4 is harmonious with the structure of the psalm, as a glance will show. The RSV adds **of mine** (vs. 4) so the reader will know it is not the foes who are sinless. Their hasty preparation for an attack gives his plea urgency.

'Awake to punish' (vss. 4b-7). [4b] Rouse shows the poet's strong feeling (cf. Pss. 7:6; 44:23). He is so eager that he bursts forth with a cry that the Christian finds somewhat intemperate (but which he may have occasionally been inclined to utter himself). **See** does not imply God's ignorance, but is an earnest plea for response. The author is sure that when God sees he will act. He forgets that God acts by his own counsels, not by those of men. Yet who can blame this anxious writer? The Hebrew term translated **my help** means literally "my call." The RSV has made a request into a response. This is appropriate since the call was for help.

[5] Here is the appeal for judgment, prefaced by an impressive divine address. The use of **God** (Elohim) with **of hosts** is quite unusual. The **God of hosts** (angelic minions or

earthly armies) is able to help, and because he is the **God of Israel**, he will aid his covenant people. It is **the nations** against whom he is implored to act, so the psalm is now broadened from the writer's personal troubles. The Hebrew phrase translated **spare none** means literally "do not be gracious to any (all)." [6] The viciousness and insatiable greed of evil people is likened to a pack of dangerous scavenging **dogs** (cf. Pss. 22:17; and especially 1 Kings 14:11; 2 Kings 9:36). This image is repeated in verse 14, but with a different sequel.

[7] Howling, prowling, **bellowing, snarling**—the canine figure is combined with that of a reflective man in the last part of the verse. The activities are open because they feel that they are immune from retribution. The Hebrew word for bellow basically means "pour forth," and some would render it "slaver." The Hebrew expression translated **snarling with** means literally "swords in" (RSV note). The literal translation is nonsensical. (Cf. Pss. 52:2; 55:21; 57:4; 64:3.) The concept may combine the ideas of **snarling** dogs and men with evil tongues. The RSV adds **they think** to the last line. The Hebrew literally means "who is hearing." Some would interpret all the details of this verse as referring to men. This is possible, though it is not the approach taken by the RSV.

The God of vindication (vss. 8-13). [8] The problem and plea behind him, the poet now asserts his faith in God's response. The menace of the nations is countermanded by a power so much greater that God laughs at their machinations (cf. Ps. 2:4). The contrast is impressive. [9] This and verse 17 are a refrain. The Hebrew word rendered **Strength** is from the same root as that rendered "fierce" in verse 3. On **fortress**, see verse 1 ("protect"). The RSV changes the Hebrew "his strength" to **my strength** to agree with the ancient versions. **Sing praises** results from emending one letter of the Hebrew word for "watch" (cf. RSV note). The result provides agreement with verse 17 and seems to be a more sensible reading.

[10] The RSV renders the literal Hebrew "God of his steadfast love" as **God in his steadfast love**. None of the

versions support the change, and verse 17 has "God of my steadfast love." An appropriate reading would be "God of kindness (or gracious God) will help." The appeal is to the covenant. The RSV adds **in triumph** (cf. Pss. 54:7; 118:7). **Enemies** implies "those who lie in wait."

[11] The call for judgment is renewed, with emphasis on the evil receiving the due consequences of their deeds. Some have suggested emending the Hebrew phrase translated **slay them not** to read "spare them not," on the assumption that a call for limited judgment is not harmonious with the passage. But the call may be for an unhurried judgment, by which men can see the consequences of an evil course in a world ruled by a God of righteousness. This would be a continuing reminder of God's action. **Totter** may suggest an army in confusion after a defeat.

[12] These wrongs of the tongue could be personal or national. May they **be trapped** by their own deeds! The Hebrew word translated **sin** is the same as that rendered "fault" in verse 4, and it may be repeated to contrast the innocence of the author with the guilt of the enemies. On **pride**, see the proud words of verse 7. Some think this whole curse may be to counteract the cursing of the enemies. Cursing was believed to be efficacious in bringing misfortune; it was not viewed simply as coarse, abusive language. The RSV adds **for** at the first of this verse; the **for** in the last line translates the Hebrew preposition usually rendered "from." [13] The call to judgment is to vindicate **God** and his relation to his covenant people. **Men** is added by the RSV. The last two lines could mean that all men would know that God ruled Jacob, or that all would know that the God of Jacob ruled all the earth.

'They howl like dogs' (vss. 14-15). Verse 14 is the same as the first of verse 7, but the image is extended differently from the last of verse 7. The stress here is on their need to satisfy their greed, while in verse 7 it was on their supposed freedom from opposition. The Hebrew word translated **growl** here is elsewhere rendered "murmur," as with the reference to Israelites in the wilderness (Exod. 15:24; Num. 14:2; 16:11; 17:5).

God My Strength (vss. 16-17). [16] This jubilant ending resumes the faith of verses 8-10. The Hebrew word rendered **might** here is cognate to that rendered "fierce" in verse 3 and "strength" in verse 9. The praise may imply proclamation to the congregation, perhaps in a morning service. Though the judgment on the enemies was not yet accomplished, we might suppose that this triggered the praise. The author's satisfaction in God is an interesting contrast to those growling in their dissatisfaction (vs. 15).

[17] This verse repeats verses 9-10 with the differences previously noted. Verses 9-10 seem to indicate anticipation, while the emphasis here is on the praise that is uttered when the anticipation has been fulfilled.

Psalm 60: 'With God We Shall Do Valiantly'

The people cry for God to reverse a national defeat. Verse 9 may indicate that the Edomites were the foe, and verse 10 may reflect a failure to re-engage them successfully. Yet this is only conjecture, for it is not possible to date this psalm exactly. It may have been composed for use in some liturgy of prayer or fasting subsequent to the defeat. The struggle between despair/lamentation and reassurance finally emerges in a victorious outlook.

In verses 1-3 the psalmist bewails the defeat, which is due to God's anger. Verse 4 could refer either to the defeat or to an offer of hope. Verse 5 contains a prayer for deliverance. Verses 6-8 contain a divine word, affirming God's control of peoples, and implying that he will aid his beloved (vs. 5). There follows renewed lament centering on Edom (vss. 9-10), further prayer (vs. 11a), and a final triumphant note of victory through God (vss. 11b, 12). The last of the psalm (vss. 6-12) is identical to Psalm 108:7-13.

A God against us (vss. 1-3). [1] A threefold depiction of agony precedes the author's cry (cf. Ps. 44:9, 24). The assumption is that **God** should give his people victory. Therefore, defeat is described as God breaking the **defenses** (cf. 2 Sam. 5:20). Even more than defeat, the people seem concerned with God's anger. There is no specific note of penitence, unless the plea of helplessness without God (vs. 11) be so construed.

[2] The defeat is likened to an earthquake. The second line seems to speak of the weakened walls, in danger of collapsing completely unless repaired. The author may feel that God's reputation has been damaged by the defeat, so he prays that there be no further deterioration; or the people may be saying that they can stand no more.

[3] Two more images complete this forlorn picture. The Hebrew word translated **suffer** means literally "see." The RSV seems to strengthen the term by its translation. Wine may refer to drugged **wine**, which caused inebriation more easily (cf. Ps. 75:8), or they may have drunk to excess. At any rate God renders them unable to function. (On the cup of God's wrath, cf. Isa. 51:17, 22; Jer. 25:15.)

Hope for deliverance (vss. 4-5). [4] Some consider that this difficult verse continues to speak of defeat (cf. the ancient versions). Thus, it either sarcastically refers to God mustering his people only to send them to defeat, or, more likely, depicts him helping them escape from the worst. This view suggests that **Selah** concludes the "woe" section of the psalm, and verse 5 begins the hope section. Others see here a statement of hope. The people **rally to the banner** in hopes of successfully engaging the enemy. The interpretation depends, in part, on how the last line is understood. One rendering could be "to take flight before" (defeat). Assuming another Hebrew root for the verb, the translation could be "to be displayed because of the bow" indicating the regrouping of the people. **Rally** seems to imply the latter, but might be understood in either sense. The Hebrew word translated **bow** means "truth" (cf. RSV note), an unusual word that also occurs in Proverbs 22:21. That reading is possible, but some suppose that the term may be an Aramaic form of the word "bow," since the words are quite similar.

[5] **That** (or "in order that") in the beginning of verse 5 seems to imply that this verse should be translated in a hopeful sense. Here is positive hope, based on the covenant. People of faith continue to be convinced of God's

concern, even though immediate surroundings seem to indicate otherwise (cf. Ps. 44).

God is in control (vss. 6-8). [6] The rest of this psalm is virtually identical to Psalm 108:7-13. Since that is a composite psalm (from Pss. 57 and 60), this might be the original text, though it is impossible to be sure. God affirms his sovereignty. Some groups are to be blessed (vs. 7), and some are for punishment (vss. 6, 8). The passage may refer to the original conquest of the land, as a means of reaffirming God's power; or it may have had contemporary relevance for the author. **Sanctuary** (cf. note), if the accepted reading, could imply a liturgical context for verses 6-8. **Shechem** was in central Palestine. The **Vale of Succoth** was east of the Jordan (cf. Gen. 33:17-18).

[7] The locations here may represent areas north and south, on both sides of the Jordan. It is all God's, so Israel should not fear her foes, as if God were weak and powerless. Of these four, three are tribes of Israel and **Gilead** is a location. God is pictured as a warrior in the last half of the verse. The **scepter**, or commander's staff, likely indicates **Judah** as the kingly tribe. In battle, therefore the tribes are not alone, but are the implements of the Lord God. [8] By contrast, three of Israel's neighbors are humbled and disgraced. A **washbasin** was used to pour water over the master's hands and feet. The casting of the **shoe** could refer to kicking off the sandals so that the slave could do the washing. Others consider the giving of the shoe to be a symbol of taking possession (cf. Ruth 4:8-9). This role was appropriate considering the pride of which **Moab** and **Edom** were sometimes accused. The Hebrew word translated **over** means literally "over me," which is awkward. The RSV follows the Syriac and Psalm 108:9 for a less difficult reading.

'O grant us help' (vss. 9-12). [9-10] Despite the oracle in verses 6-8, the tone of lamentation now recurs, as doubt and faith struggle. Perhaps because of the oracle, renewed prayer is encouraged. **Edom** is problematic. Some suggest flight to her from another enemy. More likely Edom was the foe, and the fortified city a mountain fastness there (cf.

Obad. 3-4). On this view the people want a divinely led resurgence to counter the defeat of verse 10 (cf. vss. 1-3).

[12-13] If there is **help**, it must be from **God**. No other source is considered. If not that, then defeat must be final. Thus this strong assertion of faith comes out of darkness. Yet verse 12 dispels the gloom with the light of hope. The future will be different. Though deliverance is not yet theirs, the people possess a precious oracle, a renewal of God's covenant promises, upon which to build an optimistic future.

Psalm 61: The Rock Higher Than I

This psalm includes lamentation, thanksgiving, prayer, and vow. Opinion is divided whether lament or thanks is dominant (cf. notes on vs. 5). Also verses 6-7 seem intrusive, but could be explained if the author was a king. Others feel these verses may be a later interpolation, inserted for worship purposes (cf. vs. 6).

Verses 1-4 are a prayer for security by one who calls "from the end of the earth." Verse 5 is thanks for God's blessing. The blessing on the king is in verses 6-7, and verse 8 is a promise to praise God with song and paying of vows.

'Listen to my prayer' (vss. 1-5). [1-2a] Cry might even be translated "yell"—a strong indication of the writer's distress. **From the end of the earth** could indicate an exile from Jerusalem (cf. Pss. 42, 43), or it could be a figurative expression of one who feels far from help. It has been suggested that this is a figure for the entrance to the underworld—another way of saying "I am near death." **My heart is faint** underscores the helplessness of the author.

[2b-3] Here are three images of God's protectiveness and of safety. A bewildered traveler, in danger, wants direction to a safe eminence (**rock**). He craves safety (**refuge**), for there is an **enemy** (mentioned only here in the psalm). This is a strong statement of faith from a frightened soul, who has found divine aid in the past and seeks it again. Another translation of the last of verse 2 is "to the rock that is too high for me!" This would imply he wants access

to the inaccessible. He needs help, for he cannot reach safety alone.

[4] Tent may refer to the hospitality of a protector host (cf. Ps. 23:6), or to the temple, confirming the view that he is far from Jerusalem. **For ever** (an unusual plural) is a strong way of saying he wants God's help, beyond the immediate problem, throughout his life. **[5]** Some consider this as thanks for past blessings, which the author sees as assurance that **God** will act similarly in the future. Others see it as gratitude for resolution of the problem described in verses 1-4. Thus the psalm could be either a lament or a thanksgiving, depending on the interpretation adopted. **Vows** were often made in association with prayers for deliverance, and a number of laments refer to them. **Heritage** is problematic, since all Israel received the land, not just those fearing God's **name**. Some believe there was a ceremony in which the land promise was renewed, or that the author stirs himself to fresh appreciation of God's blessings. Others would change one letter in the Hebrew text and emend the word for **heritage** to that for "desire."

Praise the king (vss. 6-8). [6] Verses 6-7 interpose a petition for the king's well being, enigmatic in its connection to the context. Some feel it is an interpolation. But Babylonian parallels reveal similar intercessions in an apparently foreign context. Perhaps the psalmist feels God's blessing on him involves the whole people, who are epitomized in the monarch. The first line means literally "days unto days of king add," which the RSV translates freely. Long **life for** a good king meant extended well being for the nation.

[7] Kingship in Israel was invested with religious significance. The house of David was promised an everlasting dominion (2 Sam. 7:16). The king was God's vicegerent. The blessings of **steadfast love and faithfulness** imply the monarch possesses the character which God approves. A survey of the many bad kings in the history of Israel shows why fervent prayers for a good king such as this would be uttered. As the leader, so the people. **[8]** This verse could express general praise for God's covenant mercies, or else have reference to the writer's particular deliverance.

Psalm 62: God My Rock and Salvation

Though this author struggles with deceitful and destructive foes (vss. 3-4), his dominant expression is neither complaint nor cry for help. The problem fades into the background, in the assurance that God will requite all men for their works. This insight into the true center of life he must share with others. The psalm includes an impressive collection of descriptions for God, strong statements of personal trust, and contrasts between possible life ideals.

In verses 1-2 (also vss. 5-6), the poet confesses the great resource he finds in God. This overshadows the depiction of his troubles in verses 3-4. Verse 7 strengthens the repetition of the refrain in verses 5-6. Verses 8-12 call the people to trust God (vs. 8), reflect on the inadvisability of placing final trust in man (vs. 9) or riches (especially ill-gotten gain, vs. 10), and conclude with an affirmation of God's power, steadfast love, and judgment (vss. 11-12). The last line of the psalm vindicates all previous statements. God's requital gives the universe purpose. How a life is lived matters enormously.

'I shall not be moved' (vss. 1-2). [1] The author introspectively affirms his faith, vis-à-vis the problem which verses 3-4 describe. **Alone** is also in verses 2 ("only"), 4-6 ("alone"), and 9 ("but"). There is nowhere else he will turn, for that would abandon his hope for salvation, and place him in jeopardy of unsettling forces (vs. 2). **In silence** could refer to the inner peace given by **God**, or to the fact that he had exhausted his plea, with no more to say. **Waits** is added by the RSV from verse 5. **[2]** Three consecutive terms in Hebrew underline the poet's confidence (**rock, salvation, fortress**). Contrast these with "men of low estate" as they are described in verse 9. God-given stability overpowers any threat, no matter how great.

The enemies (vss. 3-4). [3] Verses 3-4 are the only verses directly addressing the enemies (vss. 9-10 may refer to them obliquely). His words are less a complaint than an appeal to them and a depiction of the futility of their actions. The Hebrew word translated **set upon** occurs only here in the OT. The RSV gives a generalizing translation.

Other suggestions include "shout at," "threaten," and "overwhelm with reproaches." **Shatter** often refers to the killing of an enemy. The **wall** is usually understood as the psalmist, beset by enemies like a besieged city. The **wall**, though weakened, will not fall (vs. 2), so the attackers are due a surprise. Or the **wall** could refer to the enemies, unstable in comparison with the psalmist. [4] From direct address the writer turns to third person description. **Eminence** could indicate he was a person of some prominence. His deceitful opponents are now unmasked, to betray him no more.

The resources (vss. 5-7). [5-6] The refrain of verses 1-2 is repeated, with some changes. **In silence** is imperative (though the RSV does not so translate) and may be a self-exhortation to continue to practice the spirit expressed in verse 1. **Shaken** (vs. 6) renders the same Hebrew verb as "moved" in verse 2. The key words about the enemies are bracketed by these affirmations of trust. After verse 7, the psalm consists of instruction. [7] Four descriptions of God strengthen the words of verses 5-6. The Hebrew word translated **deliverance** is from the same root as that rendered "salvation." **Honor** is everything giving a man importance and standing among the people. On **mighty rock**, see verse 2. With such security the poet need not be disturbed by his foes.

Trust in God alone (vss. 8-12). [8] From his own experience the author offers instruction, and gives in verses 9-10 reasons why ultimate confidence in men or in wealth is inadequate. This verse seems to indicate a public act of **trust**. The **people** are invited to bare their lives to **God** (cf. "silence" in vss. 1, 5). Even the inmost secrets of the **heart** can be safely laid before him.

[9] One dare not invest ultimate hope in humans, all of whom are of so little substance **a breath** would outweigh them. The image is unforgettable, and a remarkable contrast to the descriptions of God in verses 5-7. The Hebrew word rendered **breath** here is often translated "vanity" in Ecclesiastes, and that translated **delusion** is rendered "falsehood" in verse 4. **Men of low estate** and **men of high**

estate translate two Hebrew phrases, both of which mean "sons of men," but which use different words for "men" ('*adham* and *ish*). See the discussion of Psalm 49:2.

[10] The Hebrew verb translated **Put . . . confidence** is the same as that rendered "trust" in verse 8, making a strong antithesis. Love for material things insidiously claims men. But not only are they an inadequate object of trust, they can turn men into criminals. One sure way to avoid the latter is by "**heart** control." The verbs in this verse are plural, indicating an exhortation to the whole congregation (in worship?). The Hebrew phrase rendered **set no vain hopes** is from the same root as that translated "delusion" in verse 9. The RSV adds **on them.**

[11-12] In proverbial style (**once . . . twice**) the psalm returns to prayer. **Once . . . twice** may refer to the refrain of verses 1-2, 5-6. A true grasp of God's nature must always attempt to hold his **power** (vs. 11) and his **steadfast love** (vs. 12) in balance. Such a **God** is able to requite a man as his works deserve—thus finally dispelling all deceit (cf. vss. 4, 9-10). This is a powerfully **God**-centered psalm. It implores men to recognize where the center of reality is to be found, and to focus there; for what a man sows he must reap.

Psalm 63: Strength in Time of Stress

This author is troubled by foes (vss. 9, 11), but their threat seems minor compared with his magnificent statements of trust and thanks (vss. 1-8). His vision of God makes the writer so sure of deliverance he seems almost to dismiss the danger—it seems nearly an afterthought. Since verse 11 refers to the king, some suppose that David was the writer, or that another wrote on his behalf.

Verse 1 vividly shows the author's yearning for God, built upon remembrance of worship and upon God's covenant with the people (vss. 2-4). Further nocturnal reflection upon God's help nourishes the author like a rich feast (vss. 5-7), and calls forth a strong affirmation of rewarded trust (vs. 8). Then the mood changes. There are enemies (vs. 9a), but their doom is sure and terrible (vss. 9b-10).

The last verse refers to the king's joy in anticipation of deliverance.

A heart set on God (vss. 1-4). [1] This opening word brings us from any prosaic assessment of religion into a world of tingling intensity. The poet's desire for **God** challenges the reader to new realizations (cf. Pss. 42:1; 143:6; Matt. 5:6). We suppose from the juxtaposition of past experience and present desire depicted in verses 1-2 that the more he has known God, the more urgently he wishes to know him. He is like a man nearly collapsed in a parched **land**, who will faint without sustenance. Some suppose he is far from the temple and longs desperately for the experience of God there. But the language may simply be showing the strength of his desire. He seeks, not a mystical experience of God, but an awareness of his nature (vss. 2-3), his deliverance (vss. 7-8), and to praise him (vss. 3-5). This man is absolutely wholehearted, and his heart is set on God.

[2] **In the sanctuary** there was concentrated in ritual and communal experience that which was most meaningful in his life. How did he look upon God? Was there a theophany, or the cultic symbols of his presence, or reflections stirred within the worshipper? In some of these ways, or others, God's **power and glory** were indelibly imprinted on his soul. [3] God's covenant **love** is valued more **than life**. The author's understanding may be illumined by particular evidences of divine grace in his own life. **Steadfast love**, realized in its full import, cannot but lead to praise.

[4] Praise and dependence will be his enduring characteristic. **Lifting up hands** (cf. Pss. 28:2; 141:2; 1 Tim. 2:8) may have been derived from the expectation that God would "fill" them with divine blessings. **And call** is added by the RSV.

A heart satisfied with God (vss. 5-8). [5] From desire the poet moves to satisfaction, contemplating experiences which respond to the longing expressed in verse 1. The Hebrew word translated **feasted** is from the verb meaning "to be satisfied." **Marrow and fat** imply a sumptuous and thoroughly satisfying banquet. One could want no more.

Praise is given joyfully. [6] One's mind moves to more profound reflection at day's end, and thoughts go to deeper levels than their accustomed course through the day. More than meditations upon retiring, these words could represent a **night** of anxious concern, or a **night** of prayer and meditation, crowned by surpassing convictions of God's goodness.

[7] Here the subject of his reflection is indicated. God gives **help**, security, and joy. On **shadow of wings**, see the discussion on Psalm 17:9, and see Psalms 36:7; 57:1; 61:4.

[8] If this verse had not been written, we should know it was the psalmist's commitment from his previous words. **Clings** beautifully bespeaks utter dependence. He holds to God, and God **upholds** him.

A life vindicated (vss. 9-11). [9-10] If opposition was the author's main purpose for writing, then immersion of his **life** in God was his main response. Verses 9-11 seem to be a commentary on "help" (vs. 7) and "upholds" (vs. 8), and projects similar divine help into the future. The author counters the threat with three pronouncements of doom, the last two of which (vs. 10) explain the first (vs. 9). **Depths of the earth** equals Sheol, or death. (Contrast "more than life," vs. 3.) The destroyers are destroyed. Either this is literal defeat before the king (in which case the psalm takes on a national character) or the martial experience is a figure. Slain, abandoned, and devoured by scavengers is their ignominious fate.

[11] As in Psalm 61:6-7 a reference to **the king** intrudes into the text (cf. the discussion there). The fortunes of **king** and people were closely bound together. We do not know whether the **liars** were personal enemies of the author, or of **the king**, or of the nation, nor in what the lies consisted. Perhaps there was a false accusation. **Swear by him** could either be an oath by **God** or by **the king**. Paul seems to have had this verse in mind in Romans 3:19.

Psalm 64: 'Preserve My Life'

This poet knows that God penetrates to the inmost recesses of the heart. His righteousness must inevitably punish the evil, to their surprise. The writer is confident that his situation will be resolved (he is blameless, vss. 4, 10). God will be vindicated among all men (vss. 7-9). The wicked (vss. 2-6) are so smug and set in their intents, and they are so wrong!

Verses 1-6 comprise a lament. After a prayer (vs. 1), the secret plots of the wicked are mentioned (vs. 2). Their wrongdoing is largely verbal (vss. 3-4). They arrogantly pursue their intentions, believing they will not be detected, and consequently, not punished (vss. 5-6). Verses 7-9 assure divine response in which the wicked are repaid in kind. The consequence of their sudden wounding (vs. 7) will be widespread glorification of God (vs. 9). The psalm ends with a call to the righteous to trust the Lord (vs. 10).

The plots of the enemy (vss. 1-6). [1] The writer is caught up by anxiety, **in dread of enemy** cunning, craft, and cruelty. **Complaint** can also indicate the idea of musing, so that his troubled thoughts are stressed. **Dread**, a strong word, sometimes indicates those who are practically immobilized (cf. 2 Chron. 17:10; 20:29; Job 13:11). The Hebrew word rendered **preserve** could also be rendered "you preserve," and thus express trust. However, such an expression may be premature at this point in the psalm.

[2] He knows his enemies are making plans, but not when or how they will act. He prays to be hidden, and thus protected. The Hebrew word translated **secret plots** can indicate either the plans or the planners, and that rendered **scheming** can also mean "throngs" or a raging mob. The RSV translation parallels the first line of the verse. [3] On the language of verses 3-6, see Psalms 11:2; 55:21; 57:4; 59:7. The tongue can be used as devastatingly as a weapon of war. **Arrows** may suggest poisoned arrows. This unforgettable description prepares the reader for the contrasting greatness of God (vss. 7-9). The Hebrew word translated **aim** is usually rendered "bend" (a bow). Here it is transferred to the arrow.

[4] The apprehension continues; he fears attackers who feel they can act with impunity (**without fear**). The writer asserts his innocence (cf. vs. 10). Some say the archer

symbolizes malicious charges, while others even suggest
magical curses hurled against the author (the latter, though
rejected by most commentators, is probably based on
"purpose" [literally "word"] in vs. 5). [5] Now attention is
focused on the thoughts of the wicked. **They hold fast** their
purposes, either by hardening their hearts, or by encouraging each other. The Hebrew word rendered **thinking** means
literally "they say," presumably to themselves. The RSV
note ("them") could refer to snares or plots. The RSV text,
on the basis of the Syriac, is smoother, but the Hebrew is
not impossible.

[6] This verse is difficult to translate. The RSV text enables the continuation of the quotation, and involves only a
slight change in a verb. The reading given by the RSV note
also makes sense, but is not as smooth. **We have thought
out** is difficult. Some think it should be third person, agreeing with the Hebrew of verse 5. Others suggest (with several manuscripts) "they have concealed." The Hebrew
translated **cunningly conceived plot** means literally "a
searched out search." In fact, the Hebrew word for **search**
is used three times in this one clause. The last line offers an
interesting psychological insight. Whatever man's
deepest thoughts, and however he tries to hide them, God
knows, as the rest of the psalm shows!

God's retaliation (vss. 7-9). [7] The tables are turned!
How impressive the use of the same language earlier used
to describe the wicked (vs. 4)! The enemies acted covertly
but were not concealed. They **suddenly** received what they
planned to give. Inner confidence that one is unobserved
does not, in this case, correspond to the fact. Those who
see verse 4 as a curse against the poet see verses 7-9 as a
countercurse uttered by him.

[8] The misuse of the **tongue** now brings God's wrath. If
the footnote to line one is accepted, there arises a question
of whom "they" would be. Would God have compatriots in
judgment? Not likely, unless some earthly force be assumed that would mete out punishment. The conjecture
represented by the text involves a slight change in the Hebrew verb. Wagging the **heads** may be in derision or in

shocked concern. [9] The psalm may be anticipating judgment, or seeing it as already accomplished. This verse picks up the thought of the last half of verse 8. **All men** may have reference to Israel, or it may be a universal expression. Perhaps it is the latter, with verse 10 referring to the covenant people. Compare **fear** to "without fear" (vs. 4). God's deeds will be declared and pondered.

Praise for refuge (vs. 10). So shall it be for both the evil and **the righteous.** This psalm makes a triumphant progression from verse 1 to 10. In the RSV verse 10 is made imperative, though it could as well be translated as future. Verse 10 probably indicates the psalm was to be employed in worship.

Psalm 65: Praise to God in Zion

God is praised for his lordship in creation and history, with the description of a bountiful harvest being the focal point (vss. 9-13). This psalm was employed in worship (vss. 2, 4), in which forgiveness of sins was sought (vs. 3). It is not clear whether this was thanks for a bountiful harvest, or a prayer that one might be forthcoming (perhaps even after famine).

Verses 1-4 praise God for his forgiveness and for the privilege of worshiping him as his people. He is extolled for his redemptive and creative powers (vss. 5-7) and influence over the peoples of earth (vs. 8). Verses 9-13 are a rhapsodic picture of the joy of an overflowing harvest.

Praise in worship (vss. 1-3). [1] Those who have petitioned and were answered now respond by **praise** and the performing of **vows.** If the harvest (vss. 9-13) is the controlling motif of the psalm, it might be supposed that a good crop occasioned this praise. But verse 3 speaks of sins and forgiveness, and verses 5-8 of God's great actions in blessing his people and controlling nature. Perhaps reflection on the **God**/man relation suggested by a good harvest (man's obedience and God's consequent blessings) leads to broader concerns of the same sort. Thus, thanks for a good harvest implies all God does for man. Another suggestion is that, in famine, the people come asking God's forgiveness and renewal of nature's bounty. However, the psalm seems inadequate in its expression of repentance to support this view. The translation **is due** represents a change from the Hebrew text. The original means "silence," but attempts to read that are forced.

[2-3] **All flesh** (vs. 2) may be universalistic (cf. vss. 5, 8), but it could designate only Israel, since the context is Israel's cult. The rendering **on account of sins** is a free translation of a Hebrew phrase that means literally "(with) things/words of sins." The RSV adds **when** as a transition to the rest of the verse. Another possibility is "(with) words (i.e., confessions) of sins," which would harmonize with a plea for famine relief (cf. vs. 1). The dominant note of the verse is grace. Man needs divine forgiveness, and when he cannot supply his own need, God will. [4] In language reminiscent of the Levitical privileges (cf. Num. 16:5), we have an exalted and joyful reflection, no doubt triggered by God's covenant mercies to his people, made real by forgiveness. God's **house** may symbolize all God's blessings to his people. The centralizing point is the worship which is conducted there.

Praise for deliverance (vss. 5-8). [5] The picture is enlarged as we move from the temple to the breadth of **earth** and **sea**. **Dread deeds** may imply the history of God's people (cf. Exod. 34:10; 2 Sam. 7:23; Pss. 66:3; 106:21-22; 145:6; Isa. 64:3). Yet there is probably reference to events immediate to the writer, as well. God's creative and sovereign power is especially stressed in verses 7-8. He is **the hope of all** men (a strong assertion). **Hope** (from the same Hebrew root as the word rendered "trust") may be the author's desire that all men would have confidence in Yahweh. [6] In faith's eyes nature speaks of an even larger **might** of the Creator. **Mountains** are strong, permanent, and reliable, but less so than God. **Girded with might** could describe either the mountains or God.

[7] **The seas** bear similar witness. This may refer to the waters of chaos which God bound at creation (cf. Job 38:5-11). This last line changes to **the peoples**, and continues that discussion in verse 8. Some believe **the seas**

may symbolize tumultuous mankind. Others think the meaning is that the God of nature can also control men.

[8] God's **signs** could refer to nature, or to God's blessing his people and controlling the nations. Thus God is both sign and hope (vs. 5) to men at **earth's farthest bounds.** Whether or not these people recognize Yahweh, the signs are impressive, and perhaps only await a word of interpretation that men might know him who causes them. The last of the verse has been understood as God's power in creation (RSV) or as paralleling **those who dwell at earth's farthest bounds** in the first half of the verse.

Praise for the harvest (vss. 9-13). [9] Now the psalm moves to the harvest theme. The beautiful description in verses 9-13 would warm the heart of any farmer. Verses 9-10 stress the importance of **water** for a good crop (cf. vs. 7). **River of God** may be a way of saying God gives water—it does not just come. **Providest** and **prepared** both translate the same Hebrew verb. [10] In beautiful procession this verse has four verbs and their objects. One gets the impression of the farmer watching cultivation, **growth,** and harvest. The rainy season in Palestine was October-May, with the first two and last two months having the sparsest fall. The autumn rains were important for the preparation of the soil, and the spring rains for the maturing of the crops. Here the earth received a continuous supply during the necessary period until the sprouts appeared.

[11] The climax is a generous harvest. The Hebrew phrase translated **with thy bounty** means literally "of thy goodness." The last line seems to picture a cart so heavily laden its contents spill on the ground. The RSV adds **thy chariot** to explain **the tracks.** [12] Verses 12-13 survey the land (**pastures, hills,** meadows, valleys), finding all blessed by God's largess. **Pastures** and **hills** were normally drab and dry, but this time they are so richly clad they seem to rejoice in their grassy cover. It will be a good year for the cattle, as well (vs. 13). [13] **Flocks** and crops increase. The picture is a beautiful revelation of the best of times. Shouting and singing respond to nature's generosity, but it is never forgotten that God gives all.

This psalm is redolent with God's goodness, seen by the author on all sides. This goodness operates in creation and God's holy history, and gives forgiveness, sustenance, and abundance.

Psalm 66: Personal and National Pride

Verses 1-12 of this thanksgiving psalm express national gratitude, while verses 13-20 are the thanks of an individual. Though some have conjectured that two separate psalms have been joined, it may be supposed that the author was the king or a national leader, whose personal experience in trial was a typical part of a larger national problem. Thus he links the two to give his personal testimony and to call the people to a stronger realization of their blessedness as God's chosen. Steadfast love (vs. 20) indicates this covenant relation, and links individual and nation, thus uniting the psalm. It is written for public worship, and may be antiphonal, with both group and individual contributions.

An exuberant opening calls all the earth to praise God for his terrible deeds (vss. 1-4, which are depicted, with a warning to the rebellious not to exalt themselves against God (vss. 5-7). Though God has tested his people, he has never abandoned them, and is therefore to be praised (vss. 8-12). In verses 13-15 an individual refers to the payment of vows made to God when he had been troubled. Then he refers to his previous prayer and gives thanks for God's answer, reminding the hearers of God's demands for purity (vss. 16-19). A burst of praise closes the psalm (vs. 20).

Make a joyful noise! (vss. 1-4). [1-2] On the opening call to worship, see Psalms 98:4; 100:1. Shouting and singing respond to God's deeds and power (vs. 3). It is a wholehearted summons, issued universally. Verse 2 speaks of the **praise** befitting the divine nature (**glory**). The RSV adds **to him.** A variant translation of line two is "make glory his praise."

[3] God **is so great** that the author calls all the earth (vs. 1) to praise him. **Terrible** implies fearful and awe-inspiring, not in the sense of stark terror, but of amazed praise.

Enemies, so the author dreams, see their power as nothing compared with Israel's God. [4] This verse sums up the section. The last line here is a repetition of the thought of the previous line, not an imperative.

Praise the God of the Exodus (vss. 5-7). [5] Picking up the word **terrible** (vs. 3), the author turns to the exodus as a showcase of God's **deeds**. These verses demonstrate to "all the earth" the general premise stated in verse 3. [6] Passing through the Red **Sea** (as most believe) stirs the joy of Israel. God's people are continually under the blessing of the doer of terrible deeds. [7] The exodus (and later the entry into Canaan) were powerful judgments on **nations** around Israel. By extension, God is the ruling watchman of all people for all time. Thus **rebellious** peoples must consider the consequences of undue self-exaltation. They ought to submit to Yahweh and live in peace with Israel.

The testing of the people (vss. 8-12). [8] Some say the nations continue to be addressed here on the basis of verses 1-7. Others believe, because of verses 9-12, that Israel is meant. The latter seems preferable. Thus the people, gathered in worship, are called to reflect on those same acts of God which have, the author envisions, impressed the rest of the world. If so with the nations, how much more so with Israel, and with how much more dedication ought they to praise God.

[9] The people had faced hard times but were never abandoned. God's care was constant. Israel still lives! Verses 10-12 elaborate this theme. [10] This verse begins a series of metaphors for difficulties experienced by the people. This first refers to the refining of **silver**. If God had sent hard times, it was to purge his people. These illustrations may indicate specific difficulties recently experienced, deliverance from which may be the occasion for the psalm. It is also possible that in verses 13-20 an individual offers thanks for his part in the deliverance, or a national leader speaks as one for all.

[11] **Net** envisions the people as prey of a hunter. The Hebrew word used here might also be translated "stronghold" or "dungeon." The Hebrew word translated **affliction**

occurs only here in the OT. The meaning is problematic, but may imply the idea of pressure. **Loins** probably refers to one's strength and vigor (Deut. 33:11; Job 40:16), so the idea here is that strength has been lost (see Isa. 21:3; Ps. 69:23).

[12] The first image here may imply men thrown to the road, in battle or otherwise (cf. Isa. 51:23). (On **fire and water**, see Isa. 43:2.) Despite all these tests, the people are among the living. The last line of this verse catches up the premise of verse 9. Some would keep "saturation" (RSV note) as indicating the abundance of God's salvation. The RSV, on the strength of the ancient versions, suggests a slight change to obtain a more sensible reading. The sense of God's concern, even through difficulty, is still basic.

Sacrifices to God (vss. 13-15). [13] Now the psalm changes to an individual emphasis. The speaker will bring his offerings to **pay vows** made when he was in trouble (and, no doubt, prayed God for deliverance). Verse 14 offers further comment on the vows (cf. also Ps. 22: 22-26), and verse 15 on the **burnt offerings**. Burnt offerings were wholly consumed, except for the hide. [14-15] We do not know the nature of the **trouble**, though we might compare the tests noted in verses 10-12. Apparently numerous sacrifices were offered, perhaps indicating a man of some wealth. The abundance of his offering may indicate the intensity of the previous trouble and of the present gratitude. The Hebrew word rendered **smoke** literally means incense, or the odor of the **sacrifice**.

God has heard (vss. 16-20). [16] A profoundly grateful man proclaims God's blessedness, hopeful that it will strengthen others. Deliverance leads to praise. Such proclamation was perhaps part of the vow (cf. Ps. 22:25; and note Pss. 32:8; 40:9-10). [17-19] He recounts how he had prayed and praised. In addition to noting that God hears only the righteous (of whom he is one), he may also have **extolled** God because he was so sure of his saving power. Verse 18, rather than being egotistical, is his means of declaring God's nature, in expectation of a like response from the people. God is not morally indifferent. This is a lesson to the hearers for their lives. The Hebrew word translated **cherished** (vs. 18) literally means "seen."

[20] **Steadfast love** may be the key to the entire psalm, though found here for the first time within it. Through all national and personal difficulties, God has blessed his covenant people. This gives meaning to all national and personal experience. The author is not just grateful for individual deliverance, but for unshakable fellowship with God.

Psalm 67: Let the People Praise Thee

A good harvest suggests all of God's blessings, and in praise Israel's attention is turned from the physical abundance to God himself. In joyous mission spirit, all men are called to praise God for his goodness to Israel and his promise of equitable judgment among men. These reflections no doubt accompanied a communal time of thanks for harvest—perhaps the Feast of Tabernacles. Flushed by God's goodness, they pray for its continuance.

An opening call for God's blessings, in priestly language (vs. 1), leads to the concern that all men may know of (vs. 2) and praise (vs. 3) God for his equity and guidance (vs. 4). Verse 3 is repeated in verse 5 (perhaps it also ended the psalm but has been lost in transmission). Verses 6-7 dwell on the immediate harvest with a final call to all the ends of the earth to fear God.

'May God be gracious' (vss. 1-3). [1] This opening is like the priestly benediction (Num. 6:24-26), which must often have been repeated in temple worship. The author appropriates it to begin his thanksgiving on behalf of the nation. See Psalms 4:6; 29:11; 31:16; 80:3, 7, 19. God's shining **face** indicates his favor (Pss. 44:3; 89:15).

[2] May God's goodness to Israel have universal repercussions. Good news longs to be shared. The author affirms God's mission to the **nations** through Israel. The focus is not the gift, but the Giver. Israel should not be self-centered, but God-centered. [3] The refrain here is repeated in verse 5. Verse 4 expands the thought, giving further reason for **the peoples** to **praise**. A time is conceived

when Israel and the nations have a common bond of praise to **God.**

Let the nations be glad (vss. 4-7). **[4]** In God's equitable judgment and guidance, men can find a stability on which to build and a hope of just government. The Hebrew word translated **guide** might also mean "trust kindly, care for." We do not know the full implication of the term, but it is probably a parallel statement to the previous line.

[6] The giving of earthly bounty probably spurred the larger sense of gratitude with which the first five verses were concerned. The RSV indicates a past harvest (**has yielded**). Some suggest rendering the verb as future, either expecting a good harvest or praying for one because crops had not been good. This latter view sees verses 6b-7 as prayer or expectation. The normal translation of the verb, however, indicates completed action. In fact, it is the only such verb in the psalm. The other verbs in verses 6b-7 are imperfects, indicating incomplete action. The RSV renders them as past, however, on the basis of **has yielded.** Of course incompleted action could mean that the earth has yielded, and still yields. **[7]** This verse repeats previous parts of the psalm, adding only the reference to **fear.**

Psalm 68: The Awesome God

There are many problems in this psalm, both because of the difficulty of translating certain words and the difficulty of making good English sense from the Hebrew syntax. There are marked stylistic variations. There is also wide diversity of opinion (and despair) concerning the meaning of the psalm as a whole.

However, some things can be established. The focus is on God in his victories for his people, with special stress on the exodus, and with calls for such victories to continue. Much of the psalm suggests parts of Judges 5. Numerous passages are concerned with Egypt (was it originally used in connection with a threat from Egypt?). Passages throughout indicate liturgical use. Indeed, it has been suggested that some of the obscurities could be explained if we knew more of the rituals with which this psalm was employed. There are various conjectures as to the worship occasion. Some commentators believe it describes the various stages of a festal procession. Others, failing to find sufficient discursive unity, have conjectured that the psalm may be a mosaic, wrought from parts of other poems and songs (as if one should construct a pastiche from favorite passages in a modern hymn book). Despite the frustration to the interpreter, the psalm has a powerful impact. Its imagery is strong, and the overall impression is dramatic.

The psalm is best outlined by a brief characterization of each of its segments. Verses 1-3 contain a prayer for God to scatter his enemies, causing the righteous to rejoice. Verses 4-6 praise God as the one who cares for the helpless. Verses 7-10 review the exodus, with its attendant marvelous divine actions. Verses 11-14 depict God commanding his hosts in mighty victory. Verses 15-16 describe the glory of Zion, God's eternal dwelling. Verses 17-18 show God coming in victory, leading a train. Verses 19-20 bless the God who saves. Verses 21-23 describe God's decisive victory over his foes. Verses 24-27 depict a festival procession. Verses 28-31 call for God to destroy the foes, probably Egypt. Verses 32-35 praise the powerful and terrible God of Israel.

The victorious God (vss. 1-3). [1] God's victory is stated at once. The RSV renders the verbs as imperatives (jussives) but they could also be translated as indicating incomplete (perhaps future) action. The ancient versions take both positions. In the very similar language of Numbers 10:35, the verbs do have an imperative form. These are the words used with the procession of the ark, which would suggest God's victorious care for his people. Whether a procession accompanied the use of this psalm is debated (cf. vss. 24-27), but at least such an event forms part of the conceptual background.

[2] The series of woes against God's enemies continues. The images indicate their complete defeat, like vanished **smoke** (ephemeral at best, cf. Ps. 37:20) and molten **wax** (cf. Ps. 97:5; Mic. 1:4). [3] On the other hand, the rising of God produces ecstatic **joy** amongst **the righteous**. What

could cause greater celebration! Four **joy** words (out of seven in the Hebrew) stress the point. Contrast **before God** in verse 2 with verse 3.

The God of the unfortunate (vss. 4-6). [4] The psalm turns to another vision of God's victorious coming. The second line presents two possible translations (cf. RSV note). **Lift up** can refer either to casting up a highway (as Isa. 57:14; 62:10) or lifting **a song** (if the RSV is correct here), so that **song** or "highway" (note) is an added interpretive word, not in the original text. The Hebrew word rendered "deserts" (RSV note) can be easily emended to a word meaning **clouds**, and some maintain the legitimacy of that meaning even without emendation. Given the first line of the verse, the parallels in verse 33, Psalm 18:11, and Deuteronomy 33:26, the RSV text may be preferable. The Canaanite Baal was called "rider of the clouds," and this author may borrow and purge the term to show that Yahweh, not Baal, rules. Another "hybrid" possibility is to retain "cast up a highway" (note) in the first part, with **clouds** in the latter part of the line. The Hebrew word translated **Lord** is an unusual form involving a prefix and a shortened form of Yahweh. The shortened form is found only five times outside the Old Testament poetry, and the prefix remains puzzling.

[5] Verses 5-6 show the other side of the picture given in verse 2—God is fierce in judgment, yet tender in mercy. Social concerns were always strong in Israel. **Holy habitation** could be the temple, seen as a center of that faith which cared for the **fatherless and widows.** [6] Some scholars have suggested that verses 6ff. contemplate specific past events, others current problems, others that these were general observations. **The desolate** could be a man with no family, or, according to one suggestion, an unmarried man with no bride price. The Hebrew word rendered **prosperity** occurs only here in the OT. Other suggested translations are "with music" or "skillfully." **The rebellious** were probably within Israel. **God** is concerned to rectify social needs, either in provision or punishment.

The God of the wilderness (vss. 7-10). [7-8] Verses 7-10 review God's past care, centering in the exodus and the events at **Sinai**. Verses 7-8 parallel Judges 5:4-5, Deborah's song. **God** is now addressed in the second person, and the section is almost a thanksgiving. The RSV adds the second **quaked** (vs. 8) to give **yon Sinai** a verb, since it seems out of place in the verse otherwise. On **quaked**, see Exodus 19:16-18; Psalm 18:7-8. The deluge could be an oblique reference to the continuing need of the people for moisture. Thus, in worship this psalm could imply the people's concern that rains continue to come.

[9-10] Refreshing moisture makes a parched land fit for habitation. The exodus and wandering motif may be continued, or these verses may move to the possession of Canaan. Since **rain** is not a significant event in the exodus story, some would interpret it figuratively as the manna and quail. Others see it as an image for all his blessings. The Hebrew word rendered **flock** (vs. 10) is a dubious word which could refer to animals or to men. The RSV solves the problem by seeing God's people as a flock.

He scatters kings (vss. 11-14). [11] The psalm shifts again. Verses 11-14 open with the king's voice ringing authoritatively, either to direct his forces (cf. vs. 33), or to release the news of his triumph. At that word a great host bears **the tidings. Great . . . host** is a feminine plural, and could refer to the women in many places taking up the news with song and dance (cf. Judg. 5). [12] The jubilant message announces the rout of the Lord's foes, and the disappearance of danger. **Kings of the armies** (literally "hosts") are no match for the God of hosts. Another change of scene looks on the aftermath, as **the women** (the tiding bearers?) **at home divide the spoil.**

[13] The picture continues. This verse is not difficult to translate but is hard to interpret meaningfully. Why were the women **among the sheepfolds**? Some suggest this refers to tribes who went into battle only after reflection, or even not at all (cf. Judg. 5:16). Some would emend the Hebrew word translated "women" (vs. 12) to a word meaning "donkey"—"why lie about like a donkey?" Lines 2 and 3 are also enigmatic. One conjecture is that they are frag-

ments of a longer poem, lost to us. Does the **dove** depict Israel in victory, or the enemy in flight, or is it a figure for God's glory? Perhaps the reference is to some of the finery captured, and we see the women admiring themselves in their new wardrobes. Again, some object (a statue?) in the booty may be admired. And what is **green gold**? Perhaps it is another way of referring to yellow gold.

[14] Various attempts are made to explain this verse. **Scattered** is a forced translation of a Hebrew verb that usually means "spread." **Snow fell on Zalmon** is variously explained as (1) an otherwise unknown battle, perhaps one in which God helped his people through a blizzard; (2) a reference to the bleached bones on enemy skeletons; (3) the snowy appearance of abandoned armor; (4) defeated kings fleeing like driven snow-flakes against a dark background (**Zalmon** means dark); (5) the way God appeared among the people; or (6) as a fragment of a longer poem. **Zalmon** here probably has no connection with the man by that name mentioned in Judges 9:48.

The God of Zion (vss. 15-16). [15] Zion, physically, was only a hill. Loftier peaks might seem to represent God better, because of their greater size. But the importance of Zion made it so tower above the others that they are depicted as looking on enviously. This reflection on Zion's greatness may have accompanied some religious services on Zion. The Hebrew word rendered **mighty** (vs. 15) means literally "God" (Elohim). The translation "mountain of God," however, would lose the contrast the psalm intends. It has been suggested that God was once worshipped on **Bashan**, which was later supplanted by Zion. If that suggestion were valid, then **Bashan** could be called mountain of God in the past sense.

The exact mountain meant by **Bashan** is unknown. Suggestions include Jebel Druze and Mount Hermon (which has three peaks). The Hebrew term translated **many-peaked** occurs only here in the OT, and its exact meaning is somewhat doubtful. Note the prominence of mountains in this psalm—verses 8, 14-18. [16] The Hebrew term rendered **look with envy** (vs. 16) also occurs only here in the

OT. The ancient versions interpreted it variously, indicating some problem in knowing its exact meaning.

The exalted God (vss. 17-20). [17] The OT speaks of no such event as that recorded here. The language may be figurative for God's greatness, capsuling the history of the people **from Sinai** until the temple of Solomon, and investing it with appropriate glory. The vast **chariotry** might be a heavenly army, or a sweep of all Israel's forces. Perhaps we see here the magnificence of **Sinai** now being transferred to the temple. The last line has been emended in the RSV by adding one letter and dividing a word differently. Another possibility, keeping the Hebrew, would be "The Lord is among them, the God of Sinai. . . . "

[18] This may be military imagery reviewing the history of God's blessings from Sinai to the temple. Judges 5:12 has similarities to parts of this verse. **Captives** could be conquered peoples, or Israelites, now freed. **Gifts** may have been spoils of war or tributes to the victor. The word usually refers to offerings, which may imply the latter. The RSV adds **among** to smooth a difficult reading. Ephesians 4:18 uses these words of the victorious Christ enduing the church for its task. However, in Ephesians God gives, not receives, gifts. Verses 19-20 of this psalm do speak of gifts God gives men. The difference between the word translated "receives" and "gives" in Hebrew is only the order of the first two letters. The ancient Syriac version has "gave." Still, we do not know the complete history of the change from this text to Paul's usage.

[19] In verses 19-20 the psalmist blesses **God** for his gifts of **salvation.** Another translation could be "Blessed by God day by day, he bears us up." **Bears** indicates the idea of God carrying a load (cf. Isa. 46:1-4; 63:9). Compare with this verse Judges 5:2, 9. [20] **Salvation** is defined as **escape from death. Salvation** and **escape** are both plural, perhaps indicating repeated divine deliverances. The last line is awkward to translate and interpret. Was it escape from peril, or escape in battle? Was it an affirmation that even **death** is subject to God? Or is **death** a figure for any threat,

from which God removes the terror, to give security? The last may be the best understanding.

God is triumphant (vss. 21-23). [21] With unsparing pictures, verses 21-23 denote the certain victory of **God** over **his enemies** (cf. vss. 11-14, Judg. 5:26; Hab. 3:13). Shattered **heads** indicates absolute defeat. The Hebrew term rendered **hairy crown** occurs only here in the OT and other readings have been offered (cf. Deut. 32:42). Perhaps this refers to the growing of the hair for certain kinds of battles.

[22] A divine oracle is given, either about the enemies being brought from the places to which they have fled, or about Israel being brought home victorious, or (less likely) brought back from captivity after God freed them. **Bashan** and **the depths** may refer to the victory over Og, and the passage of the Red Sea, thus returning the psalm to the exodus motif. Others think the locales symbolize heights and **depths**, that is, God is with his people and gives victory in any circumstances. [23] The victory is gory. The first line is probably figurative, yet we must recall that those killed were the guilty (vs. 21). The difference between the RSV text and footnote is only one letter in a Hebrew verb.

The holy procession (vss. 24-27). [24-25] Verses 24-27 describe a cultic procession, caught up in praise (escorting the ark? Cf. 1 Chron. 13:8; 15:16-28). There is obviously a connection between the meaning of this procession and the psalm's theme of God's victorious procession through Israel's history. The text suggests that worshipers, viewing this parade, think of the greater march of God through the centuries. **God** is extolled as **king** for the first time in the psalm. **Seen** can be rendered as past tense (cf. RSV note). The Hebrew implies completed action. The idea may be that a given procession, viewed in the ceremony at which the psalm was sung, represented much more than just the one event.

[26] Though the RSV makes this the song of the procession, we must recall the Hebrew had no quotation marks. The Hebrew word translated **congregation** is plural, and could mean **great congregation** (as RSV; cf. Ps. 26:12) or

"in companies," referring to the various parts of the procession. **Fountain** can mean source (cf. Jer. 2:13; 17:13), so the reference may be to Israel (Jacob) as the father of the people (cf. a similar usage in Isa. 48:1; 51:1-2).

[27] **Benjamin** and **Judah** are from the south, and **Zebulun** and **Naphtali** from the north. These four may represent the entire nation. **Benjamin** was Saul's tribe, and **Judah** that of the Davidic dynasty. **Zebulun** and **Naphtali** are important in Judges 5, which is closely related to this psalm. The phrase **in the lead** translates a difficult Hebrew word, which literally means "rules over them." Some see here a reference to Saul's reign. The Hebrew expression rendered **in their throng** is also difficult. Other suggested translations include "honest spoken," "a heap of them," and "in their colored garments" (supported by one Hebrew manuscript and the Targum).

'**Show thy strength**' (vss. 28-31). [28] If verse 31 governs this section, verses 28-31 may be a prayer for victory over Egypt and Ethiopia. The psalmist clearly prays for God's power to be exhibited, whatever the occasion. The psalm has amply described God's power in past deeds. Now may the present and future be so blessed. There are various ways to translate this verse (cf. the modern versions). The first **God** renders "your God" in Hebrew (the RSV deletes "your"). However, many ancient versions support the RSV rendering. [29] This verse is similar to verse 18 and has affinities to Isaiah 18:7; 60:3-9; 66:20. God's glory, manifest through history, and symbolized by the **temple**, ideally draws tribute from other earthly monarchs. The Hebrew of the first line of this verse is difficult to render sensibly. Numerous readings have been offered, most of which are in harmony with the basic thought of the RSV.

[30] This verse is difficult in many aspects (cf. RSV note). Its gist is the power of God. The RSV refers to some oppressor power, perhaps Egypt (vs. 31). Others see the verse as a mythological reference to God's past victories (cf. Ps. 74:12-14; and regarding the calf, Exod. 32:21; Deut. 9:21), offering encouragement in the present situation. **Beasts** is interpreted as hippos or crocodiles. **Reeds** could

recall the crossing of the Red (Reed) Sea, thus the victory over Egypt. The Hebrew word rendered **bulls** means literally "mighty ones" (also Ps. 22:12; Isa. 10:13; 34:7). They, and **the calves**, no doubt symbolize nations from whom Israel was endangered. **The calves** may have been tributary nations to the **bulls**.

The third line varies widely in the ancient versions, indicating interpretive problems from early times. The Hebrew text literally means "trampling pieces of silver." The first two words, however, are dubious. If "trampling" is kept, it could refer to the animals in the previous lines, or to a self-trampling (groveling, cf. Prov. 6:3, note) by the defeated enemy as he offers **tribute**. The RSV makes it a prayer to God. It also renders the last line of the verse quite freely. The last line may explain the first three. The RSV changes **scatter** from the original Hebrew sense to an imperative, with the support of the ancient versions.

[31] Here the psalmist continues praying for the homage and tribute of the nations; he may have in mind the gifts of verse 29. On the submission of the Egyptians, see Isaiah 19; 43:3; 45:14. The translation **bronze** is based on a close similarity of the Hebrew to an Egyptian word with that meaning. **Hasten to stretch out** implies both submission and supplication.

Ascribe power to God (vss. 32-35). [32] The closing hymn (vss. 32-35) draws together main themes of the psalm and reiterates the call to praise (vs. 4). All men are bidden to celebrate God's victorious power wrought for and through his people.

[33-34] On rider of **the heavens**, see verse 4. On his **voice**, see verse 11. Compare also Psalm 18:10-13. As God rules the nations, so **Israel** is exalted. Their **power** is in the one who has all power. **Power in the skies** could imply natural phenomena. [35] God is awe-inspiring, as his **power and strength** touch earth. The **sanctuary** could be the temple (cf. vss. 15-18, 24-27) or the heavenly throne (cf. vs. 33).

Psalm 69: A Plea for Pity

This psalm, frequently quoted in the NT, shows a vulnerable man subjected to painful abuse, and desperate because of it. His cause is God's cause (vs. 9). The references to Zion and Judah, as well as verse 9, could imply the postexilic community, and an author whose religious zeal was evidenced in that context.

A cry for help in verses 1-4 shows the desperation of the poet's situation, and the power of his foes. After laying himself open before God (vs. 5) and praying on behalf of the faithful (vs. 6), the author depicts his situation in verses 7-21 (shamed, alienated, insulted, ridiculed, etc.). This is interspersed with prayer for redemption (especially vss. 16-18). Verses 19-20 particularly impress us with the depth of his agony. Verses 22-28 call a curse upon the foes. A transitional prayer leads to the praise in verses 30-36. By this point relief has come, or faith has grown to know it will come, and the psalm concludes with a universe-spanning summons to worship, with assurance that God will save (vs. 35).

'Save me, O God' (vss. 1-4). [1] Metaphors in verses 1-3 show the author's situation. Like a man almost drowned he faces death, the greatest enemy. The Hebrew expression rendered **up to my neck** means literally "up to life" (cf. vss. 14-15). [2] Mired, he cannot get adequate purchase to extricate himself. This may suggest a man trying unsuccessfully to ford a river, or one caught in sudden floods. Or verses 1-2 may contain figures for the threat of the netherworld—another way of describing the danger of death.

[3] If the figure of verses 1-2 continues, we imagine the trapped man screaming for help until exhausted, his strained **eyes** searching for succor. These images powerfully convey his emotional state.

[4] The author's foes are numerous, powerful, and unscrupulous. They disregard his innocence (**without cause**), perhaps preferring false charges against him. Verses 6-12 (especially vs. 9) indicate he was persecuted for his religious zeal. The last sentences of the verse may refer to a false charge, or express injured innocence, or be a declarative statement (i.e., he even gives up his rights).

Transitional statements (vss. 5-6). [5] Our author knows his humanness and does not try to hide his frailties from God (cf. Ps. 51:3-5). Let God condemn him if he must (cf. vs. 26), but he will not concede the condemnation of his foes. The poet may feel that such self-exposure is the appropriate prelude to petition, but the theme is not really developed within the psalm. [6] Though the exact meaning is unclear, the psalmist apparently wishes to see God's nature vindicated through resolution of his own problems. He has suffered for God (vss. 7-12), and, without divine response, others who hoped in God could be shamed and mistreated by hostile persons.

Shame and insults (vss. 7-21). [7-8] Though verses 7-8 may be a key to understanding the author's circumstances, they do not yield as much information as one might wish. It is clear that **reproach, shame,** and estrangement from his own family were the price of his fidelity to Yahweh. Zeal for God's house was also involved (vs. 9). **An alien** (vs. 8) was one foreign born, and to be thus isolated was especially serious in a society where the family group was so central. [9] **Zeal for thy house** (only here in the OT) may be a general statement for great dedication. The obvious meaning is that here was burning concern for temple reform, or for the rebuilding of the temple (if postexilic), or for the purification of worship. On the other hand, **house** could be a figure for the land or people, in which case the author could be disturbed by corruption in the nation. Whatever his cause, fever **consumed** (a strong word) him. This passage described Jesus' zeal for the temple in John 2:17. See also Romans 15:3.

[10-11] The author's dedication is expressed even more strongly with his references to **fasting** and **sackcloth.** We do not know if these were because of his own faults, or out of concern for some cause (such as suggested under vs. 9), or even out of concern for his adversaries. The Hebrew word translated **reproach** is the same as that found in verses 7 and 9 ("insults"). His foes might have interpreted his acts as admissions of sin and ridiculed him for that. **Byword,** the term often rendered "proverb," obviously has a derogatory

meaning here. [12] Even **drunkards** gossiped about him in public (**the gate**). The **songs** were doubtless uncomplimentary and perhaps even ribald in nature. Here is a picture of utter scorn for one of sincere religious zeal. To face such public ridicule would take strong conviction. The RSV takes some liberties with the last line, which means literally "and songs drinkers of strong drink."

[13-15] The author resumes his prayer (vss. 13-18), with his basic appeal to God's **steadfast love** and faithfulness. He trusts God to be absolutely dependable, even amidst the trauma and ridicule. **Acceptable time** (vs. 13) may be whenever it pleased God to answer, or it could apply to particular cultic occasions. The images of verses 1-2, now resumed, appear more terrible since the poet's circumstances have been further depicted. The death imagery now seems stronger, assuming **deep** and **pit** are synonyms for Sheol.

[16-18] These verses restate his plea, adding a note of urgency (**make haste**) and referring to a further divine attribute (**abundant mercy**). His appeal is as God's servant. Note his progress in petition from **hide not** (vs. 17) to **draw near** (vs. 18) to **redeem** to **set free**. [19] **Thou** is emphatic, indicating assurance that the prayer will be answered and offering an antidote to the writer's shame and heartbreak (cf. vss. 6-12). Though the burden is great, God knows. All will be well!

[20] Public shame was especially devastating in a close-knit society like Israel. The picture of a man heartbroken and alone is most pathetic. His grief was augmented by apparent lack of concern from those from whom he might have expected support. No wonder he calls for haste.

[21] There are cases in the OT where **food** was offered as a measure of comfort (2 Sam. 3:35; 12:17; 13:5, 6, 10), and some see a similar custom here. Later Judaism seems to have had a meal for the bereaved. To poison such **food** would be almost beyond conceiving. The word for **poison** is not specific, though the LXX has "gall." In the OT it is usually associated with wormwood, which was a particularly bitter potion. **Vinegar** was sour wine which could produce nausea. The meal concept may be literal, or else it

may be an image for betrayal. This passage appropriately describes the treatment accorded Jesus in his passion and is therefore quoted by all four gospels (Matt. 27:34; Mark 15:36; Luke 23:36; John 19:29).

Prayer for punishment (vss. 22-28). [22] Verses 22-28 contain a curse, asking God to activate his covenant love and justice. Could the poet be counteracting a curse his adversaries placed on him? Foes who have "poisoned his food" have a similar fate called down upon them, though we are not told how **their table** would be **a snare.** In some way their worship really becomes their undoing. The last line literally means "for security for a snare" (see RSV note). The RSV text makes a slight emendation, suggested by the Targum. The original reading implies that what they trusted would be their downfall. Verses 22-23 are quoted, with variations, in Romans 11:9-10.

[23-24] On **loins,** see Psalm 66:11. Verse 24 indicates that it is God's nature, and not just the poet's difficulties, that is at stake. This side of God contrasts with that seen in verses 13, 16. Yet every man chooses to experience one or the other. [25] May they be like a decimated army or a deserted bedouin tent. This passage is cited in Acts 1:20 of the defection of Judas. [26] The RSV notes indicate the textual problems in this verse. The RSV has chosen variant readings, though some translations render the literal Hebrew. In line one the RSV has changed the pronoun "you" to the sign of the direct object, though without a footnote reference. This verse introduces an unusual note, reminiscent of verse 5. The author may be saying that he accepts chastisement from God because of its justice, but is galled if unjust suffering from enemies is added. Yet there is still considerable mystery about the exact circumstance of **smitten** and **wounded.**

[27-28] These severe words probably assume the impenitence of the wicked. The psalmists generally do not think beyond their own problems to the possibility of a change of heart by their persecutors (as Christians might). Some, to alleviate the rigor of these verses, suppose they quote the enemies' curse upon the author, here given to

expose their hostile attitude which deserved **punishment**. But that would be intrusive and would not explain the use of the plural. On the **book** (vs. 28), see Exodus 32:32-33; Daniel 12:1; Luke 10:20; Revelation 3:5. [29] This verse moves from the curse toward the praise in verses 30-36. The poet returns to his own agony with a prayer (or with an expression of trust, for the last line could be so translated). **On high** implies safety in a spot where his enemies could not reach him.

Praise to God (vss. 30-36). [30] From the grimness of verses 22-28 the psalm now turns to the glory of **praise**, reasons for which are given in verses 33, 35-36. The rest of the psalm indicates worship, doubtless in a cultic context. **Thanksgiving** can mean either a thank-offering or songs of thanks (as probably here). [31] This does not deny the efficacy of animal sacrifice, nor even contrast it with a genuine inner piety (as Pss. 40:6-8; 50:8-13; 51:16-17). The contrast here is with thanks. The author may feel that thanks would **please** God more than sacrifice, because it was a very personal response to his own problems, rather than a more general act of worship. Or the poet may suspect that the cultic worship of some was inadequate, and he makes a contrast with them.

[32-33] This call is probably uttered because God's justice and covenant love is demonstrated in the author's life. Thus, others who are oppressed can take courage from his experience. **Bonds** may suggest another aspect of the poet's affliction, or may be a general or even figurative statement.

[34-36] A call to **praise** sweeps **heaven and earth**. The poet would have all creation acknowledge their Creator and his special goodness. He rules **heaven**, as well as **Zion**. Verse 35 seems to imply the postexilic period (contrary to the superscription), unless we have here a later addition to the psalm. See the discussion of Psalm 51:18-19. The psalm moves here from personal to national concern. Perhaps the author, acutely aware of God's goodness to him as one of the covenant people, now widens his thought to God's beneficence to the whole people. thus he projects a blessed future in the land for generations to come.

(For Psalm 70, see Ps. 40:13-17, which is identical.)

Psalm 71: Petition of an Elderly Man

This is the plea of an old man, who has been full of trust throughout his life, for God now to deliver him from enemies. Structurally, this fragmentary psalm follows no one particular type, though it is most like a lament. The author's intense concern can be seen by his frequent pleas for help. Verses 1-8 are such a plea, fortified by intermingled expressions of trust in God. Enemy activity against him, occasioning the prayer, is described in verses 9-11. Verses 12-13 renew the plea with a specific call for the accusers to be shamed. Verses 14-19 contain an intensified discussion of praise and a proclamation of God's goodness, which lead to the reassurance that God will deliver him (vss. 20-21). Verses 22-24 speak of worship with instruments and song, in celebration of God's response to his plea.

Plea for help (vss. 1-8). [1-2] Trust and pleading for help are the notes with which the psalm opens, and in which it will continue. Verses 1-3 are largely identical to Psalm 31:1-3. Verse 2 slightly expands the parallel in Psalm 31. **Righteousness** becomes a favorite thought in this psalm (vss. 2, 15, 16, 19, 24). **[3]** This amplifies the idea of verse 1. The RSV note, if authentic, introduces the word "continually," found also in verses 6, 14. The RSV text is here based on Psalm 31 and the LXX. The Hebrew text of Psalm 31 and the words in question here are similar enough that one might suppose a copyist's error.

[4-5] Here is a threefold description of the adversaries. **Unjust** might imply a false accusation. The Hebrew word translated **grasp** literally means "palm." In verse 5, the writer appeals both to his utter helplessness without God and to his lifelong trust in him. Past, present, and future are all centered in God.

[6] This verse is quite similar to Psalm 22:9-10. Present faith is the stronger because of a long life (cf. vss. 9-10) of trust. God who creates can also sustain. Who would God rescue, if not such a man? The translation **took** represents an emendation of the MT based on Psalm 22:10. The original Hebrew verb means "severed." [7] **A portent** is an extraordinary sign or wonder, and in the Bible always ultimately has God as its source. Thus, he could refer to the impact upon others of a trusting life or to God's saving help in his life. The RSV, with the adversative **but**, seems to indicate that God is a **refuge** despite the sign, which might imply his foes considered him a man punished by God (cf. vs. 11). However, **but** is not in the original Hebrew. [8] Either he is constantly in a worshipful mood, or he speaks to others of God, that is, he is an edifier. This is the consequence of God's care, and the basis of the following prayer.

'Forsake me not' (vss. 9-11). [9] We learn now that he is an **old** man, **strength** gone, whose situation may therefore seem more precarious. In his enfeebled condition he pleads not only for help, but even more for God's fellowship. Despite his trust, he appears to have come to a moment when God seems remote because of the pressure upon him. See Isaiah 46:3-4. [10-11] Now he unfolds the threatening peril. He is the victim of collusion. Because of his disadvantaged condition, his **enemies** think God's help is no longer available to him. Callously they move to their own advantage. Thus, he asks God both to vindicate the divine nature and to prove the villains wrong.

'Be not far from me' (vss. 12-13). Here again is the desperation caused by the seeming absence of God. See Psalms 22:11; 35:22; 40:13-14. The threefold imprecation in verse 13 asks that his enemies face their just deserts (cf. Pss. 35:4, 26; 40:15; 109:29). This is the only word against the adversaries in the psalm, for the author is more concerned to express trust than to curse. The Hebrew word rendered **accusers** is from the same root as that translated "Satan" (adversary).

'I will praise thee' (vss. 14-19). [14-15] Whatever his enemies do and whatever their future, this is *his* future. His response to the difficulty is increased **praise**, which includes recitation to others of God's saving **acts** (cf. vs. 8). This could be his continual practice, or a vow attendant upon his deliverance, or perhaps both. The last line of verse 15 means literally "though I know not tellings"—almost more impressive than the RSV's free rendering.

[16] The Hebrew word translated **praise** means literally "cause to remember." He offers back to God the grace he has received, which is all man can ever do. But this author realizes it, and that makes all the difference.

[17] Verses 15-19a deal with proclamation, using a series of terms to describe what **God** has done. **Thou hast taught me** may refer to his participation in the worship of the people. He continues to do what he has always done.

[18-19] He asks not to be hindered by opponents, for there is work yet to do. The RSV seems to be based on Psalm 22:30. However, **thy power** could be put with the previous thought—that is, "proclaim thy might to a generation, thy power to all that come." God's works are beyond comprehension and comparison!

Revival is near (vss. 20-21). [20] This verse introduces an unusual note, for the author sees God at the root of his troubles. Rather than complaint, this is a strong recognition that whatever happens is under God's oversight. The important thing is the hope for being revived and brought **up** (these two verbs could also be rendered in a jussive sense, that is, Revive! Bring up!). **Depths,** or waters below **the earth,** no doubt symbolize death, the ultimate foe. Even that is no barrier to God's power and the author's hope. Here is the height of faith. The endings on the Hebrew verbs translated **see, revive,** and **bring up** could be either plural or singular. The RSV accepts the latter, but some think this verse changes to consider the nation, perhaps for liturgical reasons. All in all, the RSV seems best. [21] The Hebrew word translated **honor** here is elsewhere always used of God (except in Esther). It may mean the gifts of God making life secure and enjoyable.

A celebration of God (vss. 22-24). [22-23] Verses 22-24 describe the public **praise** promised by the writer in response to God's **faithfulness** in delivering him. It is both vocal (vs. 22a) and instrumental (vss. 22b-23), thus involving the entire person. **Holy One of Israel** is a title found most often in Isaiah. [24] This verse sums up the concerns of the psalm. On the fate of the enemies, see verse 13, where **shame** and disgrace are also found. Their fate is described with Hebrew words indicating completed action, but the author may be speaking of what God will do, as if it were already accomplished. Note similar language in Psalm 35:26, 28.

Psalm 72: At the Crowning of the King

This is a royal coronation psalm, but it also may have been used between coronations in reminder and rededication. It sets forth the king's responsibilities and qualities, and the beneficent effects of his rule upon the people. Indeed, the vision is of the perfect ruler. The whole is predicated upon God's action through the monarchy, and therefore the king's obedience to God. The Targums later interpreted this of the coming messiah. It is the only royal psalm that deals at length with the king's responsibility to the poor, and can therefore be associated with Psalms 82 and 146.

Verses 1-4 pray for God to give the king justice and righteousness so he can rule well. Verses 5-7 bless the king with long life, and as benefactor to the land. Verses 8-11 stress his universal dominion. Verses 12-14 return to the king as the keeper of social justice. Verses 15-17 once more note the blessings upon the land and to all men from him. The last three verses are a doxology to Book II of the Psalter.

Prayer for righteous rule (vss. 1-4). [1] Righteousness and **justice** are derived from **God**, who is the ultimate ruler of the people. Thus, the psalm centers in the One whose gifts make possible the proper governance of the people. This significance is unfolded as the psalm progresses, especially in verses 2-4, 12-14. The Hebrew expression translated **royal son** means literally "son of the king," and it is here probably a synonymous parallel for **king**. **[2]** Verse 2 adds the monarch's concern for the **poor** (cf. vss. 4, 12-14). Thus, social justice is of paramount importance. Note the fourfold repetition of **thy** and also the repetition of **righteousness** in verses 1-3.

[3] **Prosperity** of a **people** under such a favored ruler is described as fruitful **mountains** and **hills** (whether crops or a lush cover of grass). Perhaps the implication is that material prosperity is God's intention when matters operate as he has ordained. **Prosperity** is *shalom*, "peace."

[4] This verse expands verse 2. The Hebrew term translated **defend the cause** is cognate to that rendered "justice" in verses 1-2. The presumption is that **the poor** and **needy** had been reduced to their state by injustice and unrighteousness. The king's role here expresses a twofold significance of civil government—delivering **the needy** and crushing **the oppressor.**

Blessings on the king (vss. 5-7). [5] Long live the present king (cf. vss. 7, 17; Ps. 89:37), and may the dynasty continue. The reading in the RSV note is possible, especially in light of the end of verse 4, but it does not fit the total thrust of the verse as well as the LXX (RSV text), which assumes a transposition of two letters of the original Hebrew word. The first line means literally "with the sun," which the RSV renders idiomatically.

[6] From blessing on the king, the text considers the blessing which the king is to the people, **like rain** upon which agriculture and therefore sustenance was so dependent. As rain encourages growth, so a good king encourages the good life. Some feel that rain would not benefit **mown grass**, and suggest the idea of grass ready for mowing. The Hebrew word rendered **water** literally means "dripping," so the RSV makes a slight emendation to arrive at its reading. [7] The ideal reign of the king offers a glorious picture of an almost utopian society. The reading **righteousness** is based on some Hebrew manuscripts and the versions. The text most often found in Hebrew is "a righteous man," perhaps indicating the king produces righteous subjects. The reading **abound** represents a slight emendation of the Hebrew.

Prayer for strong rule (vss. 8-11). [8] Verses 8-11 emphasize the ideal of the king's universal dominion. The Hebrew word translated **have dominion** has the same consonants as "falls" in verse 6—a possible play on words. The verbs allow this section to be rendered as a wish, like the RSV, or as future—"he will have, etc." **The River** is probably the Euphrates (cf. 1 Kings 4:21). **Sea to sea** could be from the Mediterranean to the Indian Ocean, or it could be a mythological reference to the cosmic seas surrounding Israel. The meaning, in any case, is a universal rule. Zechariah 9:10 is virtually identical with this verse.

[9] Here begins a series of descriptions of rival monarchs in homage before God's ruler. The reading **foes** (cf. RSV note) represents an emendation to square with the parallel in the next line. The original Hebrew word refers to an unknown desert creature (cf. Ps. 74:14).

[10-11] We do not know why these locales have been chosen to illustrate universal kingship. **Tarshish** is in Spain. **The isles** are probably those in the Mediterranean, **Sheba** (cf. vs. 15) was in southeast Arabia. The location of **Seba** is uncertain, but may be on the west coast of the Red Sea (Josephus said Ethiopia). The names are reminiscent of Solomon's reign, and there may be a deliberate allusion to his glory as a model for the current monarch. Israel never literally ruled all these areas. Verse 11 is a reprise of the theme of verses 8-10.

The king's justice (vss. 12-14). This section returns to the ideas of verses 1-4, stressing the king's concern for **the poor** and **needy**. He will see to it that **oppression and violence** do not displace justice in his kingdom, and look to the rights of those whom self-serving men of importance would ignore. Let any oppressor take care!

'Long live the king' (vss. 15-17). [15] The prayer of verses 5-11 resumes here (though the verbs in this section could also be translated as futures). The RSV adds **long** (cf. vs. 5). **Gold** may be a precious commodity chosen to symbolize the **blessings** of the last line. Those **blessings** are enumerated through verse 17. [16] Some of the ideas of verses 6-7 are reintroduced here. The good life is insured by a righteous king, and thus God rules the moral realm and the natural world. The Hebrew word translated **abundance** is difficult, and is used only here in the OT. **Grain** does not usually grow on moutain **tops**, so this may be poetic for overflowing crops. The Hebrew verb translated **wave** sometimes describes the tremors of an earthquake. Some would suggest for it here the meaning "grow thickly." It seems to go with the next line, but since that makes little sense, the RSV moves it to the present location. The RSV adds **men** in the fourth line of the verse, since the verb lacks a subject, and **grain** would not fit. The meaning is difficult, but may refer to a growing population.

[17] See verse 5. The Hebrew word rendered **fame** is literally a repetition of that translated **name**. Some prefer **name** and would refer it to the king's posterity. **Continue** is a dubious reading. Another possibility is "have issue, be productive," which could be interpreted of his successors. The king would be a blessing to all **men**. Thus the psalm closes uniting the concept of the king with the blessing of Abraham (Gen. 12:3; 18:18; 22:18), so that he fulfills God's purpose in electing a chosen people.

A doxology (vss. 18-20). [18-19] Most scholars believe the remaining verses are a doxology to Book II of the Psalter (cf. Ps. 41:13). These verses are also appropriate, however, to the theme of Psalm 72, since it is **God** who makes the king what he should be! The RSV omits an extra "God" from line one of verse 18, in accordance with the LXX. On **wondrous things**, see Psalms 9:1; 40:5.

[20] Since many of the psalms in Books I and II have Davidic superscriptions (fifty-five of seventy-one), these words indicate subsequent psalms would not be of that type (with occasional exceptions—the next is Ps. 86). This ending may have originated when, in the formation of the Psalter, no other psalms **of David** followed.

Psalm 73: On the Prosperity of the Wicked

This psalm probes the question of the prosperity of the wicked, as the author moves from a nearly destructive doubt to a height of faith. He speaks for and to any in Israel who may have faced the same difficulty in their understanding of God.

The writer begins by stating his conclusion (vs. 1), after which he speaks of a problem so severe that he "well nigh slipped" (vss. 2-3). It was the increasing popularity of wicked, arrogant men, resulting in a popular skepticism regarding God's moral judgment (vss. 4-12). The writer, a righteous man, was rankled because his goodness seemed unavailing (vss. 13-14). Yet he held his peace, though his inner turmoil grew (vss. 15-16), until, in the temple, resolution finally came (vs. 17). Eventually God would judge the wicked (vss. 18-20), and the author berates himself for having doubted (vss. 21-22). Further, the psalmist's fellowship with God transcended anything the wicked might have (vss. 23-26). Thus, the psalm concludes where it began, reminding the readers that those far from God shall perish (vs. 27), but that the man near him is blessed (vs. 28).

The problem stated (vss. 1-3). [1] It is well that the author opens with the statement, for, as he moves in the opposite direction, we can recall that he is in the process of coming back to this opening point. His faith is hard won. He will learn that God's goodness is more substantial than the personal material prosperity an Israelite might have expected. Purity of **heart** (inner singleness of dedication) is far more important than wealth. The Hebrew word for "Israel" (cf. RSV note) has been divided by the translators into words meaning **upright** and **God** for the sake of meter and parallelism. Though some translators keep **God**, thus finding it twice in the verse, the RSV drops it. The footnote reading would imply that all within Israel were **pure in heart**, which the rest of the psalm shows was not the case.

[2] With striking frankness the author notes how he almost lost his faith, like a man so befuddled and hindered he could hardly walk. Though not an easy statement to make, his is one with which many readers can identify.

[3] Would it not seem logical that God's blessings would be disbursed to those serving him most faithfully? Was that not God's covenant promise to Israel (Deut. 28:15-19)? But the opposite was happening, to the author's perplexity. Not only was his very concept of God challenged, but his desire for life's bounty led to envy.

The apparent state of the wicked (vss. 4-12). [4] A lengthy description of the wicked expands on verse 3.

They are the paradigm of health and prosperity. The first line, in Hebrew, means "for there are no pangs in their death," which the RSV emends by a change of one letter and a different word division. The RSV implies that they have no illnesses or afflictions while they live, while the Hebrew indicates they died peacefully. The change assumes it would be out of place to speak here of the death of the wicked (cf. vss. 17-20). The last line means literally "and fat their body." [5] Free from the misfortunes that strike others (does the author have himself in mind—cf. vs. 14), it almost seems that God is specially blessing these people, rather than simply refraining from punishing them. Of course, the author's feelings have no doubt led him to exaggerate.

[6] The prosperity of the wicked intensifies their defiance of God, as verses 6-12 point out. The **necklace** was sometimes a status symbol. **Violence**, to them, was as natural as their own clothing, or characterized them as completely as clothing **covers** one. They are blatant with their arrogance. [7] This poet is a master of description, as he depicts the avaricious oppressor, obese from his **follies**. The picture is either of protruding **eyes** or of **eyes** glistening from puffy, shining cheeks. Contrast **follies** (literally "conceit," "imagination") with the author as portrayed in verses 13-14.

[8] Scoffing, **malice** (literally "evil") and arrogance (cf. vs. 3) are added. Scoffing sets the stage for the more complete depiction in verse 9. [9] They are guilty of unconcealed irreligion, which consequently influences the people (vs. 11). However, the Hebrew preposition translated **against** could also be rendered "in," that is, they speak as if they were gods, in control of the world. The substantial difference in the two translations may not be that great. **Struts** freely renders the Hebrew verb usually translated "walks." It pictures men who think they can do as they will with impunity. Polemics against misuse of the **tongue** are often found in the psalms.

[10] This verse literally means "therefore his people return thither [or "he will bring back his people here"], and

abundant waters are drained by them." Attempts to understand it arrive at varied interpretations. Some see a restoration of **the people**, perhaps from the depredations of the
wicked, but this is hard to relate to the next verse. Others
find a reference to the evil drowning men, or to men
"drinking up" wickedness. The RSV has chosen, instead,
to emend slightly the Hebrew text for a smoother reading
which fits the thought of verse 11.

[11] For a pious person, one of the worst results of evil
lives is their effect upon society. Other people conclude
that **God** is uninvolved in relating morality and blessing. If
one were to evaluate life from this worldly perspective, of
what use would faith be? This puzzled the psalmist. What
reason would there be for a moral base to society, or for
adherence to Yahweh? [12] This verse ends the description
of **the wicked**. There seems no cessation to the doleful
situation. They are prosperous for ever (**always at ease**),
and their wealth increases. It is a galling experience for the
poet, especially for the reason he is about to reveal.

[13] Why should he struggle to be pure if people were
right in saying that God has no moral concerns? Circumstances seemed to vindicate them. Not that the author
wanted reward—he rather wanted meaning. [14] Not only
have his activities been vain, he has been **stricken and
chastened**, as if he were the sinner. Matters seem topsy
turvy. We do not know what the writer's suffering was,
unless it was the inner agony he has been describing. The
RSV has changed the verb in the last line from active to
passive by a slight emendation.

The true end of the wicked (vss. 15-20). [15] Now the
psalm turns and we are told how the problem was worked
out. He felt strongly the power of tradition and the community, and out of regard for them constrained his doubts. He
did not wish to damage the faith of others (contrast vs. 11).
He could not deny God's past actions, though they seemed
inconsistent with the present. [16] His mental struggles
continued, growing increasingly tiring (the last line means
literally "trouble it in my eyes." He could neither abandon
nor mentally reconcile the faith. Yet in view of the subse-

quent resolution, we suppose his thinking was leading to an answer even while he was unaware of it. [17] Then—**the sanctuary**, and resolution! There is no indication that the external circumstances changed. But in that place where the whole relation of God and his people, as well as one's personal piety, focused, the writer changed within. In the place where faith was affirmed, his own found heart's ease. What happened? A word, an act, a ritual? We do not know. But eternal realities were reaffirmed and the poet was enabled to see beyond the present. He probably did not learn a new truth, but rather broke through to a truly meaningful acceptance of an old one. He saw the **end** (literally "their afterward") of the wicked. He recognized the inevitable outworkings of the divine purpose. What this was he explains in the following verses.

[18] First (vss. 18-20), the doom of the wicked is sure. Their footing will not sustain, no matter how surely they seem to stand (cf. Ps. 35:6; Jer. 23:12). Surely the author was intellectually aware of this before. But he had to be inwardly convinced and experience a reaffirmation of his trust that God was indeed what Israel claimed he was.

[19] The wicked will come to a swift, decisive, calamitous demise. The second line of the Hebrew stresses this by the use of two verbs. The author still does not know why God's judgment has been delayed, but that is no longer his basic concern. God's eternal nature is a more decisive datum than the scene around him. The wicked will discover **terrors** (cf. Job 18:11, 14; 24:17; 27:20; 30:15).

[20] The RSV contrasts what seemed to be the stability of the arrogant with their true state when the illusory is stripped away. What he so colorfully depicted in verses 4-12 he recognizes as dreams and **phantoms** (literally "images") to be given no real heed, but despised. This translation in the RSV, based on an emendation, is problematic. Many would retain "Lord" (RSV note) and attempt a translation centering on the idea of the Lord despising the phantoms of the wicked.

Faith despite the problem (vss. 21-28). [21-22] Now he describes a new stage in his pilgrimage. He reflects on his previous attitude and recoils with disgust. He has been delivered from his former bitterness. **Beast** (vs. 22) is plural in Hebrew, probably to intensify the idea. On **stupid**, see Psalms 49:10; 92:6; 94:8.

[23] This great statement of personal faith in verses 23-26 is one of the high points of the entire Psalter. His second reason for his change of attitude is that he knows a fellowship with God that the wicked do not enjoy. It includes God's intimate care, counsel, glory, and strength. Again these are inner realizations of spiritual reality, for externals regarding the wicked seem unchanged. Verses 23-26 contrast with the fate the wicked must ultimately face, and the contrast is summed in verses 27-28. The poet does not explain how he can **continually** be **with** God and still have his problems. Instead, he rises to a higher level. Part of his reassurance no doubt comes because of heightened awareness of what it means to be one of God's covenant people. So with intimate image he envisions God holding his **right hand**.

[24] The Hebrew word translated **afterward** is the same as that rendered "end" in verse 17—an interesting contrast. Just what is the author's expectation? Some argue that **glory** (or "honor") means he contemplates vindication in this life. But many feel that he affirms that if divine concern is so sure, and it does not seem obvious in this life, might it not be worked out beyond life? Is he not also God over death? Recall Enoch (who was also "received up"—the same Hebrew word appears both here and in Gen. 5:24), Elijah, Elisha, and Ezekiel 8:14. True, the Hebrew word rendered **glory** is used nowhere else in the OT in the sense of heavenly or eternal, and the LXX sees no future life here. Yet it is possible that a germinal thinker forged beyond the boundaries of most Hebrew thought of his time. This may be what he would have when heart and flesh failed (vs. 26). Compare the similar thinking in Psalms 16:11; 49:15.

[25] Material things no longer make him envious as before. **Nothing upon earth** (and perhaps no pagan deity) can win his heart. He who has God has all else, save rebellion.

When and how he will have anything, he leaves to God. The RSV translates somewhat freely. **But thee** is added to complete the sense in English. **[26]** Now the poet truly trusts him who sustains **for ever**, not in that which is ephemeral (contrast vs. 14). The Hebrew word rendered **strength** means literally "rock" (cf. RSV note). **Portion** probably indicates that his possession (parcel of land) is God, not riches. The poet has not lost sight of his suffering, but has transcended it.

[27-28] The thought returns to the fate of the wicked (vss. 17-20). This is where the author might have been had he surrendered his faith (the Hebrew term translated **false** in vs. 27 literally means "commit fornication"). Instead he knows the blessings of verse 28. The contrast of these two verses is caught in the terms **far** and **near**. In his pilgrimage he has come from skepticism to evangelism (**tell . . . works**), which flows from his own experience and insight.

Psalm 74: The Desolation of the People

The temple has been destroyed, the people have been cast off, there is no responsive prophetic activity, and the name of God is dishonored. Yet the people recall God's saving acts of yore, and plead for their repetition upon the present occasion. See Psalms 79 and 137, which are similar to Psalm 74.

The most likely view sees this psalm as a response to the destruction of Jerusalem in 587/586 B.C. Verse 9 may argue against this, but see the discussion there. Other scholars have suggested the reign of Artaxerxes Ochus (359–338 B.C.), the Maccabean period (now generally rejected), or an otherwise unknown event of the fifth through second centuries B.C. A non-historical interpretation holds that the psalm refers to a ritual drama connected with the New Year festival. The date of 587/586 B.C. seems most likely, though the psalm may have been edited for later use. The use of the psalm in worship may have been accompanied by fasting (cf. 1 Sam. 7:5-6; 1 Chron. 20:1-19; Zech. 7:1-6; 8:18-19).

Verses 1-3 call for God's saving power to be reaffirmed for

the "forgotten" congregation, with special attention to the ravaged sanctuary (vss. 3, 4-8). There is no longer any prophet (vs. 9). How long will God allow this state of affairs (vss. 10-11)? Then a splendid hymn of God's creative, governing, and saving power is interspersed (vss. 12-17), no doubt as a rationale for the prayer. Verses 18-23, with various modes of appeal, again call upon God to act for the sake of his name, his people, his covenant, and his cause.

The author often notes that it is God's interests that are being damaged (vss. 1-4, 7-8, 10-11, 18-22). The central appeal is for God's sake, not the people's. But action for his interests will also be to their benefit.

'Why dost thou cast us off?' (vss. 1-3). [1] The people have suffered long, and they feel the time for relief is certainly overdue (note "perpetual" or **for ever** also in vss. 3, 10, 19). There is no word about the injustice of their adversity, but only wonder that it continues. Did they believe they had suffered long enough for their sins, or had they repented and thus expected the load to be lifted? We cannot say. The perplexity is not resolved within the psalm. However, it is illumined by a faith that God would act. The reference to **sheep** may be a plea for the shepherd's tenderness to replace wrath.

[2] Appeal is made to God's choice of his people (**congregation** equals nation), referring to the exodus and the choice of **Zion** (see 2 Sam. 7:12-13; 1 Kings 6:11-13; Ps. 132:13-14). Why choose them, if he is not going to preserve them? May his original grace again be decisive in reversing untoward circumstances! It is God's cause that is at stake.

[3] OT poetry sometimes exaggerates to make a point. God knew about the ruined **sanctuary**, but the people urge him to notice the destruction, assuming he will then surely act! **Perpetual** again stresses the long continued situation, and wonder at the divine inactivity. Perhaps they feared that if God did not act, people would draw the wrong conclusion about his nature and power. Like a tour guide, the author recounts the razing of the temple in verses 4-8. The last line means literally "all the evil (of) the enemy in the

holy place," which the RSV has rendered more freely for clarity.

The desecration (vss. 4-8). [4] We flash back and see the ravaging of the **holy place** by manlike beasts. Or, if another interpretation of the word for **holy place** be accepted, the appointed feasts were desecrated. For the appropriate furniture (ark, holy utensils?), enemy **signs** are placed. Various suggestions have been made regarding these (military standards, pagan religious symbols), but their true nature is unknown.

[5] The RSV translates this verse as apparently describing the destruction of the temple woodwork, relying on the ancient versions, since the Hebrew text is most obscure (cf. RSV note). **[6]** The carvings (the RSV adds **wood**, but the reference could be to engravings on metal or stone) were chopped and beaten away. If this were **carved** work, overlaid with gold (cf. 1 Kings 6:21-22, 29), then the metal might have been stripped away. This spoliation of physical treasure was a sad symbol of the greater value which was being desecrated.

[7] Worse was the conflagration destroying the temple. What did it imply of God that the **dwelling place of** his **name** was reduced to ashes? **[8]** The foes felt that the people could be subdued if their cultic activity were terminated, but the very presence of this psalm shows how wrong they were. The faith was not so simply put down. The Hebrew term translated **meeting places** is the same word rendered "holy place" in verse 4. It can also mean "appointed feasts," but that meaning here would require a different verb.

'How long?' (vss. 9-11). [9] The outlook is bleak. The **signs**, whatever they were (religious, military, civil), symbolized the way life had been and was no more. Absence of a **prophet** is the reason that some deny that this psalm describes the destruction of the temple in 587/586 B.C. (which it otherwise fits so well). Ezekiel and Jeremiah were still active. But absence of prophecy might be meant in other senses, as appears from Lamentations 2:9 and Ezekiel 7:26. The verse might simply reflect the despondent mood of the time. Also, from the time Jeremiah was carried away into Egypt, there was no prophet in *Israel* (Ezekiel was in Babylon). Or perhaps the meaning was that **no prophet** knew **how long**. There are enough possible explanations to warrant the conclusion that this verse could refer to the fall of Jerusalem in 587/586 B.C.

[10-11] The description of the travail ends in verse 10. The final profanation is of the very **name** of **God**. If his people were captured and his temple destroyed with impunity, might not the foes reason he was unconcerned, or powerless, or worse? A strong appeal is made for God to act to vindicate his **name** (vs. 11). The last line of verse 11 means literally "and your right hand from the midst of your bosom consumes" (cf. note). But why should God's hand be consumed? The RSV, by changing one letter in the Hebrew, arrives at the meaning in the text.

Hymn of faith (vss. 12-17). [12] An individual voice now breaks in with a hymn to God's power over creation—it is a striking interlude amidst the deep emotion of the lament. This is the **God** the people know. Surely he will vindicate himself in the present case. Compared with the mighty deeds of **God** portrayed in verses 12-17, the oppressor previously described seems small indeed. Israel's monarch is still the most powerful of kings.

[13] In verses 13-17 ten statements are made about God. Division of **the sea** could refer to creation, or to the exodus, or to both. **Dragons** could symbolize the primeval chaos which God ordered in the beginning. Or they could represent the Pharaoh (as in Ezek. 29:3; 32:2), if the exodus is in mind. The psalmist may have deliberately combined the two events for effect. [14] **Leviathan** (the crocodile) is also a mythological creature (in the Canaanite epics, he is slain by Baal), here perhaps representing the Pharaoh. A later Jewish legend said that the pious, in a future age, would receive the flesh of Leviathan as a festal meal. The **food** could be the goods which the departing Israelites took with them from Egypt. It could also refer to the carcasses of the Egyptians, consumed by scavengers. The RSV assumes that "people" (cf. RSV note) is a refer-

ence to animals, since there was no cannibalism with the Egyptian corpses. The NEB has "sharks."

[15-16] God opens up water sources (cf. Exod. 17:6; Num. 20:8) and dries others (the Red Sea, the Jordan). The forces of nature are under his control. Also he controls the heavenly bodies (vs. 16). The Hebrew word rendered **luminaries** is singular, so that it could refer to the moon. Or it could be a collective for all heavenly bodies besides **the sun**. As the seasons continued, so God's power continued to be manifested. So, the poet hopes, it would be with God's saving power.

[17] **Boundaries** could refer to national boundaries. Or they could be divisions of seasons, as in the last of the verse. Whatever the meaning, the general reality is God's sovereign governance of all men and the universe. In this hymn, the author goes beyond the immediate agony to a highly exalted vision, which offers a renewed perspective on the immediate situation.

'Arise O God' (vss. 18-23). [18] The remaining verses of the psalm, harking back to verse 2, contain a prayer for deliverance. Scoffing and reviling pick up the thought of verse 11. Thus, the description of God (vss. 12-17) is bracketed by similar references to the indignities paid Yahweh. **Impious** translates the Hebrew word *nabhal* (also vs. 22), which refers to the impudent and shameless. The term is often translated "fool," as in Psalm 14:1. [19] It would seem that the **dove** had already been delivered **to the wild beasts**, since the city was destroyed. Perhaps the key word is **for ever**—that is, do not let the situation continue without surcease. The same Hebrew word is translated both **wild beasts** and **life**. Perhaps the author intended a play on words, with the same term (out of only four words in Hebrew) expressing both the danger and the preservation of God's people.

[20] **Dark places** probably symbolize locales away from the light of the divine countenance. Some have suggested hiding places where fugitives from the city were tracked down. Others see a figure for the portals of death. It is no doubt a way of saying any place they have gone confronts

them with the same tragedy reflected in the destruction of the sanctuary. [21] The humiliation is intense, and **the downtrodden** and **needy** beg it be continued no longer. How can they **praise** in their terrible circumstances? They long to worship God for deliverance.

[22-23] A final plea is almost a curse. A last time **God** is besought to defend his glory and **cause**. The **foes** are, in the final analysis, God's foes. The people identify their cause with him, and his seeming failure makes their lot hard to bear. This is one of the more pessimistic laments, with its suffering undiminished (cf. Pss. 39, 88). Yet there is still prayer and faith, and this may be the main way it speaks to believer through the ages.

Psalm 75: God the Righteous Judge

Though this psalm begins as a thanksgiving, much of it has a prophetic ring. It seems also to indicate a worship context, so that some consider it a prophetic liturgy.

There are several speakers. In verse 1, it is the congregation. In verses 2-5 a divine word is given. Verses 6-10 come from an individual, perhaps a temple official. If this latter figure also delivers the divine word in verses 2-5, then we have a congregational statement in verse 1, with an individual responding from varying perspectives.

The theme is the sovereignty of God in judging, with emphasis on the exaltation of the righteous and the bringing down of the wicked (cf. 1 Sam. 2:1-10 and Luke 1:46-55). These words call Israel to trust in such a God, not in any other power. After the congregational thanks and reference to God's wondrous deeds (vs. 1), the Lord speaks of his stabilizing governance of the world (vss. 2-3 which leads to a warning against arrogance (vss. 4-5). The same themes are restated in verses 6-8, with the culminating reference to God's cup of judgment (vs. 8). A final reprise brings the central concerns of the psalm into the praise of God (vss. 9-10).

Introduction (vs. 1). The congregation expresses **thanks to God**, though the particular occasion is unknown. Does **wondrous deeds** imply some specific episode? God's acts may have been recounted in worship. However, the RSV footnote reading is also possible.

'Do not boast' (vss. 2-8). [2] The theme of God as **judge** is introduced. Judgment is not subject to human whim or caprice. God sets the time and does that which is entirely fair. Only those who had known the sting of injustice could fully appreciate this confidence in God. [3] The foci of this verse are instability and stability, **the earth** and God. Behind all that trembles is that which is beyond any shock. Such a God, upon whom all order, moral and otherwise, is dependent, can surely be trusted to judge with equity.

[4-5] These verses, apparently under the image of a thick-necked, mightily horned bull, warn the boaster against exalting himself. In fact, the concept of exaltation is extended in verses 6-7, 10. The **horn** symbolizes strength and pride (cf. Pss. 18:2; 89:17; 92:10; 112:9; 132:17; 148:14). [6-7] The speech of God ends, but the argument against pride continues. **Lifting up** is God's prerogative (vs. 7). Therefore, any earthly power, despite its claims, is impotent to control history ultimately. The Hebrew term translated **lifting up** (vs. 6) could also be translated "mountains." Some, seeing **wilderness** as signifying the south, interpret mountains of the north, and thus find here the four points of the compass.

[8] The image in which judgment is depicted changes now to **a cup** of **wine** given to the wicked (cf. Pss. 11:6; 60:3; Isa. 51:17; etc.). The content of the **cup** is doubtless God's wrath. **Mixed wine** contained ingredients that made it more intoxicating. It will be drunk **to the dregs.** We can picture the drinkers staggering about in a God-induced stupor. He has controlled them. Thus, the idea of God's sovereignty is continued from earlier verses. This is the only place in the psalm that Yahweh **(Lord)** is used.

Praises to God (vss. 9-10). An individual concludes the psalm with praise. This is followed by a reiteration of the judgments on the **wicked** and the **righteous** with which the psalm has been concerned. For the first time, **the horns of the righteous** (cf. vss. 4-5) are noted, perhaps showing they are given strength from **God. Rejoice** (vs. 9, cf. RSV note) involves a change of only one letter from the MT, and fits the parallel, **praise**, better. However, "declare" is not impossible. The "wondrous deeds" (vs. 1) may have been the subject of the declaration.

[10] In verse 10, the RSV changes "I" (note) to **he**, since the author would hardly be the one to accomplish the judgments of which the verse speaks. To retain the Hebrew, one would need to suppose that the Lord speaks in verse 10, while a different "I" speaks in verse 9.

III

Psalms 76–150

Clyde M. Miller

Psalm 76: God Is Glorious, Majestic, and Terrible
"To the choirmaster," used frequently in the psalm titles, could be translated "for the leader," and could refer to the leader of the temple singers, to a priest, or even to a king. The word "neginoth" (KJV) refers to stringed instruments in contrast to wind instruments. "A psalm of Asaph" could mean a psalm written by Asaph or by one of the members of his guild of temple singers, or it could mean a psalm authorized or collected by the Asaph guild. This guild extended from David's day into postexilic times. A "song" (Heb. *shir*) refers to a happy, joyous song. Since many, if not most, of the psalm titles were added long after the writing of the psalms, it is better to interpret each psalm on the basis of its text rather than by its title.
This psalm treats a familiar theme in the Psalms: God, as king, is triumphantly victorious over his enemies. God's enemies are frequently also Israel's enemies; therefore God's victory is theirs as well.

There is no way to determine what specific event, if any, prompted the writing of the psalm. The title in the LXX, "A Song for the Assyrian," suggests that it refers to Sennacherib's defeat in his effort to destroy Jerusalem in 701 B.C. However, verse 1 would seem to suggest a time during the period of the United Kingdom. The psalm could well reflect the glorious days of David after God had given him rest from his enemies round about (2 Sam. 22; Ps. 18).

This psalm blends historical, cultic, and eschatological material. The first two stanzas look back to past deliverance granted by Yahweh (vss. 1-6). In the third stanza (vss. 7-9), there is a glimpse of the final judgment at which time all the earth will be judged and all the oppressed liberated. The cultic element is emphasized in the fourth stanza (vss. 10-12), where the paying of vows in response to divine deliverance is stressed. The prophets and psalmists often use past judgments of God as evidence of the final judgment of the world. This contemplation leads to exhortations to be faithful to God.

The psalm is symmetrically divided into four stanzas of three verses each. As frequently, God is pictured as dwelling in Jerusalem where he had chosen to put his name (vss. 1-3). This feature identifies the psalm as a Zion psalm (cf. Pss. 46–48, 84, 87, 122). God accepted David's choice of Jerusalem as a permanent resting place for the ark of the covenant (cf. 2 Sam. 7; 1 Kings 8; Pss. 24, 132). God was thought to dwell symbolically over the cherubim overshadowing the mercy seat (cf. Exod. 25:22). God is highly praised because of a great victory won for his people (vss. 4-6). God is terrible when his anger is aroused, and no one can stand against him (vss. 7-9). When man recognizes God's wrath as but a manifestation of his mighty power, proper homage will be paid to God (vss. 10-12).

The psalmist expands his spiritual horizons from a consideration of God's provincial care of Israel (vss. 1-6) to his universal control of humanity (vss. 7-12).

God's presence in Zion (vss. 1-3). This stanza contains three synonymous couplets, which means that each verse contains a single thought. **[1] Is known** and **is great** are synonymous phrases indicating God's renown. **Judah** and **Israel** include the whole covenant people. **[2] His abode** (Heb. *sukko*) could be from the Hebrew word *sokh*, meaning a natural thicket, covert, or lair; or it could be from *sukkah*, meaning a man-made thicket, tent, or tabernacle (KJV, NASB, NEB). **His dwelling place** (Heb. *me'onatho*) is from the feminine noun *me'onah*, which derives from the verb *'un*, to dwell. The noun, in either the masculine or feminine, can refer to the lair or den of wild beasts, or in a figurative sense to desolated, depopulated cities. It can also refer to human habitations or to the divine dwelling place, as in the present passage. "Battle-quarters" (NEB) is without textual warrant. **Salem**, an old name for Jerusalem (cf. Gen. 14:18), is synonymous with **Zion**, often used to indicate the entire city rather than merely the specific hill of Zion. **[3]** God's presence in Jerusalem is demonstrated by his defending the city from foreign armies. **Flashing arrows**, literally "fiery shafts of the bow" (NASB, margin), is likely a poetic metaphor either for fire-tipped arrows or for the lightning speed of the arrows. **Weapons of war** is literally "battle," but frequently means the necessary things for carrying on warfare. In this context where **the shield** and **the sword** are mentioned, the latter definition applies. These terms are used synonymously in this passage. It is God's defense of Jerusalem or the nation that causes his name, that is, his character, to be known in Israel (vs. 1).

Though God is omnipresent, that is, everywhere at once (Ps. 139:1-12), he is represented as symbolically dwelling in Jerusalem. Solomon, in his prayer of dedication for the temple, recognized the fact that God cannot be contained in material structures (1 Kings 8:27).

The foe falls at the Lord's rebuke (vss. 4-6). This stanza contains four synthetic couplets in which the second line of each couplet adds something to the thought of the first line. **[4]** Drastic emendation of the text is not necessary. (NEB omits 4b.) Our text, which follows the LXX, is sufficiently clear, although the Hebrew for **the everlasting mountains** reads "the mountains of prey" (KJV, NASB). Our text assumes that the word '*adh*, which can mean either "prey" or "everlasting," was misinterpreted by a copyist who then inadvertently wrote the word *tereph*, "prey." While it is true that the phrase **the everlasting mountains** is a common Hebrew expression (cf. Deut. 33:15; Hab. 3:6), there is nothing difficult in the Hebrew text of our passage as it stands. "The mountains of prey" can be understood as the place from which God had taken spoil as he conquered the foe. "This may be a compressed expression for the mountains which are the haunts of predators" (Derek Kidner, *Psalms 73–150,* TOTC, p. 274, n. 2). **[5-6]** The word **sleep** is apparently an allusion to death (KJV, NASB), as is the word **stunned**. God's glory and majesty (vs. 4) are manifested in his victory over the enemy. The word **rider** (cf. NASB, NEB) is from *rekhebh,* meaning "chariot" (KJV). Probably "charioteers are intended" (A. Cohen, *The Psalms,* SBB, p. 244). It is hardly appropriate to say that chariots **lay stunned,** or "were cast into a dead sleep" (KJV).

God's universal judgment (vss. 7-9). This stanza extends the central idea of the first two, in that it looks to the judgment of all men. It employs synthetic parallelism and is pregnant with temporal and purpose clauses emphasizing the divine purpose in judgment. The change from the second person (vss. 7-8) to the third (vs. 9) demonstrates the change from prayer in the form of praise to a didactic element uttered for the edification of the congregation at worship.

[7] God's **anger is roused** against the arrogant oppressors. **Terrible** (Heb. *nora'*) is not too strong a translation in this context. **[8]** When God utters judgment, the world fears (*yare'ah,* a cognate of *nora',* vs. 7). **From the heavens** reveals that the psalmist understood that God's throne is actually in heaven (cf. vs. 2). **Thou didst utter** is literally "thou didst cause to be heard" (KJV, NASB). The meaning is that God pronounced sentence (cf. NEB) against the evildoers. **[9]** God's purpose in his judgment was **to save all the oppressed of the earth.** The translations **oppressed** and "meek" (KJV) or "humble" (NASB, NEB) reflect a possible difference in meaning between the Hebrew words *'ani* and *'anaw,* but it is likely that they are only two different forms of the same word (cf. BDB, p. 776). When the oppressed are declared to be saved by the Lord, it should be understood that in addition to their state of oppression they also humbly trust in God, for these are the only ones whom God will deliver (cf. Ps. 18:27). The universal element so characteristic of biblical eschatology involves the whole world, so that **the earth** fears and is still (vs. 8), and God saves **all the oppressed of the earth** (vs. 9).

Human response to divine wrath (vss. 10-12). This stanza employs synthetic (vs. 10), climactic (vs. 11), and synonymous (vs. 12) parallelism. Emphasis is here placed upon homage which the world should give to God.

[10] The boldness of the language creates a problem of interpretation. The Hebrew, however, as rendered in our text, does not need emending. Verse 10 may be elliptical, meaning that God will take vengeance upon those who oppress the righteous, which will in turn cause the righteous to praise him. Or it could be that the psalmist is saying that the defeated nations will serve as involuntary witnesses to God's power. The first line is not difficult to interpret. **Wrath** could also mean "fierceness, raging anger." Fierce nations, such as Assyria and Babylonia, vented their wrath against Israel and Judah, but God worked providentially to so magnificently deliver his people from their enemies as to cause Israel to praise God (cf. Isa. 10:5-19; 31:6-9; 32:16-20; 38:1-20; 48:14-21).

The second line of verse 10 is difficult. **Gird upon** is incorrectly rendered "restrained" (KJV). The word means to bind in the sense of girding a garment upon oneself (cf. Ps. 109:19). It makes little difference whether **the residue of wrath** is God's or man's. If it is the residue of *man's* wrath, the meaning is that after man has partially destroyed himself through his sin, God finishes the destruction to his own glory. The prophets continually emphasize both the permissive judgment of God whereby Israel is permitted to suffer the natural consequences of her sins (cf. Hos. 5:5-7, 15; 5:11-12; 12:14; 13:3, 12) and also the judgment of God whereby he steps into the picture and completes the destruction (cf. Hos. 5:13-14; 7:11-12; 8:8-10; 9:7, 17; 10:5-7; 13:14-16). If **the residue of wrath** refers to *God's* wrath, the passage means that God will continue his work of destruction until it is complete. The same practical results follow from either interpretation.

By changing the vowels of *'adham,* "man," to *'edhom*, "Edom," and taking the word for wrath *(chamath)* as a proper name, signifying the Syrian state north of Israel, the NEB derives the following translation:

> For all her fury Edom shall confess thee,
> and the remnant left in Hamath shall dance
> in worship.

This is a possible translation of the consonantal Hebrew text, but such drastic change is not necessary.

[11] Vows can be made to God with confidence because God will always keep his promises to Israel. Vows were voluntary, but once made had to be kept (Deut. 23:21-23). The completion of the vow involved the offering of votive offerings, a special kind of thank-offering made in thanksgiving to God who had granted the worshiper's desired deliverance (cf. Lev. 7:16; 22:18-27; 27:1-13; Num. 6:13-21). Under certain circumstances, a man could render void the vow of his wife or daughter (Num. 30). **Gifts** (Heb. *shay*) could also be translated "tribute," referring to gifts brought by non-Israelite people (cf. Isa. 18:7; Ps. 68:30). Chronicles implies that neighboring nations brought such gifts to Yahweh following the defeat of Sennacherib (2 Chron. 32:20-23). **All around him** probably refers to nations bordering on Israel.

[12] The relative clauses in our text are declarative statements in Hebrew. Rather than **who**, the Hebrew text has "he" (so KJV, NASB). Verse 12 assigns a reason for all men to bring gifts and worship the Lord God. The word "for" (NEB) shows this syntactical relationship between verses 11 and 12. In verse 12, the present tense seems to be the best way to translate the Hebrew imperfect (vs. 12a) and participle (vs. 12b).

There is little evidence to justify the theory that here and frequently elsewhere the psalmists are setting forth a pantomime or dramatic portrayal of the enthronement of Yahweh acted out in Israel's worship. It is more likely that nothing more than figurative language is intended here.

EXCURSUS

The Wrath of God

From their Scriptures Israel could recall great events when divine anger had been manifested, sometimes against them and at other times against their enemies. God's fury consumed Pharaoh's army (Exod. 15:7-8) and caused the inhabitants of Philistia, Moab, and Canaan to be struck with terror (Exod. 15:14-16). Moses' intercession caused God's wrath to be turned away from the nation of Israel (Exod. 34:9-14), but the persons guilty of idolatry were slain (Exod. 32:25-29). God's jealously prompted such action (Exod. 34:14; cf. Exod. 20:4-6). God's anger was kindled against Miriam and Aaron in their rebellion against Moses, so that Miriam was stricken temporarily with leprosy (Num. 12:9-16). God's wrath prevented the unbelieving Israelites from entering Canaan (Ps. 95:7-11). Even Moses and Aaron so angered God that they were banned from the promised land (Num. 20:12; Ps. 106:32-33). The NT also emphasizes the wrath of God (Rom. 1:18; 2:4-11; 1 Thess. 2:14-16; 2 Thess. 1:5-10).

But Israel also understood the remedial purpose behind God's wrath manifested within history. One psalmist begs God not to vent his full anger against him (38:1-2), and he expects God to hear and forgive (38:15, 17-18, 21-22). God is slow to anger and he will not keep his anger for ever against those who repent (Exod. 34:6-7; Ps. 103:6-18). Hezekiah knew that God's wrath and fierce anger could be turned away from Judah by their sincere repentance and reformation of life (2 Chron. 29:8-10). Habakkuk could pray with confidence, "In wrath remember mercy" (Hab. 3:2). The biblical doctrine of propitiation and atonement grows out of the need to assuage the wrath of God through the atoning blood offered on behalf of the guilty sinner (Lev. 17:10-11; 17:1-7; 2 Chron. 29:3-11; Rom. 3:21-26; Eph. 2:1-10).

Psalm 77: Grief in Historical Perspective

"To the choirmaster" and "a psalm of Asaph" are explained in connection with Psalm 76. "According to Jeduthun" (cf. Pss. 39, 62) refers either to a director of the temple choir (cf. 1 Chron. 16:41-42) or to a certain tune to which the psalm was to be sung.

In this national lament the psalmist voices both his and the nation's feelings in a time of crisis. It is impossible to determine with certainty what that calamity was. If the psalm is of north Israelite origin, it could fit the time between Tiglath-Pileser III's devastation of much of Israel in 732 B.C. and the final downfall of Israel in 722 B.C. If Judean in origin, it could fit the time immediately prior to Sennacherib's siege of Jerusalem in 701 B.C., or the time of Jeremiah when it was becoming obvious that Judah would soon fall to the Babylonians. The reference to Joseph and Jacob (vs. 15) could mark the psalm as being from North Israel (cf. Amos 7:2, 5; 5:6, 15; Hos. 10:11), or it could refer to the twelve-tribe nation prior to the division between Israel and Judah (cf. Pss. 76:6; 78:5, 21; Obad. 18).

This psalm is generally recognized as containing the seemingly antithetical elements of lament and praise. This fact need not lead to the conclusion that two or more psalms or fragments have been pieced together, for the same feature is to be found in Psalms 9–10, where an alphabetic arrangement running through the two psalms demonstrates that they were originally one, as the LXX indicates by assigning only one number to them. Psalm 44 also contains praise (vss. 1-8), lament (vss. 9-22), and petition (vss. 23-26). In Psalm 77 the order is reversed, the lament (vss. 1-9) preceding the praise (vss. 11-20). Here the psalmist realizes that his wrong has been in supposing that God has changed from his steadfast love of old. Having rediscovered the goodness of God, he now recounts God's glorious deeds. Leupold observes that the psalmist begins by talking *about* God, and it is only as he begins to talk *to* God that his attitude toward God changes significantly (H. C. Leupold, *Exposition of the Psalms*, p. 555).

The stanza divisions in this psalm are not easily discernible, but the following arrangement satisfactorily allows for the development of the theme.

Loud cries of distress (vss. 1-2). This paragraph employs stairlike (vs. 1) and synthetic (vs. 2) parallelism. **[1]** The emphatic phrase **aloud to God** is repeated in the second line for emphasis. The Hebrew is elliptical, and reads:

My voice unto God, and I cry;
My voice unto God, that he may give ear to me.

Our text compresses this thought into fewer words without destroying the essential meaning. The verbs to be supplied are better put in the present tense (cf. **I cry aloud** with NASB "My voice rises") than in past time (KJV, NEB). This verse seems to be an introduction stating his present circumstances. Crying aloud to God as a result of deep distress is normal and was so done by the Savior (Heb. 5:7). The last clause is best taken as a purpose clause, **that he may hear me. I cry** (a Hebrew frequentative imperfect) indicates a continual crying. **Hear** (a Hebrew perfect) suggests a decisive answer from God. It is also better to translate the verbs in verses 2-5 in the present tense (against KJV, ASB, NEB), indicating a continuing state in the present. **[2]** He continuously implores God without receiving divine aid, yet his faith will not allow him to grow weary. **In the day** and **in the night** are Hebrew idioms indicating a continuous state or continuous action (cf. Pss. 19:2; 22:2). **My hand is stretched out** describes a familiar gesture used in prayer to symbolize the longing of the heart for God's blessings (cf. Pss. 28:2; 141:2; Lam. 3:41). **Without wearying** is literally "and was not numbed." "My sore ran in the night, and ceased not" (KJV) and "I lay sweating and nothing would cool me" (NEB) employ alternative meanings of the key words (*naghar* and *pugh*), which results in translations which make little sense in the present context. His **soul refuses to be comforted** until a favorable answer comes from God.

Mournful musing about God (vss. 3-10). This paragraph employs synonymous (vss. 3, 5-9) and synthetic (vss. 4, 10) parallelism. **[3]** His thoughts of God, who has not acted on his behalf, cause him to **moan**, and his **spirit faints. [4]** His trouble makes him sleepless and speechless.

[5] He tries to bolster his faith and calm his spirit by reflecting upon God's help in the past. [6] Verse 6 has been emended and partially deleted in our text. The NASB faithfully renders the Hebrew, except that the present tense fits the context better than the future tense. Hence we derive the following translation:

> I remember my song in the night;
> I meditate with my heart;
> And my spirit ponders.

This translation yields a synonymous triplet which expands the thought of verse 5.

[7-9] Here the content of his musing is given in three synonymous couplets, all of which say in effect: Will God never again bless Israel? (For the concept of the wrath of God, see the excursus at the end of Psalm 76.)

[10] The psalmist indicates the turning point in his quest for understanding of the divine riddle. The startling thought strikes him that it is he and not God who has changed. Now he recognizes that though the ways of God are sometimes incomprehensible to man, nevertheless God does act according to recognizable principles. The principle of historical continuity, which the psalmist is able to bring to bear on the situation at hand, enables him to preserve his faith and to wait patiently for God's deliverance from the present distress. **Grief** could also be translated "weakness." **Changed** is better than "years" (KJV, ASV [1901]).

Mitchell Dahood (*Psalms II*, AB, pp. 228–29) takes quite a different view of verse 10. He suggests that in verses 9-10 three synonyms are used: *shakhach*, *qaphats*, and *sheneth*, "all conveying the literal idea of 'drying up' but metaphorically expressing the thought that God's compassion and power have become ineffectual." He takes the suffixes as third masculine singular, as he does in verse two. Thus he translates:

> [9] Have the inmost parts of God dried up,
>   or his bosom shrunk in his anger?
> [10] Perhaps his sickness is this:
>   the right hand of the Most High has withered.

This should be compared with the translation of the NEB:

[10] 'Has his right hand', I said, 'lost its grasp?
     Does it hang powerless, the arm of the
          Most High?'

This would deny that a change of heart has come over the psalmist in verse 10. However, there does seem to be a transition in thought in verse 10, since in the rest of the psalm there is a noticeable confidence and also an absence of the complaints found in verses 1-9.

Fruitful reflection upon the past (vss. 11-15). This paragraph employs synonymous (vss. 11-12, 14-15) and synthetic (vs. 13) parallelism. The psalmist resolves to reflect upon the past in a more positive way by looking at God's works of the past. In each verse there is a parallel between God's general **deeds** and **work** on the one hand, and his **wonders** and **mighty deeds** on the other. The latter could refer to miracles or other extraordinary deeds.

[13-15] Only God can rightly claim to be the holy wonderworker and redeemer. Emphasis is here placed on the period of the exodus from Egypt when God redeemed **the sons of Jacob and Joseph.**

Elaboration on the scene of the exodus (vss. 16-20). This paragraph employs four synthetic triplets (vss. 16-19) and one synthetic couplet (vs. 20). [16-19] It would appear that the psalmist moves from an allusion to God's separation of the waters in the creation (vs. 16) to the parting of the waters of the Red Sea at the time of the exodus (vss. 17-19). The thread which ties these two events together is the divine appearance which reveals the majesty of God. This majesty should be recognized by the peoples contemporary with and contiguous to Israel (cf. vss. 12-15). [20] God, the chief shepherd, led his people through the wilderness by means of the leadership of his servants, **Moses and Aaron** (cf. Ezek. 34; 1 Pet. 5:1-4).

EXCURSUSES

Canaanite Baalism

In verses 13-15 the psalmist enters sympathetically into the prophetic tradition reflected in several psalms as he engages in a polemic against Canaanite Baalism. Israel had frequently lapsed into Baalism, primarily because of a double attraction which this cult held out to degenerate man. First, it was supposed that Baal controlled the fertility of the field, animals, and persons. Therefore, to please Baal meant to insure prosperity. Second, the fleshly attraction of cult prostitution corrupted Israel's morals. Israel's pre-exilic history is discolored with Baalism. At Baal-peor before the conquest of Canaan (Hosea 9:10; Num. 25:1-18; Deut. 4:3; Ps. 106:28-31), during the period of the Judges (Judg. 2:13; 6:25, 31), in the ninth century (1 Kings 16:31; 18:21-40), and throughout the Prophets, Baalism is emphatically condemned.

Because of the syncretistic nature of Baalism which allowed men to cling to their old gods but also include Baal, it was necessary for the prophets (cf. Hos. 2:5-13; 4:11-14; 9:10-14; 11:1-4; 13:4-6) and the psalmists (see Pss. 86:8-10; 95:3-5; 96:3-6; 97:7-9; 115:3-11) to insist that Yahweh is the only God who through his works has demonstrated his reality.

Universalism

God has manifested his might among the peoples (Ps. 77:14), not merely in Israel; hence universalism is a frequent theme in the Psalms. God wants all men to know and worship him (96:2-3,7-9). God has revealed himself to the peoples through the created world (97:6) and through his dealings with Israel (98:1-3). All men are depraved sinners (14:1-3), and no one is righteous before God (143:1-2). But God's grace, mercy, and love resulting in forgiveness are extended to all who call upon him throughout the whole world, the realm of his dominion (103). The psalmists were not narrow-minded nationalists. They understood God's interest in all humanity.

The Supplementation of History in the Psalms

Frequently the Psalms mention things which are omitted from the historical books of the OT. For instance, in 77:17-18 the psalmist refers to a thunderstorm in connection with the parting of the waters of the Red Sea, which is omitted in Exodus. Some think that the psalmist has exercised poetic license in embellishing the text, while others suggest that he is filling in the history from extra-biblical sources. There is nothing inconsistent with either view. Similarly, Psalm 105:18 mentions Joseph's neck being put in a collar of iron, 105:22 recalls that Joseph taught Pharaoh's princes, 137:7 tells of a day when Edom encouraged the Babylonians as they razed Jerusalem, 132:1-2 refers to David's oath in connection with his plans to build a temple, and 110:4 mentions God's oath to David concerning his perpetual dynasty. None of these items is included in other parts of the OT. The historical books do not propose to give every detail of Israel's history, but the authors indicate that they have selected material from extant written records (cf. 1 Kings 11:41; 14:29; 15:7; etc.). The psalmists could easily have had access to these written records or to the oral tradition taught by the priests and Levites.

Psalm 78: Didactic Reflection Upon the Past

The word *maśkil* in the title seems to mean "skill" or "skillful," and doubtless refers either to the skillful rendition to be given by the musicians or to the requirement of deep meditation in order to grasp the significance of the message.

This psalm is written in the style of an epic poem relating the adventures of Israel's past. It has a didactic aim of exhorting present and succeeding generations not to perpetuate the mistakes of the past. It is written in the style of a wisdom poem whereby the parents instruct their children in the knowledge of God. Two divine characteristics are blended here. The longsuffering love of God in forgiving a decadent people is balanced with a consideration of the holiness of God which must discipline a wayward people.

The psalm needs to be dated shortly after David's reign,

at which time the religious center of the nation had been removed from the tribes of Joseph and placed in Jerusalem in the tribe of Judah. Emphasis is placed upon God's selection of David to replace Saul. Ephraim (North Israel) was removed from the position of glory because of her unworthiness and Judah was chosen because of David's loyalty to God. Thus the didactic aim is well served by stressing the principles of divine governance of the nation. Righteousness is blessed and sin is punished.

The psalm's twofold purpose (vss. 1-8). Two purposes are set forth in these introductory verses: the first (vss. 1-4) is to warn Israel against following the past sins of the nation; the second purpose is to exhort the present generation to pass on their heritage to succeeding generations (vss. 5-8).

[1-2] Synonymous parallelism is employed. **Parable** here simply means a comparison which seeks to discover principles in God's dealings of the past which are applicable to the present generation. **Dark sayings** (or "riddles") is synonymous with **parables.** The term does not refer to esoteric or enigmatic language, but to the incomprehensibility of the depths of the degradation of sin and the corresponding divine remedy provided for forgiveness.

[3-4] These teachings have been handed down by oral transmission from generation to generation. The urgency of perpetuating these traditions reflects Deuteronomy 6:6-7. The spiritual significance of the precepts and rituals, which were memorials of God's acts of righteousness and salvation (Exod. 13:8, 14; Deut. 6:20-25; Josh. 4:6-7), are to be kept alive. So Christians need to keep alive the significance of Christ's death, burial, and resurrection.

[5-8] Both positive and negative results will be forthcoming when a proper historical perspective is perpetuated. They will **not forget the works of God** and thus be **stubborn and rebellious**, but will **hope in God** and **keep his commandments.**

Results of forgetting God (vss. 9-16). [9-10] It is not certain what sin of Ephraim is intended in the allusion here, or whether Ephraim stands for North Israel. Verses 67-68 seem to suggest that all the northern tribes are intended.

The historical allusion may be to the period of the Judges, when the Ephraimites sought prominence and glory (Judg. 4:24–8:3) and yet were reluctant to bear the brunt of the battle (Judg. 12:1-6). Or the allusion may be to the mountains of Gilboa, where Saul met his death in battle against the Philistines (1 Sam. 31; cf. ch. 15). At any rate, the psalmist is saying that the weakness manifested in the northern tribes (cf. vs. 59) resulted in God's choosing Judah (vs. 68) and David (vs. 70).

[11-16] These verses cover the period of the miracles in Egypt up to Israel's arrival at Sinai (cf. Exod. 7–17). **Zoan** (vs. 12), an ancient capital of Egypt, stands here as a synonym of Egypt.

Results of murmuring against God (vss. 17-31).

[17-20] The allusion to the miraculous provision of water (vs. 20; cf. vs. 15) is to the incident at Rephidim (Exod. 17), and the allusion to miraculous provision of food (vss. 18-19, 20b) relates to the incident related in Numbers 11. The irony which the psalmist sees in the situation is that Israel did not believe God could provide meat for them in spite of the miraculous provision of water which had preceded their craving for meat.

[21-31] This paragraph also relates to the record in Numbers 11, but here the emphasis is on Israel's unbelief and God's anger which caused him to send a plague along with the meat which they craved.

Shallow repentance (vss. 32-39). [32-37] With words of flattery rather than sincerity, Israel pretended repentance in time of trouble, but **their heart was not steadfast toward him,** nor were they **true to his covenant.** Hosea 6:1-6 should be read in this connection. **[38-39]** Yet God, **being compassionate, forgave** them because he remembered human frailty (cf. Ps. 103:6-14).

The sin of ingratitude (vss. 40-53). [40-43] They rebelled against God because they forgot the significance of his redemptive acts at the time of the exodus. **Provoked** (41b) is a better translation than "limited" (KJV; cf. "pained," NASB; "grieved," NEB). The Hebrew word can mean "to set a mark upon," or "to cause pain, provoke anger." **The**

Holy One of Israel is an expression seldom used outside Isaiah (cf. Pss. 71:22; 89:18; Jer. 50:29; 51:5), but which is found twenty-five times in Isaiah (1:4; 5:19, 24; 10:20; 12:6; 17:7; 29:19; 30:11, 12, 15; 31:1; 37:23; 41:14, 16, 20; 43:3, 14; 45:11; 47:4; 48:17; 49:7; 54:5; 55:5; 60:9, 14). "The Holy One in Israel" is found in Ezekiel 39:7. This phrase emphasizes both the transcendence (separateness) and immanence (closeness) of God (cf. Isa. 57:15). From man's viewpoint, God's holiness demands reverence and obedience, which qualities were so sorely lacking in Israel at the time contemplated in the psalm. **[44-53]** The psalmist mentions seven of the ten plagues of Egypt, but not in the order given in Exodus 7–12. Verses 46-48 make use of synonymous parallelism, so that a single plague is referred to in each verse: locusts, hail, and murrain on the cattle. Verses 49-50 anticipate the tenth plague of verse 51. The psalmist again refers to the crossing of the Red Sea (vss. 52-53; cf. vs. 13), which event followed shortly after the tenth and last plague.

Continuing ingratitude (vss. 54-66). [54-55] Holy land and **mountain** are synonymous. **The mountain,** therefore, is not Mount Sinai, but Mount Zion. This is in anticipation of verses 68-69. The conquest and settlement of the land are attributed to God and not to Israel. **[56-58] Testimonies** (vs. 56) refers to ceremonies and statutes of a character to remind Israel of God's acts of grace and mercy toward her; for instance, Passover, Tabernacles, etc. But they rejected the testimony and became **like a deceitful bow** (vs. 57). This refers to a warped bow which causes the arrow to veer off and miss the target. So Israel, through spiritual insensitivity to God's saving acts (cf. Mic. 6:1-5), has missed the mark which God set for them. But now, in Canaan, the sin is not primarily one of discontent such as characterized her wilderness journey, but it is the sin of idolatry (vs. 58), the very sin against which God was attempting to shield them by driving out the pagan nations before them.

[59-66] The background of this section is 1 Samuel. The first allusion is to the capturing of the ark by the Philistines (vss. 59-61; see 1 Sam. 4:17-22). **Dwelling** and **tent** are synonyms of the tabernacle or ark (vs. 60), as are **power** and **glory** (vs. 61). So Phinehas' wife called the ark the "glory" (1 Sam. 4:22). The second allusion is to the death of Hophni and Phinehas, sons of Eli, the high priest (vss. 63-64; 1 Sam. 4:17) and to the stunned silence of Phinehas' wife who could only exclaim, "Ichabod (No Glory)!" (1 Sam. 4:21). The third allusion is to the plague of tumors and mice which God sent against the Philistines in order to make them return the ark to Israel (vss. 65-66; 1 Sam. 5–6).

Ephraim rejected, Judah chosen (vss. 67-72). God **chose Mount Zion** as his sanctuary **for ever**, which can only mean "for a long period of time." History shows that the temple was destroyed in 587 B.C. by Nebuchadnezzar the Babylonian, and the rebuilt temple was again destroyed by the Romans in A.D. 70. The Scripture teaches that even the earth is not eternal (cf. Ps. 102:25-27). God **chose David** of the tribe of **Judah** to be **his shepherd.** See the notes on 77:20 for the concept of God's servants as shepherds. Note the emphasis which is placed on David's **upright** and **skilful** reign. This emphasis shows the didactic aim of the psalm, which is to encourage Israel to be faithful to God.

Psalm 79: Jerusalem and the Temple in Ruins

This is a psalm of national lament following the devastation of the temple and the city of Jerusalem (vs. 1). The only time which adequately fits this description is the exilic period following the burning of Jerusalem and the temple by King Nebuchadnezzar of Babylonia in 587 B.C. (2 Kings 25:8-12). There is no clear historical evidence for a siege of Jerusalem in either 485 B.C. or 344 B.C., as some have contended. The apocryphal book of Judith seems to allude to the 344 B.C. date, but there are too many historical anachronisms in that book to justify our taking the story seriously. The psalm does not refer to the desecration of the temple by Antiochus IV Epiphanes in 167 B.C., for neither the temple nor Jerusalem was destroyed in his day. The fact that verses 2 and 3 are quoted in 1 Maccabees 7:17 indicates that these words are already used as sacred scripture, which precludes a Maccabean date for the psalm. Since vengeance has not yet been taken on Israel's enemies (vss. 11-12), the psalm fits the exilic period better than the postexilic. It would seem that the psalmist is among those left in the land (vs. 4; cf. 2 Kings 25:22) rather than among those deported to Babylon.

In his lament (vss. 1-4), the psalmist complains about the defilement of the temple and the devastation of Jerusalem (vs. 1), and the defilement of the holy land through bodies left unburied (vss. 2-3). The taunts of Israel's enemies following her military defeat add insult to injury (vs. 4).

In the petition (vss. 5-13), there are the elements of lamentation (5, 7, 10a), imprecation (vss. 6, 10b, 12), petition for forgiveness (vss. 8-9) and deliverance (vs. 11), and promise to praise God following deliverance (vs. 13).

Desecration of temple and city (vss. 1-4). In this paragraph, the psalmist enumerates the adverse conditions brought on by Israel's enemies. [1] In true piety he recognizes the land as God's inheritance. In one sense, all the earth belongs to Yahweh (Exod. 19:5; Ps. 24:1-2) by virtue of divine creation. However, Israel had been purchased by God (Exod. 15:16-17); therefore, the land of Israel was God's special possession (Lev. 25:23). The most terrible thing about this foreign invasion is not that Israel is suffering, but that God's holy possession has been defiled. It is God's holy temple which has been desecrated.

[2-3] God's **servants** and **saints** (*chasidim*, "loyal ones"; cf. NEB "loyal servants") have been shamefully treated. Since dead bodies left unburied defiled the land, the people were to bury corpses the same day on which death occurred (Deut. 21:23; Num. 19:11-19). The apocryphal book of Tobit attaches a great deal of merit to the character of Tobit because of his zeal in burying bodies which the heathen oppressors had left unburied (Tobit 1:17-20; 2:3-7). Or the allusion to the shame of unburied bodies may reflect the distress suffered over human indignity in such a situation. Jeremiah warned that God would bring such shame on the ungodly because of their cumulative national sins (Jer. 7:33; 8:1-2;14:16; 16:4). There is little justification for

the idea that Israel believed the soul would suffer in Sheol if the body were left unburied. [4] In addition to the physical distress of the time, Judah had to suffer the indignity of the taunts of her enemies, the various pagan peoples near her borders.

How long before deliverance? (vss. 5-7). [5] The plaintive cry **How long?** was often upon Israel's lips in time of distress (cf. Pss. 13:1-2; 74:10; 80:4; Isa. 6:11). The expression **for ever** should be taken here to mean a period of long duration (cf. the notes on Ps. 78:69). **Jealous wrath** is doubtless an allusion to Exodus 20:5. The psalmist knows that God takes vengeance on evildoers. But the wrath was not intended to be for ever. See the note on the wrath of God at the end of Psalm 76. [6-7] On the basis of the concept of degrees of wickedness, the psalmist prays that God will not let peoples more wicked than Israel torment them. But greater opportunity brings greater judgment for failure (cf. Amos 3:1-2; Lk. 12:48). Again see the note at the end of Psalm 76 and compare Habakkuk 1-2. But the psalmist is not completely ignorant of this principle, for he confesses the sins of his people.

Cumulative national sins (vss. 8-10). [8] The expression **iniquities of our forefathers** could also be translated "our former iniquities" (KJV), but it seems better to follow the majority of the versions in their understanding that cumulative sin is under consideration. It is cumulative sin perpetuated through many generations which destroys a nation (Jer. 7:21-26; Lam. 5:7; Dan. 9:16). We may be called upon to suffer the *consequences* of the sins of others (Exod. 20:5; Jer. 32:17-18), but God does not hold us guilty for sins which we have not personally committed (Deut. 24:16; Jer. 31:29; Ezek. 18:1-4, 20). When the cup of iniquity is full, God destroys a people (cf. Job 21:19-21; Gen. 15:16; Matt. 23:29-36; 1 Thess. 2:14-16). The word "prevent" (KJV) is an archaic usage meaning "precede" (cf. 1 Thess. 4:15, KJV), corresponding to the Hebrew "come before" or "come to meet."

[9] The petition for forgiveness is not based in Israel's supposed worth, but on God's compassion (vs. 8b) and

God's honor as one who keeps covenant. [10] **Where is their God**, or something similar, is an expression frequently used by Israel's enemies in her time of shame and defeat (cf. Pss. 42:3, 10; 115:2; Joel 2:17; Mic. 7:10). This reaction resulted from Israel's continual boasting in her God (Ps. 44:8). The imprecation in verse 10b should be understood in light of the emphasis on God's honor. The NT as well as the OT recognizes the fact that God is a God of vengeance (Rom. 12:19-20; 2 Thess. 1:5-10).

Praise for deliverance (vss. 11-13). [11] Now the psalmist appeals to God on the basis of his people's suffering. The phrase **groans of the prisoners** is no doubt a poetic device used to describe the mental anguish of shame and disgrace. The Hebrew expression "children of death" in verse 11b **(those doomed to die)** should be understood in a similar way. Not all the exiles were executed or even imprisoned; most were allowed a relative amount of freedom, provided they lived peaceable lives (cf. Jer. 29:1-14; Ezek. 11:5-12, 14-21). [12] The sevenfold vengeance simply means complete, or full, vengeance (cf. Gen. 4:24).

[13] The promise of thanksgiving following deliverance is an expression of belief in the fact that God will answer his people's petition. Israel's postexilic history is ample testimony to the fact that this faith did not go unrewarded. A deeper religious insight, such as that manifested by Shadrach, Meshach, and Abednego (Dan. 3:16-18), would allow the sufferer to praise God even if deliverance should not come.

EXCURSUS

Imprecations in the Psalms

To the Christian reader, it seems inappropriate for the psalmists to beg for God's mercy for themselves while at the same time praying for evil to come upon their enemies. Two things need to be understood. (1) We should examine the psalms in light of other scriptures for a fuller understanding of the nature of these imprecations. (2) We should remember that in these prayers man is speaking to God rather than God speaking to man; therefore, we are not obligated to agree with everything which the psalmists say.

Moses' psalm of rejoicing (Exod. 15:1-18) includes praise to God for the discomfiture of the enemy (vss. 4-10) because God's glorious majesty is thus manifested (vss. 11-12) and because overthrow of the enemy was an essential part of God's working for the salvation of Israel (vss. 13-17). Frequently, imprecations in the national psalms of lamentation emphasize either the glory of God (cf. 9:20; 10:2, 15-18; 55:9, 15, 19; 109:6-31; 139:19-24) or God's compassion manifested toward Israel as fulfilment of his promise to be loyal to his covenant people (cf. 7:1-17; 69; 79). There are other psalms of lament in which the imprecation seems to be more personally motivated (cf. 35, 38, 137). It would appear that the idea of a curse psychologically carried great force in ancient days. The mere wishing of evil brought it to pass (cf. Num. 22–24). Since Israel's enemies often cursed her (cf. 109:17), the only way to nullify the curse was to counter it with a stronger curse. However, there were some psalmists who understood that it is only God's word which is powerful, and he is to be trusted to act according to his own character. Some of the psalms of lament do not contain a curse, but trust God to do the right thing (cf. Pss. 3; 4; 6; 11; 12; 13; 22; 26; 27; etc.).

The prophets, who were delivering oracles of God, frequently pronounced evil upon Israel's enemies who were also God's enemies (cf. Amos 1–2; Isa. 13–23; Jer. 46–51). But, significantly, the prophets refrained from formulating these predictions in the form of human curses pronounced upon these nations. On the contrary, there is often to be found in their predictions the elements of pathos and even lamentation over the evil which is coming. Furthermore, these predictions came from God himself, with the prophets being nothing more than his spokesmen.

These prophetic predictions should be compared with the one book of prophecy in the NT, where similar predictions of divine wrath coming upon the wicked are to be found (cf. Rev. 6:12-17; ch. 9; 14:9-11; 16:4-7; 18:1–19:8;

etc.). Paul's pronouncements (Acts 13:4-12; 23:3; 2 Tim. 4:14) belong in the same category.

The ultimate goal of divine discipline executed within history is the salvation of men (Ezek. 18:23; Dan. 4:25-27; Jonah 3:10; 4:1-6, 11; Rev. 15:3-4; cf. the note on the wrath of God at the end of Psalm 76). Both the OT (Exod. 23:4-5; Lev. 19:18; Job 31:29-35; Prov. 25:21-22; Jer. 17:16; 18:20) and the NT (Lk. 23:34; Acts 7:60; Rom. 12:19-21; 2 Tim. 4:16) indicate that man is to return good for evil. David did so (1 Sam. 24:16-19). The Christian will do well to follow the perfect example of his Lord and Savior.

Psalm 80: Prayer for Restoration

"According to Lilies" probably indicates a certain tune to which the psalm was sung. "Testimony" means primarily a recitation or cultic act which reminds Israel of God's dealings with her and the significance of their acts of worship. For the rest of the title, see Psalm 76.

This is a public lamentation written in a time of national crisis, although identification of the crisis is uncertain. The distress is so great that it appears God has forgotten his covenant relation to Israel. Three refrains (vss. 3, 7, 19) divide the psalm into its several parts and lay stress on the central idea of the psalm, namely, an urgent prayer for restoration.

Considerable difference of judgment prevails concerning the immediate audience intended, whether the psalm originated in North Israel or in Judah. Three principal interpretations should be considered. (1) The psalm is exilic and was written from the standpoint of the prophetic promises of the union of Israel and Judah (cf. Ezek. 37:15-22; Jer. 31:1-21; Hos. 1:11). This is based on the assumption that the vine looked at in retrospect (vss. 8-11) is the same vine which the psalmist prays for God to restore (vss. 14-17). (2) The mention of Joseph, Ephraim, Benjamin, and Manasseh (vss. 1-2), with no reference to Judah, suggests that the psalm originated in North Israel. (3) The psalm was written by a Judean out of sympathy for North Israel. The second interpretation seems the most likely.

It is possible that the historical event lying behind the psalm was either the fall of Gilead and Galilee to Assyria in 732 B.C. (2 Kings 15:29), or the fall of Samaria to Assyria in 722 B.C. (2 Kings 17:1-6), at which time the northern kingdom of Israel came to an end. The LXX title, "concerning the Assyrians," intends to refer to these or similar circumstances.

Three motifs, found often in the OT, are here combined. (1) God is Israel's shepherd and Israel is his flock (1a; cf. Gen. 49:24; Pss. 77:20; 78:52; 79:13; Isa. 40:11; 63:11; Mic. 2:12; 4:8). (2) God is king and Israel is his protected people (1b; cf. 1 Sam. 8:7; Mic. 2:13; Isa. 6:5; Ps. 24:7-10). More often, however, God is presented as king of the whole world (cf. Pss. 93:1-2; 95:3; 96:10; 97:1-5; 99:1-5). (3) God is the husbandman and Israel is his vine (8-15; cf. Hos. 10:1; Isa. 3:14; 5:1-7; Jer. 2:21; 12:10; Ezek. ch. 17). Ezekiel allegorizes the vine, as does the author of this psalm.

Petition for restoration (vss. 1-3). [1] The invocation (vss. 1-2) includes "hymnic predicates" which describe God as Israel's tender shepherd and mighty king. **Shepherd** sometimes refers to Israel's king (cf. 78:71). These shepherds, however, frequently failed to provide Israel with proper guidance and protection, so God had to take matters into his own hands (cf. Jer. 33; Ezek. 34). God is frequently designated as Israel's shepherd (see introduction above). God promised to lead Joseph like a flock (Gen. 49:24), as he also promised to lead Judah (cf. Isa. 40:11). **Israel** and **Joseph** are here synonymous, referring to North Israel (cf. vs. 2). God was thought to dwell symbolically upon (or above, not "between," KJV) the cherubim overshadowing the mercy seat (see Exod. 25:21-22; Num. 7:89; 1 Sam. 4:4; 2 Sam. 6:2; and notes on Ps. 76:1-3). From this symbolic throne he watched over Israel. There is no reason why North Israel could not have had a cherubim in her sanctuaries. [2] **Ephraim, Benjamin,** and **Manasseh,** all descendants of Jacob through Rachel (Gen. 35:24; 48:1), were grouped together on the west side of the tabernacle (Num. 2:18-24) in Israel's wilderness wandering. In the psalm, these three are synonymous with **Joseph** and **Israel**

(cf. vs. 1). The primary petition is for God **to save us.**

[3] The Hebrew word for **restore** can include restoration of external circumstances such as exile, and it can also refer to the turning of man's heart to God (cf. "turn us again," KJV). God must turn favorably toward Israel before Israel will be able to turn to God (cf. vs. 14). If God will so turn and save them, they will never again turn away (vs. 18, *nasogh*) from him. Verses 14 and 18 suggest that salvation in this context includes forgiveness as well as restoration to the home land. **Let thy face shine,** connected with the plea for salvation (cf. Ps. 31:16), is a prayer for God to be gracious to his people and bless them, as the synonymous phraseology of Numbers 6:24-25 and Psalm 67:1 (cf. vs. 2) indicates.

Bread of tears (vss. 4-7). [4] God is angry with them in spite of their tears and prayers. The verb **be angry** literally means "smoke," and may be used with anger as the subject (cf. Deut. 29:20 [Hebrew 19]; Ps. 74:1). God's anger, which scatters his enemies, may be implied in the word, even though not stated (cf. Ps. 144:5-6). "Resist" (NEB) is not a necessary emendation here. [5] Their distress is described poetically as **the bread of tears,** and they have been given **tears to drink. In full measure** literally reads "a third part" (NASB note). "Threefold" (NEB) is too strong. The word doubtless refers to a specific measure which is the third part of another specific measure, but what measure is uncertain (cf. Isa. 40:12).

[6] They are made an object of strife, or contention, to their neighbors round about. The word **scorn** is an emendation of the text following the Syriac, which changes *madhon* to *manodh*, corresponding well with the parallel thought of verse 6b. The Hebrew word *madhon* literally means "strife" (KJV) or "an object of contention" (NASB). **Neighbors** could refer to the Assyrians, if Israel is in exile, or to Philistia, Syria, etc., if Israel is in Palestine.

[7] The expression **O Lord God of hosts** (vss. 4, 19), a variant of **O God of hosts** (vss. 7, 14), need not be thought strange. Dahood (*Psalms, II,* pp. 58–59) compares the expression with Psalm 59:5, and, on the basis of Ugaritic

parallels, contends that the absolute form *'elohim* (rather than the construct *'elohe*) results from wrong vocalization of the word. But if *'elohim* has been substituted by an editor for an original *Yahweh* (vss. 7-14), why was Yahweh retained in verses 4 and 19? Progression of thought is indicated in the refrain (vss. 3, 7, 19). From the idea of *'elohim,* the mighty Creator, the psalmist advances to the idea of God as leader of Israel's hosts, and finally to the idea of Yahweh as Israel's covenant God who cares for her.

The ravaged vine (vss. 8-13). [8-9] God cleared the land by removing its former inhabitants, and planted it with a choice vine, Israel and Judah (cf. 78:54-55; Isa. 5:1-7).

[10-11] Israel's occupation of the land extended from the southern **mountains** to **the mighty cedars** of Lebanon in the north, and from the Mediterranean, **the sea** to the west, **to the River**, the Euphrates in the northeast. God had promised to extend Israel's borders to the Euphrates (cf. Gen. 15:18; Deut. 1:7; 11:24; Josh. 1:4), and he fulfilled it in the days of Solomon (cf. 1 Kings 4:21, 24). [12-13] Isaiah (5:1-7) had a ready answer to the question of verse 12. God removed his protection of the vine because the vine inexcusably bore wild grapes. This is the only place the wild **boar** is mentioned in the OT, although Dahood gives Canaanite parallels which use the term in a metaphorical sense (*Psalms II,* p. 259). Here in the psalm it refers to Israel's enemies.

Final plea for restoration (vss. 14-19). [14] Though God symbolically sits enthroned over the cherubim (vs. 1), his throne is actually in heaven (cf. 76:1, 8). [15] It is not necessary to omit, with some, the second line of verse 15 (RSV, NEB), which reads, "and upon the son whom thou hast reared for thyself." This seeming intrusion does not destroy the imagery. Here allegory and interpretation mingle. Israel is frequently thought of as God's son (cf. Exod. 4:22-23; Hos. 11:1; Jer. 31:20). "Branch" (KJV) is a metaphor for God's son, whether referring to Israel (cf. Isa. 14:19; 60:21) or the Messiah (cf. Isa. 11:1; Jer. 23:5; Zech. 3:8; 6:12). It is not likely that the Messiah is intended here.

[16] On the significance of imprecations in the psalms,

see the excursus at the end of Psalm 79. **[17] Man of thy right hand** is here a term of endearment indicating Israel's covenant relationship to God. The expression is likely a play on the word Benjamin (meaning "son of my right hand"), referring here, however, to Israel. **Son of man** refers to a human being (cf. Ps. 8:4), used here of Israel.

[18] The psalmist is not contending that they have not turned back from God (NEB), but he is promising that the nation will henceforth be faithful to God if he will deliver them. **Turn back** (*nasogh*) refers to apostasy.

Psalm 81: Israel Must Listen to God

"According to the Gittith" is uncertain in meaning. The Targum connects *gittith* with the Philistine city Gath and takes the title to indicate a musical instrument or melody of Philistine origin. The Midrash relates Gittith to the Hebrew *gath* (vineyard), and takes it to refer to a tune associated with vintage songs. For the rest of the title, see Psalm 76.

The psalm apparently celebrates the Feast of Tabernacles. The *shophar*, or ram's horn (vs. 3), was blown at the new moon of the seventh month (Num. 29:1), in contradistinction to the blowing of silver trumpets (Heb. *chatsotseroth*) at each new moon throughout the remainder of the year (Num. 10:10). Hence, the month of celebration under consideration is not the first month of the religious calendar in which the Passover was celebrated (Lev. 23:4-8), but the seventh month, during which the Feast of Tabernacles was begun on the fifteenth day when the moon was full (Lev. 23:33-36). The special significance of blowing the *shophar* in the seventh month accounts for the synonymous parallelism of verse 3, giving significance to the new moon and the full moon. The Feast of Tabernacles not only celebrated the autumn harvest festival, but also reminded Israel of her divine protection during the wilderness wandering (Lev. 23:39-43) after they had come out from Egypt.

The psalm consists of a festive hymn (vss. 1-5b) and a prophetic oracle (vss. 5c-16). Like Psalm 95, it lays stress on the necessity of obedience accompanying Israel's praises. The exodus from Egypt (vss. 5a, 6-7a, 10) and the period of wilderness wandering (vss. 7bc, 11-12) provide the historical perspective out of which come admonitions for the present (vss. 8-10, 13-16).

The festive hymn (vss. 1-5b). **[1-2]** A summons is given to praise the God of Jacob who made a covenant with the patriach and his descendants, the Israelites. God is frequently referred to as Israel's **strength** (cf. 18:1; 21:1; 31:1-2; 46:1; 59:16-17). For the expressions **sing aloud, shout for joy,** and **raise a song,** see the notes on Psalm 98:4-6. **[3]** For the significance of blowing the trumpet **at the new moon** and **at the full moon,** see the introduction to the psalm. "At the appointed time" (KJV) is incorrect.

[4] This verse involves synonymous parallelism, so **statute** and **ordinance** are synonymous. **[5ab]** God made the festival **a decree** (or "testimony," KJV, NASB) **in Joseph. Decree** here equals the **statute** and **ordinance** of verse 4, just as **Joseph** refers to **Israel** of verse 4. Verse 5 may refer to God's going **out over the land of Egypt** in bringing about the death of the firstborn of the Egyptians (cf. Exod. 11:4). The rendering "when he came out from the land of Egypt" (NEB, LXX), involves a change of prepositions or a resort to Syriac, a cognate language (Dahood, *Psalms II*, p. 264). The problem with the traditional translation is that while the decree for the Passover festival was given in connection with the last plague, the death of the firstborn (Exod. 12), the psalm seems to reflect the Feast of Tabernacles, which was instituted later. However, since both Passover and Tabernacles were connected in a general way with the exodus from Egypt, this is no insurmountable obstacle. Verse 3 refers to Tabernacles and not to Passover (see the introduction to the psalm).

The prophetic oracle (vss. 5c-16). **[5c]** The **voice** is God's voice to the prophet, and in the following verses the prophet relates the content of God's word to him. This introductory statement should not be expunged from the text (cf. NEB). **[6-7] Burden** and **basket** are synonymous. Though **basket** does not appear in the Exodus account, ancient pictures discovered by archeologists indicate that

Oriental women carried baskets on their shoulders or heads, and the men carried them at their side. "Pots" (KJV) translates the usual meaning of the Hebrew word, but **basket** is better here. **Your** is "his" in Hebrew (cf. KJV, NASB, RSV), referring to Israel at the time of the exodus. The order of the verbs is important: **relieved, freed, delivered, answered, tested**. Only after God delivered Israel from Egyptian bondage (Exod. 13) did he answer them with his covenant requirements at Sinai (Exod. 19–23) and test them in the wilderness. Two places came to be called **Meribah** (strife, contention). Rephidim was situated between Egypt and Sinai (Exod. 17:1-7), and Kadesh was reached after Israel left Sinai (Num. 20:13). In either case, God did not test Israel until after he had delivered her from Egypt. The notes on Psalm 95:7d-11 should be compared. According to the book of Exodus, Israel tested or tried God with their impatience. However, God also tested Israel's faith by letting her temporarily suffer deprivation. **The secret place of thunder** refers to the covering of Mount Sinai with smoke at the time of God's appearance (Exod. 19:16-18; 20:18-20). The transposition of verses in NEB is unnecessary.

[8-10] The Feast of Tabernacles included a reading of the law every seventh year (Deut. 31:10-13) so that each generation could hear it. Verses 8-10 reflect some of the salient points of this memorial reading of the Law. There is tenderness in the rebukes of verse 8. The warning against idolatry echoes Deuteronomic legislation and exhortation reflected in the second account of the Decalogue (Deut. 5:6), in the "Shema" ("Hear, O Israel," Deut. 6:4), and in the Song of Moses (Deut. 32:12, 16, 39). Verse 10c reflects Deuteronomy 8:3-10, which sets forth the divine purpose behind Israel's deprivations and God's miraculous care in the wilderness. Psalms 78 and 106 are also instructive on this point.

[11-12] The psalmist again reflects upon two great biblical principles. God permits man freedom of choice (vs. 11), but holds him responsible for the consequences of his choices (vs. 12). [13-16] The psalmist reiterates the prom-

ises of God in Deuteronomy 28, to bless Israel if she would only obey him. Verse 15a has a difficult phrase. **Would cringe toward him** involves a Hebrew word *(kachash)* with an interesting history. The word basically means "to dwindle away," resulting in that which has no substance (cf. 109:24b, "My flesh is lean, and has no fatness"). From this it comes to mean physically that which fails (cf. Hos. 9:2; Hab. 3:17). Ethically it means that which is deceptive or false (Hos. 4:2), such as feigned obedience (Josh. 24:27). And finally it refers to God's enemies whose arrogant resistance to his power has been removed (cf. Deut. 33:29; Pss. 18:44; 66:3). The last definition fits the present psalm passage. Pretended obedience (cf. NASB) does not fit the context as well as our text. **And their fate** [better than "time," KJV, NASB] **would last for ever** conveys not the insincerity of Israel's enemies, but their loss of political ascendancy (cf. Jer. 27:7) resulting from their unbelief in Yahweh's claims upon all mankind (cf. vs. 9). The idea of obedience (pretended or otherwise) of the nations is not in the verse.

The final verse reflects Deuteronomy 32:13-14, where the phrases **finest of the wheat** and **honey from the rock** are given in reverse order. The word **finest** literally means "fat" (Heb. *chelebh*) and in the Deuteronomy passage is similar to the word "milk" (Heb. *chalebh*), thus providing an interesting wordplay.

Psalm 82: God Judges Human Judges

For the significance of "Asaph" in the title, see the comments on Psalm 76.

Three principal interpretations have been given to this psalm. (1) It presents God's judgment against heathen deities, placing them in a subordinate role to that of God and threatening them with death. (2) It is a portrayal of the disorders caused in the world by "the spiritual hosts of wickedness in the heavenly places" (Eph. 6:12), that is, by Satan and his angels. (3) It is polemic against human judges and rulers in Israel.

In regard to the first interpretation, the primary problem centers around the question of the identity of the spokes-

man in verse 6. The pronoun "I" is in the emphatic position in Hebrew, "It is I who have said...." God is the
spokesman. It is incredible that God would acknowledge
the reality of pagan gods, even in relegating them to a
dethroned status.

The second interpretation carries more weight, since the
Bible does teach the reality of satanic powers which affect
men (Job 1–2; 1 Chron. 21:1; Zech. 3:1-2; Lk. 22:3, 31;
Acts 5:3; 2 Cor. 12:7, 35; etc.). However, no biblical reference presents these powers and personalities as pronouncing judgment on men, as do the 'elohim of Psalm 82:2-4.

It seems most likely that the third interpretation is the
correct one. One major objection to this interpretation has
been that the word 'elohim would not be applied to human
beings. However, the word is definitely used of a Davidic
king in Psalm 45:6-7, which we give here with the word
'elohim transliterated.

[6] Your throne, O 'elohim, is for ever and ever;
A scepter of equity is the scepter of your
kingdom.
[7] You have loved righteousness and hated
wickedness;
Therefore, 'elohim, your 'elohim, has
anointed you
With the oil of gladness above your fellows.

Since both verses are addressed to the same person, the
pronouns **your** preceding 'elohim in verse 7 shows that the
'elohim of verse 6 refers to the king (cf. 45:1). Since human
judges in Israel stood in the place of God in their role as
judges (cf. Deut. 1:17; 2 Chron. 19:6-7; Exod. 22:8-9), the
judge, as God's deputy, may be called 'elohim.

Verse 7 is also said to be a major hindrance to the concept of human judges, but the present writer believes that
this verse, along with verses 2-4, actually confirms the interpretation, as the exegesis will show.

For the viewpoint that the psalmists are strictly mono-
theists, see the note on Canaanite Baalism at the end of
Psalm 77 and compare Psalm 81:9-10.

The congregation of God (vs. 1). For the sake of clarity, we give a literal translation of the verse, but transliterate the terms generally applied to deity:

> *'elohim* stands in the congregation of *'el*;
>   in the midst of the *'elohim* he judges.

Obviously the second *'elohim* cannot be God. The word **council** is a mistranslation which presents a misleading idea, as does the expression "the court of heaven" (NEB). "The congregation of the mighty" (KJV) is an acceptable translation, but "mighty" is ambiguous. "His own congregation" (NASB) is better, but "the congregation of God" is best. It is significant that the singular word *'el*, rather than the plural form, *'elohim*, is used here. The singular removes any doubt as to the identity of the one to whom the psalmist refers. "The congregation of God" should be compared with the "congregation of Yahweh" (Num. 27:17; 31:16; Josh. 22:16-17), referring to Israel. "The congregation of Israel" is a frequent expression (cf. Exod. 12:3, 6, 19, 47; Lev. 4:13; Num. 16:9; 32:4; Josh. 22:18, 20). Since human judges were a part of "the congregation of Israel," which is also "the congregation of Yahweh," these rulers doubtless are the ones referred to both in the expression "the congregation of *'el*," and in the phrase "in the midst of the *'elohim*."

The scriptures which are often used as evidence of God's calling a council of the angels are not convincing. True enough, "the assembly (*qahal*) of the holy ones" (Ps. 89:5) can be equated with "the council (*sodh*) of the holy ones" (Ps. 89:7), but these subordinates who stand "in the council (*sodh*) of Yahweh" are there to perceive God's word and obey it (Jer. 23:18), and then proclaim it to others (Jer. 23:22). No one counsels God on anything (Isa. 40:13-14 = Rom. 11:34). The council in Jeremiah is composed of God and his prophets, just as in Psalm 82:1 "the congregation of *'el*" is composed of God and his judges in Israel.

Indictment of the judges (vss. 2-4). [2] The indictment here is a common one in the scriptures. Rulers are condemned for judging unjustly (cf. Isa. 1:23; 3:13-15; Jer.

22:1-5, 13-17; Amos 5:10-13, 24; 6:12; Mic. 2:1-11; 3:1-4, 9-12). **[3-4]** The same requirement for rulers to defend the defenseless is found elsewhere, often with a promise of divine blessing attached, in Deuteronomy (14:28-29; 16:11-12, 14; 24:19-22; 26:12-15; 27:19), the Prophets (Isa. 1:16-17; Jer. 7:5-7; Ezek. 22:9; Zech. 7:8-14), and the Psalms (10:14, 18; 68:5; 146:9). God is especially the champion of the defenseless and he demands the same concern on the part of his leaders.

The foundations are shaken (vs. 5). The pronoun **they** must refer to the unjust judges of verses 2-4. **Knowledge** of God includes the practice of justice (Jer. 22:16). Those who fail to give every man his rights are without **understanding** (Ps. 14:4) and **they walk about in darkness** (Isa. 59:9). However, the pronoun **they** could refer to the victims of these unjust judges. In this case, the passage means that the oppressed do not understand why such conditions are allowed to continue in a nation governed by God (cf. vs. 8). The darkness would not be the darkness of moral ignorance, but of misfortune (cf. Isa. 8:21-22). **The foundations of the earth** here refers to civil and moral order, which have been destroyed by unscrupulous leaders (cf. Ps. 11:1-3, where the synonymous word *shathoth* is used).

Princes die like commoners (vss. 6-7). **[6]** For the use of *'elohim* in referring to human deputies of God, see the introduction to this psalm. **Sons of the Most High** reflects upon the fact that Israel is God's son (cf. Hos. 1:10; 11:1; Jer. 31:20; Isa. 1:2; Exod. 4:22-23); therefore, these rulers can also be referred to as his sons. **[7]** "And fall like any one of the princes" (NASB) best translates the meaning of verse 7b. **You shall die like men** refers to rulers dying as commoners (cf. Jer. 22:18-19); compare the expression "like any other man" (Judg. 16:7, 17). **Princes** (plural in Hebrew) refers to Davidic rulers who were also judges (cf. 2 Sam. 15:1-4; 1 Kings 7:7; Ps. 72:1-2, 4, 12-14).

Petition for God to judge the earth (vs. 8). Here *'elohim* refers to Yahweh, who is judge of the earth. He judges the world of righteousness, truth, and equity (cf. Pss. 94:2; 96:10, 13; 98:9).

Psalm 83: A Coalition of Enemies

It is impossible to determine with certainty the historical background of this psalm. Since Assyria is included as an enemy of Israel (vs. 8) but Babylonia is not, the psalm must have been written after Assyria began her westward march in the eighth century B.C., and before Babylonia became a world power at the overthrow of Nineveh in 612 B.C. In all likelihood, the psalm is meant to be a composite picture of Israel's enemies, past and present, and the purpose is to bolster faith for dealing with present problems.

Israel's enemies are God's enemies (vss. 1-8). [1] Do not keep silence and **do not hold thy peace or be still** are phrases meant to implore God not to be inactive in Israel's time of distress. **[2-5]** They remind God that these are **thy enemies who hate thee** (vs. 2), who **against thee make a covenant** (vs. 5). The enemies **are in tumult,** that is, in a state of agitation (vs. 2), they are **crafty** (vs. 3), **they consult together** (vs. 3b), and **conspire with one accord** (vs. 5a) against Israel. They intend to **wipe Israel out as a nation** so that her **name** will **be remembered no more** (vs. 4). And all of this is being planned against God's **protected ones** or his "treasured ones" (NASB; vs. 3).

[6-8] Edom, the Ishmaelites, Moab, and **Ammon** were blood relatives of Israel (Gen. 25:19-30; 16:15; 11:31; 19:36-38), but they were also traditional enemies of Israel. **Edom, Moab,** and **Ammon** bordered Israel on the south and the east. **The Ishmaelites** were a semi-nomadic people who sometimes settled among various Arab tribes south and east of Israel. **The Hagrites** were apparently descendants of Abraham by Hagar (Gen. 16:10). They dwelt east of the Jordan and east of Gilead (1 Chron. 5:10, 18-20). **Gebal** was situated north of Edom and south of the Dead Sea (Josh. 13:5). **Amalek** was the father of nomadic tribes who roamed from the Sinai peninsula to the territory east of the Gulf of Aqabah. They were also hostile toward Israel (Exod. 17:8-16; Num. 24:20) and were marked by God for destruction (1 Sam. 15:1-3). **Philistia,** located southwest of Israel, was an inveterate foe. **The inhabitants of Tyre,** situated northwest of Israel, were generally conciliatory toward the Israelites, and sometimes made alliances with them (1 Kings 7:13-14). At other times, however, they were hostile enemies (Amos 1:9-10; Joel 3:4-8). The prophets frequently announce the certain downfall of Tyre (Isa. 23:1-17; Jer. 25:22; 47:4; Ezek. 26–28; Zech. 9:3-4). **The children of Lot**, Moab and Ammon, are the chief instigators of this coalition against Israel (vs. 8b).

'Destroy our enemies' (vss. 9-12). [9-10] The psalmist here refers to the victory of Deborah and Barak over **Jabin**, king of Hazor (Judg. 4–5). No specific mention is made of **Endor** in Judges, but since it is near Mount Tabor, which figured prominently in the battle, it is likely that Endor was also involved. The Greek reads *en harod*, "the spring of Herod" (cf. NEB), the place of a Midianite defeat.

[11] A second event referred to is the victory of Gideon over the Midianite nobles, **Oreb and Zeeb** (Judg. 7:25; 8:3), and the princes, **Zebah and Zalmunna** (Judg. 8:4-21). The psalmist is following a usual form employed in blessings and curses whereby one recites instances of past happiness or misery and prays that something similar may happen in the present. **[12]** These foes boasted that they would **take possession of the pastures of God**, that is, dispossess the Israelites and take over their grazing grounds and all their possessions (cf. vs. 4).

'Put our enemies to shame' (vss. 13-18). [13] Whirling dust may possibly refer to a tumbleweed (RSV note), or a wild artichoke which, when dry in the summer, rolls in the wind like a tumbleweed (cf. NEB "thistledown"). The thought is that the **dust** and the **chaff**, because they have little substance, are easily displaced by the wind. So may Israel's enemies be displaced.

[14-15] May God **terrify them** like a forest **fire** or a **hurricane. [16-18]** May the enemy **be put to shame and dismayed for ever** and **perish in disgrace**. It is difficult to reconcile these sentiments with the phrases **that they may seek thy name** and **know that thou alone…art the Most High over all the earth**. It would appear on the surface that the psalmist is interested in the conversion of the enemies, but that idea is hard to reconcile with a wish for their complete extermination. Perhaps the psalmist feels that the massive destruction of the present generation of these mad warriors must take place in order for their children to see the truth about God. See the note on imprecations in the Psalms at the end of Psalm 79.

Psalm 84: Longing for the Temple

"A Psalm of the Sons of Korah" indicates a psalm written, authorized, or collected by one or a group of the sons of Korah, who were authorized by David as temple singers and musicians, gatekeepers and caretakers of the temple (1 Chron. 15). For the rest of the title, see the notes on Psalms 76 and 81.

The reference to the king (vs. 9) and the mention of temple singers (vs. 4) and possibly official doorkeepers (vs. 10) suggest that the psalm was written sometime in the monarchical period but not earlier than David.

The psalm is a hymn of praise to God who meets his people at the temple. In this respect it can be compared with Psalms 42–43. The psalmist there was prevented from going to the temple and leading the procession of pilgrims as had been his custom. This is possibly the circumstance in Psalm 84, although the evidence is not clear.

The psalm is symmetrically divided into three stanzas of four verses each. Each stanza is built around a beatitude (vss. 4, 5, 12). These three beatitudes serve to emphasize the development of the theme, as the outline reflected in the headings below indicates.

Blessed are those who dwell in God's house (vss. 1-4).

[1] God's **dwelling place** in this context is the temple where **the courts of the Lord** (vs. 2) and his **altars** (vs. 3) are located. The emphasis in all three phrases is on God rather than the facilities for worship. Truly the temple was **lovely**, but the psalmist is likely reflecting upon the fact that the temple is beloved (cf. NEB "dear") to him because God is there (cf. Isaiah 5:1, where the same root is used). "Amiable" (KJV) suggests the fellowship available at the temple. For the phrase **O Lord of hosts** and its variants (vss. 3, 8, 12), see Psalm 80. **Hosts** may refer to Israel (Exod. 12:41)

or any nation (Josh. 10:5), to armies (1 Kings 15:20), or to angels (Ps. 148:2; Lk. 2:13). Here it refers to Israel.

[2] The interpretation of the psalm hinges on the meaning to be attached to three key words in this verse, all of which are capable of varied connotations. **Longs** (Heb. *kasaph*) can mean to be depressed or disappointed according to cognate languages, but in the Bible it means to be eager or yearn for (Gen. 31:30; Ps. 17:12). **Faints** ("yearns," NASB; Heb. *kalah*) can mean to fail or languish (Lam. 4:17) or be accomplished or fulfilled (Ezra 1:1). **Sing for joy** ("crieth out," KJV; Heb. *ranan*) means to give a ringing cry either in joy or exultation (Jer. 31:7), or in distress or anguish (Lam. 2:19). Since the third word is used regularly in the psalms to mean a cry of joy, it seems best to interpret the other two words in the positive sense of yearning. There is nothing here to require the conclusion of some that the psalmist is prevented from going to the temple at the appointed seasons. Verses 8 and 9 could reflect a time of distress, but not necessarily so. **Soul, heart,** and **flesh** are variants indicating the whole person rather than suggesting that man is a threefold being (cf. Matt. 22:37; 1 Thess. 5:23). **The living God** (cf. Ps. 42:2) is the only God who has reality and who can bless man (cf. Isa. 38:14-20).

[3-4] The word for **sparrow** literally means "bird" (NASB), but is used here in a specific way to correspond to the word **swallow. Home** (vs. 3) and **house** (vs. 4) are from the same Hebrew word, but **nest** shows that it means **home** in verse 3. There may be an intentional play on the word to indicate that even birds' nests, as well as the facilities for worship, demonstrate the hospitality of God. The beatitude in verse 4 summarizes the thought of the stanza. How blessed are those who never have to long for God's house because they are continually there!

Blessed are those who journey to Zion (vss. 5-8).

[5] While the beatitude in the first and third stanzas is given at the end, this one is given at the beginning. The phrase **to Zion** is an addition to the Hebrew text. "Of them" (KJV) adds little to our understanding. "Pilgrim ways" (NEB) takes the word for **highways** to mean a raised

road or main thoroughfare over which the pilgrims would journey. Verses 6 and 7 indicate that a pilgrimage to Jerusalem is intended. **Strength** doubtless has primary reference here to the weariness of the journey which can only be offset by the joyous anticipation of arriving at God's house (cf. vs. 7).

[6] There is no known **valley of Baca** in Palestine. The word probably refers to a place of balsam trees (cf. 2 Sam. 5:23), an arid place which the pilgrims psychologically **make a place of springs.** "They find water from a spring" (NEB) departs from the Hebrew text. The causative verb stem indicates not something ready at hand, but that which they created in their hearts. **Pools** involves a different vocalization of the consonants for "blessings" (MT, NASB). **Early rain** (Heb. *moreh*) can also carry an alternative meaning, "teacher." Thus the LXX translates "the teacher (or lawgiver) will give blessings." If the festival contemplated is the Feast of Tabernacles, the early rains would soon begin and turn the dry region into a watered place. Anticipation of this may have prompted this poetic strain.

[7] **From strength to strength** seems to suggest that the nearer they approach the temple the more strength they receive as a result of their anticipation of the glorious fellowship to be enjoyed there. Compare "grace upon grace" (John 1:16), which refers to our coming into a greater fulness of Christ, and Paul's "from one degree of glory to another" (2 Cor. 3:18), which anticipates the final glory to be received (cf. 2 Thess. 1:10-12). God promises to renew the strength of those who trust in him (Isa. 40:31). "From outer wall to inner" (NEB) assumes that *chayil*, "strength," should be revocalized to read *chel*, "rampart." This turns the passage into a physical, rather than a psychological, consideration. The general tenor of verses 5-7 is against this unnecessary emendation. **The God of gods will be seen** literally reads "he appears before God" (cf. NASB, KJV). The word for "to" or "before" sounds much like the word for "God" (*'el* with a short vowel for the preposition and a long vowel for the word "God"). The latter, followed by *'elohim*, could mean **God of gods.** The

niphal form of the verb "to see" can mean "appear" or "be seen." Either interpretation states a truth. Every male was commanded to appear at the temple for the annual festivals (Exod. 23:17), and God would be seen there in the sense of being present and meeting Israel in fellowship (Exod. 29:42-43; 30:6, 36; Num. 17:4).

[8] Earnestness is indicated by the phrases **hear** and **give ear**. Such terminology is frequently employed in time of trouble (cf. Pss. 17:1; 54:2; 55:1; 86:6). The psalmist may be unable to go to the temple (cf. vs. 2), or he may be making an earnest petition for strength and protection on the wearisome journey to Jerusalem (cf. vss. 5-7).

Blessed are those who trust in God (vss. 9-12). [9] Shield and **anointed** are synonymous words used of the king. Though God may be designated as Israel's shield (cf. vs. 11), so may the king (cf. 89:18; 47:9). **Behold** and **look upon the face** implore God to act with favor. [10] The word **elsewhere** (cf. "without," NASB) is an addition to the Hebrew text but is essential to complete the thought. The verbal phrase **be a doorkeeper** could also be translated "stand at the threshold" (NASB; cf. "linger," NEB). It is not certain, therefore, that an official doorkeeper is intended. There is a cognate nominal phrase, "keeper of the threshold" (Heb. *shomer hassaph;* Jer. 35:4; 2 Kings 12:9; 22:4=2 Chron. 34:9; 2 Kings 23:4; 25:18-19=Jer. 52:24), which refers to a lesser official at the temple. There were some four thousand gatekeepers or porters (Heb. *sho'arim*, 1 Chron. 23:5), who had various duties, among them that of acting as attendants for the ark of the covenant (1 Chron. 15:23, 24). Since verses 1-4 reflect upon the glory of the temple servants, **be a doorkeeper** likely refers to an officiant at the temple. If so, the contrast is not between the lowly work of such an officiant and an exalted position elsewhere, but between the righteous work of the doorkeeper and **the tents of wickedness**. Even temporary service at the temple for only **a day** would be **better than a thousand** days spent elsewhere, especially in wickedness. There is another thought here, too. The layman could approach no closer than the altar of burnt offering outside the sanctuary proper (Num. 1:47-54). Even the Levites who were not officiating priests could not enter the sanctuary but performed their services outside the sanctuary (Num. 18:1-7). The contrast, therefore, may be between only being able to *approach* the holy sanctuary and dwelling *in* the tents of wickedness.

[11] God is frequently referred to as a **shield** (cf. Gen. 15:1; Deut. 33:29; Pss. 3:3; 18:2, 35; 28:7; 33:20; 59:11; 91:4; 115:9, 10, 11; 119:114; 144:2; Prov. 30:5), but seldom as a **sun** (cf. Isa. 60:19-20; Mal. 4:2). This restraint doubtless is an effort to avoid any taint of pagan thought, since most of the ancient nations worshiped the sun. God is Israel's source of **favor** and **honor** (more literally, "grace and glory," KJV, NASB). God will **withhold no good thing** from his own (cf. 34:10; Rom. 8:32). But the precondition of divine blessing is that one **walk uprightly**, for sin alienates man from God's good things (Isa. 59:1-2; Jer. 5:25).

[12] The final beatitude reaches to the heights of spiritual perception. Though he does not live in God's house (vs. 4) and possibly cannot presently make the pilgrimage to the temple, or at least cannot remain there long (vs. 5), the psalmist can and will trust in God, for this is the greatest blessing of all. This beatitude implies that God is present to bless his own even when they are not at the sanctuary. This thought does not discredit public assemblies (cf. Heb. 10:25), but emphasizes the fact that religion should be a daily experience.

Psalm 85: 'Revive Us Again!'

See Psalms 76 and 84 for the phraseology used in the title. This psalm has been interpreted as eschatological, referring to the messianic age when righteousness and peace will prevail. The psalm has been conversely interpreted in a cultic sense as a psalm sung at the New Year Festival in the autumn. The psalm would then consist of a confession of sin and a prayer for God's blessings during the coming year. It seems better, however, to take the psalm as historical, perhaps reflecting the time of reconstruction following the exile. The rejoicing over God's favor in allowing Israel to go back home was marred by the internal problems and external enemies which they encountered, as reflected in Ezra and Nehemiah, and by the resulting delay in the completion of the temple, as reflected in Haggai and in Zechariah 1–8.

The psalmist recalls the past situation when God forgave their sins and restored them to their land (vss. 1-3). Then he prays for restoration, revival, and salvation in the present circumstances (vss. 4-7). He resolves to listen for God's answer and expresses confidence in God's constancy (vss. 8-9). Either through a prophetic oracle, or by reflecting upon the nature of God, a vision of complete concord comes to him (vss. 10-13).

There is an interesting and informative use of the word "turn" (*shubh*) in this psalm (cf. Ps. 80). It is translated "restore" (vss. 1, 4) and "turn" (vss. 3, 8), and is the basis of the word "again" in verse 6. God turned from his anger (vs. 3) and restored Israel (vs. 1) in the past. So, on the basis of faith in God's constancy, the prayer goes up for God to "restore" (vs. 4) and "revive" (vs. 6) Israel again. But Israel must "never turn back to folly" (vs. 8). The concept of God's turning in favor toward those who turn in penitence is a theme frequently elucidated in the Scriptures (cf. Jon. 3:8-10; Jer. 18:5-11).

Reflection upon the past (vss. 1-3). [1] The phrase **thou wast favorable** means basically to count as acceptable. There had been a time when they were not acceptable because of their wandering into sin (cf. Jer. 14:10, 12). But when they repented, God accepted them and restored **the fortunes** [or "turned the captivity," KJV] **of Jacob,** that is, Israel. [2] **Forgive** (literally "lift up and carry away") and **pardon** (literally "cover") are synonyms, as are **iniquity** (literally "distortion") and **sin** (literally "missing the mark"). [3] This verse also employs synonymous parallelism. God's anger resulting from Israel's former sins has now been removed.

Simple past tense (RSV, NASB), as well as present perfects (KJV, NEB), convey the thought of action completed in past time. The Hebrew perfects are translated as aorists (simple past) in the LXX, but the Hebrew perfect can carry the force of the Greek perfect, indicating past actions with continuing results. The word **all** (vss. 2b, 3a) leaves no doubt with regard to the completeness of their restoration and forgiveness. There is no conflict between verses 1-3 and 4-7. Verses 1-3 speak of forgiveness of the sins which brought on captivity. Restoration to the homeland is proof of their forgiveness. There may be a distinction intended between **their** (vs. 2) and **us** (vs. 4). The word **again** (vs. 4) is an addition to the Hebrew text (cf. KJV, NASB, NEB). Perhaps the psalmist means that the former generation was fully forgiven and restored to the homeland, but the work of reconstruction has suffered because of later sins of those who returned (cf. Haggai).

Present estrangement (vss. 4-7). [4] For the word **again**, see the comments above. Imperatives used in supplications carry the connotation of earnest pleading rather than that of commanding. Synonymous parallelism is employed in this verse and the next. **Restore us** to your favor (cf. vs. 1) and **put away thy indignation** (cf. vs. 3) as you did in the past. [5] Plaintive questions frequently accompany supplications for forgiveness and restoration (cf. 79:5; 80:4). These questions reveal little about the length of the suffering, for Isaiah could raise the cry "How long, O Lord?" (Isa. 6:11) even before the calamity came. Nor do these questions reveal impatience or mistrust (cf. vss. 7, 10-13), but rather the earnestness of the petitioner. [6] **Revive us again** reflects the common Hebrew concepts of historical continuity whereby the present generation is linked to the past (cf. **thy people**, vss. 2, 6), and community solidarity whereby the sins of some affect the welfare of all. But the psalmist also understands and acknowledges the concept of social responsibility whereby each generation and each individual is responsible for preserving the covenant blessings through faithfulness to their covenant obligations (cf. vss. 8b-9). [7] **Steadfast love** (*chesedh*, covenant loyalty) and **salvation** are here synonymous. God's love causes him to go beyond strict covenant obligation and to manifest his grace and acts of mercy (*rachamim*); compare Psalm 51:1, which begins in Hebrew, "be gracious," and Psalm 103:8, where "merciful," "gracious," and "steadfast love" are combined.

Waiting for God's answer (vss. 8-9). [8] **Speak** seems to suggest a vocal answer given through a prophetic oracle, although that is not necessarily the case. **Saints** (*chasidim*) are God's faithful covenant keepers. Apparently **his people** and **his saints** are identical here. The word "and" preceding the latter phrase (KJV, NEB; omitted in RSV) could better be translated "even." "But let them not turn back to folly" (RSV note represents the Hebrew) is a warning against repetition of the same kind of folly which brought on past and present misfortunes (cf. 80:18). The line does not need to be emended according to the Greek (cf. NEB).

[9] "Worship" (NEB) is unsuitable because it is more restrictive in meaning to the modern English mind than **fear**, which means total reverence and obedience in all walks of life (cf. Prov. 1:7; Pss. 111:10; 112:1). **Glory** probably refers to the rebuilding of the temple, a reversal of the departure of God's glory at the beginning of the exile (Ezek. 10:4; 11:22-23; cf. 1 Sam. 4:19-22).

Future glory (vss. 10-13). [10-11] **Steadfast love** and **faithfulness** are companion terms, as are **righteousness** and **peace**. Verse 11 shows that **faithfulness** refers to Israel and righteousness refers to God's righteousness which comes down to man. **Righteousness** used in this sense can mean vindication (cf. Deut. 25:1; 1 Kings 8:32; Pss. 24:5; 43:1; 103:6, 17-18) or justification (cf. Gen. 15:6; Ps. 32:1-2; Rom. 4:1-8; Pss.143:1-2; 130:3-4). God's **steadfast love** will meet with man's **faithfulness** (not "truth," KJV, NASB), and God's **righteousness** (justification) will result in man's **peace** (cf. Isa. 32:17; Rom. 5:1). **Kiss each other** refers to making a covenant. [12] As usual, material blessings attend spiritual concord (cf. Hos. 2:14-23; Matt. 6:33).

[13] God's **righteousness** will go before him as a herald goes before the king, and **make his footsteps a way** for his subjects to pass over (cf. Isa. 40:3-11; Matt. 3:3; Luke 3:4-6). Though messianic connotations are couched in such language, these verses also had an immediate application

to the people of the psalmist's day. Complete restoration of the homeland would follow the establishment of complete concord between God and Israel.

Psalm 86: Prayer for God's Grace

For the phrase "of David" in the title, see Psalm 76. The word for prayer in the title and in verse 6, and the root of the word for supplication in verse 6, set the tone for this psalm. The psalmist is pleading with God to manifest to him His grace, mercy, and love (cf. vs. 15). The root of the word for "supplication" (*tachanunoth*, plural in Hebrew) is the same as that for the noun "grace" (*chen*), and for the adjective "gracious" (*channun*, vs. 15), and the imperative verb "be gracious" (*chonnen*, vss. 3, 16). For a discussion on the significance of the meaning of these words, see the notes at the end of the psalm.

Another interesting feature of this psalm contributes to our understanding of its tenor. In referring to deity, besides the word *'elohim* (mighty ones, vss. 2, 8, 10, 12, 14, 15), there is an interchange between LORD (Yahweh, vss. 1, 7, 11, 17) and Lord (*'adhonay*, vss. 3, 4, 5, 8, 9, 12, 15). The last word is used in the OT of earthly masters and of God and *'elohim* in verse 8 refers to pagan gods. The word *'adhonay* connotes mastery and suggests the subordination required of the subjects of the master. But the mighty God (*'elohim*) is known to Israel as the eternal covenanter and he is merciful, gracious, and abounding in steadfast love; therefore, submission is a joyous rather than grievous experience. This thought permeates the entire psalm.

Since this psalm is reflected in many other psalms, some have conjectured that it was composed to serve as a liturgy to be used by individual worshipers in times of distress. It is not likely that David, who possessed creative talent as a poet (cf. 1 Sam. 16:18-23; 2 Sam. 1:17-27; 3:33-34; ch. 22; 23:1-7), would have borrowed so freely from others. However, it may be that others have borrowed from this psalm.

Supplication of one who trusts (vss. 1-7). [1] **Incline thine ear** suggests God's condescending nature which causes him to listen to and answer man's pleadings. **Poor and needy** are terms often used of individual Israelites or the nation Israel to describe the humble petitioner who is in urgent need of divine assistance. (For the word **poor** [*'ani*], see Pss. 9:18; 10:2, 9; 12:5; 14:6; 34:6; etc. For the word **needy** [*'ebhyon*], see Pss. 49:2; 69:33; 107:41; 109:31; 112:9; 132:15; 140:12. See the companion word *dal*, "poor, weak," Pss. 41:1; 72:13; 82:3, 4; 113:7.) These words, as used in the psalms, do not necessarily reveal the financial circumstances of those described, but indicate recognition of the need for help from God. In Psalm 86, the need is to be delivered from insolent enemies (vss. 14-17) and possibly also to be forgiven (vs. 5).

[2] **Preserve my life** suggests that his life is in danger (cf. vs. 14). **For I am godly** (*chasidh*, "loyal") appeals to God's faithfulness, as verse 1 appeals to his compassion. (Cf. "holy," KJV, which better translates *qadhosh*. "Constant and true" [NEB] is an effort to include the two principal meanings of the word.) The psalmist, however, does not trust in himself, but in God (vs. 2b). On **servant**, see the comment on verse 16. **Thou art my God** may be syntactically connected to verse 2 or verse 3. **God** (*'elohim*) here suggests a mighty protector and deliverer. [3] **Be gracious** (cf. vs. 16, Hebrew) is better than "be merciful" (KJV). The motives for expecting an answer from God are three-fold in these opening verses, as indicated by the word **for**. His undone condition (vs. 1b) and his incessant prayer (vss. 3b, 4b) are linked with God's forgiving love (vs. 5) and constancy (vs. 7b). [4] Expectancy of a favorable answer anticipates the gladness that will accompany deliverance. **Soul** (cf. "heart," NEB) frequently indicates the person himself (cf. Gen. 46:15; Exod. 1:5; Ezek. 18:4; KJV).

[5] **Good** here means "kind" (NEB), one who is **forgiving**. [6] Verse 6 employs synonymous parallelism. For the discussion of the key terms, see the note below on prayer.

[7] The present tense is best here, for the recurring experience of the psalmist is indicated by the Hebrew frequentative imperfects.

God's sovereignty the basis of trust (vss. 8-13). [8-10] See the notes on Canaanite Baalism and universalism at the end of Psalm 77. **Works** (vs. 8) likely refers to God's acts of creation, and **wondrous things** (vs. 10) probably refers to miraculous deeds done within Israel's history.

[11] Pious Israelites recognized the need for divine help in doing right (cf. 119:33-40), and also human responsibility in utilizing the strength given (cf. 119:57-64). **Walk** suggests a bent of mind and way of life. **Truth** and "faithfulness" (vs. 15) translate the same Hebrew word. **Truth** is the abstract teaching which results in faithfulness. The context must determine the way the word is translated. **Unite my heart** indicates the need for singularity of purpose in following God. "With those who revere thy name" (NEB) expands the Hebrew text and alters its meaning. [12] **With my whole heart** indicates the undivided and sincere thanksgiving which will characterize one whose heart has been united by God. [13] God's past preservation of the psalmist's life provides the basis for his present trust and hope (cf. vss. 2, 5, 7). Or the perfect Hebrew tenses could be understood as indicating the certainty of future deliverance. In this case, the psalmist might be referring to resurrection (cf. 49:15; 73:23, 24), although this is highly unlikely. **The depths of Sheol** may indicate the place of deepest darkness in the nether world (cf. Ps. 88:6), or it could refer simply to death, or to the grave as being under the earth as the heights of the heavens are above it. "The lowest hell" (KJV) is misleading to the modern reader because of the common tendency to attach the concept of conscious punishment to the word "hell." The word did not necessarily carry that connotation in 1611, when the KJV was first published. There is no idea of conscious punishment in the Hebrew word *sheol*.

Lamentation over present troubles (vss. 14-17). [14] Such narrative statements in prayer are not meant to inform the omniscient God, but are part of a suppliant's plea as he presents his case before God's tribunal for adjudication. See the note on prayer below. **Insolent men** are those who arrogantly disregard God's laws, and **ruthless men** are those devoid of human compassion. Since compassion is a characteristic of God to be imitated by men, the last line of the verse, **and they do not set thee before them,** can be understood as a summary of the two preceding lines. [15] In contrast to these godless persons, God is **merciful, gracious, and abounding in steadfast love and faithfulness.** This is an exact quote from Exodus 34:6b. See the note below on God's grace, mercy, and love. [16] **Take pity on me** is better translated **be gracious to me** (as in vs. 3). **Save the son of thy handmaid** could be a reflection upon the godliness of the psalmist's mother (cf. 116:16), but it is more likely a humble way of stating his complete and loving submission as comparable to that of a slave born in the house of his master. [17] **Sign** can indicate any visible manifestation, not necessarily a miracle. **Favor** ("good," MT, KJV, NASB) can mean "kindness" (NEB; cf. vs. 5). The psalmist is asking for evidence (cf. NEB "proof") of God's kindness in granting his petition. His enemies will **be put to shame** when they see his deliverance.

Excursus

Prayer in the Old Testament

The most common word for prayer in the OT is *tephillah*, which derives from the verb *palal*, used in the titles to Psalms 17, 86, 90, 102, and 142, and in many psalm passages. The synonymous parallelism of Psalm 86:6 connects *tephillah* very closely with *tachanunoth*, "supplications." *Tephillah* is used about seventy-five times in the OT, more than thirty times in the psalms. The word often refers to one who pleads for vindication from God (Ps. 109:6-7; Jer. 7:16; 11:14; 14:11; 29:7-12; 42:2, 20; etc.). The verb is also used in contexts which emphasize the idea of pleading before a superior and is variously translated as "interposed" (Ps. 106:30), "punished by the judges" (Job 31:28), "grant justice" (Isa. 16:3), "mediate for," and "intercede for" 1 Sam. 2:25). The language of the law courts gave this word its color. Though the word is frequently used in non-legal contexts, the idea of pleading is usually retained.

The second key word in Psalm 86:6, *tachanunoth*, "supplications," and its cognates are also popular in the language of prayer. The nouns derive from *chanan*, which means to be gracious or generous. The various nouns which derive from this verb are used almost forty times, with ten of them in the psalms. When used with reference to prayer to God, the words mean a pleading for grace or mercy.

A third term, *pagha'*, and its derivatives are not used in the Psalms but are found ten times in the OT in the sense of "intercede" (Jer. 7:16; 15:11; 27:18; 36:25; Gen. 23:8-9; Ruth 1:16; Job 21:15; Isa. 47:3; 53:11-12; 59:16). When one intercedes on behalf of another, he pleads that person's case.

It can be seen, therefore, that the three most common OT words for prayer or praying carry the idea of pleading. The imperative mode so often attached to these words needs to be understood in the sense of an inferior pleading with a superior on his own behalf or that of another. Figurative expressions often used in prayer, such as "I lift up my soul" (Ps. 25:1; 86:4; 143:8), or "I lift up my hands" (Pss. 28:2; 63:4; 134:2), also connote sincere pleading. Also, the word "cry," used as a noun (cf. Pss. 5:2; 17:1; 18:6; 34:15; 39:12; 40:1; 88:2; 102:1; 106:44; 119:169; 142:6) or as a verb (cf. Pss. 22:2; 27:7; 28:2; 34:17; 57:2; 86:3), and the word "call" (cf. Pss. 4:1, 3; 86:5; 99:6; 102:2; 145:18) suggest pleading for an answer. Pleading is always the tone of Hebrew prayers. Thanksgiving and praise are not generally stated to be prayer in the OT.

God's Grace, Mercy, and Love

Chesedh is used 245 times in the OT, and often in the Psalms. It is generally translated "steadfast love"(RSV), "lovingkindness" (NASB), or "mercy" (KJV). It may be used in conjunction with "faithfulness" or "steadfastness" (cf. Pss. 25:10; 40:11; 57:3; 61:7; 85:10; 86:15; 89:14, 24; 98:3; 115:1; 138:2), with one or both of the words "righteousness" and "justice" (cf. Hos. 10:12; 12:6; Isa. 57:1; Jer. 9:24; Mic. 6:8; Pss. 36:10; 101:1; Prov. 21:21), with "mercies" (*rachamim*, cf. Pss. 25:6; 103:4; Hos. 2:19; Jer. 16:5; Dan. 1:9; Zech. 7:9), with "grace" (Esth. 2:17; Gen. 19:19; Pss. 77:9; 109:12), or with "love" (*'ahabh;* cf. Jer. 2:2; 31:3; Isa. 63:7-9). It is obvious that "steadfast love," or some such hybrid phrase, is necessary to catch the full meaning of the word. *Chesedh* means basically loyalty and love manifested to God's covenant people. It often goes beyond strict covenant obligation to express God's free, unfettered grace and mercy.

Rachamim, "mercies," and its cognates express God's compassion on the undeserving. The word is used in all its forms at least sixty-five times in the OT, usually of God's mercy (cf. Pss. 25:6; 40:11; 51:1; 69:16; 77:9; 79:8; 103:4; 119:77, 156; 145:9).

The varied forms of the word for "grace" are also used over sixty-five times in the OT. The adjective "gracious" (cf. Pss. 86:15; 103:8; 111:4; 112:4; 116:5; 145:8), and the verb "be gracious" (cf. 26:11; 41:4; 56:1; 57:1) indicate God's generosity and kindness in doing for man what he cannot do for himself. The unfortunate rendering "be merciful (KJV) obscures the distinction between grace and mercy. As the sins of Israel required, God bestowed more and more grace (Rom. 5:20-21) until Christ came as the full expression of God's grace (John 1:16-17).

Psalm 87: Glorious Zion!

For the title, see the comment on "A song" in Psalm 76, and for the rest, see Psalm 84.

This is a song of Zion which lays special stress on the temple and palace, the spiritual and political capital of the nation (cf. Pss. 24, 46, 47, 48, 84, 122). These psalms, like the enthronement psalms (Pss. 93, 95-99), seem to contain three major elements. (1) They frequently look back to historical beginnings, in this case to the time when David made Jerusalem the spiritual and political capital of Israel. (2) They actualize the past in the present praise of Jerusalem because of the wonderful things which occur within her walls. (3) They sometimes look to the future glory of Zion when all nations will come and bow before their

Creator and Sustainer. Hence, historical, cultic, and escha-tological elements frequently blend in the psalms of Zion.

The multitudes of Jews streaming to the temple from various nations where they had migrated could have prompted the psalmist to reflect upon the glorious prophe-cies about the future of Zion. Some of the messianic prophecies in Isaiah (2:2-4; 19:19-25; 56:3-8; 60:10-14; ch. 62; 66:7-14) and Jeremiah (3:11-18; 23:5-6; 33:15-16) may have influenced the psalmist.

The mention of Egypt ("Rahab") and Babylon (vs. 4), with no mention of Assyria, would suggest a date for the psalm after 612 B.C., when Assyria fell to the Babylonians.

The text of the psalm is terse and elliptical, which makes it difficult to interpret. However, the text can be under-stood without resorting to transposition of verses. Some freedom, however, must be allowed the translator.

Zion, the city of God (vss. 1-3). [1] The elliptical Hebrew reads, "His foundation . . . in the mountains of holi-ness." One must supply something or understand the verse to introduce verse 2. **Stands** and **city** are supplied in the RSV. God is said elsewhere to be the founder of Zion (Ps. 78:69; Isa. 14:32). This doubtless refers to God's accep-tance of Zion, a choice made by David (cf. 2 Sam. 6:16-19; 7:1-17; Ps. 132), and figuratively to the salvation and pro-tection of Zion, representing by metonymy and synec-doche the nation (cf. Isa. 26:1; 28:16-17). [2] The Lord is not partial, but Zion is the place where God symbolically dwells, and where he meets with his people at the ark of the covenant (cf. 1 Kings 8:1–9:5). [3] The phrase **glorious things** has a messianic ring to it. See the third paragraph in the introduction above. It is God who makes the city holy (vs. 1a) and this fact makes the phrase **O city of God** appro-priate (cf. 46:4; 48:8).

Jerusalem, the mother city (vss. 4-6). This paragraph is in the form of a prophetic oracle with God as a spokesman.

[4] **Know** means to acknowledge, experience, and obey. These nations are pictured as converts to monotheism. Some take verses 4-6 to refer to Jewish proselytes, while others believe that only Jews who came from these nations

to worship at Jerusalem are under consideration. However, the messianic age when all nations have equal access to the kingdom of God is likely under consideration. **Rahab** is a reference to Egypt (cf. Ps. 89:10; Isa. 30:7; 51:9), the mighty dragon which devoured Israel during the period of the bondage. **Babylon** is the other great persecutor of Israel in the days of the psalmist. **Philistia** was a perennial enemy of Israel, and **Tyre** was sometimes an enemy (see on Ps. 83:7). **Ethiopia** (Hebrew Cush) on occasion had assailed Israel (2 Chron. 14:9). These nations stand as typical of all of Israel's enemies. But the psalmist envisions a time when they will say of Jerusalem, **This one was born there**. This phrase implies the ancient registries in which the names and nationalities of natives and foreigners were kept (cf. 2 Chron. 2:17; Ezra 2:62; Neh. 7:5; Jer. 22:30; Ezek. 13:9). The place of registry is Jerusalem (vs. 5), and God is the recorder (vs. 6). The claim made here is too strong to indicate proselytism, for these claim to be natural-born citizens.

[5] God not only founded Jerusalem (vs. 1), but he **will establish her**, that is, renew and sustain her (cf. Isa. 65:17-25). The LXX has the additional phrase "my mother," following the clause "of Zion it shall be said" (cf. NEB). This may be reflected in Galatians 4:26. The Hebrew word for "my mother" (*'emi*) is much like **it shall be said** (*ye 'amar*), which could have caused a scribe to inadvertently omit "my mother." **[6]** God personally registers the peoples born in Jerusalem. This comes close to the idea of regeneration, or a new birth which would give the Gentiles a claim on God. Though the doctrine of regeneration is not explicitly taught in the OT, several passages delineate a similar idea (cf. Ps. 51:6, 10, 12; Isa. 63:5, 8-9).

Response to the glorious promises (vs. 7). Singing and dancing were two of the most exuberant forms of praise and thanksgiving in Israel (see Exod. 15:20; Judg. 11:34; 21:21; 1 Sam. 18:6; 21:11; 29:5; 2 Sam. 6:14; Pss. 30:11-12; 68:25; 149:3; 150:4). **Springs** are the sources of spiritual life and strength (cf. Isa. 12:3; Ps. 36:9; John 7:38). Redeemed Jerusalem is the source of living water because God is in her (cf. Joel 3:18; Zech. 14:8). The New Jerusalem is so pictured (Rev. 21:1-4; 22:1-5).

Psalm 88: The Hopelessness of Death

Machalath le'annoth in the title means literally "sickness to afflict." It may reflect the subject matter of the psalm, or could suggest a cultic use of the psalm. For the word *maśkil*, see Psalm 78. "Heman the Ezrahite" presents a problem. Heman, a Levite temple musician, is mentioned in 1 Chronicles 15:17, 19. There is a wise man named Heman, connected with Ethan the Ezrahite (1 Kings 4:31 [Hebrew 5:11]; cf. Ps. 89, title). For the rest of the title, see Psalm 76.

Like several others, this psalmist cries out of the depths of despair (cf. Pss. 7:1-2; 22:1-2; 31:1-2; 61:1-2; 130:1-2); but unlike the others, this psalmist sees no hope for better days. His faith prompts him to continue praying, though he has no hope for deliverance.

The continual pleading (vss. 1-2). [1] I call for help emends the word *yeshu'athi* (my salvation) to relate it to the verb *shu'a,* "cry out." The emendation is plausible and requires little change in the Hebrew text. **By day** and **in the night** express his continual calling upon God (cf. vs. 9; Ps. 22:2). **[2]** This verse implies that he receives no favorable answer from God (cf. vss. 5, 14).

The gloomy prospects (vss. 3-12). [3-5] Sheol (vs. 3) and **Pit** (vs. 4) are synonymous, as are **the dead** and **the grave** (vs. 5). **Pit** (Heb. *bor*) refers to the **grave,** but, in conjunction with **Sheol** and **death,** can refer to the state of the dead. He feels that he is forsaken, forgotten, and disfellowshiped by God (vss. 4-5). **[6]** Sheol, or the **Pit,** is a dark, gloomy place (cf. Pss. 6:5; 30:9; 115:17; Job 10:20-22; 17:13-16). **[7]** God's **wrath,** the cause of the psalmist's suffering, is **heavy** and can be figuratively described as a flood (cf. 42:7). **[8a-b]** Because his companions consider his sin the cause of his calamity, they shun him (cf. Pss. 31:11-12; 38:11; Job 19:13-19; 30:10). **[8c-9a]** Worst of all, there is no escape from his sorrowful plight. **[9b-c]** For the significance of stretching out the hands in prayer, see the note on prayer at the end of Psalm 86. **[10-12]** All these rhetorical questions expect the answer no. **The shades** (vs. 10b; Heb. *repha'im*) means the weak, helpless ones, and refers to the powerless state of the dead. **Abaddon** (vs. 11) is a synonym for Sheol (cf. Prov. 15:11; 27:20; Job 26:6) or **the grave** (cf. Job 28:22).

A lifetime of affliction (vss. 13-18). **[13] In the morning** suggests the urgency of his prayers (cf. Pss. 119:147, 148; 143:8) and their regularity (cf. Pss. 5:3; 59:16). **[14]** The idea of being **cast off** is frequent in psalms of lament (cf. 43:2; 44:9, 23; 71:9; 74:1; 89:38; 108:11). Hiding the face can mean not to remember one's sins (cf. Ps. 51:9), or not to answer one's prayers (cf. Ps. 34:15-16), or not to bless man (cf. Ps. 30:7). **[15]** The word for **helpless** (*pun*) is only used this one time in the OT, and its meaning is uncertain (cf. "distracted," KJV; "overcome," NASB; "cower," NEB). **[16-18]** Compare verses 7-8.

EXCURSUS

The Hebrew Concept of Immortality

Christ is declared to be the one who "brought life and immortality to light through the gospel" (2 Tim. 1:10). This does not mean that nothing was known about the afterlife before this time, but Christ gave further information and verified some truths which had already been learned and accepted by some in his day.

Little information is given in the OT concerning the afterlife. Only one passage (Dan. 12:2) clearly reveals bodily resurrection, and that came during the exilic period (587–536 B.C.). Several passages on resurrection are figurative of national restoration of Israel from exile (cf. Isa. 25:6-9; 26:12-19; 27:12-13; Ezek. 37:1-23). It is not likely that Job 19:23-27 is a resurrection passage. Textual ambiguities render uncertain the meaning of verses 25-26. Furthermore, the passage ends on the same somber note as preceding and succeeding references to Job's problems (cf. Job 14:7-17; 21:23-26; 24:1, 22-25).

A few references indicate that some may have had deeper insights than others. One passage says that God is present even in Sheol (Ps. 139:8), and two references (Pss. 49:15; 73:24) may possibly refer to resurrection, although both passages are capable of other interpretations. In Psalm 49, the psalmist is certain that the grave will be the eternal home of the wicked (vss. 10-12). Verse 15 probably refers to preservation from an untimely death (and so, Pss. 16:10; 71:20). The word "glory" in Psalm 73:24 could be translated "honor," and does not necessarily refer to a time following death. The use made of Psalm 16 in Acts 2:25-31 does not answer the question concerning a general resurrection of the dead in Hebrew thought. Nor did miraculous resurrections reveal insights concerning a general resurrection (1 Sam. 28:8-19; 1 Kings 17:17-24; 2 Kings 4:32-37; 13:20-21).

Sheol, to the Hebrew mind, was generally a place where God could not be praised (Pss. 6:5; 88:10-11), where God was not remembered (Ps. 6:5), and where God did not remember the dead (Ps. 88:10a, 12b). There is no clear distinction anywhere between the fate of the righteous and of the wicked in Sheol. In fact, the book of Job presupposes that there is no such distinction. The eternal fire of Isaiah 66:24 (cf. Mark 9:48) was apparently not interpreted to mean eternal punishment for the wicked until intertestamental days.

Intertestamental Jewish literature developed a concept of bodily resurrection and conscious peace or punishment in Hades, the place of the dead in Greek thought (cf. 2 Macc. 7:9-38; 12:43-45; 1 Enoch chs. 22, 51, 54, 98). The Pharisees accepted belief in a resurrection and in rewards and punishments; but the Sadducees, who did not accept the validity of the oral tradition and intertestamental writings, rejected these concepts (Matt. 22:23; Acts 23:8; Josephus, *Wars*, 2.8.14; *Ant.*, 18.1.4).

The careful student of the OT will not read NT ideas back into OT settings, but will attempt to see the development of thought as God continued to reveal his will to Israel and the church (cf. Heb. 1:1-2).

Psalm 89: The King's Crown is Defiled

For the title, see Psalm 88. This is one of several royal psalms to be found in the Psalter (cf. Pss. 2, 16, 18, 20, 21, 45, 72, 110, 132). Not all these psalms were written by a king, but the king is in every case the subject about whom the psalm is written. These psalms emphasize six important points with regard to the king. (1) He is inducted into office and anointed by the Lord (2:2, 6). (2) He is adopted as God's son (2:6-7; 89:26-27). (3) He is given the promise of the continuance of his kingdom for ever (89:1-4, 28-37; 132:11-12). (4) The king is to be endowed with God's righteousness and justice and to utilize these qualities as he governs his people (45:6-7; 72:1-2; 89:14). (5) He has priestly functions (110:4). (6) He is promised victory over his enemies (2:8-9; 20:6-8; 21:8-12; 45:4-5; 132:18).

All of these six major features of royal psalms have messianic overtones. These ideals are only partially fulfilled at best by the Davidic kings. It is the Christ who perfectly fulfils them in his spiritual kingdom, the church. These psalms contain an *idealistic hope* for the future at which time God's righteousness and justice will prevail (72:1-4). There is the expression of *universalistic hope* which includes all nations in God's plan of salvation (72:8-11; 2:8-9). There is the expression of *eschatological hope* which extends God's plan of salvation to the end of time (72:5-7; 89:36-37).

The emphasis in Psalm 89 is on the promise that the kingdom would endure for ever (vss. 1-3, 19-37). Yet there is an apparent breach of covenant (vss. 38-45). Considerable time has elapsed between the days of David and the writing of the psalm (vss. 19, 49). The walls of Jerusalem have been breached and its strongholds laid in ruins (vs. 40). Though the king is young, he has been dethroned and shamefully treated (vss. 44-45). The time between the captivity of Jehoiachin (597 B.C.; 2 Kings 24:8-17) and the fall of Jerusalem (587 B.C.; 2 Kings 25:8-12) best fits the setting of this psalm. Zedekiah, the last king of Judah, was nothing more than a puppet of the Babylonian Empire.

Introductory summary (vss. 1-4). The main themes of the

psalm are set forth here. [1] **Thy steadfast love, O Lord** reads in Hebrew, "the steadfast love of the Lord." However, the emendation is advisable to balance the lines of poetry and address both lines to God. [2] The theme of God's **steadfast love** and **faithfulness** is frequently applied to the Davidic covenant in the psalm (vss. 5, 8, 14, 24, 28, 33, 49). [3-4] God's promise to David is found in 2 Samuel 7:1-17 and is elaborated in this psalm (vss. 19-37). **Thou hast said** is supplied since there is no formal introduction to the word spoken by God in the Hebrew text. The concept of the **covenant** made with his **chosen one, David** his **servant**, is repeated in the psalm (vss. 19, 20, 28, 29, 34-36, 39, 49-51). There is no record of an oath being used by God when he chose David (vs. 3b). This may be poetic license used to emphasize the unconditional nature of the covenant, or it may be that the book of Samuel left out the detail of the oath. See the note at the end of Psalm 77 on the supplementation of Israel's history in the Psalms. **For ever** (vs. 4a) is also repeated in the psalm (vss. 1, 2, 21, 28, 29, 36, 37, 46). With the possible exception of verse 2, **for ever** must mean "for a long time." The kings are all dead, the kingdom has ended, and the Jewish era has passed. This phraseology is doubtless idealized hyperbolic language used to gain an intensive effect (cf. Ps. 72:5, 15, 17). However, the psalmist here seems to have taken the phrase literally. See the final paragraph at the end of the psalm.

The throne of God (vss. 5-18). [5-8] The majesty of God is set forth in these verses. Verses 5 and 6 employ synonymous parallelism. **Wonders** and **faithfulness** (vs. 5) suggest those divine manifestations which show God to be faithful to his covenant promise. **The assembly of the holy ones** (vs. 5b), **the heavenly beings** (literally "sons of God," vs. 6b), and **the council of the holy ones** (vs. 7a) all refer to the angelic hosts in **the heavens** (vs. 5a) and **skies** (vs. 6a; cf. Deut. 33:2; Dan. 7:10). The language may be mythological in origin, referring to the inferior gods which counseled with the chief god in pagan thought. However, the Scripture demythologizes these concepts and purifies them so that God is supreme and unique (cf. Isa. 14:12-14). See the

312 / PSALM 89:9-20

note on Canaanite Baalism at the end of Psalm 77 and the note on Psalm 82:1. No one is as mighty as God (vs. 8).

[9-13] The mastery of God is here set forth. God controls the world he created. **Rahab** (vs. 10), like Leviathan (Ps. 74:13-14; Job 26:12), stood as a symbol of the ancient sea monster subdued by the chief God in creation. But **Rahab** in Israelite literature stands for Egypt (see Ps. 87:4), and Leviathan stands for Assyria or Babylonia (Isa. 27:1). **The north and the south** (vs. 12) may also be a reference to the mythological language of Canaanite paganism which pictured the supreme god as enthroned in the north on Mount Saphon (Hebrew for "north"). Here it merely means throughout the land. **Tabor** (1,900 ft.) and **Hermon** (9,000 ft.) are symbols of the glory of God. The idea that four mountains are named here (NEB) is unconvincing.

[14-18] The moral nature of God is here set forth. **Righteousness** and **justice** (vs. 14) come from the legal language of the law (cf. Deut. 25:13-16; Lev. 19:35-37). God always administers righteousness and justice in keeping with his **steadfast love** (Hebrew covenant loyalty) and **faithfulness** to his covenant with Israel. The king is expected to possess and utilize these characteristics in the administration of his office (cf. Pss. 45:6-7; 72:1-2). **The festal shout** (vs. 15) apparently refers to a celebration of the king's victory, recognizing the king as God's representative (cf. 1 Sam. 4:5-6; 18:6-7), or to God pictured as a victorious king (cf. Pss. 47:5-7; 98:6). **Horn** and **shield** (vss. 17-18) refer to the king's strength and the protection he provides for the people as he relies upon divine help (cf. Pss. 18:1-3; 21:1-7). **Our shield** and **our king** are synonymous. **Belongs to** faithfully represents the Hebrew (cf. KJV, NEB).

Terms of the covenant (vss. 19-37). (Cf. 2 Sam. 7:1-17.)

[19] **Thy faithful one** is plural in Hebrew. This could be taken as a plural of majesty, referring to David, or it could refer to Samuel and Nathan through whom God's wonderful promises came to David. **Crown** (Heb. *nezer*, cf. vs. 39) is an emendation of the Hebrew text, which reads "help" (*'ezer*). [20] David is God's **anointed** (1 Sam. 16:1, 13; 2 Sam. 5:3), as are his successors to the throne.

[21-25] The usual promises of success granted to the king are here related. [26-27] In this adoption formula (cf. Ps. 2:6-7), the king accepts God's guidance in his kingly functions and God makes him **the firstborn, the highest of the kings of the earth**. The last phrase is in apposition to the first. **Firstborn** has reference to rank rather than order of birth (cf. Col. 1:15-20). The psalmist is doubtless reflecting upon the fact that Israel as a nation was chosen as God's firstborn son (Exod. 4:21-23), and as long as Israel was obedient he would be exalted above all the nations of the earth (Deut. 28:1). What was originally said of the nation is here declared of the king.

[28-37] A distinction is made between the unconditional promise of the continuance of the Davidic dynasty (vss. 28-29, 33-37) and the discipline which would be executed upon a disobedient king (vss. 30-32). The psalmist apparently failed to apply his discernment in his following complaint (vss. 38-51).

[37] RSV emends the Hebrew ("and be steadfast as the witness in the sky") but preserves the thought.

Apparent breach of covenant (vss. 38-51). [38-45] The king has been rejected and renounced (vss. 38-39), despoiled and defeated (vss. 41-43), dethroned and defamed (vss. 44-45). [46-48] The familiar plaintive cry **How long?** (vs. 46; cf. Pss. 13:1; 79:5) is a plea for restoration of the king, as is the reference to human frailty (vss. 47-48).

[49-51] Here the psalmist appeals to God's loyalty (vs. 49) and love (vss. 50-51). Verses 50-51 are probably words put in the mouth of the king by the psalmist. The psalm appears to be *about* the king rather than *by* him (cf. vss. 1-18).

It is difficult to understand in what way the psalmist feels that God has broken covenant or been unfaithful to the king of Israel. He may feel that the untoward circumstances of the present indicate that the dynasty is about to come to an end. If Jehoiachin is the king who is the subject of the psalm, the kingdom did come to an end as a political entity ten years later and was never restored. God's promise to continue David's house "for ever" was apparently misunderstood to mean that the political kingdom would endure for all time to come.

[52] This is a doxology closing Book III of the Psalter. God has raised up the booth of David (Amos 9:11-12; Acts 15:16-17), and all nations are blessed by the Branch of David, the Messiah (Isa. 11:1-3, 10; Acts 13:23; Rom. 15:12). The fulfillment of the Davidic promise has far exceeded Israel's fondest hopes.

Psalm 90: Man's Transient Life

There are numerous literary correspondences between this psalm and the song of Moses (Deut. 32) and the final blessing of Moses upon Israel (Deut. 33). These correspondences are pointed out in the comments on the psalm. The similarity of language between Moses and the psalm has led to two divergent conclusions. Some insist that these phrases verify the accuracy of the title which attributes the psalm to Moses. More likely is the view that these phrases, probably borrowed by the psalmist, influenced the collectors to attach the present title to the psalm. Since Moses lived 120 years and died as a result of God's judicial intervention while yet in his vigor (Num. 20:12; Deut. 34:7), it seems unlikely that he would designate the normal span of life in his day as seventy, or at best, eighty years (vs. 10). Aaron died when he was 123 years of age (Num. 33:39).

The psalm is written in the style of a community lament, and it involves numerous contrasts which emphasize on the one hand the eternal constancy of God and his judgment on sinful man, and on the other hand the temporality and frailty of sinful man. Death is viewed as the divine judgment upon sin.

The eternity of God (vss. 1-2). [1] Where the Hebrew text designates God as a **dwelling place** (*ma'on*), the Greek LXX and Latin Vulgate have "refuge" (representing the Heb. *ma'oz*; cf. RSV note). However, in comparison with Deuteronomy 33:27, the Hebrew text can stand as it is. Compare "rock of refuge" (71:3, *letsur ma'on*; 31:2, *letsur ma'oz*). The concept of God as a refuge (*machas*) and a habitation (*ma'on*) is paralleled in Psalm 91:9. One living in

the presence of the eternal God finds an adequate counterpart to his own temporality; hence, these introductory
verses provide a good foundation in faith which can serve
to temper the lament and petition which follow. **In all generations** refers to mankind in general, not to Israel in particular (cf. vs. 2).

[2] **Brought forth** pictures creation as a birth, and the
Hebrew word for **thou hadst formed** is the same as that
used in Deuteronomy 32:18 of Israel's birth as a nation.
These metaphors should not be interpreted in the pagan
sense, for God is never described in the Bible as literally
marrying and procreating children. The metaphor of birth
lays stress on the fact that the universe is the product of
God's sovereign will (cf. Job 15:7; 38:8). God, as Creator,
existed before his creation, and he will survive it. In fact,
he is **from everlasting to everlasting**, which means that he
always has been and always will be. The transcendent Creator who is distinct from his creation is also the immanent
God who takes up his personal abode among men (cf. Isa.
57:15; John 14:23). Though our psalmist does not go quite
this far, he does recognize that man is allowed to come into
the presence of God.

The temporality of man (vss. 3-6). In stark contrast to the
eternity of God stands the temporality of man. These
verses emphasize God's control of everything, even the life
span of man; and they anticipate the fact that death is the
result of divine judgment upon sinful man (cf. vss. 7-12).

[3] **Dust** here refers to death (cf. Gen. 2:7; 3:19, where a
different word for dust is used). [4] **A thousand years** in
God's sight are but like a day to man, or even as **a watch in
the night**, a third of the night according to Jewish calcula-
tion. The latter phrase shows that the psalmist was not
setting forth the epochs of world history as a week of
thousand-year days. The passing of time is of little consequence as viewed from the vantage point of eternity. However, since man cannot yet fully comprehend eternity, his
fleeting life can seem futile. [5-6] The figures of the swift-
ness of a flood, the transiency of a dream [Hebrew

"sleep"], and the short life cycle of grass are used to emphasize the brevity of life.

Sinful man under judgment (vss. 7-12). Man needs to take seriously the divine judgment upon sin which has greatly shortened the span of life compared with ancient days and which has filled life with problems and anxieties.

[7-8] Verses 7 and 8 employ synonymous parallelism. **Iniquities** refers to the deviate mind or the straying footsteps. **Secret sins** (*'alumenu*) refers to those trespasses which overtake us without our full awareness of them (cf. Ps. 19:12 [Hebrew 13], *nistaroth*; cf. Gal. 6:1-2). Whether sin is intentional or unintentional, it is ever under God's judgment. **In the light of thy countenance** means that men's hearts and lives are under the close inspection of God, and he will smile with favor or frown with disfavor in keeping with their obedience or disobedience (cf. Ps. 34:15-16).

[9] **Our days pass away** (Hebrew "decline toward the evening"), and "we bring our years to an end" (cf. RSV note) **like a sigh** (not "tale" as in KJV). [10] The span of life is brief and full of trouble. **Span** in Hebrew is "pride," doubtless referring to pride in a long life which characterized the patriarchs (cf. Gen. 25:8; 35:29).

[11] Synonymous parallelism is employed here. Man has a tendency to take too lightly the connection between mortality and sin. **According to the fear of thee** here refers to fear of the consequences of sin which ought to deter man from sinning as he contemplates the anger and wrath of the holy God. [12] **To number our days** is to use each day wisely as we contemplate the brevity of life (cf. vs. 12b; Deut. 32:29).

A plea for God's favor (vss. 13-17). Return, O Lord! How long? is a common mode of expression in psalms of lament when a plea for God to reverse the present circumstances is under consideration (cf. Pss. 6:3-4; 74:10; 89:46). **Have pity** could also be translated "repent" (KJV), but the former fits the context better. [14] **Satisfy us in the morning** means "give us a fresh start in life." The blessing of God's steadfast love will result in rejoicing and gladness (vs. 14b). [15] Synonymous parallelism is used here and in verse 16. The petition is that God will balance the evil with good things. **[16] Work** and **glorious power** doubtless refer to the kind of great things which God performed at the time of the exodus, wilderness wandering, and settlement of the land. The correspondence between the psalm and Moses' farewell message (see the introduction to the psalm) suggests a conscious borrowing of the exodus motif. **[17]** This final plea, taken in conjunction with the opening verses (1-2), suggests that life is not futile when the divine presence smiles in blessing upon us.

Psalm 91: Under God's Wings

Although the Hebrew has no title, the LXX attributes the psalm to David. Because of literary correspondences with Deuteronomy 32, some attribute the psalm to Moses, and have concluded that it is a happy sequel to the gloomy picture presented in Psalm 90. However, there are no clues in the psalm which identify the author or time of writing. The viewpoint of Rashi, a medieval Jewish commentator, that Moses authored the whole series of Psalms 90–100, is untenable.

The psalm is a psalm of confidence or an affirmation of trust. First, the psalmist states his personal trust (vss. 1-2), then he teaches others to trust in God (vss. 3-13). Finally, God responds with a solemn promise of protection and salvation (vss. 14-16). This is a beautifully constructed psalm which compresses many wonderful thoughts into a small amount of space.

Declaration of trust (vss. 1-2). The syntactical relationship between verses 1 and 2 in the Hebrew is difficult and the RSV emends the text. The verses could be literally translated as follows:

> [1] He who dwells in the shelter of the Most High
>   abides [or, will abide] in the shadow of the
>   Almighty.
> [2] I will say of the Lord, "My refuge and my
>   fortress;
>   my God, in whom I trust."

In well-balanced poetic strains, the psalmist employs four frequently-used metaphors to describe divine protection. **Shelter** refers to a covert or secret hiding place which evil forces and personalities cannot invade. God's **shadow**, frequently used in the phrase "the shadow of thy wings" (Pss. 17:8; 36:7; 57:1; 63:7), suggests the picture of a mother bird sheltering her young (cf. vs. 4). God is a **refuge** in which are all necessary provisions and where evils that would harm are not allowed to enter. God is a **fortress** which can successfully withstand the battering assaults of the enemy.

Four divine names fortify this portrayal of divine protection. **The Most High** is an ancient name for the deity (cf. Gen. 14:17-24), and emphasizes the supremacy of God as Creator and Sustainer of the world. **Almighty**, another ancient name used by the patriarchs, also emphasizes the power of God (cf. Exod. 6:3). **Lord** (Yahweh) is the covenant name by which God made himself known to Israel. This word indicates both the eternity and the providential working of the God who keeps covenant loyalty (cf. Exod. 3:13-22; John 8:58). The name **God** (Elohim), a plural form, magnifies the manifold expressions of the divine power. Though this word was also used by the Canaanites of their pagan deities, the pronoun **my** shows that the psalmist refers to the unique God of Israel.

Protection from every foe (vss. 3-13). Vivid metaphors portray potential dangers that lurk unseen on every hand and which may strike without warning. **[3] The snare of the fowler** suggests evil schemes and plots which evil men may execute against us (cf. 119:110; 124:7; 140:1-5). **The deadly pestilence** refers to a plague which suddenly destroys men in large numbers (cf. 78:50). **[4] Shield** is here a metaphor of protection, just as **buckler** is a metaphor of security, since the buckler holds the soldier's armor in place.

[5-6] Synonymous parallelism is employed here. **The terror of the night** and **the arrow that flies by day** may refer literally to attacks at night and in the daytime, or they could be metaphors for secret and open attacks respectively. It is not necessary to assume that attacks by demons are here considered, as the LXX and later Jewish exegetes supposed.

[7-8] Verses 7-8 may well be an allusion to the exodus from Egypt when the Israelites witnessed the destruction of the Egyptians armies in the Red Sea. **Thousand** and **ten thousand** are synonymous, referring poetically to a great multitude. A poetic device called "ascending numeration" is employed. In some examples, the second numeral is to be taken literally, the first numeral merely providing poetic balance (cf. Prov. 30:18-19, 21-23, 29-31). In other cases, neither numeral is to be taken literally (cf. Amos 1:3–2:8). Large numerals, such as those employed in this psalm, indicate large numbers of people, but not necessarily the precise number indicated. In some cases, a contrast is indicated by the numerals employed (cf. 1 Sam. 18:7).

[9-10] Those who trust in the Lord and abide in him are protected from evil. A textual problem is created in the Hebrew text by a change in pronouns from "my refuge" to "your habitation." The verb translated **you have made** requires the second person pronoun in verse 9b. If this verb is to be supplied in verse 9a, the pronoun needs to be emended to the second person. Other psalms (cf. 37, 49, 73) deal with limitations of the sweeping promise made here. The righteous may suffer, but God will grant deliverance (Ps. 34:19).

[11-12] God will intervene on behalf of his saints. Whether this means to suggest miraculous intervention or divine providence is not clear. Since it appears to be a universal promise to the righteous, divine providence is probably intended. Jesus' encounter with Satan shows how this promise could be abused (Matt. 4:6). Angels attended Christ when he needed them (cf. Matt. 4:11; 26:53-54), just as they sometimes came to the rescue of OT worthies (cf. Dan. 3:24-28; 6:16-22). **[13]** **The lion** and **young lion** doubtless are metaphors of strong enemies, while the **adder** and **serpent** suggest stealthy foes.

The divine response (vss. 14-16). This response may have come by means of a prophetic or priestly oracle at the temple, or the psalmist may have sensed divine response by meditating upon the Scriptures as he heard them read and proclaimed in the temple exercises.

[14] The inverted synonymous parallelism indicates that **he knows my name** means **he cleaves to me in love**. This love is the effectual cause of God's deliverance. [15] The climactic triplet lays stress on the manner in which God will answer him; he will **rescue him** from his trouble and **honor** him. [16] **Salvation**, in light of the psalm, means protection and deliverance.

Psalm 92: Praise of God's Faithfulness

The title indicates that this psalm came to be used in connection with sabbath observances. The content suggests those things which Israel needed to reflect upon frequently. The use of the psalm was probably attracted by the theme, rather than the psalm having been written for the express purpose of celebrating the sabbath.

The psalm combines features of a praise hymn (vss. 1-9, 12-15) and a psalm of thanksgiving (vss. 10-11). This is a pattern frequently followed in praise hymns whereby the psalmist enlarges upon God's special deliverance of him as a person, then turns the psalm into a national hymn of praise for all God's wonderful works. This pattern reveals the keen spiritual insight of the psalmist, who sees in particular saving acts of the Lord evidence of his constant loyalty to his people.

Constant praise of God (vss. 1-4). Each couplet in this paragraph employs synonymous parallelism so that a single thought is contained in each verse. [1-2] It is good to constantly thank the Lord and praise him **in the morning** and **by night**. These phrases lay stress on the frequency of such activities and may possibly be an allusion to the burnt offering made every morning and evening by the priests at the temple (Exod. 29:38-42; Num. 28:1-8). Praises accompanied those sacrifices, at least from David's day forward (1 Chron. 16:1-6, 37-41). God is to be praised for his **steadfast love** (covenant loyalty) and his **faithfulness** to Israel. For the names **Lord** and **Most High**, see the comments on Psalm 91:1-2. [3-4] God is pleased with our gratitude (cf. Ps. 69:29-31), and such gratitude helps us to be **glad** because of God's works.

The dullness of the stupid (vss. 5-9). [5] Not only is the psalmist filled with gladness as he reflects upon God's works (vs. 4), but he is led into deeper reverence as he thinks of the great mind of God which produced and maintains the universe. **[6]** But **the dull man** (*ba'ar*, one who is brutish like an animal) and **the stupid** (*kesil*, the intellectual dullard) cannot understand this. The psalmist is not referring to one who is incapable of knowing, but to one who refuses to exercise his mental and spiritual capacities. Verse 6 employs synonymous parallelism, so that **dull** and **stupid** are synonyms, as are **know** and **understand**. The word **this**, in its usage in the OT, may refer to what follows (Gen. 42:18; 43:11; etc.), or it may look back to what precedes (Ps. 78:32; Isa. 5:25; 9:12, 17, 21; 10:4; Jer. 3:10; etc.). **[7]** The insertion of the word **that** in our text results from the assumption that the word **this** in verse 6 points forward. According to this interpretation, the psalmist is saying that the dullard does not properly reflect upon the brief duration of the prosperity of the wicked. But it is possible that the psalmist meant to say that the dullard does not properly reflect upon God's greatness as seen in his creation (vs. 5; cf. "when," vs. 7, KJV). A frequent theme in the OT is that the wicked may prosper for a time, but eventually they will get their just deserts in the form of calamity resulting from divine visitation. **[8-9]** Since God is **on high for ever**, that is, in complete control of his universe, his **enemies shall perish**.

Deliverance of the psalmist (vss. 10-11). [10] Horn is a symbol of strength. The **fresh oil** was used on festive occasions as a symbol of gladness (Pss. 23:5; 45:7), also as part of the priestly healing ceremony for one who had been afflicted with leprosy (Lev. 14:10-20), and for medicinal purposes (Isa. 1:6). It is not clear in what sense the psalmist alludes to his anointing. Verse 7, which focuses attention on the downfall of his enemies, would seem to suggest that he is figuratively describing the joy that he felt when God vindicated and delivered him.

[11] Historical continuity is employed here. Since God has delivered him in the past, he will continue to do so. The concept of community solidarity is also involved, as the psalmist applies the lesson to the entire worshiping community (vss. 12-15).

The prosperity of the righteous (vss. 12-15). [12] The **palm tree** is doubtless the date palm which is known for its fruitfulness and durability. The **cedar** was known for its stateliness, especially the majestic cedars of Lebanon.

[13] The **house of the Lord** and **the courts of our God** are synonymous. The antecedent of the pronouns in verses 13 and 14 is **the righteous** of verse 12. This verse employs a metaphor whereby the lives of the priests who live at the temple are considered to be representative of all Israel under God (cf. Ps. 84). [14] In contrast to the wicked who are doomed to destruction (vss. 7-8), the righteous continue to bear fruit in old age (cf. 2 Cor. 4:16-18).

[15] All these blessings demonstrate that **the Lord is upright** and that **there is no unrighteousness in him**, that is, he blesses the righteous and punishes the wicked (cf. Exod. 20:5-6).

Psalm 93: The Lord Is a Mighty King

Psalms 93, 95–99 (and possibly 100) form a group of psalms which are frequently called "enthronement psalms" because they emphasize God's role as king of the universe. Three basic interpretations have been given to these psalms. (1) Some believe that these psalms imply an enthronement ceremony similar to the practice of the Canaanites and the Babylonians. In the autumn, the fertility god dies and in the spring he is resurrected to life again. The king plays the role of the god in a cultic ceremony in which he is symbolically buried in the autumn and resurrected the following spring. However, no evidence has been presented for any such cultic activity in Israel. (2) Others believe that these psalms were part of a New Year's celebration in connection with the Feast of Tabernacles in the autumn. Israel offered praise for a bountiful harvest and rededicated themselves to the Lord for the coming year. This viewpoint is more tenable than the first, but it, too, is based on conjecture. (3) Others believe that these psalms point to the final judgment of the world when righteousness and justice will reign supreme. According to this viewpoint, these psalms have no direct reference to Israelite society. It appears, however, that these psalms contain both historical allusions and eschatological hope. God's judgments of the past provide an insight into his continuing moral government of the world, and these judgments are but a foretaste of the great judgment to come.

God's moral government (vss. 1-2). The Lord reigns could also be translated "the Lord has become king." However, our text is the better rendering, for God's eternal reign is acknowledged in this psalm (vs. 2). This phrase is apparently meant to be a proclamation of Yahweh's kingly rule. Similar phrases are used to announce new kings in Israel (2 Sam. 15:10; 2 Kings 9:13). In these enthronement psalms, however, the proclamation does not designate one who has recently become king, but indicates man's increased awareness of God's kingship—an awareness which grows out of his acts of deliverance of his covenant people.

The Lord **robed in majesty** and **girded with strength** is a poetic picture of the Lord in joyous procession. Because God is king of the whole world, there is a discernible moral order in the universe (vs. 1c). **It shall never be moved** does not mean that the world will stand for ever (cf. Ps. 102:25-27), but that the moral government of the world is coextensive with the duration of the world (cf. vs. 5; 96:10).

Tumultuous floods and storms (vss. 3-4). In climactic parallelism, the roaring of the flood waters (vs. 3) is shown to be inferior in might to **the Lord on high** (vs. 4). The thundering flood waters could be a veiled reference to initial creation when God proved his power over the forces of chaos (Gen. 1:2-10). Language borrowed from Babylonian mythology may be reflected here (cf. Pss. 74:12-17; 89:9-10), but if so, it is only used figuratively to designate the historical fact of creation. It is also possible that the flood waters here, as elsewhere, reflect some time of great distress from which God has delivered the nation. Flood waters may figuratively refer to anguish experienced in time of chronic illness (Ps. 38:4a), to distress suffered at the hands of enemies (Pss. 66:12; 69:1-2, 13-15; 79:3; 88:17; Isa. 8:5-8), and perhaps as a figure of trouble in general (Ps. 46:1-3). The specific allusion in our psalm is not clear, but the important point is that God is more than equal to the task of granting deliverance from any trouble.

God's holy decrees (vs. 5). The word for **decrees** (Heb. *'edhuth*) might better be translated "testimonies" or "affirmations." God's works of creation and providence affirm his claims to sovereignty, and the believing, worshiping community testifies to this sovereignty in their cultic acts and hymns of praise. Thus **holiness befits** God's **house.** These testimonies **are very sure,** or reliable. They will stand the test of time and of eternity.

Psalm 94: The God of Vengeance

This psalm is not written in the literary form of an enthronement psalm (see introduction to Ps. 93), but rather in the form of a psalm of lament and petition. The fact that God is here portrayed as a mighty warrior implies the role of God as king, which is also the major theme of enthronement psalms (cf. Pss. 93, 95–99). This thematic similarity doubtless accounts for the placement of Psalm 94 among the enthronement psalms.

The form of Psalm 94 is unusual in that it begins with a community lament (vss. 1-15) and ends with a personal lament (vss. 16-23), which is a reversal of the usual pattern. The concept of community solidarity, whereby the fortunes of the individual and of the community intertwine, is involved. It should be noted that the individual lament is both an invitation and an exhortation for the community to stand with the psalmist in his opposition to evil.

There is in this psalm a perfect blending of urgent immediacy and reflective confidence. Based on the conviction that the divine nature is immutable, the psalmist can trust God to deliver the unfortunate as he has in the past. But the intensity of his present frustration and that of the nation causes him to urge God to hasten to their help.

God the Judge (vss. 1-3). **[1-2]** In stairlike parallelism, the Lord is set forth as the **God of vengeance**. As **judge of the earth**, God should **rise up** and let the light of his truth **shine forth** in the form of judgment against **the proud**.

[3] In stairlike parallelism, the familiar plaintive cry **How long?** lays stress on the urgency of the situation (cf. the notes on Ps. 79:5). The Pentateuch bears testimony to the fact that God was recognized as the judge of the earth (Gen. 18:25) and as an avenger (Deut. 32:35).

Arrogance of the wicked (vss. 4-7). Not only do such wicked men commit acts of callous brutality (vss. 5-6), but they also boast that they will not be called into account for it (vss. 4, 7). Such attitudes of unbelief and pride could be manifested by pagan nations (cf. Ps. 10:4, 13, 15-16), or on occasion by apostate Israelites (cf. Ps. 50:19-21).

God does see! (vss. 8-11). **[8]** These dullards and fools are morally insensitive. **[9-10]** The Hebrew text better fits the English verse divisions, so that **He who teaches men knowledge** is in apposition to what precedes and should be followed with a period (cf. Ps. 50:21). **[9]** Surely the creator of the **ear** and **eye** does **hear** and **see**. **[10]** **Chastens** (*yoser*) can also mean "instructs" (cf. 1 Chron. 15:22), and **chastise** (*yokhiach*) can also mean "rebuke, correct" (cf. Ps. 50:8; 105:14). God has placed within all men an innate capacity for moral discernment (cf. vss. 2:12-16). Verses 8-11 seem to be applied especially to Israel (cf. "people," singular, vs. 8, and see vss. 12-15). **[11]** **A breath** could also be rendered "vanity."

The blessedness of discipline (vss. 12-15). **[12-13]** These verses involve external parallelism in which the second couplet (vs. 13) provides a reason for what is said in the first couplet (vs. 12). **Chasten** (or "instruct") and **teach** are synonyms. **To give him respite** could also be rendered "to give him rest, or quiet" (cf. Isa. 7:4). **[14-15]** Verse 15 explains how God will care for his people, the positive counterpart of the negatives in verse 14. **Righteous** and **upright** are synonyms. **Justice** here means the rendering of the right verdict, fairness, equity.

God the only sure champion (vss. 16-19). **[16]** Others are invited to join him in his effort to eradicate wickedness.

[17-19] But God is the only one capable of preserving one from death and consoling the troubled heart.

Wicked allies (vss. 20-23). **[20]** The rhetorical question obviously expects an emphatic no in response. **[21]** **Condemn** suggests that these wicked rulers utilize apparently legal means of disposing of their enemies by suborning false witnesses to testify against them in the courts of law.

[22] **Stronghold** and **refuge** here refer to places of protection and safety (cf. 1 Sam. 22:1-5; Ps. 18:1-3). **Rock** (*tsur*) is frequently used of God as a support and deliverer (cf. Deut. 32:4, 15, 18, 30, 31, 33-38). **[23]** This protection will be provided by God's executing his sentence against the unscrupulous wicked.

Psalm 95: Acceptable Worship

Two essential elements of acceptable worship are here combined. Gratitude and humility must characterize those who worship God (vss. 1-7c), and only obedient lives can demonstrate the homage which man needs to give to his maker and provider (vss. 7d-11). In this respect, Psalm 50 follows the same general pattern, looking first at the sin of ingratitude (vss. 7-15) and then at the sin of disobedience (vss. 16-21).

In the hymnic portion of the psalm, there is a double summons to worship, the first (vss. 1-5) calling the worshipers into the presence of God, and the second enjoining them to manifest the proper spiritual posture as the worship actually begins (vss. 6-7c). The third and final stanza (vss. 7d-11) extends the concept of submission to the daily walks of life.

Summons to enter God's presence (vss. 1-5). This stanza strikes a familiar theme in the praise hymns of Israel.

[1-2] Israel is to enter into God's presence with joyful **songs of praise** and happy songs of **thanksgiving. The rock of our salvation** (vs. 1b) suggests the constancy of God's saving acts on behalf of Israel. **[3-5]** God is the King of kings who providentially watches over his creation. There is no acceptance of a multiplicity of gods in the phraseology used here (cf. 96:4-5).

Summons to prostration (vss. 6-7c). [6] The word translated **worship** so frequently in the OT means to prostrate oneself. The word is often accompanied by one or both of the other two words used here: to **bow down** and to **kneel**. All three words signify the willing humiliation of body and soul which must characterize sinful man's approach to the holy God.

[7a-c] God is both Israel's Maker (vs. 6b) and her shepherd (vs. 7). Doubtless the close connection attained by the use of the word **for** (vs. 7a) indicates that in this context the major thought focuses on the new creation of Israel as God's covenant people (cf. Ps. 51:10; Isa. 43:1, 7).

Exhortation to obedience (vss. 7d-11). [7d] The focal point of interest in this stanza focuses on the word **today**. The author of the book of Hebrews in the NT quotes 7d-11 (Heb. 3:7-11) and interprets the word **today** in terms of the days of Moses, the days of David, and the Christian era (cf. Heb. 3:12–4:13). Since verses 8-11 in our psalm are put in the form of an exhortation, the lesson to be learned can be applied to every age.

[8] The historical allusions to **Meribah** (contention) and **Massah** (testing) would be readily understood by Israel (cf. Exod. 17:1-7; Num. 20:1-13). On these two occasions Israel contended with Moses because of a lack of water in the wilderness journey and so they tried sorely the patience of God. [9] Both psalmists (cf. Pss. 78, 106) and prophets (cf. Amos 3:1-2) point out the grave duty of Israel to assume the responsibilities which accompany the special privileges of those who had seen the works of God in a special way. [10] **That generation** was not allowed to enter the promised land because of unbelief which led to disobedience (cf. Heb. 3:18-19). [11] Even after the settlement in Canaan the people did not enjoy true **rest** because of divine discipline sent in response to their continued disobedience. Though they lived in the place of rest (Heb. *menuchah*, 11b), they did not enjoy the favor of God during their times of apostasy. Thus the people in the days of the psalmist are

exhorted to hearken to God **today** so as not to incur his disfavor. This admonition is still applicable to us.

Psalm 96: The Lord Is Judge of the World

Some believe that Psalms 96–99 alone are to be classed as enthronement psalms. Others consider Psalms 93 and 95 in this category also. This commentary takes the latter view. Included in the summons to praise God (vss. 1-6) is the charge given to Israel to proclaim the knowledge of God among the Gentiles (cf. vss. 10-13). The middle stanza of the psalm (vss. 7-9) and verse 10 give the content of the proclamation.

The Lord's glory (vss. 1-6). [1-2] The triple invitation to **sing** sets the tone for this beautiful hymn of praise. New songs were composed to celebrate new deliverances or saving acts performed by the Lord (cf. vs. 2b). **[3]** The **glory** of God is the manifestation of his many-faceted personality, but especially is it a manifestation of his holiness. Verse 3 employs synonymous parallelism, so that **glory** and **marvelous works** are to be treated as synonyms, as are **nations** and **peoples**. This shows that God's glory is manifested in his marvelous works. **[4-5]** The psalmist gives no credence to polytheistic ideas, for he declares that the **gods of the peoples are idols** (literally "things of nought"). God's supremacy is set forth in the declaration of verse 4b. God is to be worshiped as the only true God who created the universe (vs. 5b). **[6]** God's greatness (vs. 4a) and majesty (vs. 6) are sufficient motivation for man to praise him. The words **strength** (*hodh*) and **beauty** (*hadhar*) provide an excellent example of alliteration in Hebrew (vs. 6b).

Invitation to praise God (vss. 7-9). [7-8] In stairlike parallelism, the phrase **ascribe to the Lord** is emphasized by repetition. Notice that the invitation is addressed to the **families of the peoples**, namely, **all the earth** (vs. 9b). The means of ascribing praise to God is to **bring an offering** (vs. 8b) to him. Gentiles were not forbidden to offer sacrifices at the temple (cf. Num. 15:11-16, 27-29). **[9]** The **holy array** (literally "adornments of holiness" in Hebrew) may refer to the priestly ornaments (Exod. 28:2), or else may be a reference to the necessity of moral purity on the part of the worshipers (cf. Ps. 50:23). The exhortation to **tremble before him** seems to suggest the latter.

Let all nature worship God (vss. 10-13). [10] The kingship of God and the resulting orderly world are to be proclaimed (cf. vs. 13). [11-13] All creation should praise God because of his righteous judgment.

On universalism in the psalms, see the excursus at the end of Psalm 77.

Psalm 97: Our Lord Is Supreme

To the responsive rejoicing emphasized in Psalms 96–98, Psalm 97 adds the dimension of terror awaiting the wicked in the day of judgment (vss. 3-5, 7).

The presence of God (vss. 1-5). The exodus typology involving a theophany (appearance of God) is employed as a symbol of the divine presence in Israel (cf. Exod. 13:21-22; 19:16-18; Ps. 18:7-15; Isa. 6:1-4; Ezek. 1; Nah. 1:5). The actual theophany at the time of the exodus is employed figuratively by the psalmist. [1] For **the Lord reigns**, see Psalm 93:1. **Earth** (*'erets*) sometimes means the land of Israel (cf. Deut. 5:16), but the synonymous phrase, **the many coastlands**, shows that here it means the world at large. **Coastlands** could also be translated "islands," and the Hebrew word is often used of places remote from Israel (cf. Isa. 24:14-16; 40:15-17; 41:5; 42:4, 10). [2] Concerning God's **righteousness** and **justice** exercised in his judgments, see Psalms 33:4-5; 45:6-7; 72:1. [3] **Fire** is frequently used by the prophets to symbolize God's judgments (cf. Amos 1:1–2:5; 4:11; 7:4; Joel 1:19-20; 2:3; Obad. 18; Nah. 1:6; Zeph. 3:8; Isa. 30:27; 66:15-16; Jer. 5:14; 23:29; Ezek. 21:32). [4-5] The figurative language used here describes God's power to humble mighty men and nations in the face of his judgment (cf. Mic. 1:4; Nah. 1:5; Isa. 64:1-2).

The exaltation of God (vss. 6-9). [6] The **peoples behold the glory** of God as a result of the heavenly proclamation of his **righteousness**. **Glory** indicates the visible manifestation and **righteousness** indicates the moral aspect of God's holiness (cf. Isa. 5:16). **[7] Images, idols,** and **gods** are interchangeable here. For the word **idols,** see the comments on 96:5. God often demonstrated his reality and power in contrast to impotent idols (cf. 1 Kings 18:17-40). **All gods bow down before him** is accommodative language used to declare the supremacy of God. (It is not clear whether Hebrews 1:6 dquotes Psalm 97:7 [LXX] or Deuteronomy 32:43 [LXX], where the Greek has the additional line, "And let all the angels of God worship him.") **[8] Daughters of** means "the people of" (cf. Jer. 46:24; 49:3; Pss. 9:14; 137:8; Isa. 62:11; Jer. 6:2; Zeph. 3:14; Matt. 21:5; Lk. 23:28).

[9] Most high (*'elyon*) is synonymous with **exalted,** and is not here employed as a proper name for God (cf. NEB, KJV, against NASB).

The Lord grants deliverance (vss. 10-12). [10] The note in the RSV (cf. KJV, NASB) renders the Hebrew of the first line. The slight emendation in the RSV (cf. NEB) matches the form of the two succeeding verbs. However, exhortation and declaration are often mixed in the psalms (cf. vss. 11-12). Hating evil is the natural antithesis of loving good (cf. Prov. 8:13; Rom. 12:9). **[11] Dawns** (Heb. *zarach*) is the usual way of referring to sunrise, although "is sown" (KJV, NASB, NEB; Heb. *zarua'*) can be justified as a figure of speech (cf. NASB "like seed"), indicating the sowing of the light of God's truth in the human heart. **Light,** as a metaphor of divine blessing, may refer specifically to life (Ps. 36:9), prosperity (Job 29:3), enlightenment (Ps. 119:105, 130), or deliverance (Ps. 43:2-4). **Righteous** and **upright** are synonyms. **[12]** The **righteous** should **rejoice** in the greatness and goodness of God and be thankful for his righteous judgments.

Psalm 98: The Lord Judges in Righteousness

The emphasis here is on the lesson to be learned by the nations as they see God's deliverance of Israel. Doubtless some particular historical event is in mind, probably the deliverance from Babylonian exile. Surely on this occasion the nations could see the handiwork of God, especially if the prophetic predictions concerning the return had reached the ears of Israel's pagan neighbors (cf. Isa. 41–42; 44:24–45:7).

This psalm is composed entirely of praise. All mankind, and even all nature, are encouraged to praise the Lord. Though this psalm does not specifically refer to God's reign, God is designated as king (vs. 6) and judge (vs. 9). The past, present, and future reign of God is implied. God has revealed his kingship in his past acts of deliverance (vss. 1-3). God is King in the present (vs. 6), and as King he will judge the world in the future (vs. 9).

The victory of God (vss. 1-3). [1] A **new song** is appropriate to celebrate God's marvelous acts of deliverance (cf. 96:1). God's **right hand** and **holy arm** signify his divine strength and the holy cause in which this strength is exercised (cf. 44:3; Isa. 52:10). [2] Verse 2 employs synonymous parallelism in which **victory** and **vindication** are synonymous. The word for **victory** (*yasha'*) is frequently translated "salvation" and the word for vindication (Heb. *tsedhaqah* or *tsedheq*) is often translated "righteousness." The latter word is frequently used in the enthronement psalms (cf. 96:13; 97:2; 98:9; 99:4). Righteousness and salvation are frequently connected in Isaiah in parallelistic structure (45:8; 46:13; 51:5, 6, 8; 56:1; 59:17; 62:1). The RSV translation of 98:1-3 is an excellent rendering in this particular context. The basic meaning of "salvation" is deliverance of whatever nature, and the word "righteousness" basically means to be put in the right. The context sometimes suggests a specific kind of salvation or righteousness. **Has made known** is a causative verb form in Hebrew, emphasizing that God was the cause of the **victory**. **He has revealed** is an intensive verb form, suggesting some noticeable act of God.

[3] The reason for God's granting victory and vindication to Israel is twofold. First, God **has remembered his steadfast love** (*chesedh*, covenant loyalty) **and faithfulness** toward Israel. These two covenant terms are frequently found together in the OT (Gen. 24:27, 49; 32:10; 47:29; Exod. 34:6; Josh. 2:14; 2 Sam. 2:6; 15:20; Pss. 25:10;

40:11; 57:3; 61:7; 85:10; 86:15; 89:14, 24; 98:3; 100:5; 115:1; 138:2; Prov. 3:3; 14:22; 16:6; 20:28). They emphasize previous commitment between the two parties to a covenant. God has promised never to utterly forsake Israel, but that he would restore her when she repented (cf. Ezek. 18:30-32). The second reason given for God's restoring Israel is that this deliverance may serve as an object lesson to the pagan peoples.

Let all humanity praise the Lord (vss. 4-6). **[4] Make a joyful noise** means basically to shout for joy, and was used in an acclamation of a king (Zech. 9:9). **Break forth into joyous song** is literally "break forth and sing for joy" (cf. NASB). **Break forth** is used by Isaiah in anticipation of Israel's deliverance from captivity (14:7; 44:23; 55:12). **Sing praises** means literally to make melody. **All the earth** is equivalent to **the world** and **the peoples** (vs. 9).

[5-6] The *kinnor* is likely the small **lyre** (NASB) rather than the larger harp (KJV, NEB). **The sound of melody** is rendered "the voice of song" in Isaiah 51:3 and is connected with songs of thanksgiving. The **trumpets** were silver instruments (Num. 10:2), and the **horn** was the ram's horn (Heb. *shophar*).

Let all nations praise the Lord (vss. 7-9). These verses should be compared with 96:11-13. The inarticulate praise which nature renders to God results from the fact that nature does what God created it to do. **[7]** The natural roaring of the sea is equated with the articulate praises of men. **[8]** The slapping of the flood waters against the banks of the rivers or the shores of the seas is likened to the clapping of the hands in joyous acclamation of Israel's king (cf. 1 Kings 1:39; 2 Kings 11:12, 14), the Lord of the earth. And so the whispering of the wind in the hills suggests the figure of joyous songs. **[9]** All this chorus of praise is offered in anticipation of the coming of the Lord in judgment.

Excursus

The Redemption of the Earth

In Romans 8:18-25, Paul anticipates the complete redemption of creation, including the human body. The creation was subjected to futility by God as the result of the entrance of sin into the world (cf. Gen. 3). But it was subjected in hope of sharing the glory of God. Since we are not given specific information as to how this transformation will occur, the subject should not be allowed to degenerate into idle speculation. It is enough to know that there will be a new environment in which righteousness will dwell (2 Pet 3:10-13; Rev. 21:1-4). Nature as we now know it is not the world which God created, but the world rendered degenerate through sin. The eternal abode of the righteous will be in an atmosphere cleansed of all evil and enshrouded with the holiness of God for all eternity (Rev. 7:13-17; 21:27).

Psalm 99: The Holy Lord Pardons and Avenges

A refrain (vss. 3, 5, 9), which is progressively lengthened, emphasizes the holiness of God as manifested in his reign as king (vss. 1-3), in his equitable judgment (vss. 4-5), and in his forgiveness and vengeance (vss. 6-9).

God enthroned as king (vss. 1-5). [1] See the notes on 93:1 for the phrase, **the Lord reigns.** For the idea of God **enthroned upon the cherubim,** see the comments on 80:1.

[2-3] Though Israel's God was thought to reign in Zion, **he is exalted over all the peoples,** meaning all the world. Therefore, all men should praise God's **great and terrible name.** In Hebrew idiom, one's name identifies his personality and defines his character. Since God is great (vs. 2a), so is his name (vs. 3a). He is great in his supremacy (vs. 2b). The words **terrible** (Heb. *nora'*) and **holy** (Heb. *qadhosh*) are used together in 111:9, where the psalmist connects these divine attributes with God's redemptive acts toward his covenant people (cf. 98:1-3).

[4] Though God is supreme, he does not rule as a des-

pot but his strength is tempered with justice. The phrase **let them praise** (vs. 3) may be meant to carry over to this verse (Cohen, *Psalms*, p. 322). some emendation seems necessary to make good sense out of verse 4. "The strength of the king loves justice" (cf. KJV, NASB) obscures and does not explain the passage. "Let them praise the strength of the king who loves justice" (Cohen) may be best. **Thou** is emphatic in Hebrew.

[5] God's **footstool** may refer to any place where his glory is manifested over his subjects. It is sometimes applied to the ark of the covenant (1 Chron. 28:2), the temple (Ps. 132:7), Zion (Lam. 2:1), or the earth (Isa. 66:1). It is the earth that is meant in the present context.

Forgiveness and vengeance (vss. 6-9). [6] Apparently the clauses **were among his priests** and **was among those who called on his name** are meant to be treated as synonymous expressions emphasizing the priestly function of intercession and mediation exercised by Moses (Exod. 14:15-18; 17:11-13; 32:30-34), Aaron (Num. 16:44-48), and Samuel (1 Sam. 7:8-11; 12:16-23). In addition to Aaron, Moses (Exod. 24:6-8; 40:22-27; Lev. 8) and Samuel (1 Sam. 7:9-11) offered sacrifices, but that does not seem to be the primary thing emphasized here. The emphasis is on the fact that their intercession was effectual before God. The psalmist is encouraging every faithful Israelite to thus call upon God with the assurance that his prayer will be heard (cf. James 5:16b-18). [7] Only Moses and Aaron received revelations **in the pillar of cloud** (Exod. 33:9; Num. 12:5); but though this visible symbol was not present in the case of Samuel, it is evident that God was hearing and answering him. The last two lines of verse 7 employ synonymous parallelism, so that the phrase **they kept** applies to both lines, and the words **testimonies** and **statues** are used interchangeably. For a discussion of the technical meanings of several words used to describe the law, see the introduction to Psalm 119.

[8] It is not incongruous for the psalmist to refer to God's forgiveness and vengeance in the same connection. The NEB, on the supposition that these two items are

incompatible, emends **an avenger** (Heb. *noqem*) to "holding them innocent" (Heb. *noqam* from *naqah*). Forgiveness, which results from God's mercy and grace, restores fellowship between man and God, but it does not erase all the consequences of sin (see Num. 14:20-25; 2 Sam. 12:1-23). Each individual is held guilty only for his own sins (Ezek. 18:1-4, 20), but the consequences of one's sins may be visited upon succeeding generations (Exod. 20:4-6). **[9]** God's holiness, as manifested in his punishing and pardoning, is cause for man to **worship** and **extol** God.

Psalm 100: Gladness and Joy in Worship

It is not certain that this psalm was written as a summary of the enthronement psalms (see the introduction to Psalm 93), but it is likely that the collector of Book IV of the Psalter (Pss. 89–106) intended that the psalm should serve that purpose. The concept of God as king (Ps. 93:1; 95:3; 96:10a; 97:1; 98:6; 99:1, 4) and that of impending world judgment (96:10b, 13; 98:9), so prominent in the enthronement psalms, are not explicitly set forth in Psalm 100. The concepts of the gladness of worship (100:2, 4; 95:1-2; 96:11-13; 97:1, 12; 98:1, 4-6, 7-9; 99:3, 5, 9), of God as Creator of the world (100:3; 95:5-6; 96:5) and shepherd of Israel (100:3b; 95:7), and of monotheism (100:3a; 95:3; 96:4-5; 97:7, 9) are common property to the group of Psalms 93, 95 –100. However, these concepts are also frequently found in non-enthronement praise hymns (102:12, 25; 103:19; 104:24; 105:2-3; 107:33-43; 115:3-8, 16-18).

The word *todhah* in the title could refer to the thank-offering (Lev. 7:11-18), or it could refer to thanking God in a psalm of thanksgiving (vs. 4). From David's time forward, such songs accompanied the thank-offering and other communion sacrifices (1 Chron. 16:37-42; 25:1-8).

First summons to thanksgiving (vss. 1-3). [1] The word **lands** is singular in Hebrew and could be translated "earth," meaning all the world, or "land," meaning Israel. The context of the psalm favors the latter (vs. 3), but the possible position of the psalm as a conclusion to the enthronement psalms favors the former (cf. 96:1, 7-9; 97:1;

98:4; 99:1-5). For the meaning of **make a joyful noise**, see the comments on Psalm 98:4-6. **[2]** The expressions **serve the Lord** and **come into his presence** are synonymous and are related to the beginning clause of verse 1. Service in the form of worship and in daily living are enjoined in the OT and in the NT (Exod. 12:25-27; Deut. 6:13; Jer. 30:8-9; Matt. 4:10; Rom 12:1-2).

[3] The Hebrew employs an emphatic pronoun (unfortunately omitted in the RSV), in order to separate God from false gods. The Hebrew reads, **Know that the Lord, he is God!** The second line of verse three is elliptical. Either **we** (RSV, NEB) or "we ourselves" (KJV, NASB) must be supplied in translation. Some manuscripts and versions of our passage read "his" (Heb. *lo*) and others read "not" (*lo'*). Obviously a scribal error has been made, but the original reading is difficult to determine. **His** seems to fit better into the following context. Three things are asserted in verse 3. (1) God is revealed as Yahweh (**the Lord**), One who, as Israel's covenant God, reveals his personality and character in his words and works (cf. Exod. 3:13-17, RSV note, "I will be what I will be"). (2) Next, Israel is reminded of her own origin and nature. (3) Finally, Israel is reminded of her favored position as God's covenant people. The word **know** can mean to be aware of (51:3), or to acknowledge or confess (32:3, 5). The double summons to thank and praise God in this psalm would suggest that the latter meaning is intended here.

The second summons to praise (vss. 4-5). Perhaps the first stanza (vss. 1-3) was uttered as the worshipers approached the temple, and the second (vss. 4-5) at the time they actually entered the temple court. **[4] Thanksgiving** and **praise** are often used interchangeably, as here. The only way man can bless God's name is to **give thanks to him**. **[5]** The first two lines of verse 5, which combine God's goodness and his **steadfast love** (*chesedh*, covenant loyalty), are found elsewhere in slightly different form (106:1; 107:1; 118:1, 29). The author adds the dimension of **faithfulness** to further emphasize the constancy of God's covenant loyalty.

Psalm 101: The Ideal Ruler

In Book IV (Pss. 90–106) of the Psalter, only Psalms 101 and 103 are attributed to David. Whether these titles suggest authorship, or refer to authorization by royalty, or suggest that the psalm is about a king, is not clear. It is clear that Psalm 101 is written by an official, perhaps a king. The psalm reflects the high ideals of Israelite kingship as generally reflected in the career of David, and the psalm could well be his.

Avowal of personal integrity (vss. 1-3a). Before one can lead others effectively, he must demonstrate his own ability and willingness to follow the regulations imposed upon his followers. This the psalmist recognized. [1] His song will be about **loyalty** (*chesedh*) and **justice** (*mishpat*), two great covenant terms. **Loyalty** (usually "steadfast love" in the RSV) is often used in conjunction with "faithfulness," and **justice** is frequently used in connection with "righteousness." **Loyalty** emphasizes one's covenant commitments and the **justice** lays stress on the administration of those precepts and principles which relate to covenant commitments. Since the psalmist sings to the Lord of these qualities, we can assume that he recognizes the divine origin of his responsibilities. The movement from verse 1 to verse 2 indicates that **loyalty** and **justice** in this context refer to human attributes.

[2] The word **blameless** (*tamim*) does not demand absolute perfection, but suggests a well-rounded person who acts with integrity. The question in the middle of verse 2 poses a problem in this particular context. The inquiry would be more at home in a psalm written in a time of distress, but seems strange in a psalm of confidence. Some have thought that it may reflect David's sense of alienation from God following his sins with Bathsheba and Uriah (cf. 2 Sam. 11–12; Pss. 32:3-4; 51:1-17). The greatest objection to this interpretation is that this confident, happy psalm would hardly have been written during David's time of despondency. Apparently the question here is nothing more than an appeal for divine guidance in the exercise of his public functions. Solomon's humility at the beginning of his

career can well illustrate the point (cf. 1 Kings 3:1-14).

[2c-3] The Hebrew word rendered **integrity** (*tam*) is from the same root which is translated **blameless** in verse 2a. The Hebrew word for **base** (*beliya'al*) is the root from which we get the word "Belial." It means that which is perverse and devoid of any good (cf. Judg. 19:22; 20:13; 1 Sam. 2:16, KJV). The word came to be used of Satan, the ringleader of wickedness (cf. 2 Cor. 6:15). Here it is the exact opposite of the person characterized by **integrity of heart** (vs. 2c).

Avowal of public integrity (vss. 3b-8). [3b-4] There is some question whether verses 3b-4 provide a transition from the king's private life to his public functions. The decision hinges on the meaning of the phrase **those who fall away** (vs. 3b). This translates one word (*setim*) in Hebrew, which seems to mean "revolters," "apostates." The phrase literally would read "the works of the revolters." This seems to suggest that the theme has shifted from a description of the king's private life to a consideration of his choice of public ministers. However, it is still possible that the phrase is meant to be understood in the abstract, and could be translated "disloyalty" (NEB). One's decision on this matter will not greatly affect the overall interpretation of the psalm. Verse 4, in the light of the above, could refer to the king's own character or to that of his ministers.

Verses 5-8 definitely speak of the characteristics of the righteous king's chosen ministers. [5] The king is judge of the supreme court in Israel. As such, he might deputize some of the princes to assist him in judging the people (cf. Ps. 82:2-7). Both king and princes, as well as all the judges, are expected to render right judgments. Perhaps the one **who slanders**, etc., refers to a judge or to a person who is hailed into court because he has falsely accused his neighbor. The righteous king must see to it that such mistreatment of the righteous is not allowed to continue.

[6] By contrast, **the faithful, blameless** person will be selected to be the king's minister. **Dwell with me** (vs. 6b) is to be equated with **shall minister to me** (vs. 6d). [7] So, **dwell in my house** (vs. 7a) and **continue in my presence**

(vs. 7b) also refer to those who serve in the king's court. The deceitful liar shall have no place there. **[8]** Bold language is employed here. The Hebrew word *labbeqarim* should be understood as containing "the article of totality" and translated "every morning," or, in the distributive sense, **morning by morning** (Leupold, *Exposition,* p. 301b). It is preposterous to suppose that any earthling would imagine himself capable of destroying every day all the iniquitous in the land. The boldest hyperbole could not be allowed to carry that meaning. But it is possible for a supreme ruler to eradicate such undesirables from his administration

Psalm 102: A Prayer for the Afflicted

The title suggests a liturgical use of the psalm. It is meant to be used as a source of comfort and consolation for any troubled person who feels the need to plead with God for help. The average Israelite would not possess the necessary literary skill and training to compose a beautiful poem to adequately express himself before the Lord, but he could utilize the products of the skills of others. All the psalms came to be used as types of similar problems or blessings which attended individual Israelites or the nation.

Plea for help (vss. 1-2). The choice of verbs and their objects employed in these opening verses reveals the fervency with which the prayer is uttered. **[1]** The word for **prayer** (*tephillah*) refers to a plea made before a judge in a court of law. The **cry** is obviously a cry of distress (cf. vs. 2). The imperative **hear** is tempered by the imperfect jussive **let come**. In combination, these varied modes of expression reveal the urgency of the need and the humility and reverence with which mortal man should approach the holy God. The latter part of the verse means "Give attention to my cry." **[2]** God's hiding his face is a figure used to express his refusal to grant the petition (cf. Ps. 34:15-16). In another context, the expression may refer to God's granting deliverance or forgiveness (cf. Ps. 51:9). **Incline thy ear** suggests the condescending nature of God who stoops down to lift man out of his sinful condition. The adverb **speedily**, in conjunction with the adverbial clause **in the day when I call**, stresses the need for immediate help, and should not be interpreted to indicate impatience on the part of the petitioner.

Plaintive description of distress (vss. 3-11). Hyperbolic language is generally characteristic of laments. This feature makes it difficult at times to determine the real life situation of the psalmist. However, there are usually sufficient clues to enable the careful student to discern between exaggeration and reality. The clear statements in verses 23-24 reveal the fact that the psalmist fears that his life will be cut short in his prime. From verses 13-17 we get the picture of one in exile hoping for restoration to the homeland. The highly descriptive language in verses 3-11 should be interpreted in light of these identifiable facts.

[3-4a] Three figures illustrate the brevity of life. As **smoke** quickly evaporates into the air, as **bones** are quickly consumed in a furnace (or conflagration), and as **grass** quickly withers in the hot, dry Oriental summer, so the days of our lives quickly pass and life is spent. The brevity of life may also be pictured aś swifter than a weaver's shuttle, a breath, and clouds that soon vanish (Job 7:6-10). The days of one's life are also described as swifter than a runner, like skiffs of reed, and an eagle swooping down upon the prey (Job 9:25-26). The action in the drama of life is momentary and fleeting. Especially to one in the face of death, the brevity of life becomes paramount (cf. Gen. 47:9). The additional circumstances of physical and mental distress often cause contemplation of the brevity of life to become an obsession.

[4b-5] The distracting distress has caused him to fail to nourish his body so that his **bones cleave** to his **flesh** because of his skinniness. **Because of my loud groaning** is an elliptical phrase. The same distress which causes the loud groaning also causes him to fast, which in turn causes his **bones** to **cleave** to his **flesh**. **[6]** His loneliness is described as being **like a vulture** (or pelican) **of the wilderness**, or **like an owl of the waste places**. The birds here mentioned cannot be definitely identified, but the synonymous terms **wilder-**

ness and **waste places** suggest regions uninhabited by man.

[7] This loneliness is further pictured as being like **a lonely bird on the housetop**, apparently without its mate.

[8] His enemies contemptuously use his name as a curse. [9] Here is a picture of one sitting on the ash heap in mourning (cf. Job 2:8) with the wind whipping the **ashes** into his food. Or, perhaps he has put **ashes** on his head in mourning (cf. 2 Sam. 13:19; Esth. 4:1), and they keep falling into his food. And his **tears mingle** with those **ashes**.

[10] The language here must be analyzed carefully. The psalmist does not state the cause of God's **indignation and anger**, but only focuses on the results of God's displeasure. **Thou hast taken me up and thrown me away** is a veiled reference to the exile (cf. vss. 13-17). God was perfectly justified in being angry with Israel because of her cumulative sins committed throughout many generations (cf. Ps. 106). Israel's sins may well be implied in the first half of verse 10 (cf. Ps. 38:1-4). [11] **Evening** is literally "lengthened," as the **shadow** would appear in the lateness of the day. The figure of withered **grass** suggests that though he is not old, life seems to be almost over (cf. vss. 23-24). For other expressions of the brevity of life, see verse 3.

Zion's appointed time (vss. 12-22). [12-17] The eternal God can easily bring to pass what he decrees according to his timetable. The psalmist doubtless was aware of the prophecy of Jeremiah (25:11-12) concerning a seventy-year captivity. Daniel (9:1-2) calculated the time and discovered that it was time for God to restore the exiles to their homeland. Apparently the psalm was written about the time of Daniel's reckoning. [12] While the Hebrew word rendered **enthroned** means literally to "sit" or "dwell," its frequent use in the technical sense of one enthroned is to be understood here (cf. Pss. 9:7; 10:16-18). [13] On the basis of God's faithfulness in keeping his word, **Zion** will now become the object of God's **pity**. [14] Though Zion is in ruins (cf. 79:1-4), God's **servants** still love her. [15-17] Because God regards **the prayer of the destitute** (vs. 17), he will **appear in his glory** and **build up Zion** (vs. 16), which will cause the **kings** and **nations** of the earth to **fear the name of the Lord** (vs. 15).

[18-22] This paragraph extends the thoughts of the former. [18] It is not certain whether the pronoun **this** refers to the rebuilding of Zion (vs. 16) or to the psalmist's trust recorded in this psalm. At any rate, both the glorious event of the restoration of Zion and the psalmist's declaration of trust have been recorded for generations far removed from his day. [19-22] These verses reveal the content of the wonderful things worth recording. [19] The holy God who inhabits the high and lofty heavens condescends to look down on man in his lowly estate (cf. Isa. 57:14-21). [20] In his compassion, the loving Lord sets free the prisoner **doomed to die** (literally "the sons of death"; cf. Ps. 79:11).

[21-22] As a result, God will be praised by all men in Jerusalem (cf. Ps. 79:9-10, 13).

The eternal and the temporal (vss. 23-28). [23-24] The psalmist returns from his meditations about Zion's great past, present ruins, and future glory to the reality of his own sorrowful state in exile (cf. vss. 3-11). Whether the psalmist is in the throes of death or only imagines as much in his state of mental depression is uncertain. But the pain of the latter state is as real as that of the former. To die **in mid-course** was considered a divine judgment upon one for his sins (cf. Ps. 55:23; Jer. 17:11; Isa. 38:1-6, 9-11, 17). To contemplate such an end would be extremely depressing. Surely the eternal God can spare mortal man a few more years!

[25-28] Orientals love vivid descriptions. In a culture where God's creative acts can be so beautifully described as God's clothing himself with light, stretching out the heavens like a tent, laying beams upon the waters, and setting the earth on its foundations (Ps. 104:1-6), the language here is not surprising. The consummation is the opposite of the creation. These garments **will wear out** and need to be changed (vs. 26). Foundations eventually give way, even though they seem so permanent (vs. 25). But God is eternal. **Thou art the same** reads literally **thou art He.** God is the unique one, the only true God in the

universe whom Israel knew as eternal. And because the Israelites are a special object of care in the heart of their eternal God, they and their posterity **shall dwell secure.**

Psalm 103: All God's Benefits

God's benefits (vss. 1-5). [1] Many have noted that Psalms 103 and 104 begin and end the same way (see the introduction to Ps. 105). This could indicate that the two psalms have one author, that one borrowed from the other, or that both were using expressions common to the worshipping community. This personal exhortation is doubtless meant to kindle a spiritual awakening in the heart of each worshiper. Man needs to give his best effort to God in worship and service. The shift from personal (vss. 1-5) to national (vss. 6-14) to universal (vss. 15-22) considerations show that this is a community psalm.

[2] Though God's benefits cannot be enumerated or adequately praised (Ps. 40:5), it is well to keep them in mind as best we can. The word for **benefits** refers to blessings which manifest themselves through deeds and actions, as the relative clauses (Hebrew participial clauses) which follow indicate. [3-5] It must be recognized that the reception of these benefits is conditional. God must will it so and man must meet whatever conditions God has stipulated.

[3] God wills to forgive all who come to him in his appointed way (cf. Acts 2:21, 38-39; Rev. 22:17). God sometimes chooses to heal our physical diseases, but in other cases he chooses to let the problem remain while at the same time providing the strength of his grace to let the affliction serve God's good purpose (cf. 2 Cor. 12:1-10).

[4] The word for **Pit** (*shachath*) could be derived from the verb *shachath*, "to go to ruin," in which case the noun would mean "destruction." Or the noun could be derived from the verb *shuach*, "to sink down," and the noun would mean "a pit." The word is frequently used in conjunction with Sheol, and can mean the grave or the realm of departed spirits (cf. Pss. 30:3, 9; 88:3-6). Apparently, the psalmist means nothing more than that he has been delivered from an untimely death. God's **steadfast love and**

mercy emphasize his loyalty to his covenant commitments and his compassion toward sinful, suffering man.

[5] **As long as you live** is based on an emendation of the Hebrew, which reads "your ornament." The Hebrew has been taken to mean the mouth or the soul, the latter interpretation taking "your ornament" in the same general sense as "my glory" (cf. Pss. 30:12; 108:1 [KJV, NASB]). Our text reads the Hebrew as from '*ad*, "duration," "perpetuity," "eternity." The long life of the eagle and his ability for long flight provide a suitable metaphor for a vigorous and long life (cf. Isa. 40:31; Exod. 19:4; Deut. 32:10-12).

God's mercy (vss. 6-14). [6] **Vindication** is an excellent rendering of the Hebrew here in a context where **justice** is used in the forensic sense of a verdict in a court of law. Deliverance from oppression is intended. As frequently, the word refers here to the righteousness of God which manifests itself in his saving acts. [7] **Ways** and **acts**, in the present context, refer to the marvellous ways in which God manifested his character and will by means of his deliverance and protection of Israel. Revelation through saving acts is the primary meaning of the name Yahweh (Jehovah, or Lord, cf. Exod. 3:13-15; RSV note). [8] This verse reflects God's portrayal of himself to Moses in the wilderness (Exod. 34:6). God's grace, mercy, and love are explicitly set forth here as throughout the OT and NT.

[9] **Chide** translates a Hebrew word which means "contend," and, like the key terms in verse 6, was at home in the law court. It means basically "to try a case in court." God does not keep one on trial for ever. [10] The thought is extended by emphasizing that God does not deal with the penitent sinner on a legal basis of acquitting the innocent and condemning the guilty. "If a man does not repent, God will whet his sword" (Ps. 7:12), but when the sinner repents and strives to obey God (cf. vss. 17-18), God freely forgives.

In emblematic parallelism, the psalmist in three figures vividly declares the completeness of forgiveness (vss. 11-13). [11] As the distance from heaven to earth cannot be measured, so the **steadfast love** of God is immeasurable.

[12] Forgiveness is absolute, just as **the east** is completely removed **from the west**. [13] God, the loving Father, **pities his children**. To pity means to have compassion on the undeserving. [14] The physical frailty of man stands as a type of man's moral and spiritual weakness. Though "every transgression and disobedience received a just recompense of reward" (Heb. 2:2), God's justice is tempered with mercy for the penitent.

Man compared with God (vss. 15-18). [15-16] As the Oriental summer winds can wither the herbage of the field in just a few days, so man's life is brief. [17-18] But God's **steadfast love** is for ever present for **those who fear him** and **keep his commandments**. It may seem strange that two things which are not exact opposites should be so contrasted. The opposite of God's loyalty (*chesedh*) is man's disloyalty, but the latter is not considered. The opposite of man's weakness is God's strength, but the latter is not considered. The apparent inconsistency disappears when one understands that man's temporality is only an elaboration of verse 14, in which man's physical weakness is used as a type of his moral and spiritual weakness. Man's moral weakness is the opposite of God's moral fidelity (*chesedh*, **steadfast love**). God's imputed righteousness manifested in forgiveness (cf. Rom. 3:21-26; 4:20-25) is the opposite of man's unrighteousness or moral imperfection (cf. Pss. 130:3-4; 143:2).

God's universal dominion (vss. 19-22). The purpose of these verses is to show that God blesses all men, not just Israel; therefore, all creation should praise God. [19] God is frequently set forth as King of the universe (cf. Pss. 93:1-2; 95:3-5; 97:9). [20] The **angels** who are in the very presence of God and see his works should praise him.

[21] **Hosts** probably refers to the celestial bodies rather than to the angels (cf. Deut. 4:19). These heavenly bodies are frequently included in an invitation for the whole creation to praise God (cf. Pss. 96:11-13; 148:1-6).

[22] **Works** means created things. The psalm ends as it began, with the author's self-exhortation.

EXCURSUS

A Note on Forgiveness

The OT declares that men were forgiven (Lev. 4:20, 26, 31, 35; 5:6, 10, 13, 16, 18; 6:7; Isa. 1:18; 6:7; 38:17; Mic. 7:19). David knew he was forgiven (2 Sam. 12:13; Ps. 32:1-5) and Paul verifies David's conclusion (Rom. 4:6-8). The NT nowhere contradicts this idea. It declares that animal sacrifices could not take away sin (Heb. 10:1-4), but it does not say that God by his free grace could not forgive sin or was not in fact forgiving it. Pious individuals in OT days knew that sacrifices alone could not atone for sin (cf. Pss. 40:6-8; 50:12-15, 23; 51:16-17; 69:30-31; 1 Sam. 15:22-23). Christ's blood cleansed those under the Old Covenant who were obedient and penitent, just as it cleanses those living today (Heb. 9:15-17). In his divine forbearance, God "passed over former sins" (Rom. 3:25); that is, he did not exact the penalty for sin upon the righteous, but waited until Christ could bear their sins. Jesus declared Abraham and Lazarus to be in a state of blessedness (Lk. 16:19-25). God's truth is always consistent and should be so interpreted.

Psalm 104: God, the Master Architect

For comments on the opening and closing lines, see the introduction to Psalm 103. The psalmist bases his reflections upon creation on the record in Genesis 1. Initial acts of creation are reviewed in relation to God's present acts of providence whereby the Creator continues to protect and guide his creation. The emphasis in the psalm is on the Creator rather than on the creation. The psalmist manifests a keen awareness of the habits and habitats of wild animals and birds. Being close to nature has brought him close to God.

God's majesty in creation (vss. 1-4). [1] This introductory verse sets the tone for the whole psalm. God's greatness, **honor**, and **majesty** are magnified. **[2]** Participial clauses employed in the Hebrew text of verses 2-4 show that the initial act of creation is regarded as continuing into the present in God's providential governance of his world. The **light** which God created on the first day continues to surround and glorify him. As a king adorns himself with royal garments, so God clothes himself with **light** which is his very essence (cf. 1 John 1:5). God, who sent physical life to adorn the earth, has also sent his spiritual light to enlighten our spirits (John 1:1-9). The vertical separation of the waters above and beneath the firmament on the second day is here described poetically as stretching out a tent.

[3] God's abode in the heavens is pictured as **chambers** erected upon the celestial **waters**. Though God was recognized by Israel as omnipresent and permeating the whole universe (cf. 1 Kings 8:27; Ps. 139:7-10), he is pictured here like a great king going forth in his **chariot** to survey his kingdom. He can command **the clouds** and **the wind** to serve his purposes. And from his lofty height he can look down upon the earth and have regard for his creatures (cf. Ps. 102:18-20). [4] In synonymous parallelism the psalmist describes the **winds** and **fire** as God's **messengers** and **ministers**. In Hebrew, the word *ruchoth* (like the Greek *pneuma*) can mean "wind" or "spirit," and the word *mal'akh* (like the Greek word *angellos*) can refer to an earthly or heavenly messenger. This accounts for the play on words in the book of Hebrews, which quotes the passage from the LXX (Heb. 1:7). The contrast between Christ as Son of God and the angels as ministers is emphasized in the book of Hebrews (cf. 1:5-14). However, the context of the psalm shows that the psalmist had the physical elements in mind.

Creation and utilization of the earth (vss. 5-9). [5] In language common to his day, the psalmist describes the **earth** as **set** upon **foundations**. Job, by contrast, thinks of the earth as hung upon nothing (Job 26:7). One need not assume in either case that the language is intended to be understood literally. However, since in Job and in our psalm the Scriptures record the thoughts of man, it is possible that these passages present alternative viewpoints in regard to the earth. Genesis 1 does not tell us exactly how the earth is held in place. This was left for modern man to discover in his divinely ordained quest for understanding his environment (cf. Gen. 1:26-27). **[6]** This verse pictures the earth before God separated the dry land from the waters on the third day of creation. Apparently the psalmist thinks of **the mountains** as existing before that separation took place.

[7] In synonymous parallelism the psalmist pictures God rebuking the reluctant waters, **the deep.** This may reflect the mode of expression employed by the ancient Babylonians that Marduk, the chief God, had to subdue Tiamat, the great sea dragon, before his work of creation could proceed. If there is such a reflection of language here, there is no reason to suppose that the psalmist has embraced Babylonian mythology. This psalm portrays Yahweh as in complete control of his creation. **[8]** This verse, in the light of verse 6, seems to suggest that though the **mountains** already existed previous to this separation of water and dry land, they became higher and **valleys** became deeper on this third day of creation. While the psalmist is not writing from the vantage point of a modern scientist, there is nothing known to modern science which contradicts this poetic portrayal.

[9] The Scriptures often speak of the "bounds" of the seas as some kind of barrier beyond which they cannot **pass** (cf. Isa. 54:9; Jer. 5:22; Prov. 8:27-29; Job 38:8-11).

In these first two paragraphs, the psalmist has focused on the first two and one-half "days" of creation. He has mentioned the four basic elements out of which the universe was created according to the ancients: earth (vs. 5), air (wind, vss. 3b, 4a), fire (vs. 4b), and water (vss. 6b-9).

Provision for animal life (vss. 10-23). [10-13] Here the creation of vegetation on the second part of the third day is mixed with animal life created on the fifth and sixth days, since vegetation was created at least in part to sustain animal life. The Hebrew participles which open and close this paragraph indicate that the intervening verbs describe a present state of things. **[10]** No creation of **springs** of water is mentioned in Genesis 1, but the psalmist cannot conceive of anything existing without the exercise of the divine will. [11] The psalmist is familiar with the instincts of beasts **of the field** which allow them to find the life-sustaining waters.

[12] The waters make possible the trees which become a habitation for certain **birds.** [13] For the idea of God dwelling in his upper chambers, see verse 3. Abundant water makes possible plenteous vegetation which sustains the needs of man (cf. vss. 14-15).

[14-16] God provides **grass** and **plants** for the benefit of **man** and **cattle.** [14] The middle line of this verse in the RSV represents an emendation of the Hebrew, which reads: "and plants for the service of man." [15] The three most important areas of human life are reflected here: **wine** for man's times of refreshment, **oil** for its pleasant aroma at the banquet table, and **bread** as a symbol of the necessities of life. Wine was an acceptable beverage to be used in moderation at meal time (cf. Eccl. 10:19; John 2:1-11), and could also be used for medicinal purposes (cf. Prov. 31:6-7; Luke 10:34; 1 Tim. 5:23). However, the excessive use of wine and strong drink has always been condemned in the Scriptures (Prov. 20:1; 23:29-35; 1 Cor. 6:9-11), as has the excessive use of food (Prov. 23:20-21; Tit. 1:12-13). Christ put his stamp of approval upon the value of aesthetic enjoyment and the love that may be expressed through the giving of that which cannot be strictly considered necessities of life (cf. John 12:1-8).

[16] **The cedars of Lebanon** stand as a symbol of God's great bounty, since they were among the best cedar in the world.

Animal instincts are especially singled out in verses 17-23. The psalmist recognizes God as the provider for these creatures. [17-18] The animals which live in remote regions especially reveal to the psalmist God's providential care, since it is obvious that man is not responsible for the care of these as he is of his domesticated animals (cf. vs. 14). [19] The mention of **the sun** and **moon** which were created on the fourth day introduces the distinctions between the habits of nocturnal animals and man.

[20-22] Nocturnal animals hunt their food while man

sleeps. [23] But **man** works while these animals sleep. This situation does not fit modern man in western civilization, but it did fit the psalmist's time.

The works of God (vss. 24-30). [24] The ancient Israelites recognized the **wisdom** and understanding required to create this orderly universe (cf. Ps. 136:5). So enamored were they with this concept that they sometimes personified **wisdom** and treated her as the agent through which God created all things (cf. Prov. 8:22-31). That God's **wisdom** is continuing to order the universe is also recognized (cf. Job 28). This use of personified wisdom is not to be equated with the NT revelation that God created the universe through Christ (John 1:1-14; Col. 1:15-17; Heb. 1:2).

[25-26] The vastness of the seas fills the psalmist with awe and wonder. **Leviathan** is a term describing the mythical ancient sea monster, but in the Bible the idea is demythologized and applied to great evil kingdoms controlled by Satan (cf. Isa. 27:1), or the term refers to great sea creatures which struck fear in the heart of man or filled him with awe (cf. Job 41). The latter meaning is likely the one to be attached to our psalm passage. Here, and in the following paragraph, the psalmist' reflects upon the sea creatures which were created on the fifth day.

[27-28] God's providential care of these sea creatures is no less evident than for the rest of his creation.

[29-30] Two figures are mixed. Death is pictured as a withdrawal of **breath** by the Lord (vs. 29). The regeneration of animal life (vs. 30a) and the renewal of vegetation in the spring (vs. 30b) are pictured as God's again infusing the life-giving principle. **Breath** (vs. 29) and **Spirit** (vs. 30) derive from the same Hebrew word (*ruach*). In the present context, the word means nothing more than the life-giving principle.

Concluding prayer and vow (vss. 31-35). These lines are for the most part in the form of a wish, and so should be translated "may" or "let" as in the RSV. Verse 33 is the one exception. This verse is a declaration of the psalmist's avowed purpose. The prayer is threefold, expressing the desire that the Lord may be pleased with and glorified through his creation (vss. 31-32), that the psalmist's reflections on God as Creator may please him (vs. 34), and that the incongruity of wickedness in the universe may be removed so that harmony can be restored (vs. 35). This last wish recognizes that God's creation was good before sin entered the human family (cf. Gen. 1:12, 18, 21, 25, 31), but sin has changed the order of things (cf. Gen. 3:14-19; Rom. 8:18-25).

[33] The psalmist knows that life-long praise of God is the only response which he can give to the glory and majesty of the Creator. [35c] Therefore, he ends as he began, with a personal admonition to himself.

[35d] This is the first time the Hallelujah (**praise the Lord**) appears in the psalms, and the psalms are the only OT literature that employs the term. By NT days the term had become popular and has continued in use among Christians and Jews. Note the introduction to Psalm 105.

Psalm 105: The God of Abraham, Isaac, and Jacob

In all likelihood the Hallelujah at the end of Psalm 104 was originally the beginning of Psalm 105. In this case, each of Psalms 103–106 ends by repeating the opening line. Psalms 105 and 106 are both historical praise hymns, but there are significant differences between them. Psalm 106 begins where the historical psalms usually begin, with Israel's national beginnings at the time of the exodus from Egypt. Psalm 105 is unique in that it begins the historical retrospect with God's promise made to Abraham, and ends abruptly when the history has progressed far enough to demonstrate God's fulfilment of his covenant promise made to Abraham in the event of the successful conquest of Canaan. Psalm 78 is a didactic historical psalm which ends the historical retrospect with God's choice of David and the tribe of Judah as the religious capital of the nation. Whereas Psalm 105 emphasizes God's goodness to Israel while ignoring Israel's sins, and Psalm 106 emphasizes God's love for Israel in spite of her sins, Psalm 78 combines these two elements of God's covenant loyalty and

Israel's waywardness. It is instructive to make a careful comparison of these three historical psalms.

Invitation to praise (vss. 1-6). The invitation is issued to those who seek the Lord (vs. 3b), namely, the offspring of Abraham (vs. 6a). [1] The summons to **give thanks to the Lord** is frequently made the opening thought in psalms of praise and thanksgiving (cf. 66:1; 95:1-2; 96:1-2; 106:1; 107:1; 118:1; 136:1). Israel's pious leaders felt keenly the responsibility to share her blessings from God with the nations of the world. God's works on behalf of Israel demonstrated his desire to bless the whole world. [2] God's **wonderful works** are **his miracles** (cf. vs. 5). [3] **Name** stands for personality, character manifested through action.

[4] God's **presence** means that his **strength** is available to his trusting ones. [5] God's **judgments** include his blessings on the faithful and his chastisements upon the wayward.

The covenant God (vss. 7-11). [7] Though God's **judgments are in all the earth**, he is Israel's special covenant God. This concept of God as a covenant God was unique in Israel's religion. [8] The **covenant** relationship assures Israel that God will be true to his commitments to them. **Word** refers to the promise made by the superior party who also sets the terms of the covenant (cf. vss. 9b, 11). **Thousand** stands for "many," or a limitless number (cf. Exod. 20:6; Deut. 7:9; Ps. 50:10-12). **He is mindful** is better than "he has remembered," since mental activity is thought of as a continuing state. [9a] God's initial **covenant with Abraham** (Gen. 12:1-3) was renewed and extended to assure Abraham that his descendants would inherit Canaan (Gen. 17:6-8). It was still later renewed and confirmed with an oath which made the promise unconditional (Gen. 22:15-18; Heb. 6:13-20). [9b] **His sworn promise to Isaac** (cf. Gen. 26:2-5) reaffirmed the fact that the covenant included Abraham's descendants through Isaac.

[10] The divine election involved further selection of Jacob and his descendants (cf. Gen. 28:13-15), who constituted the nation, Israel. **Everlasting** must be taken to mean "of long duration" (cf. Heb. 8:6-13). **For ever** (vs. 8a) is from the same Hebrew word and bears the same connota-

tion in this context. [11] This promise was made to each of the patriarchs, Abraham, Isaac, and Jacob. For a NT interpretation of divine selectivity in God's covenant choices, see Romans 9:9-13. Now God's covenant is extended to all men of every nation who will accept its terms (Rom. 9:25–10:4).

God's protection (vss. 12-15). [12] The patriarchs were only **sojourners** with no legal rights and at the mercy of the local inhabitants. They were comparatively **few in number** (cf. Gen. 28:4; 34:30). [13-15] These verses allude to the migrations of Abraham to Egypt (Gen. 12:10-20) and Gerar (Gen. 20:1-18), and to Isaac's migration to Gerar (Gen. 26:1-22) in time of famine. The patriarchs could figuratively be called God's **anointed ones** because God revealed himself through them. They could be designated God's **prophets** because they interceded on behalf of men (cf. Gen. 20:7).

Joseph as savior (vss. 16-22). God worked providentially to prepare Joseph for the role which he was to play in revealing God's wisdom and ways. And God prepared Egypt for the acceptance of Joseph's role. [16-17] The antecedent of the pronoun **he** is God (vs. 7). **He had sent** is an excellent translation of the Hebrew perfect in this context. There is no differentiation in Hebrew between the simple past and the past perfect tense, but the historical facts indicate that God sent **Joseph** to Egypt and prepared him for his role before he **summoned** the **famine** (cf. Gen. 37:25-28; 39:1–41:45). The psalmist, like all pious Israelites, viewed everything as being under the guiding providence of God. God was using the jealousy of Joseph's brothers, the lying tongue of Potiphar's wife, and the dreams of Joseph, the imprisoned butler and baker, and the Pharaoh for his own glory and to accomplish his purpose with his covenant people. [18-19] There is no mention in Genesis of the specifics mentioned in verse 18. The psalmist may be relying on oral tradition for this information, or he may be exercising poetic license by embellishing the historical record in keeping with the treatment generally accorded a prisoner of that day. The psalmist sees the imprisonment of Joseph as a testing from God. Joseph's endurance under duress demonstrated his faith in God and his loyalty to ethical principles.

[20-22] Following his interpretation of the dream of the chief butler and baker and that of the Pharaoh, Joseph was brought out of prison and made overseer of the grain collection in preparation for the coming famine which God had revealed to the Pharaoh through Joseph's interpretation of his dream. When the time came for someone to be selected for this oversight, the Pharaoh said of Joseph, "Can we find such a man as this, in whom is the Spirit of God?" (Gen. 41:38). The divine preparation of both Joseph and the Pharaoh was successful. [22] There is no mention of these specifics in Genesis, but it was a common practice for the Pharaohs to so utilize intelligent slaves. Apparently Moses was trained for such a task (cf. Acts 7:22).

God's care of Israel (vss. 23-45). [23-25] Jacob's family was forced to go to Egypt for their livelihood during the time of famine, and during the time of Joseph were treated as honored guests by the pharaohs. Under these favorable circumstances the Israelites multiplied more rapidly than the Egyptians, filling the Egyptians with fear that they might conquer them. So they made slaves of the Israelites, but they multiplied all the more (Exod. 1). The psalmist, with his faith in the sovereignty of God, attributes all of these happenings directly to God. God does not induce men to do evil (James 1:13), but with his divine foreknowledge, utilizes the sinful tendencies of men to discipline his people and to accomplish his purposes.

[26-36] God gave **signs** of his presence through the miracles which he enabled Moses and Aaron to perform. This was God's way of preparing both the Israelites and the Egyptians for Israel's departure by the decree of God. Eight of the ten plagues recorded in Exodus 7-11 are enumerated, but not in the order given in Exodus. Possibly the plague of **darkness** is mentioned first because of the tremendous impression which it made on the people of Egypt (cf. Exod. 12:29-36).

[37-39] God's providence caused the Israelites to depart

Egypt not emptyhanded, but with provisions supplied by the Egyptians. **[40-42]** In the wilderness sojourn, God miraculously cared for Israel. He was proving to Israel his own reliability and faithfulness in keeping the covenant promise which he had made with Abraham (cf. vss. 7-11).

God thus freed his people from bondage and caused them to inherit Canaan. **[43]** The psalmist reflects upon the song of victory which Moses and Miriam sang with the Israelites after their miraculous crossing of the Red Sea and the destruction of the Egyptian army (cf. Exod. 15:1-21). **[44]** Moses, in a farewell sermon to Israel, placed great stress on the exercise of God's grace and love which would allow Israel to inherit **the fruit of the peoples' toil** (cf. Deut. 6:10-12; Josh. 24:13; Neh. 9:25). **[45]** Israel's response to God's grace must be manifested in obedience and grateful praise (cf. vss. 1-6).

Psalm 106: God's Love for Wayward Israel

Opinions differ regarding the literary form of this psalm. Its beginning and ending, however, identify it as a praise hymn. There is the element of confession in the historical retrospect, but this element is employed in praise to God (cf. Ps. 103; Neh. 9:5-37) and in didactic psalms (cf. Ps. 78), as well as in laments (cf. Ezra 9:1-15; Dan. 9:3-19). In all these instances, pious Israelites were expressing their faith in the constancy of God's covenant loyalty toward Israel (cf. 1 Kings 8:44-53).

The question is also raised as to whether this psalm was originally intended to be used for liturgical or private purposes. The use of plural pronouns (cf. vss. 3, 6-7, 47) and the didactic element in the historical retrospect suggest that the psalm was intended to be used publicly, whether in a cultic or devotional sense. The interjection of a personal plea (vss. 4-5) expresses the psalmist's desire to be included in the restoration of the nation.

Verse 47 places the psalm most naturally in the exilic period (587–538 B.C.). The similarity of language between the contemporary confession of Daniel, the late phraseology used by Ezra and Nehemiah, and our psalm suggests a liturgical formula used in public confessions, although this is not certain.

It is of singular interest that Israel's sins are enumerated in a praise hymn, but this stresses the importance of praising God for his grace, mercy, and love, as well as for his power manifested in his creative and providential acts.

Invitation to praise (vss. 1-3). [1] This psalm, along with Psalms 105, 111-113, 115-116, and 146-150, bear the subtitle "Praise the Lord!" [Heb. *hallelujah*] either at the beginning, or end, or both. For that reason, they have been designated Hallel or Hallelujah Psalms. Verse 1 is found in identical form in 107:1; 118:1, 29; 136:1. This repetition seems to suggest a liturgical formula used in Israel's praises. **Good** is a very general term suggesting the full complement of divine attributes, but the special emphasis here is on God's **steadfast love**, that is, his covenant loyalty.

[2] The psalmist recognizes human inadequacy in rendering praise commensurate with the divine attributes and the saving acts of the Lord (cf. 40:5; 116:12). [3] But he recognizes that man glorifies God when he emulates in his own life the divine attributes of **justice** and **righteousness** (cf. 45:6-7; 72:1-2; 89:14).

Personal plea for restoration (vss. 4-5). [4] The Hebrew word for **favor** *(retson)* comes from a verbal root which means to be pleased with, or to express good will toward, to be gracious or propitious. It is connected here with God's salvation (cf. KJV, NASB). The latter term can mean physical deliverance, success, or prosperity, as well as restoration of spiritual fellowship granted in forgiveness. The immediate context suggests the first definition here, although the element of confession in verses 6-46 indicates that the spiritual connotation may also have been intended.

[5] **Prosperity** (cf. NASB, NEB) is the likely meaning of the Hebrew word translated "good" in the KJV.

Sin and deliverance (vss. 6-12). [6] The first line literally reads, "We have sinned with [KJV; "like," NASB, NEB] our fathers." The thought seems to carry the idea of cumulative sin committed and continued by succeeding generations, including the present one. [7] The Israelites so soon forgot God's wonders in Egypt as to rebel **at the Red Sea** a few days after leaving their homes in Egypt. The Hebrew text reads "the sea, the sea of reeds," the repetition being used for emphasis (cf. KJV, NASB). The name Red Sea derives from the LXX version. Note how ingratitude led to rebellion.

[8] Though Israel did not deserve deliverance, God acted out of grace for his name's sake; that is, **he made known his mighty power.** [9-11] This exertion of divine power resulted in the destruction of the Pharaoh's army and the deliverance of Israel. **Saved** and **delivered** (redeemed, cf. KJV, NASB) both refer here to physical deliverance from Egyptian bondage. [12] These mighty acts momentarily accomplished God's twofold purpose, namely, to deliver his people and to cause them to believe in him. Compare the praise hymn in Exodus 15:1-18. Note how this "song of Moses" looks to the past fact of deliverance and then, by faith, to the future conquest and settlement of the land of Canaan.

Rebellion in the wilderness (vss. 13-33). This grateful praise uttered in faith was soon exchanged once again for unbelief that led to serious sins which entailed serious consequences. [13-15] Their insatiable appetites (cf. NEB) demanded that they have what they wanted when they wanted it rather than patiently trusting God to care for them. The Hebrew employs a cognate accusative here ("they lusted lust") to intensify the force of the verb. The food miraculously provided filled their stomachs, but God "sent a leanness into their soul" (KJV). This idiom suggests **a wasting disease** (cf. NASB) or "wasting sickness" (NEB) which would result in diminished strength instead of increased vigor. This was a judicial act of God utilized to cause Israel to see the fruit of her selfish desire. For the historical record alluded to, see Numbers 11.

[16-18] The second illustration of Israel's sin in the wilderness is related in Numbers 16. Korah headed a conspiracy against **Moses and Aaron**, contending that since all the nation was holy, the special privileges afforded Moses and Aaron were discriminatory. An ancient Jewish tradition

says that Korah is not mentioned in the psalm because the psalmist did not wish to bemean the Levitical priestly services, of which Korah was a part. **The holy one of the Lord** (cf. saint, KJV) refers to the fact that Aaron and his sons were consecrated for the special priestly functions (cf. NEB).

[19-23] This section reverts back to the incident of the golden calf made and worshiped at Sinai or Horeb (Exod. 32). The historical record shows that Aaron received a stern rebuke from Moses for allowing this terrible sin to occur (Exod. 32:21), but Aaron's name is omitted in the psalm passage apparently for the same reason that Korah is omitted above. [20] **The glory of God** is literally "their glory" (cf. KJV, NASB, NEB). Jewish tradition has it that the text originally read "glory of God" (cf. NEB note, Jer. 2:11; Rom. 1:23), but the scribes changed it out of reverence for the holy name of God. The second half of the verse imposes the same satirical scorn on idolatry as occasionally found in the prophets (cf. Pss. 115:3-8; 135:15-18; Isa. 40:18-20; 41:6-7; 44:9-17; 46:5-7; Jer. 10:14-15; Hos. 10:5-6; 13:2). [23] Moses' successful intercession on behalf of Israel is recorded in Exodus 32:11-14, 30-34.

[24-27] The story of the report of the spies and Israel's unbelief is told in Numbers 13–14. The psalmist says **they despised the pleasant land**. This might be translated "made light of" (NEB). Again the sin of unbelief caused them to take lightly the promise of the Lord to give them the land of Canaan as an inheritance (cf. 105:11). [26] The word **swore** is not in the Hebrew text, but the raising of the hand is an idiom used to indicate the taking of an oath (cf. Exod. 6:8; Deut. 32:40). [26-27] The verbs in verses 26b and 27a are the same in Hebrew (literally "to cause to fall"). **Disperse** is from an infinitive which means to scatter. This doubtless refers to the oath that God took at the time of Moses' farewell to his people shortly before his death, an oath that he would disperse Israel among the nations if they turned to idolatry (Deut. 4:25-27). Thus the psalmist has here compressed into one event the whole period of the wilderness wandering. Perhaps he intended to convey

the thought that unbelief in God's promises precedes apostasy in the form of idolatry (cf. Isa. 7:1-9; 2 Kings 16:1-20).

[28-31] Numbers 25 records the incident alluded to here. The reference is to a particular kind of **Baal** worship engaged in by the Moabites at Shittim just east of the Jordan over against Jericho. [28] The last half of the verse reads in Hebrew, "and they ate the sacrifices of the dead." It is not certain whether this phrase refers to idols as dead gods (cf. Num. 25:2; Ps. 115:4-8; Jer. 10:14-15; 51:17-18) or to offerings made on behalf of dead persons (cf. Deut. 26:14; Lev. 19:28; Deut. 14:1). [30] **Phinehas,** the grandson of Aaron, **interposed** ("interceded," NEB) on behalf of Israel by leading the righteous to slay the wicked perpetrators of this sin. [31] **And that has been reckoned to him as righteousness,** just as Abraham's faith was reckoned as righteousness (Gen. 15:6). David believed in imputed righteousness based on faith (Ps. 32:1-2; cf. Rom. 4:1-8). The law and the prophets, meaning the entire OT, bear witness to a righteousness of God imputed to man on the basis of his faith (cf. Rom. 3:21-22).

[32-33] The incident alluded to here is recorded in Numbers 20:1-13. The people's constant murmuring and complaining caused Moses' **spirit** to become **bitter** so that **he spoke words that were rash.** An alternative interpretation takes **him** (vs. 32a) and **his spirit** (vs. 33a) to refer to God, but it seems that the antecedent of these two pronouns is the same as **he** in verse 33b. This rashness kept Moses and Aaron from entering the Promised Land. "Inadvertently" (KJV) is too mild for this setting.

Failure in Canaan (vss. 34-46). [34-39] Israel's conquest of Canaan was followed by her own absorption of the idolatrous practices of the Canaanites. The purpose back of God's command for them to exterminate these pagan people was to prevent Israel from taking up their wicked ways (cf. Deut. 7:1-5; 20:16-18). Because Israel failed to carry out God's command, the nation was warned that these peoples would become a snare to Israel (Judg. 1:21–2:5). The history of Israel, as recorded in Judges,

Samuel, Kings, and the Prophets, provides ample evidence of the reality of Israel's lapses into idolatry.

Two features of idolatry were especially abominable in God's sight. One was child sacrifice (vss. 37-38), and the other was cult prostitution. **Demons** is from the Hebrew *shedhim*, which seems to refer to some kind of inferior spirit beings. The allusion here is from Deuteronomy 32:15-18, which is apparently alluded to in 1 Corinthians 10:19-22. A specific prohibition against child sacrifice was given in the law of Moses (Lev. 18:21). Nevertheless, at times this heinous crime was commonly practiced in Israel (cf. 2 Kings 16:1-3; Jer. 19:1-9).

Cult prostitution may be alluded to in verse 39, although harlotry is frequently used as a figure of idolatry in general. That Israel sometimes engaged in cult prostitution is clear from Hosea 4:14.

[40-46] Israel proved herself unworthy through her many lapses into idolatry. Yet many times God manifested his covenant loyalty toward Israel. This is a clear expression of God's grace. "Where sin abounded, grace abounded all the more." (Rom. 5:20-21).

Prayer for deliverance (vs. 47). New saving acts on the part of God provide new occasions for praise and thanks.

Verse 48 is an appended doxology closing Book IV of the Psalter (cf. 41:13; 72:18-19; 89:52).

Psalm 107: Deliverance from Typical Distresses

This psalm of thanksgiving was occasioned by Israel's return from Babylonian exile (vss. 2b-3). However, the psalm is not confined to the circumstances of the exiles, but rather uses those events as typical of problems experienced at any time.

God's love acclaimed (vss. 1-3). [1] The psalm actually praises God for all the manifestations of his covenant loyalty toward Israel (cf. 106:1 and the notes).

[2-3] Redeemed here is further defined by the expression **gathered in from the lands.** Redemption in the OT can mean physical deliverance or spiritual redemption in the form of forgiveness (cf. Ps. 130:8). So the NT speaks of the redemption of our bodies (Rom. 8:23) as well as redemption in the form of forgiveness (Eph. 1:7). Apparently the four directions are used here to indicate that the exiles were gathered in from wherever they had been scattered (cf. Isa. 43:5-7). The exiles might be thought of as returning from the **east** country (Assyria, Babylonia, or Persia) and from the **west** country (Egypt, cf. Zech. 8:7), or from the **north** (Assyria) and the **west** (Egypt, cf. Isa. 49:12).

Examples of distress (vss. 4-32). In beautiful poetic form, the psalmist in four stanzas names homelessness, imprisonment, sickness, and perils at sea as typical troubles from which they had been delivered. Each stanza follows an almost identical fivefold poetic pattern. There is a statement of a specific problem (vss. 4-5, 10-12, 17-18, 23-27) followed by a declaration of their supplication uttered in an identical refrain (vss. 6, 13, 19, 28). Next, a specific act of deliverance from the specific problem at hand is related (vss. 7, 14, 20, 29-30), followed by an exhortation to thank God uttered in a second identical refrain (vss. 8, 15, 21, 31). The fifth element is slightly varied. In stanzas one and two of this section, a motive for thanking God is set forth (vss. 9, 16). In stanzas three and four, the congregation is exhorted to further praise and thanksgiving (vss. 22, 32). The expression **for his wonderful works to the sons of men** shows that the psalmist intends for these specific saving acts of the Lord to be treated as representative of many others which could be enumerated.

[4-9] This stanza may refer to fugitives who fled from Nebuchadnezzar's invading armies. With no certain inhabited dwelling place, they were **hungry and thirsty** to the point of becoming faint. God heard their cry for help and **delivered them from their distress** (the Hebrew here and in verses 13, 19, and 28, is plural, "distresses," cf. KJV, NASB). The Hebrew uses a cognate accusative in verse 7 to connect very closely the **way** (*derekh*) with God's leading (*yadrikh*) them. Poetically, God is said to go over the way before them so that they could follow safely. In the last half of the verse, **a city to dwell in** is literally "a city of habitation" (so also vss. 4 and 36; cf. KJV, NASB). Note how the deliverance (vs. 7) and motive for thanksgiving (vs. 9) are vitally connected with the specific problem described in verses 4-5.

[10-16] The second stanza in this section deals with imprisonment. Not all the captives were literally imprisoned, but some were (cf. 2 Kings 17:4; 23:31-33; 24:10-12; 25:7). Isaiah thinks of the captivity itself as a form of imprisonment (Isa. 42:6-7; 49:8-9), and Jesus applies the Isaianic passages to his own role of setting men free from the prisonhouse of sin (Lk. 4:18-21; Isa. 61:1-2). Jehoiachin, after an imprisonment of thirty-seven years, was freed and honored by Evil-merodach, king of Babylon (2 Kings 25:27-30). But the psalmist has in mind the restoration of the nation after the captivity was over.

[17-22] Sickness resulting from sin is the third example of distress from which the Israelites were delivered.

[17] The Hebrew word translated **sick** means literally "fools" (cf. KJV, NASB, NEB). The following verses indicate that the psalmist refers to those who brought sickness upon themselves through their own foolish ways (cf. Ps. 38:3-10). Wandering in trackless wastes (vss. 4-5), or living in unsanitary conditions in prison (vs. 10) could have brought disease and illness upon them. But these conditions were the result of their sinful ways (vss. 11, 17).

[20] The Hebrew word rendered **destruction** is plural (cf. KJV, NASB), apparently indicating the several kinds of illness which overtook them (cf. Deut. 28:15-22).

[22] Thankofferings, or **thanksgiving** as a sacrifice, and **songs of joy** are to be offered up to the God who delivers.

[23-24] Perils at **sea** provide the last illustration of specific dangers from which God delivers. [25-26] God brought on the storm in order to manifest his greatness (cf. vs. 24). [27] Apparently the first half of the verse describes seasickness. The second half reads in Hebrew, "And all their wisdom was swallowed up," which might be paraphrased, "and their seamanship was all in vain" (NEB). **And were at their wits' end** is another effort to capture the thought in English idiom. [29] Divine interven-

tion which exerts power upon nature is clear evidence of God's greatness and goodness (cf. Ps. 29; Matt. 8:23-27). God brings spiritual calm to those who trust in his redeeming love and in the atonement offered in Christ.

[31] "Goodness" (KJV) is too general a translation of *chesedh*. "Loving kindness" (NASB) is better, but **steadfast love** or "enduring love" (NEB) is best. The Hebrew word applies to those in a covenant relationship. But the word in this context, as frequently elsewhere, goes beyond strict covenant obligations to reveal the gracious, enduring love of God toward Israel even when through her sin she no longer deserved that love. [32] Public praise is a proper response to community deliverance.

God's control of nature (vss. 33-38). [33-34] Soil samples from the Sinai Desert, from North Africa, the western desert area in the United States, and many other parts of the world, reveal that these regions were once well-watered places. Precisely what physical circumstances wrought these changes is not known, but the psalmist knows that God is in control of all these physical forces and that he utilizes them as a discipline upon sinful man (cf. Gen. 3:17-19; Rom. 8:18-22). The **salty waste** ("barrenness," KJV, is inadequate here) is doubtless a reference to the region of Sodom and Gomorrah which are thought to be buried under the southern end of the Dead Sea (Salt Sea in the OT, cf. Gen. 13:10-12; 19:24-29). [35-36] Oases in the **desert** seem to be alluded to here. Or possibly irrigation projects are in the mind of the psalmist.

[37-38] Because of God's blessings, cities may prosper in arid regions and cattle may fare well.

God's control of history (vss. 39-42). Doubtless the psalmist has reverted to the event which originally prompted the writing of this psalm of thanksgiving—the deliverance from captivity. Special emphasis is given in the Psalms to God's special interest in the weak and defenseless who are oppressed by the powerful nobility and royalty (cf. 9:9-12, 18-20; 10:17-18; 37:32-33; 105:12-15).

Summary exhortation (vs. 43). This verse doubtless sums up the entire psalm. Such concluding exhortations are

364 / PSALM 109:1

often found in psalms of thanksgiving (cf. 32:11). Hosea (14:9) concludes his prophetic ministry in much the same way. The first and last verses of the psalm, as well as the refrains (vss. 8, 15, 21, 31), lay special stress on God's **steadfast love** for his covenant people. The **wise** will **give heed** and **consider** these things so that they may help him to attain and maintain a mature faith.

Psalm 108: Steadfast Confidence in God

With minor variations, verses 1-5 are identical with Psalm 57:1-11, and verses 6-13 are identical with Psalm 60:5-12. For the interpretation of Psalm 108, see the comments on these passages.

Psalm 109: Prayer for Vengeance

This psalm, along with Psalm 69, contains the strongest imprecation against enemies to be found in the Bible (see the excursus at the end of Ps. 79). A curse is pronounced upon the entire family of the enemy (vss. 9-10) and upon his posterity (vs. 13). Even in the NT, God promises to vindicate his enemies who persecute his faithful people (Lk. 18:1-8; Rev. 6:9-11). In both testaments, however, man is discouraged from taking personal vengeance on his enemies (Lev. 19:18; Rom. 12:19-21; Deut. 32:35; Prov. 25:21-22). The recognition of God's judgment on the wicked (Acts 23:3; 2 Tim. 4:14; 2 Thess. 2:8-12) is coupled with prayer on their behalf (Lk. 23:34; Acts 7:60; 2 Tim. 4:16). The full revelation of God in Christ reveals a final day of judgment followed by the sealing of the destinies of men. Those who have done evil and failed to repent of it will enter into eternal torment (2 Thess. 1:1-10). These facts, plus the example of our Lord, make it easier for the Christian not to avenge himself. Perhaps the greatest element in these cries for vengeance in the OT is the recognition that divine justice demands that the righteous be vindicated and that the wicked be destroyed. The fact of the matter is that God's forgiveness of the wicked is always contingent upon their repentence.

The complaint (vss. 1-5). [1] Be not silent means do not let the wrong go unpunished (cf. 50:3, 21). The psalmist declares his innocence. **[2]** His enemies speak deceitful lies against him, for the charges brought against him and the slander spoken against him are not true. **[3]** They **attack** him **without cause,** for he has done nothing to provoke their hatred. **[4-5]** He is rewarded **evil for good** and **hatred for love. Even as I make prayer for them** (vs. 4b) is an interpretation of the Hebrew text which reads literally, "But I am [all] prayer" (cf. KJV, NASB). "Though I have done nothing unseemly" (NEB) departs completely from the Hebrew text. The elliptical Hebrew phrase does not indicate specifically that he was praying on behalf of his enemies, though the context might imply as much. In light of the total context of the psalm, this interpretation is difficult to accept, although a better explanation is lacking.

Imprecation (vss. 6-20). [6-7] The Hebrew of verse 6b reads, "Let a *śaṭan* stand at his right hand." The *śaṭan* may refer to Satan (cf. KJV), or it can mean an adversary (NASB). "Rascal" (NEB) may be a little too strong here. The psalmist has been falsely accused, perhaps even in a law court (vs. 4); therefore, he prays for the same fate to come to his accuser. **They accuse me** (vs. 4) and **my accusers** (vss. 20, 29) are from the same root. The expression **stand at his right hand** refers here to the lawyer for the prosecution, or possibly to the accuser himself, depending on how the law courts were structured (cf. vs. 31). The change from plural (vss. 2-5) to singular may suggest that one person was responsible for arousing a conspiracy against him. (Cf. Ps. 55, where there is a shift from plural enemies in vss. 2-3, 9-11, 15, 18-19, and 23 to a single enemy in vss. 12-14 and 20-21). In verse 7, the psalmist is asking that his false accuser be found to be a sinner, which would make his prayer an abomination in the sight of the Lord (cf. 66:18).

Next (vss. 8-15), the psalmist prays for the complete disgrace and obliteration of the entire family of his accuser.

[8] A short life-span was considered a judgment from God resulting from one's sins (cf. 55:23; Jer. 17:11; Isa. 38:6, 17). **[9-12]** Since the **fatherless** and the **widow** were frequently without legal rights, and since creditors often seized a person's goods in payment of debts, the very circumstances here wished for sometimes happened. The fatherless and the widows are often classed as subjects for charity on the part of Israel (cf. Deut. 14:28-29; 16:9-12).

[13] That it was a dishonor for a man to die without sons to carry on the family name can be seen in the law pertaining to levirate marriage (Deut. 25:1-10).

[14-15] In light of the context, these verses must be a prayer that everlasting disgrace attend his enemy's ancestry. God would never hold the father guilty for the sins of his children if the father did what was lawful and right (Ezek. 18:1-13, 20). The Hebrew of verse 15b reads "their memory" (cf. KJV, NASB, NEB).

[16-20] Since his accuser has relentlessly cursed and wronged him, may the accuser be continually cursed. Since he **pursued** his enemy **to their death** (vs. 16), may he find curses against himself to be like a garment worn daily (vs. 19) and like a body saturated with water and oil (vs. 18). Note that the psalmist has returned to a consideration of the group of enemies (vs. 20).

Plea for deliverance (vss. 21-29). [21-25] Three motives for God to deliver are offered. **[21]** May God's reputation for keeping his promise to protect his faithful ones be upheld. **[22-24]** The psalmist's physical distress which has greatly weakened him is cause for God to act. **[25]** And the mental agony of social disgrace is cause enough for God to deliver him.

[26-27] The psalmist prays for God to act in a fashion that demonstrates that his deliverance is God's work.

[28-29] Though his enemies **curse** him, may God **bless** him. Note the footnote in the RSV to verse 28b. It is better, however, to read, "When they arise, they shall be ashamed" (NASB). The word for "arise" is to be taken as a future perfect introducing a conditional sentence. Taken in this sense, the half verse is a declaration of trust. Our text assumes that the entire passage (vss. 26-29) employs imperatives and jussives to express a wish or desire. The

Greek translates with a plural participle, "them that rise up against me" or "my assailants" (vs. 28b).

Promise to praise God (vss. 30-31). [30] With full confidence that God will vindicate him, he contemplates the subsequent **praise** which he will render to God.

[31] Rather than an accuser standing at his right hand (cf. vs. 6b, notes), God will stand there as judge or perhaps as lawyer for the defense. Therefore, the needy will be delivered from the death penalty.

Psalm 110: The King Is a Priest at God's Right Hand

This royal psalm has messianic overtones, and verse 1 is attributed to David in the NT (Matt. 24:43-45). It appears that the psalm as a whole was written *about* a king rather than *by* one. Perhaps verses 1 and 4 are prophetic oracles concerning David, and the psalmist builds his psalm around these oracles. The word "says" (Heb. *ne'um*) in verse 1 is a technical term frequently used in the prophets to indicate a divine revelation given to a prophet. The word is used only here in the psalms. For characteristics of royal psalms, see the introduction to Psalm 89.

At God's right hand (vs. 1). Yahweh promises **my lord** (*'adhoni*), the king, victory over his enemies. The one at the right hand of a ruling monarch was considered second in command or authority. A person's right hand was a symbol of his strength and power (Judg. 5:26; Job 40:14; Pss. 21:8; 45:4; etc.), and God's right hand is frequently used in Scripture to indicate divine power (Exod. 15:6; Pss. 16:11; 17:7; 18:35; 20:6; 44:3; 48:10; 60:5; 63:8; etc.). The Davidic king is actually a prince under God's control (cf. 1 Sam. 10:1). **Footstool** indicates figuratively that which is subordinate. When applied to God's footstool, it may refer to the earth (probably universe, Isa. 66:1; Matt. 5:35), to Israel (Lam. 2:1), to the temple where Israel worshiped God (Pss. 99:1-5; 132:7), or to his enemies who would be brought into submission (Heb. 10:13).

Verse 1 is quoted or alluded to several times in the NT and applied to Christ. David is treated as a type of Christ, the Hebrew Messiah (Matt. 26:63-64; Mark 16:19; Acts

2:34-35; 5:30-32; Rom. 8:34; 1 Cor. 15:25; Eph. 1:20; Col. 3:1; Heb. 1:3, 13; 8:1; 10:12-13; 12:2). In Matthew 22:44, Jesus used the verse to set forth his pre-earthly existence, which allowed him to be David's Lord, as Christ ruled with God in heaven, and also made it possible for Christ to be David's son according to the flesh (cf. Rom. 1:3-4).

Promise of strength (vss. 2-3). [2] God, who anoints the king and inducts him into office, also sends the king out against his enemies when he goes forth with the royal scepter of equity and righteousness for the cause of truth (cf. Ps. 45:4-7). [3] When the king goes out to battle, Israel will rally behind him and be loyal to him. **Mountains** follows a multitude of Hebrew manuscripts which read *harreh* instead of *hadhre*, "adornments." The text suggests that the armies are going out over the mountains of the Holy Land, and these are holy mountains. The standardized Hebrew Bible reads "the adornments of holiness" (cf. KJV, NEB) or "holy array" (NASB), thinking of the nation as a holy, priestly nation (Exod. 19:6). There are variant readings for the rest of the verse also which cannot be pursued here fully. The final clause seems to say, "From the womb of the morning, to you [is] the dew of your youth." Or if we supply "are" instead of "is," the young men of the army are under consideration (cf. NASB). It seems better, however, to understand that the daily renewal of the king's youthful vigor will be supplied by God. (For a full discussion of the textual problems and variant readings of verse 3, see C. A. Briggs, *A Critical and Exegetical Commentary on the Book of Psalms,* ICC, vol. 2, pp. 379–80. Dahood's rather drastic reconstruction of the psalm is not convincing.)

The priestly functions (vs. 4). The oath makes the promise unconditional, as the clause **and will not change his mind** indicates (cf. 89:34-36; 132:11; Heb. 6:13-20). **After the order of Melchizedek** alludes to the fact that Melchizedek, like the Jebusite kings before him in Jerusalem, was a priest-king (cf. Gen. 14:17-24). That David (2 Sam. 6:13-15) and Solomon (1 Kings 8:62; 9:25) performed priestly functions is clear. The fact that other kings were condemned for acts of disobedience in connection with priestly functions does not negate this conclusion. Saul was condemned for violating a specific command from God through the prophet Samuel (1 Sam. 10:8; 13:8-15). Ahaz was condemned for engaging in the abominable practice of child sacrifice (2 Kings 16:1-4, 12-13). Uzziah was condemned for going into the sanctuary, which was forbidden to any except the Aaronic priests (Lev. 16:17), to burn incense (2 Chron. 26:16-21). There was more involved in their actions than merely offering sacrifices. None but the Levitical priests could go into the sanctuary; therefore, Davidic kings could not make atonement for sin, for this required blood to be sprinkled in the sanctuary (Lev. 16). But these kings could (and at least David and Solomon did) offer thank-offerings to God with divine approval. The phrase **for ever** as applied to Davidic kings would mean as long as their kingly functions continue.

This verse is treated messianically in the NT and applied to Christ as the antitype of the Davidic priest-kings (Heb. 5:6, 10; 6:20; 7:11, 15, 21). The contrast between the OT priesthood and Christ's priesthood which is made in the book of Hebrews is between the Levitical, or Aaronic, priesthood and that of Christ. The similarity between the Davidic priestly functions and that of Christ is that they were priest-kings and they derived their authority from a source other than the priestly directives in the law of Moses (cf. Heb. 7:11-22).

The king's triumph (vss. 5-7). [5] **The Lord** at the king's **right hand** is a figure of divine protection (cf. 16:8; 109:31).

[6] The pronouns here seem to refer to **the Lord** of verse 5. God will grant victory to the king. [7] The pronouns here seem to refer to the king. **Therefore** apparently reverts back to verses 5 and 6. Because God grants the king victory, the king can leisurely **drink from the brook** as he relaxes after the battle is won, and he can triumphantly **lift up his head** as he leads his victorious army home.

Psalm 111: Praise God for His Works

Psalms 111 and 112 are closely related in poetic form,

subject matter, and phraseology. Both are acrostics containing twenty-two lines, each succeeding line beginning with the following letter of the Hebrew alphabet. Psalm 111 describes God as reflected in his works, and Psalm 112 the man who fears God and properly responds to him. Some of the phraseology used in Psalm 111 to describe God is repeated in Psalm 112 to describe the God-fearing man. In an acrostic poem, the poetic form takes precedence over the development of the theme, so that the flow of thought may be uneven.

In keeping with several historical psalms (cf. 78, 105, 106), this psalm alludes to the exodus from Egypt (vss. 4, 9), the giving of the law at Sinai (vss. 7b-8), the wilderness wandering (vs. 5a), the settlement in Canaan (vs. 6b), and the covenant (vss. 5b, 9).

Several terms are used to refer to God's works: what he has made (vss. 2, 6, 7, 8), what he has done (vs. 3), and that which creates wonder (vs. 4). This might be compared with Isaiah 45:9-13, where God is described as having fashioned (vss. 9, 11), made (vss. 9b, 12), begotten (vs. 10a), and stretched out (vs. 12) the things which now exist. In poetry, technical distinctions in such varied terms are not to be stressed, but the terms are to be understood as practically synonymous.

'Praise the Lord' (vs. 1). With my whole heart means sincerely, willingly. **Company** means a group assembled for a common purpose, whether for worship, instruction, or judgment to be rendered. **Congregation** refers to the assembled nation. **Upright** is an ethical term describing the character God demands of the nation (cf. 32:11; 33:1).

The Lord's works (vss. 2-9). [2] Studied means more literally "sought out" (KJV). Searching out the wonders of the physical features of the universe and the laws which govern them has ever been a source of delight to man. As long as this searching is done in **the fear of the Lord** (vs. 10), man will be richly blessed. **[3]** God's **honor, majesty,** and **righteousness** are seen in his works. **Righteousness** in this context refers primarily to those fixed and dependable laws of nature by which God created and maintains the universe. Man must live in harmony with these laws and recognize the glory of God in the things which he has made if he would be truly happy (cf. Rom. 1:18-32). Therefore, the ethical connotation is not completely absent from the word **righteousness** even in this context.

[4] God **has caused his wonderful works to be remembered**. It is not an accident, nor is it the result entirely of human ingenuity, that these works have been remembered. God's works reveal that he is **gracious** and **merciful**. **Wonderful works** are those works of providence which cause the God-fearing man to see how God works all things together for good (Rom. 8:28).

[5] **Covenant** here could refer to the original provision which God made for man's happiness as he provided his necessary **food** (Gen. 1:26-31), but the remainder of the psalm suggests that the reference is more likely to the covenant made with Israel at Sinai. The miraculous provision of food and drink in the wilderness is elsewhere regarded as evidence of God's special care for Israel (78:11-31; 105: 8-9, 16-24, 40-41; 106:13-15). These references indicate that these blessings resulted from God's grace and mercy (vs. 4) rather than from Israel's meritorious righteousness.

[6] The conquest and settlement of Canaan were by the power and grace of God (cf. Deut. 6:10-15; 9:4-12).

[7] God was **faithful** to his promise made to Abraham (cf. 105: 8-9, 42). **Just** (or justice) here means the same thing as "righteousness" (vs. 3b), **faithful**, and **trustworthy**. These last two words are from the same root in Hebrew. God is dependable. His **works** and **precepts** which reveal his nature and will, respectively, are connected here and elsewhere (cf. 33:4, 6, 9; 19:1-6, 7-13). [8] Man is to perform God's precepts **with faithfulness and uprightness** like that manifested by God. [9] God first **sent redemption** to Israel, and then gave her a **covenant** by which to live (cf. Exod. 14:30; 19:1-6). God's **name** (reputation, character, personality) is **holy and terrible**. **Terrible** is from the same root as **fear** in verse 10. It means "awesome" (NASB, NEB) or "reverend" (KJV).

Response to the holy God (vs. 10). The fear of the Lord is the basis of the ethical teachings of the wisdom writers in the OT (Prov. 1:7; 9:10; 15:33; Eccles. 12:13; Job 28:28). The expression is the equivalent of our expression, "religion." It involves worship, the commandments of God, and one's manner of life (cf. Pss. 19:9; 34:11).

Psalm 112: What It Means to Fear the Lord

For the similarities between this and the preceding psalm, see the introduction to Psalm 111. The theme of 111:10 is elaborated here. Psalm 112 is a wisdom poem based on the nature of God set forth in Psalm 111, which is a praise hymn.

The God-fearer (vs. 1). Just as verse 1a reflects back upon 111:10, so verse 1b reverts back to 111:2. **Delights** is from the same Hebrew root as "have pleasure" in 111:2. The God-fearer not only keeps God's **commandments**, but knowing God's goodness and grace, he **delights** in doing so (cf. 1 John 5:3).

Blessings of the God-fearer (vss. 2-9). These verses contain bold and striking similarities to the description of God in 111:2-9. **[2]** Acceptance of the principle of community solidarity enhanced Israel's interest in familial continuity. A man's personality and character were to be continued through his children. The promise of a goodly progeny was considered a great blessing from God (cf. Gen. 12:1-3; 15:1-6). But these promises are contingent upon following God's precepts with faithfulness and uprightness (cf. Ps. 111:8).

[3] Prosperity comes to and remains with the person who is righteous in the use of these blessings (cf. vs. 9). The second half of this verse and verse 9 boldly apply 111:3, a description of God, to the God-fearer. No man is absolutely righteous (143:2), but some can be classed as belonging to "the generation of the righteous" (14:5) or **the generation of the upright** (112:2). These are relatively righteous because they fear God and strive to keep his commandments (vs. 1). **[4]** The **light** of prosperity and contentment **rises for the upright** and dispels **the darkness** of suffering want and guilt through his refusal to distribute to those in need. He (not **Lord**, RSV) is **gracious** (generous), **merci-ful** (compassionate toward the needy), and **righteous** (prac-ticing proper ethical behavior). The half verse here bor-rows the description of God in 111:4b and applies it to the God-fearer. **[5]** In addition to practicing **justice** or fairness, the one who fears God is also benevolent.

[6] For this benevolence, the Lord will reward him with stability so that he **will never be moved**, and **he will be remembered for ever** by those who have been helped, or at least by the Lord (cf. Matt. 25:31-46). The idea of a reward for meritorious righteousness is far from the mind of the psalmist. He is responding to God's grace and mercy (cf. 111:4b) with the same spirit toward his fellowmen (vs. 9b).

[7] Since he trusts in the Lord, no **evil tidings** can cause him to be **afraid**. **[8]** This verse seems to define the **evil tidings** of verse 7. Wicked men, out of envy and jealousy, seek his ruin, but they themselves shall come to ruin (vs. 10). **[9]** One who **has distributed freely** without any desire for reward will receive the best reward of all, namely, to be treated as a righteous person.

The fate of the wicked (vs. 10). As is frequently done in wisdom psalms (cf. Ps. 1:1-3, 4-6), the fate of the wicked is here contrasted with that of the righteous man described above. The wicked man's life is futile and his **desire comes to nought**.

Psalm 113: God's Care of the Poor

In subject matter, Psalm 113 is an excellent sequel to the two previous psalms. Psalm 111 declares that God's works reveal him to be powerful, gracious, merciful, righteous, and faithful. Psalm 112 shows how the God-fearing man emulates the nature of God as he graciously lends to the poor in his time of need. And Psalm 113 reveals that God himself cares for the poor as well as the affluent.

In Judaism, Psalms 113–118 are known as The Egyptian Hallel. Psalms 113–114 are sung before the Passover meal and Psalms 115–118 after it. These psalms are also sung at the feasts of Pentecost, Tabernacles, and Dedication (Han-nukah, or Lights).

Call to praise (vs. 1). Servants could refer to the priests or Levites, or to the nation. For the significance of **the name of the Lord**, see the comments on Psalm 111:9.

The exalted Lord (vss. 2-4). [2] For the last half of the verse, compare 115:18; 121:8; 125:2; 131:3. The expression means continually throughout one's lifetime. **[3]** Geographically, God should be praised everywhere, poetically stated as from east to west. **[4]** God, who is exalted **above** men and **nations**, is worthy of universal praise.

God helps the needy (vss. 5-9). [5-6] God is not only the transcendant (separated) one, but he is also the immanent (near) one in time of need (cf. 102:18-22; 138:6; Isa. 57:15).

[7] Dust and **ash heap** refer to the city dump, where the abjectly poor and the diseased might be forced to remain.

[8] By strong contrast, these pitifully poor ones are made **to sit with** the highest among men, **the princes** who enjoy royal luxuries. **[9]** Barrenness was considered a disgrace in ancient Near Eastern culture (cf. Gen. 30:1-3). So God is here pictured as causing one who had been disgraced to receive lasting joy.

Verses 7-9 reflect the situation with Hannah. Verses 7-8 reveal verbal similarities to the Song of Hannah (1 Sam. 2:8) and verse 9 reflects the situation with Hannah (1 Sam. 1:1–2:11). Hannah is used by the psalmist as a typical example of the way the Lord helps the destitute.

Psalm 114: The God of the Exodus Glorified

This psalm takes its place among the many which reflect upon Israel's national beginnings. But none compresses more thought into such a few words, and none so effectively captures the beauty of language with which to glorify the God of the exodus.

Those who interpret the psalms primarily with a historical approach suggest that the psalm may have been written to encourage those who had returned from captivity in those days of continual hardship and harassment as set forth in Ezra and Nehemiah. Those who interpet the psalms primarily with a cultic approach suggest that the psalm was written to celebrate the Passover. Whether this latter viewpoint is correct, the psalm came to be used for that purpose. The movement in the psalm is very rapid as the psalmist advances from Egypt to Canaan in eight short verses. The psalm is divided into four stanzas of two verses each.

Out of bondage (vss. 1-2). [1] The foreign Egyptian language added to the burdens of the Israelite slaves in Egypt.

[2] But when they settled in Canaan they became a kingdom of priests and a holy nation (Exod. 19:6). **Became** is better here than "was" (KJV), for the Exodus passage indicates action not yet completed at the time of the giving of the promise. Synonymous parallelism is employed in verse 2. **Judah** and **Israel** do not indicate separate kingdoms. **Sanctuary** refers here to the nation among whom God would dwell (Lev. 26:11-12), and **dominion** refers to the people as a nation under the kingly rule of God. No antecedent is given for the pronoun **his**, because Yahweh is obviously in mind. **Dominion** is plural in Hebrew, apparently to be understood as a plural of intensity stressing Israel's exalted position among the nations as a people under the rule of God.

From the Red Sea to the Jordan (vss. 3-4). [3] Synonymous parallelism capsules two events separated by forty years into a single idea. The parting of the waters of the Red Sea and of the Jordan (Exod. 14:21; Josh. 3:14-16) reveal the same truth. The divine purpose to settle Israel in Canaan as his holy people was accomplished by separating them from the bondage of Egypt and from the hardships of the wilderness. [4] In bold similes, the quaking of the **mountains** at Sinai (Exod. 19:18-19; Judg. 5:5) is pictured as being like frisky sheep skipping about.

A rhetorical question (vss. 5-6). Verse 5 begins in Hebrew with the elliptical inquiry, "What to you?" **Ails** is supplied by the translators. Since **ails** carries the connotation of some malady which has overtaken the **sea**, **Jordan**, **mountains**, and **hills**, it might be better to simply translate, "For what reason, O sea, do you flee?" No answer is given to the question, nor can verses 7-8 be taken as the answer. Since the theophany is being described, it is plain that these inanimate objects are personified and pictured as standing in awe in the presence of deity.

Creation's response (vss. 7-8). **[7] Tremble** is from the Hebrew word *chul*, which basically means to turn in a circle, to twirl. The word is neutral in that it can be used of happily dancing for joy or of writhing in pain or trembling in fear. The context must determine the specific use being made of the word. The context here seems to indicate trembling in amazement or awe at the glory of God. However, since these inanimate objects are personified, they might be thought of as trembling in fear because of their undone condition (cf. Exod. 19:9-25; 20:18-20; Isa. 6:1-5).

[8] As in verses 1-2 and 3-4, the psalmist, with one bold sweep of the pen, takes in the period from the beginning to the end of the wilderness period. At Rephidim, shortly after Israel had left Egypt (Exod. 17:6), and at Kadesh, when Canaan was near (Num. 20:11), God miraculously brought water out of the rock. In synonymous parallelism, the psalmist compresses these instances into a single thought. The God who can perform such wonders is worthy of the devotion of the whole universe.

Psalm 115: The Honor of God's Name

The imperatives directed to Israel, the antiphonal features, and the jussives pronouncing blessings upon Israel indicate that this psalm was composed for liturgical use in Israel's worship assemblies. The precise occasion on which it was intended to be recited is not clear. Verse 2, in a liturgical psalm of praise, need not be taken as a lament (cf. 42:3, 10; 79:10). The question, used in this context, possibly indicates that the psalm is postexilic. The psalmist wants the nation to realize that this taunting question so often put to them by their captors during the exile has ceased to be effective, for God has vindicated his name by granting Israel deliverance.

The proper object of praise (vss. 1-2). **[1]** Israel confesses her unworthiness and recognizes that only God is praiseworthy. The confessional prayer in which Daniel led the captives in Babylon at the end of the exile is instructive here (Dan. 9:1-19). Not Israel's goodness, but God's **stead-fast love** and **faithfulness** are responsible for her well-being. The imperative clause **to thy name give glory**, though addressed to God, needs to be understood as a declaration of commitment on the part of Israel. The force of the statement is "to thy name let us give glory."

[2] God has acted so as to vindicate his name and remove the stigma attached to this taunting question. See the above introduction to the psalm.

God contrasted to idols (vss. 3-8). [3] Verse 3b does not contain an expression of impudence, nor does the psalmist charge God with caprice. Rather, it is a declaration of divine omnipotence, in contrast to the impotence of idols given in the following verses. [4-7] The main feature of this diatribe against idolatry is that these idols are lifeless forms created by man, and, as such, are unable to respond to those who made them (cf. Ps. 135:15-18). So, because of false trust in lifeless idols, idolaters are as impotent as the gods of their own creation. Instructive here are those passages given in Isaiah to comfort the exiles and bolster their faith in preparation for the return home (Isa. 41:14-29; 44:9-20; 45:14-17). Israel, under siege by the Babylonians, was encouraged in similar fashion by Jeremiah (10:1-18). Habakkuk, Jeremiah's contemporary, spoke similar words to bolster Judah's faith (2:18-19).

Affirmation of faith (vss. 9-13). A call to **trust** (vss. 9-11) meets with a response in the form of an affirmation of trust (vss. 12-13). Probably the call to trust was recited by a temple official and the response was uttered by the congregation. Three groups are addressed: all **Israel**, the **house of Aaron**, which was composed of the priests and their families, and those **who fear the Lord** (cf. 118:2-4; 135:19-20). This last group might be composed of Gentile converts (cf. 1 Kings 8:41-43), of which there must have been many in postexilic Judah (cf. Isa. 56:6-7), or the truly devout in Israel (Pss. 111:10; 112:1), or the entire nation including both priests and laity. The apparent antiphonal feature of the psalm suggests the third interpretation.

Priestly blessing (vss. 14-15). The verbs in verses 14a

and 15a can be understood either as jussives expressing a wish (RSV, NASB, NEB, vs. 14), or as futures indicating an affirmation of trust (KJV). The context suggests the former. Apparently these verses are a priestly benediction on the nation.

National commitment (vss. 16-18). This closing stanza elaborates upon the central thought of the psalm, and particularly of verse 15b, that God the Creator is the living God who is faithful to his people (cf. vs. 1). This paragraph is to be understood as the declaration of Israel's commitment to Yahweh. **[16]** The background of this verse is Genesis 1. Both **the heavens** and **the earth** are God's creation (vs. 15; Gen. 1:1), but he has committed **the earth** to the stewardship of man (Gen. 1:28-29).

[17] The common belief of ancient Israel was that God could not be praised or contacted in Sheol, the realm of the dead (cf. 6:5; 30:9; 88:4-6, 10-12; Isa. 38:18). **[18]** This belief, which resulted from no clear revelation concerning the state of the dead, caused the Israelites to recognize their privilege and responsibility in praising God throughout their lifetime on earth (cf. 104:33; 146:2). Christians, in light of God's perfect revelation in Christ, praise both God and Christ in anticipation of the privilege of rendering a more perfect praise in eternity (cf. Rev. 4–5; 7:9-17; 11:17-18; 21:1-4; 22:1-5).

Psalm 116: Thanksgiving for Deliverance

Either the psalmist has been delivered from what appeared to be a fatal illness (vss. 2, 8) or from false accusers (vss. 10-11) who plotted his death. Out of gratitude for his deliverance, he thanks God publicly so that others may share in his joy and faith.

Past anguish (vss. 1-4). Remembering where we have been helps us to be grateful for present blessings (cf. 2 Pet. 1:9-11). **[1]** The Hebrew imperfect for **has heard** should be taken as a frequentative indicating action in the past, not the present (cf. NASB). Or the particle *ki* could be translated "that" and the verb rendered as introducing a conditional clause, "he should hear." It is better to consider that we have here a case of dittography whereby the letter *yodh* on the end of the preceding word has been mistakenly repeated at the beginning of the following word. Without that letter, the word would be a perfect indicating completed action, as most English translations render it. The perfect tense of **inclined** in verse 2 points in that direction. God's answering his prayer causes the psalmist to love God. [2] And it also causes him now to vow to call on God all his life. [3] This verse employs a climactic triplet in which the first two lines employ similar figures to describe death and the third line states the anguish which resulted from the contemplation of imminent death. [4] But faith prompted him to beg God to save his life, which petition was answered affirmatively (vss. 1-2, 8).

The Lord's mercy (vss. 5-11). [5-7] The Hebrews customarily delineated the attributes of God by observing God's actions. [5] God's saving acts reveal that he is **gracious**, **righteous**, and **merciful**. **Righteous**, in this context, describes one who acts out of a sense of what is right to do under a given set of circumstances. In this case, it is God's grace and mercy, not any legal right possessed by the psalmist, which causes God to act. God is acting in faithfulness to his own character (cf. Hos. 2:19-20). [6] **The simple** is here used of the inexperienced who feels a sense of helplessness (cf. 19:7; 119:130; Prov. 19:25) rather than the usual sense in Proverbs of the foolish moral simpleton who can be led astray into every sin (Prov. 1:22, 32; 7:7; 8:5; 9:4, 13, 16; 14:15, 18; 22:3; 27:12). The use made of the word in our psalm is positive in that it describes one who leans upon the Lord for knowledge and strength (cf. Prov. 3:5). [7] He exhorts himself to **return** to his former state of tranquility (as indicated by the word *menuchah*, **rest**, which suggests a permanent state of well-being). The reason is that God has **dealt bountifully with** him.

Verses 8-11 extend the thought of verse 7b. Here is an explication of God's bountiful dealing with him. [8] In progressive parallelism, the psalmist declares that the Lord has preserved him **from death** and the **tears** prompted by his contemplation of death, and he has prevented him **from stumbling** or falling. The last phrase refers to his endangered faith (vss. 10-11), which was preserved by the power of God. **[9]** Life is now seen as a precious gift from God. Verses 8-9 are almost identical with Psalm 56:13 with slight variations, the present passage adding the phrase **my eyes from tears.** **[10]** "When" (NASB) or **even when** is a better translation than "therefore" (KJV). In spite of his harrowing experience, his endangered faith (cf. vs. 8c) was preserved. **[11]** However, in his **consternation,** he lost faith in men. **Consternation** or "alarm" (NASB) is better than "haste" (KJV). **Vain hope** reads more literally "liars" (KJV, NASB). "Faithless" (NEB) or **vain hope** catch the spirit of the language.

Response in gratitude (vss. 12-19). **[12]** The psalmist confesses his inadequacy in repaying or returning to (literal meaning of the Hebrew of **render**) the Lord the service which he so richly deserves. **[13] Lift up** is more literally to bear, carry away. Here it has the connotation of taking something in hand (cf. KJV, NEB). **Cup of salvation** could refer to the drink offering offered up with an animal sacrifice (Num. 15:10), but it more likely refers to a kind of religious toast offered freely to God in connection with the payment of a vow (vs. 14). Verse 12b may indicate that the cup of salvation was nothing more than thanksgiving and praise offered to God (cf. vs. 17). **[14] Vows** were voluntary, but once made must be kept (Deut. 23:21-23; Eccles. 5:1-6). The psalmist will gladly "complete" (literal meaning of the Hebrew word *shalam*) his vow in the presence of the congregation so that they may share his joy and his faith (cf. vss. 18-19). **[15] Precious** here means costly (cf. Ps. 72:14, 1 Kings 5:17, and 7:9-11, where the same Hebrew word is used). The NEB misses the point here. **[16]** Here is the picture of a manumitted slave who volunteers to serve his master as a freedman. This figure magnifies the psalmist's gratitude and instructs us in regard to the proper response to God's grace.

Psalm 117: Universal Praise to God

As Psalm 119 is the longest chapter in the Bible, so

Psalm 117 is the shortest (if these psalms can rightly be called chapters). There is no thought in this brief hymn that is not found abundantly expressed many times elsewhere in the psalms. This psalm must have been composed, or compiled, for some special occasion, but we have no knowledge of what that occasion was. The psalm is great in the scope of its outreach.

[1] By means of synonymous parallelism, the mind is stayed on a single thought. God's praise should be universal. [2] The reason that all men should praise God is that **his steadfast love** (covenant loyalty) and **faithfulness** are great and enduring. The phrase **toward us** tempts one to surmise that the psalmist thinks of these two divine qualities as equally distributed toward all men even in his day. However, in view of the fact that **steadfast love** and **faithfulness** are covenant terms regularly applied to God's agreement with Israel, it is not likely that the psalmist had so large a vision. He probably means that the nations should see the reality of Israel's God by observing what God does for Israel (cf. 98:1-3; Isa. 52:1-10).

Psalm 118: A Processional Psalm of Thanksgiving

Interpreters generally recognize the antiphonal feature of this psalm, but there is little agreement on the specific persons who speak at different points in the recitation of the psalm. We will attempt to point out what we consider to be the most likely form of the litany, but the reader should take this as nothing more than a studied opinion. The message of the psalm is much more important than the form in which it was cast.

There is also difference of opinion as to whether the psalm is to be considered as originally an individual psalm of thanksgiving which was incorporated into public sentiments of thanksgiving, or whether it was originally a community psalm, the "I" standing collectively for Israel. Verses 5-14, 19, 21, and 28 seem to portray a great deliverance which has come to a king, possibly David himself. There are similar sentiments in Psalm 18. The king, or someone else, may have employed this individual thanks-

· giving in a composition intended for community use on the occasion of a joyous festival (vss. 22-27), or the king may have made his triumphal entry into Jerusalem with the grateful throng after victory was won. This interpretation helps explain the messianic use made of the psalm in the NT. The Davidic king more readily stands as a type of Christ than does the nation Israel. At any rate, as the psalm came to be used, it celebrates victory granted to Israel and to the church through the Messiah.

Call to thanksgiving (vss. 1-4). **[1]** Verse 1 is identical with 106:1, 107:1, 136:1, and is similar to 136:26. Psalm 118 ends as it begins, and the second part of the first verse is repeated in verses 2b, 3b, and 4b. This repetition lays stress on the enduring quality of God's covenant love (*chesedh*) toward Israel. **[2-4]** The same groups are mentioned here as in 115:9-13. See the notes there.

Chastening, then deliverance (vss. 5-18). **[5-9]** This paragraph is a summary conclusion derived from the experience of distress and subsequent deliverance. **[5] Set me free** (cf. the NEB) is more literally "with enlargement" (cf. the KJV, NASB). This may reflect deliverance from death, since Sheol was thought of as being like one in straits (literal Hebrew of 116:3 for "pangs"). Deliverance from **distress** (same Hebrew word as in 116:3) may be thought of as God's setting one in a broad place (cf. Job 36:16; Pss. 18:19, 36; 31:8; Hos. 4:16), or giving him room (cf. Gen. 26:22; Ps. 4:1). The paraphrase **set me free** changes the metaphor but preserves the essential thought.

[6] Perfect love casts out fear (1 John 4:18), and trust gives substance to one's faith (Heb. 11:1). Men cannot conquer the man of faith (Heb. 13:6; 1 John 5:4). **[7]** This statement is not an expression of personal vengeance, but an elaboration upon his declaration of faith (vs. 6).

[8-9] The comparative parallelism employed in each of these verses emphasizes the relatively superior value of putting one's confidence in God rather than in man. Only one word is changed in the repetition employed in verse 9; **man** (vs. 8) is replaced with **princes** (vs. 9). The latter narrows down the view from mankind in general to powerful princes. None can be completely trusted to always grant the help that is needed. David certainly knew from experience that a king's own sons cannot always be depended upon to do the right thing (cf. 2 Sam. 13; 15; 1 Kings 1).

[10-14] Here the psalmist elaborates threats made against him by surrounding nations. If the "I" in this paragraph and following is a collective noun referring to Israel, the psalmist is reflecting upon some time or times when Israel as a nation was being threatened. If this is a personal reflection on the part of a king, then since the fortunes of king and people are intertwined, the result would be the same. Psalm 18:16-19, 24-45 are instructive at this point.

[10] When the king fights in the cause of truth (cf. Ps. 45:4), God will grant him victory. Repetition enforces the two central thoughts of verses 10-12. **Surrounded** is used four times to emphasize the dire straits in which he found himself (cf. vs. 5 and notes). **In the name of the Lord I cut them off** is found three times so as to stress the fact that it is God who granted him victory.

[12] The stairlike parallelism extends the first part of each of verses 10-12, so that **on every side** and **like bees** intensify the picture of distress. **Blazed** is "quenched" in Hebrew (cf. the KJV, NASB), and can be explained in context, for thorns burn themselves out just as quickly as they blaze up. The RSV, following the LXX, supposes that two letters in the word for "burned" (*ba'aru*) have been mistaken by a scribe for two similar letters, making it read "quenched" (*da'akhu*). [13] **I was pushed hard** (cf. the NEB "They thrust hard against me") again follows the LXX. The Hebrew reads, "You pushed me hard" (cf. the KJV, NASB), in which case the enemy is being addressed directly. [14] This verse is borrowed from the victory song of Moses (Exod. 15:2), which shows how the exodus motif permeated Israel's thinking (cf. Isa. 12:2).

Songs of victory (vss. 15-18). [15] This verse and the following also reflect the exodus motif (Exod. 15:6). **Victory** is "salvation" (cf. the KJV, NÁSB) in the form of "deliverance" (cf. the NEB). Salvation in time of battle comes in the form of victory. **Tents** or "tabernacles" may refer to the temporary "camp" of the army (cf. the NEB), or to the temporary tents, or booths, in which Israel dwelt in the wilderness following the exodus from Egypt.

[16] The right hand of the Lord is his mighty strength (see the notes on Ps. 110:1, 5). **[17-18]** The fact of deliverance from death (vs. 18) gives confidence that God will not allow him to suffer an untimely death (vs. 17; cf. 16:10).

Procession to the temple (vss. 19-27). **[19]** The victorious king, the nation Israel, or the temple choir addresses the gatekeeper as they approach the outer court of the temple. **Gates of righteousness** may refer to the righteousness of the Lord whose presence is known at the temple (Jer. 31:23), to the righteousness imputed by the Lord to his believing covenant people, or to the ethical righteousness required of those who would worship the Lord acceptably (cf. Amos 5:21-24). **[20]** The gatekeeper replies. **The gate of the Lord** may be synonymous with **the gates of righteousness** (vs. 19a), or may be explained by verse 19b to refer to ethical righteousness.

Praise and prayer mingle in verses 21-25. **[21]** Here the theme of the psalm is restated (cf. vss. 1-4). **[22-23] The stone** is either the king or Israel. The cornerstone is either the main stone in the foundation or in the arch which holds the whole structure together. The nations (vs. 10a) sometimes derided Israel because of her apparent insignificance (2:1-3), but God honored and protected her. Christ is the antitype of this cornerstone in two respects. He was rejected by many as insignificant (cf. Mk. 12:10-11; Acts 4:11; 1 Pet. 2:7), and yet he is the cornerstone which holds everything together (Eph. 2:20-22; cf. 1 Cor. 3:11; Col. 1:15-20). The Lord has done the marvelous thing. **[24] This day** is apparently the festive occasion rather than the day of victory. **[25] Save us** is more literally "Save, please." This is the expression translated Hosanna in connection with Christ's triumphal entry into Jerusalem (Matt. 21:9 and parallels).

The priestly benediction (vss. 26-27). **[26]** This is apparently the priestly benediction pronounced upon those who enter the temple courts to worship. In the NT it is applied to Christ (see vs. 25). **[27] Light** here stands for deliverance (cf. Ps. 43:3; Esth. 8:16). **Festal procession** translates a single Hebrew word which refers to a festival. Some think that in this passage it refers to the sacrifice of the festival (cf. the KJV, NASB), while others believe it refers to the procession of worshipers around the altar (cf. the NEB). The word for **bind** can mean to order or marshal troops (cf. 1 Kings 20:14). this verse apparently refers to the *lulab* or tree branches that were brought in celebration of the Feast of Tabernacles (cf. Lev. 23:40).

Summary conclusion (vss. 28-29). [28] In synonymous parallelism, the covenant relationship between God and the psalmist, or nation, is emphasized in the twice repeated **thou art my God. I will give thanks to thee** and **I will extol thee** are synonymous expressions. **[29]** The opening verse is here repeated for emphasis.

Psalm 119: God's Glorious Word

From the standpoint of poetic artistry, this psalm is truly amazing. It is an alphabetic psalm consisting of twenty-two stanzas corresponding in order to the letters of the Hebrew alphabet. Each stanza has eight verses of two lines each and the first line of each verse begins with the particular Hebrew letter for that stanza. All eight verses of the first stanza begin with *'aleph*, the eight verses of the second stanza begin with *beth*, etc. This artificial poetic form hinders the development of a well-ordered theme. There is much repetition in the psalm. We have attempted to show some consistency in each stanza, although the effort is not too successful in places.

The psalm is entirely composed of praise of God for his revelation to Israel. Eight synonyms for the divine revelation and two additional related words describing this revelation are interspersed throughout the psalm. "Law" is a general term which means instruction or direction. It may be applied to legal precepts, but can also indicate God's promises, historical facts, and descriptions of God's nature. Two Hebrew words are translated "word," or "promise," and either can be used in a general or specific sense.

"Testimonies" refers to those affirmations which God has given of his nature and will through historical saving acts on behalf of Israel. Occasionally the word refers to cultic acts which remind Israel of God's activities within the nation or in the world. "Precepts," "statutes," and "ordinances" are used with little, if any, distinction, to mean practically the same thing as commandments.

The psalmist is no legalist who believes in the merit of lawkeeping. Rather, he knows that God must supply the strength to enable him to keep the law. God's word provides life, light, confidence, peace, and freedom from anxiety. The two companion words used with the eight synonyms above emphasize the spiritual value of the word. The word enables one to walk in God's way (or ways), the way of righteousness, justice, and uprightness. God's faithfulness gives confidence and fills the faithful covenant person with delight in doing the will of God. God's mercy, grace, and love provide the necessary guidance and discipline to keep the sincere follower in the right way.

The titles employed in the stanza divisions are only intended to be used as a point of reference. The entire stanza may contain other elements as well. Since the word "way" is frequently employed in the psalm, it appears that the psalmist is emphasizing the way of life which the word directs one to follow, namely, the way of God. For this reason, we have emphasized this key word in the headings.

The way of blamelessness (Aleph, vss. 1-8). This stanza emphasizes God's requirements and the necessary human response (vs. 4). **Blameless** (vs. 1a) persons are not those who are perfect, but those **who seek** God **with their whole heart** (vs. 2b), who are **upright** (vs. 7a), and who do not practice **wrong** (vs. 3a). The earnest petition that his **ways may be steadfast** (vs. 5a) indicates humility, and the final petition of the stanza (vs. 8b) shows that he has a sense of his own moral frailty. The next stanza emphasizes this fact and the necessity of relying upon God for strength.

The way of purity (Beth, vss. 9-16). The human tendency to sin is emphasized (vss. 9a, 10b, 11b). The righteous man recognizes that God's word is meant to shield him from sin (vss. 9, 11); therefore, he places his confidence in that word (vss. 14-16). In full anticipation of God's guiding hand, he praises the word (vss. 13, 14, 16a) and vows **not to forget** it (vs. 16b). Most of all, he praises God who has given his word (vs. 12a).

The way of divine counsel (Gimel, vss. 17-24). Insolent, accursed ones who wander from God's commandments (vs. 21) express **their scorn and contempt** (vs. 22a) for the psalmist, and **princes sit plotting against** him (vs. 23a). He seeks comfort and consolation in God's word (vs. 20). But he recognizes that he needs divine aid in keeping the word, so he prays for God to intervene on his behalf (vss. 17, 22). He also needs God's help in understanding and trusting God's word (vss. 18-19), for he delights in God's law (vs. 24). Note that his interest in the word is not merely academic, but very practical. He desires to **behold wondrous things out of** God's **law** (vs. 18) so that he **may observe** the **word** (vs. 17b) and so that God's **testimonies** will serve as his **counselors** (vs. 24).

The way of faithfulness (Daleth, vss. 25-32). In the throes of death, he prays for revival of life (vs. 25). His confidence is based on the fact that God has in the past been faithful in answering him (vs. 26). In his state of **sorrow** (vs. 28a), there is the temptation to turn to **false ways** (vs. 29a). He has **chosen the way of faithfulness** (vs. 30a), but he needs God's help in **understanding** (vss. 26b, 27a, 32b) and keeping (vss. 25b, 28b, 32a) God's law. **Run in the way of thy commandments** (vs. 32a) means to be diligent and zealous in obedience.

The way of life (He, vss. 33-40). Seven of the eight verses in this stanza begin with a hiphil (causative) verb which involves God as the outside agent who makes it possible for the psalmist to keep God's word. The alphabetic arrangement lends itself to these verb forms, but the rest of the psalm reveals a studied effort to demonstrate reliance upon the God of the word as well as the word of God. **Behold** provides an appropriate word to close out the stanza as it introduces an exclamatory declaration (vs. 40a) and petition (vs. 40b). The prayer is basically one for

understanding and guidance in the observance of God's commandments (vss. 33-35). But he also prays for a right **heart** which will enable him to keep these requirements (vss. 36-37; cf. 51:10-12). He prays further for divine deliverance which will **confirm** God's **promise** (vss. 38-39). And finally, he prays that God, on the basis of his **righteousness** (fairness and equity), **give** him **life** (vs. 40b).

The way of liberty (Waw, vss. 41-48). Liberty (vs. 45a) means to be free from distress or anxiety. The Hebrew word translated **enlargest** (vs. 32) is from the same root. The psalmist is seeking relief from **those who taunt** him (vs. 42a). He wishes to have the requisite confidence to stand before **kings** and **speak** God's **testimonies** (vs. 46). He loves and reveres God's commandments (vss. 47-48). Through constant meditation upon them (vss. 45b, 48b), he has learned to **trust** them (vs. 42b) and to **hope** in them (vs. 43b). He knows that right attitude must be accompanied by right conduct (vs. 44). And, above all, he is aware that God's **steadfast love** expressed in fulfillment of his covenant promise in the form of **salvation** (deliverance) must become effective if he is to succeed (vs. 41).

The way of obedience (Zayin, vss. 49-56). Recognition of divine **blessing** resulting from keeping God's **precepts** (vss. 51, 56) produces a triple reaction. He is filled with **comfort in affliction** because he knows he is a recipient of God's **promise** (vss. 50, 52). He is filled with **hot indignation** toward the wicked, who **forsake** God's **law** (vs. 53). And he is filled with praise for God, who protects and preserves him (vss. 54-55). His initial prayer (vs. 49) shows that his trust is in God rather than in himself.

The way of fellowship (Cheth, vss. 57-64). Portion (vs. 57a) is from a root which can mean to divide into shares. The noun, in this context, means God's sharing himself with man, hence fellowship. His **promise** to **keep** God's **words** assures a recognition of the covenant obligation which devolves upon one who enters into fellowship with God. God is treated as the suzerain who is powerful to bless, and the psalmist asks God to **be gracious** to him as the superior party to the covenant who has attached a

promise of protection to the covenant agreement (vs. 58). Because of his fellowship with God, he is also a **companion to all who fear** God (vs. 63; cf. 1 John 1:1-4). Furthermore, he is not afraid of his enemies, for God has become his protector (vs. 61). He is careful to keep his covenant obligations (vs. 60) and he is glad to do so, for he recognizes that they are **righteous ordinances** (vs. 62b). He praises God (vs. 62a) and turns to him in obedience (vs. 59) because of God's ways toward him. The final prayer (vs. 64) again shows his dependence upon God.

The way of discipline (Teth, vss. 65-72). Affliction has brought him back from a wayward life (vss. 67, 71). God has **dealt well** with him (vs. 65) and is **good** in all that he does (vs. 68); therefore, the **godless** will not overcome him (vss. 69, 70). **Gross like fat** (vs. 70a) means to have a closed heart which is unresponsive to the divine will (cf. 17:10). He needs God's help in exercising **good judgment and knowledge** (vs. 66a). Rather than being bitter about God's discipline, he considers God's laws as more precious than much **gold** and **silver** (vs. 72).

The way of mercy (Yodh, vss. 73-80). The psalmist recognizes that God's discipline is **right** (vs. 75) but he also needs God's **mercy** (vs. 77) and **steadfast love** (vs. 76; cf. vs. 41). He wishes to share with others the lesson learned as a result of experiencing God's discipline (vss. 74, 79). The **godless**, the proud who have subverted him with guile (distorted his case with falsehood), must be **put to shame** (vs. 78). Perhaps his motive here is good in that he desires that others not be led astray by the cunning of such godless persons as he may have been so led astray (cf. vss. 67, 71, 75). He hopes, through God's help, to keep his **heart blameless** (vss. 73, 80).

The way of endurance (Kaph, vss. 81-88). Too many expressions of confidence are used in this stanza for one to conclude that the psalmist is about to lose faith. He hopes in God's word (vs. 81b) and has **not forgotten** his **statutes** (vs. 83b). He knows that God's **commandments are sure** (vs. 86a), so he has **not forsaken** God's **precepts** (vs. 87b). He does not despair of faith, but of life (vss. 87a, 88a).

Godless men, proud and arrogant (vs. 85a, cf. vs. 78), **per-secute** him **with falsehood** (vs. 86b). He is "worn out" (the literal meaning of the Hebrew, vs. 81a) with waiting for God's deliverance (vss. 81-84). **A wineskin in the smoke** (vs. 83a) probably refers to a skin hung up to dry. Smoke from the room, since it has no chimney by which to escape, is absorbed into the skin. So the psalmist's eyes burn and smart under his emotional strain as if he were in a smoke-filled room (vss. 82-83). The questions of verse 84 should not be interpreted as evidence of lack of faith in or rever-ence toward God. They represent frequent idioms em-ployed for the purpose of expressing the intensity of one's longing for deliverance (cf. 6:3; 13:1-2; 35:17; 74:10; 79:5; 80:4; 89:46; 90:13; 94:3). When God addresses himself to obstinate sinners, he also employs his plaintive cry, "How long?" (cf. Exod. 10:3; 16:28; Num. 14:11, 27; Josh. 18:3; 1 Kings 18:21; Pss. 4:2; 82:2; Prov. 1:22; 6:9). But the psalmist is not such an obstinate sinner, nor is he an unbe-liever. Since he knows God's **commandments are sure** (vs. 86a), he can pray with confidence for God to exercise his **steadfast love** toward him, so that he will be able to **keep** God's **testimonies** (vs. 88).

The way of certainty (Lamedh, vss. 89-96). There is a reference in the stanza to the fact that the worlds exist and function in an orderly way because of God's word (vss. 90b-91; cf. Ps. 19). From God's seat of government, his immutable word goes forth (vs. 89), and the whole cre-ation, as God's servants (vs. 91b), must bow in submission. Though the wicked do not willingly submit to the divine directive, the psalmist is confident that God will overrule their wicked intentions to destroy him (vs. 95). His confi-dence in God's word is bolstered by the fact that God has kept his promise to protect him (vss. 92-93). There is a limit to all things temporal, but God's word is broad in scope and application (vs. 96). **Perfection** means that which is complete, accomplished, brought to an end. The word can be used in an ethical sense, referring here to the limits of man's efforts to achieve his goals. In either case, the

Lord's commandment is exalted as God's instrument by which he meets the needs of his creation.

The way of wisdom (Mem, vss. 97-104). As hate is the antithesis of love, so the one who loves God's truth hates **every false way** (vss. 97, 104). **Love** of the word prompts one to meditate upon it all day (vs. 97; cf. Ps. 1:2). And the reward is greater than tasting the sweetness of **honey** (vs. 103; cf. Ps. 19:10). **Understanding** which is derived from God's word makes one wiser than those who depend upon human wisdom (vss. 98-100). This divinely ordained wisdom is more than academic. It guides the life aright (vss. 101-102; cf. Ps. 19:11).

The way of light (Nun, vss. 105-112). The psalmist thinks of the person traveling by foot at night with a lamp attached to his ankles or feet to show him the way (vs. 105; cf. Prov. 6:23). Though he is in great danger (vss. 107, 109-110), he even dares to take an **oath** to confirm his intention to keep God's commandments (vs. 106). **I hold my life in my hand** (vs. 109) suggests the taking of great risk (cf. Judg. 12:3; 1 Sam. 19:5; 28:21; Job 13:14). This would seem to imply that he is afflicted by his enemies because of his religious devotion (cf. 69: 9-12). His primary objective, however, is to make God's word his **heritage for ever** (vss. 111-112). The verb used in Hebrew means to take as one's possession or heritage (cf. the KJV). God offers this priceless treasure and it is merely left for man to **incline** his **heart** to make this prize his own (vs. 112).

The way of fear (Samekh, vss. 113-120). The concept of the fear of the Lord is prevalent in the OT. The fear of the Lord, or its equivalent, may refer to having reverence and awe toward God (Ps. 33:8), to trusting in God's covenant loyalty (33:18), to acknowledging God's nature and will (Prov. 1:7; Ps. 111:10), to the life of reverent obedience (112:1), and to being afraid of the wrath of God (90:7-12). In short, the **fear** of the Lord is the essence of religion. In the stanza before us, emphasis is given to the wrath of God which causes pious men to be **afraid** of God's judgment (vs. 120). **I am afraid** is from the same root as "fear" in the above passages. Such godly fear helps one to keep a proper balance between confidence in God and the human tendency to be arrogant and self-righteous. The psalmist trusts implicitly in God's word (vs. 114), and he loves God's commandments (vss. 113b, 119b). He recognizes his dependence upon God to enable him to keep God's word (vss. 116-117). He believes God will remove the obstacles in his path so that he can do right (vss. 115, 118-119).

The way of justice (Ayin, vss. 121-128). The flow of thought is more awkward than in most of the other stanzas of this psalm, being hindered by the sparsity of words beginning with the letter '*ayin*. It is especially difficult to see the logical significance of **therefore** in verse 127, although the word does show a logical connection at the beginning of verse 128. Apparently the alphabetic arrangement of the psalm, rather than the flow of thought, suggested the use of the word in verse 127.

Since the psalmist has **done what is just and right**, he feels that he has a right to expect the Lord to protect him against his **oppressors** (vs. 121). He asks God to be the **surety**, or guarantor, for his welfare (vs. 122). He wearily waits for God to act on his behalf (vss. 123, 126). As a faithful **servant**, he begs for **understanding** (vss. 124-125). Verse 128a is difficult. Perhaps it could be rendered "Therefore, I esteem as upright each and every precept." This absolute devotion to the uprightness of the word causes him to **hate every false way** (vs. 128b; cf. vs. 104).

The way of steadfastness (Pe, vss. 129-136). The unfolding of God's **words** (vs. 130) must be met with deep desire or longing on man's part (vs. 131). **Unfolding** could be read "entrance" (KJV) by changing the first vowel of the Hebrew word from a short to a long *e*. The RSV text interprets the word to refer to the revealing of God's word; "entrance" takes it to refer to the reception of the word. The word **imparts understanding** (vs. 130b) to none save those who receive it. Like a hungry animal panting with open mouth, he longs for God's word (vs. 131a). God's **testimonies** (vs. 129a) affirm his character and confirm his faithfulness in keeping his covenant promises (vs. 133a). Therefore, these **testimonies are wonderful**; that is, they inspire awe and reverence (vs. 129a). This awe, in turn, prompts one to obey (vs. 129b). The psalmist prays for God to **be gracious** to him (vs. 132), and to **make** his **face shine upon** his **servant** (vs. 135) in delightful blessing and satisfaction (cf. Num. 6:24-26). God's word **gives light; it imparts understanding** (vs. 130). For **simple**, see 116:6. He needs God's help in overcoming the temptation to give up in time of trouble (vs. 133). Violation of God's law on the part of others causes the psalmist to **shed streams of tears** (vs. 136). The satisfaction he longs for includes the removal of anxiety over the unfaithful (cf. 2 Cor. 11:28-29).

The way of righteousness (Tsadhe, vss. 137-144). Since God is **righteous**, so his **judgments are right** (vss. 137-138), and since God's **righteousness is righteous for ever** (vs. 142), so are his **testimonies** (vs. 144a). **Zeal consumes** the psalmist because his **foes forget** God's **words** (vs. 139; cf. 69:9; John 2:17). Though he is **despised** by his enemies (vs. 141), he does not forsake God's law (vs. 143). **That I may live** (vs. 144) probably goes beyond a simple request for preservation from death. He longs for the fruit of righteousness—peace and contentment (cf. Isa. 32:16-18).

The way of hope (Qoph, vss. 145-152). Sincerely, wholeheartedly he cries for help because he trusts in God's promises and desires to obey his word (vss. 145-148). He prays for God to answer him in keeping with his **steadfast love** and **justice** (vs. 149). Though his wicked persecutors are **far from** God's **law**, the **Lord** is **near** to his faithful servant (vss. 150-151). The psalmist is spiritually mature in his knowledge that God's testimonies have been **founded for ever** (vs. 152; cf. vss. 142-144).

The way of vitality (Resh, vss. 153-160). The word **life** in this psalm can best be described as spiritual vitality which provides the essential incentive, energy, and satisfaction so necessary for successful living. The scattered references to this life (vss. 17, 25, 37, 40, 50, 107, 144, 149) become more concentrated in the present stanza. **Give me life** (vss. 154b, 156b) and **preserve my life** (vs. 159b) come from precisely the same Hebrew word. This threefold plea for life is based on the psalmist's faith in God's **promise** (vs. 154b). The plea here is at least in part for deliverance from **affliction** (vs. 153a) and from his **persecutors** and **adversaries** (vs. 157a), who are **faithless** with God (vs. 158). The plea is based on the psalmist's remembrance of God's law (vs. 153b) and diligence in keeping it (vss. 157b, 159a). But he still recognizes his need of God's mercy (vs. 156a). **The sum of thy word** means the same thing as **every one of thy righteous ordinances** (vs. 160).

The way of rejoicing (Shin, vss. 161-168). Not only is his obedience motivated by **awe** (vs. 161), but also by the joy resulting from a rewarding search (vs. 162), by his **love** of God's **law** (vss. 163b, 165, 167), and by the **hope** which God's promises engender (vs. 166). Love for God's truth causes him to hate falsehood (vs. 163; cf. vss. 104, 128). Though **princes persecute** him **without cause**, that is, unjustly (vs. 161a), he can **praise** God **seven times a day for** his **righteous ordinances** (vs. 164). The usual custom was to pray and praise God three times a day (cf. 55:17; Dan. 6:10). **Seven** here probably means the complete number.

The way of confession (Taw, vss. 169-176). He cries for help (vs. 169), supplicates God (vs. 170), and anticipates the praise in song that he will render to God when he answers him (vss. 171-172, 175a). Because God's precepts have been deliberately **chosen** (vs. 173), and the **law** is a source of **delight** (vs. 174), the psalmist confidently prays for revival of life (vitality, vs. 175).

How appropriate that the psalmist chose to end this lengthy encomium of God for his word with a humble confession of his sinfulness (vs. 176). Though he does not forget God's commandments and cannot, therefore, be called an apostate, he knows that no man is perfect. There have been times when he has gone astray like a lost sheep. In light of the numerous professions of loyalty to God and his word in the psalm, the psalmist can hardly be interpreted to mean that he is presently an apostate. For this reason, some suggest that this verse should begin with a conditional clause: "should I go astray." Others suggest that the verse makes no reference to spiritual straying, but describes his loneliness and helplessness under oppression.

Isaiah (53:6) uses a similar expression to describe Israel's lapse into sin, and Christ described himself and his faithful followers as those who seek the lost sheep (Luke 15:3-7; Matt. 10:6). In spite of his many professions of loyalty, the psalmist gives some scattered glimpses of his need for moral and spiritual cleansing (cf. vss. 5, 29, 36-37, 59, 67, 71, 120). As one becomes more spiritually mature, he acquires a deeper understanding of the nature of sin. Things once overlooked now become recognizable marks of imperfections (cf. Pss. 130:3-4; 143:1-2). May we learn to trust in God's righteousness and faithfulness as these pious psalmists did.

Psalm 120: Prayer for Peace

Psalms 120-134 form a group of fifteen psalms which bear the title, "A Song of Ascents." The title has been variously interpreted (see the Introduction). The view taken in the commentary is that these are psalms sung by the pilgrims as they made their way up to Jerusalem and the temple for the annual festivals. Some of the psalms in this group may have been originally written for this purpose, but it is not likely that all were.

Psalm 120 seems to be from the exilic period, since the psalmist is dwelling among the heathen (vs. 5). Yet this could be metaphorical language, indicating Israelites who act like pagans.

Prayer for deliverance (vss. 1-2). [1] The verbs could be rendered in the past tense (cf. the KJV, NASB, NEB), in which case the opening stanza (vss. 1-2) is a summary recollection of deliverance from the distress described in the remainder of the psalm. Then, the psalm is a psalm of thanksgiving written to celebrate his deliverance. If the present tense be followed (RSV), the Hebrew perfects are to be understood as characteristic perfects of experience, which would suggest that deliverance from the present distress has not yet come. In this case, the psalm is to be understood as a psalm of lament and petition. It is permissible to translate the Hebrew conjunction *we* ("and," KJV, NASB, NEB) as **that**, introducing a purpose clause.

[2] The imperatives identify the verse as containing the content of the prayer offered. The problem faced is that of **lying, deceitful** persons who cause him harm.

Punishment of the deceitful (vss. 3-4). [3] The form of the question involves a frequent Hebrew idiom, "God do so to you, and more also" (cf. 1 Sam. 3:17; 1 Kings 2:23; Ruth 1:17). The thought is that God will do something worse to these insolent liars than they have done to the psalmist.

[4] This suggests that God will answer these verbal **arrows** of the wicked (cf. Jer. 9:8) with still more powerful and destructive arrows of divine judgment (cf. Ps. 64:3-4, 7-8). Since these liars have kindled strife and contention, God's wrath will be kindled against them like the **glowing coals of the broom tree** (cf. 140:10-11). The broom tree has a low combustion point and thus blazes up immediately with intense heat.

Trouble to a peace-lover (vss. 5-7). [5] **Meshech** refers to a people in the extreme northern part of Mesopotamia, or possibly in a region near the Black Sea. **Kedar** refers to Arabian descendants of Ishmael who lived southeast of Israel. It is impossible, therefore, to think of the psalmist living in the midst of both peoples. Several attempts have been made to solve this problem. Some suggest that the **I** refers to Israel and that exiles were living in these places. However, there is no specific evidence to substantiate this conclusion. Others emend the text to "Massa" (Gen. 25:14) instead of **Meshech**. Massa was a descendant of Ishmael and the reference here, as well as to **Kedar**, could be to these Arabians. It is possible, however, that Meshech and Kedar are only meant to be metaphors for the heathen.

[6] **Too long** he has dwelt among these hate-mongers.

[7] He speaks **for peace,** but they speak **for war.** Only God can deliver from such foes (cf. vss. 1-2).

Psalm 121: The Keeper of Israel

The Hebrew title is slightly different from that prefixed to Psalms 120, 122–134. The title here prefixes a preposition to the word "ascents," whereas in the others the definite article is prefixed. However, the preposition is likely used in the genitive sense, "of," as in Psalm 122:5. In the Qumran psalm texts, the definite article is prefixed in the title to Psalm 122, and the preposition is prefixed in the title to Psalm 123 (11QPsᵃ). Apparently, there is no significant difference in meaning between the two forms.

The word "keep," used six times in various forms in this short psalm (vss. 3, 4, 5, 7 [twice], 8), designates the theme of divine protection. It is not clear whether the psalm was written as a pilgrim psalm, or adapted to that use. The universality of the trust expressed suggests the latter. Israelite worshipers were encouraged to look toward the temple from wherever they might be and to pray with the confident faith that they would be heard (1 Kings 8:31-53).

It is likewise unclear whether one or more than one voice speaks in the psalm. The change from first person (vss. 1-2) to second person (vss. 3-8) is interpreted by some to indicate a dialogue between two Israelites, two worshipers, or between a worshiper and a priest. While these conclusions are possible, they are not necessary. It may be that the psalmist's rhetorical question and answer (vss. 1-2) is projected into corporate Israelite thought, in which case there is only one voice in the psalm.

While it is possible that the psalm may contain an implied polemic against the Baal fertility cult in Canaanite worship, this is not clear. In the absence of any clear allusion to this effect, such a conclusion must be treated as conjecture.

Help comes from the Lord (vss. 1-2). [1] I lift up (present tense) suggests the customary practice of the psalmist. If the future tense is employed (KJV, NASB), it needs to be understood as a future of certainty or determination, rather than placing emphasis on future time. Verse 2 shows that the psalmist is dealing with the present recognition of the eternal constancy of the Lord. The "if" which the NEB inserts at the beginning of the clause would better be rendered "whenever." **The hills** (or "mountains," NASB) are used by metonymy for Jerusalem, where the temple, signifying God's presence with his people, was situated. (See notes on Ps. 122.) The psalmist's question in verse 1b is only rhetorical, and serves to emphasize the answer given in verse 2.

[2] **My help** is in the emphatic position. God is frequently designated Israel's helper (cf. Pss. 20:2; 27:9; 33:20 and 115:9, 10, 11; 40:17 and 70:5; 46:1; 63:7; 94:17; 124:8). He is often presented as the one **who made heaven and earth**, which embraces the whole universe (cf. Pss. 115:15; 124:8; 134:3; 146:6). Our passage refers to God's universal power to control and provide for his creation.

God never sleeps (vss. 3-4). The stairlike parallelism, which repeats key phrases, focuses on two principal thoughts. Since God never slumbers (vss. 3b, 4b), he is ever alert to his people's needs and he will keep them from ultimate harm. Though a psalmist in distress might entertain the thought of God sleeping or being insensitive to his needs (cf. Pss. 7:6; 44:23-24), these pious songsters knew that God is ever alert to their needs.

Two forms of the negative are employed in these verses, *'al* (twice in vs. 3) and *lo'* (vs. 4). The first may be interpreted as expressing a wish or as an interrogative (cf. the NEB). However, it appears that this form is used here only for emphasis.

[3] **Not** to **be moved** suggests that one stands or walks on a sure, firm footing. Metaphorically, it means to be steadfast, secure (cf. Pss. 10:6; 16:8-9; 30:6; 55:22; 62:2, 6; 112:6-7). The participial form of **he who keeps** indicates continuous action. [4] **Behold** re-emphasizes the central thought of verse 3, and the additional phrase, **nor sleep**, is an appositive repetition used for emphasis.

The Lord your keeper (vss. 5-6). [5] **Keeper, shade**, and **right hand** indicate protection. For the last phrase, see the notes on Psalm 110:5. [6] **By day** and **by night** are frequently used to mean "always" or "constantly" (cf. Pss. 22:2; 88:1). Sunstroke is a constant danger in certain parts of Palestine, especially in the Negeb and in the Jordan Valley near Jericho (cf. Ps. 91:6; 2 Kings 4:18-19; Isa. 49:10). Verse 6b may reflect an ancient superstition that lunacy (from Lat. *luna*, the moon) could result from being "moonstruck," or it could be nothing more than poetic parallelism to balance the verse. Certain diseases were thought to be caused by the moon, especially epilepsy. The Greek word for epilepsy in the NT (Matt. 4:24; 17:15) is from a word which means to be moonstruck. At any rate, the verse declares poetically that God keeps his people from all dangers of the day and of the night.

God protects (vss. 7-8). [7] **Evil** should be understood here in the sense of sorrow or distress, exemplified by death (cf. vs. 7b). [8] **Your going out and your coming in** suggests the totality of one's activities. These phrases, or similar ones, might refer specifically to armies going out to battle and subsequently returning home (Num. 27:17; Deut. 31:2), or to one's coming and going on the normal duties of daily living (Deut. 28:6; Ps. 126:6). In our psalm, the phrases might suggest pilgrimages to and from the temple. (But see the introduction to the psalm.) **From this time forth and for evermore** embraces the totality of whatever future time is under consideration in the context (cf. 113:2; 115:18; 125:2). Here it is obviously limited to one's lifetime.

Psalm 122: The Happy Pilgrims

The title in most manuscripts of the LXX and the Vulgate omit the phrase "of David." The psalm gives evidence of having been written during the monarchical period, since both palace and temple are mentioned. In all likelihood, it was written during the period of the united monarchy, since all the tribes seem to be accustomed to going up for the festivals. This psalm gives more evidence of having been written as a pilgrim psalm than any others among the Psalms of Ascents (120–134), with the possible exception of the last one. Other Psalms of Zion may refer to pilgrimages also (cf. Pss. 48, 84).

The psalmist combines three Zion motifs which may be found in Zion psalms: (1) the city as a symbol of national security under divine protection (vss. 3, 6-9; cf. Pss. 46–48); (2) the worship assemblies at the temple, where God symbolically dwelt (vss. 4, 9; cf. Pss. 84, 87); and (3) the king's

400 / PSALM 122:1-7

palace, where justice was administered (vs. 5; cf. Pss. 45:2, 6-7; 72:1-4, 12-14).

The joy of the pilgrimages (vss. 1-2). [1] This verse pictures the swelling crowd of pilgrims as they invite the residents of the towns and villages through which they pass to join them in their journey to the temple. A double joy would fill the hearts of the pilgrims: (1) the anticipation of coming into the presence of God at the temple; and (2) the fellowship of fellow-pilgrims on the journey. **House of the Lord** could refer to the tabernacle (cf. 1 Sam. 1:7, 24; 2 Sam. 12:20) as well as the temple.

[2] **Have been standing** translates the Hebrew perfect tense of the verb "to be," plus the participle for **standing**. The phrase could be understood as a perfect of experience signifying action of the past continuing into the present. This translation is better than the present tense (NASB, NEB). The future tense (KJV) is incorrect. The psalm is to be recited in the temple precincts after the pilgrimage to the temple has been completed.

Zion's threefold blessing (vss. 3-5). [3] The topography of Jerusalem, situated on four hills, made this fortified city almost impregnable against the enemy. [4] As the natural topography and human fortifications of the city bound it together securely, so the annual worship assemblies bound the nation together under God in a bond of unity. [5] And, provided the kings administered justice as God intended (see the introduction to the psalm), the palace would also be a symbol of unity and security.

The peace of Jerusalem (vss. 6-9). [6-7] It is not enough to have these outward symbols of security. Hence, Israel needs to express her trust in the Lord by praying for **the peace of Jerusalem.** Prosperity will come to those who love what Jerusalem symbolizes. There is a beautiful double wordplay involved in these two verses. In verse 6, the last part of the word **Jerusalem** (*shalam*) means **peace** (*shalom*). In verse 7, the word **peace** (*shalom*) and the word **security** (*shalwah*) involve alliteration. Such devices were intended to catch and hold the attention of the worshiper. Jesus doubtless made a similar wordplay on the word "peace"

(Luke 19:42), and may possibly have been alluding to this psalm. [8-9] A twofold motive prompts the prayer: (1) brotherly love (vs. 8), and (2) love of God (vs. 9), who symbolically dwells in the temple.

Psalm 123: Patient, Submissive Waiting

Verses 1-2 are written in the tone of a psalm of trust, but 3-4 are in the form of a community lament. However, psalms of lament usually include declarations of trust; therefore, this psalm follows the usual pattern of a lament. Significantly there is no imprecation against enemies.

The shift from singular (vs. 1) to plural (vss. 2-4) pronouns may indicate that the psalm is a liturgy, the first verse spoken by a priest and the rest supplying the congregational response. Or it may be that, as is frequently the case, the psalmist employs the concept of a community solidarity so as to identify his personal circumstances with those of the nation.

Eyes lifted up to God (vss. 1-2). [1] Lifting up the eyes to God is a frequent idiom used to describe pious longing and expectant hope (cf. 121:1). The phrase is similar to the idea of lifting up the soul in trust (cf. 25:1; 86:4; 143:8), or lifting up the hands in prayer (cf. 28:2). God **who** is **enthroned in the heavens**, unlike impotent idols, is able to do whatever he pleases (cf. 115:3). Since he is the God of steadfast love (cf. 36:5-6; 103:4-5, 11), he will act on behalf of his people.

[2] The Hebrew terms for **master** and **mistress** indicate the superior party which exercises control over others. The words **servants** and **maid** would better be translated "slaves" and "slave girl" (cf. the NEB). In emblematic parallelism, these slaves are compared with God's servants, his people Israel. As the slave looks trustingly for some favorable reaction from his master, so Israel waits patiently until God manifests his grace. "Be gracious" (NASB) is better than **have mercy** (RSV, KJV), or "deal kindly" (NEB, vss. 2-3). **Hand** often stands for power or sufficiency, and Ezra (7:6, 9, 28; 8:18, 22, 31) and Nehemiah (2:8, 18) employ the phrase "the hand of the Lord [God]" in this way.

Plea for God to be gracious (vss. 3-4). [3] The repetition of the plea indicates fervency. Superlatives are used here and in verse 4 to indicate the overabundance of **scorn** and **contempt** which they have received. **For** indicates a motive for God to act in their behalf. God is compassionate toward the oppressed, especially those who suffer unjustly.

[4] This verse elaborates the thought of verse 3. **Those at ease** are so prone to be contemptuous toward the unfortunate (cf. Job 12:5; Amos 6:1-7). Such **contempt** arouses God's compassion toward the victims (Zech. 1:15-17). The **scorn** heaped upon the returned exiles fits well into this setting (cf. Neh. 2:19; 4:1-4).

Psalm 124: Escape from a Deadly Peril

Those who insist on a Davidic composition compare the setting to David's battles against the Philistines (2 Sam. 5) or against the Ammonites (2 Sam. 10). Some Greek manuscripts and the Latin Vulgate omit the phrase "of David" in the title. Those who date the psalm in post-exilic days relate it to the era of reconstruction under Ezra and Nehemiah, or think of Israel's escape from her pagan captors. Since Israel was delivered from many perils throughout her colorful history, it is impossible to date the psalm on the basis of a particular crisis recently faced. The presence of Aramaisms does not indicate a late date for the psalm, for Aramaic influenced biblical Hebrew from very early times.

This is a beautiful psalm of national thanksgiving celebrating God's deliverance of the nation from a deadly peril which would have annihilated them had not God come to their aid.

Description of the danger (vss. 1-5). Verses 1 and 2, by means of stairlike parallelism, provide the *protasis* to the stanza, and verses 3-5 the *apodosis*. **[1-2]** In Hebrew, the sharp contrast between **on our side** (*lanu*) and **against us** (*'alenu*) is more pronounced than in English. "For us" and **against us** might better show the contrast. The NEB obscures the full force of the opening clause in verses 1 and 2. There is an implied contrast between the help of **the**

Lord and the impotence of idols worshiped by Israel's pagan neighbors.

[3-5] Vivid figures describe the danger which had confronted Israel. A monster who could swallow men alive and a sweeping flood or torrent symbolize swift, consuming dangers. Only the RSV does full justice to the Hebrew poetic structure of verses 4 and 5. The two verses form a triplet, each line of which is synonymous in thought to the other two. But the second and third lines are arranged chiastically, that is, the order of phrases is reversed so as to stress the fact that it is **over us** that **the flood, the torrent,** and **the raging waters** would have gone.

Escape from peril (vss. 6-8). [6] **Blessed be** is a passive form frequently used in the psalms to indicate divine blessings bestowed upon men (cf. 1:1) or thanksgiving rendered to God for blessings granted to his people (cf. a similar form in 103:1-5). What is stated negatively in verse 6 is declared positively in verse 7. The two similes used in verses 6 and 7 describe the slow, painful capture by a beast of prey or a bird confined by a fowler. [7] Again, only the RSV does full justice to the Hebrew poetic structure of this verse (cf. vss. 4-5). Four lines of poetry form an external chiastic arrangement, in which the first and fourth and the second and third lines correspond. By this structure, two focal points of interest are enhanced: that of **the snare** and the fact that **we have escaped.** [8] For the idea of God as Israel's help, see the notes on 121:2. **The name of the Lord** frequently stands for his renown and character discerned through his saving acts on behalf of Israel, which gave Israel confidence in the saving power of God (cf. 1 Sam. 17:45; Ps. 118:10, 11, 12; Prov. 18:10). It is likely that the covenant name, Yahweh, places primary emphasis on the character of God discerned through his acts (cf. Exod. 3:14—RSV note, "I will be what I will be"). The idea of God's eternity seems to be a developed connotation attached to this name, which comes from the Hebrew verb "to be, become." The eternal, unchangeable nature of God seems often to be connoted by the name Yahweh (cf. Isa. 40:28-31; 41:4; 43:10-11; 44:6-8). For God **who made heaven**

404 / PSALM 125:1-5

and earth, suggesting one in whom Israel can have complete confidence, see the notes on 121:2.

Psalm 125: Peace for Those Who Trust in Yahweh

The psalmist exercises keen discernment in that he makes a proper distinction between the fate of the righteous and the fate of the wicked, a favorite theme in Israel's wisdom poetry (cf. Ps. 1; Prov. 1–9). Those blessed are **those who trust in the Lord** (vs. 1), **the righteous** (vs. 3), **the good** (vs. 4a), **those who are upright in their hearts** (vs. 4b). Wicked kings (vs. 3a) and people (vs. 5) must be eliminated so that the righteous will not be encouraged to do wrong (vs. 4). This should for ever silence those who doubt that leniency toward criminals leads to a breakdown of morality in society!

The encircling love of God (vss. 1-3). [1-2] Not all Israelites indiscriminately, but **those who trust in the Lord,** are blessed; not those who trust in Jerusalem, but those who trust in the God of Jerusalem. **The mountains** offered security to **Jerusalem** and became a symbol of divine protection. **[3]** Most commentators assume that **the scepter of wickedness** refers to foreign kings and refer the reader to the situation described in Nehemiah 6. While this may be true, it is not a necessary conclusion. The prophets constantly rebuked Israelite leaders for adversely influencing the nation through their own wickedness (cf. Isa. 1:21-31; Jer. 5:1-6; 6:13-15; Hos. 4:4-10). The psalmists acknowledged the principle also (cf. 72:1-4; 78:67-72; 101:1-8).

A discerning prayer (vss. 4-5). Prayers on behalf of the corporate community, as well as those prayed on one's own behalf, must be prayed in keeping with God's will (cf. 1 John 3:22; 5:14-15). The psalmist is aware of this principle. **[4]** King and people alike must be **good** if they expect the Lord to **do good** to them (cf. 18:20-27). **[5]** But king and people alike he **will lead away with evildoers** if they are evil (cf. Hos. 3:4; 7:7; 8:4, 10; 10:3, 7, 15; 13:10-11). The final petition, **Peace be upon Israel,** presupposes that Israel will choose to follow the good way.

Psalm 126: Restoration of Zion

This community prayer is strikingly similar to the longer Psalm 85 (see the introduction to that psalm). Verses 1-3 reflect upon a past deliverance, probably the return from Babylonian captivity. Verses 4-6 plead for a further restoration from present problems, probably the hardships encountered in the reconstruction era following the return from captivity, as reflected in Ezra and Nehemiah.

By means of temporal clauses, verses 1-2 look back to a time of divine deliverance (vs. 1) and the resultant effects on Israel (vs. 2ab) and the nations (vs. 2cd). The psalmist concludes this stanza with a reaffirmation of Israel's gratitude for God's saving acts (vs. 3). In beautiful imagery, the psalmist has the nation pray for the refreshing waters of divine blessing (vs. 4), and then that their tears may be turned into rejoicing (vs. 5). He concludes the second stanza with an affirmation of trust which also includes a definite causal relationship between sowing and reaping (vs. 6).

'The Lord has done great things' (vss. 1-3). The purpose of this introductory stanza is properly understood by comparing it with the concluding stanza. Past deliverance gives hope for present salvation. **[1] Restored the fortunes of** (cf. the NEB) might also be rendered "turned the captivity of" (cf. the KJV and NASB). This clause, with slight variations, is frequently used by the psalmists (14:7 and 53:6; 85:1; 126:1, 4) and the prophets (Jer. 29:14; 30:3, 18; 31:23; 32:44; 33:7, 11, 26; 48:47; 49:6, 39; Ezek. 16:53; 29:14; 39:25; Hos. 6:11; Joel 3:1; Amos 9:14; Zeph. 2:7; 3:20). In the majority of the passages, the context shows clearly that restoration from captivity is to be understood. **We were like those who dream** is a poetic way of saying that the reality of restoration seemed too good to be true. The expression also reveals the fact that the captives had often longed for restoration. **[2]** Israel was able to sing God's praises and to rejoice at her restoration, and the nations were enabled to see the power and goodness of Israel's God. **[3]** In a time of distress, the psalmist wants Israel to remember the past favors of God so that the following petition can be prayed in faith.

'Restore our fortunes' (vss. 4-6). [4] The watercourses in the Negeb provide a fit simile by which to describe the joys of restoration. The Negeb is the southern part of Judah which extends southward toward the Sinai Peninsula. It is a very dry region most of the year. When the abundant, seasonal rains fill the wadis, there is occasion for great rejoicing. So the tribulations of the nation can be pictured in terms of that dry region, and the anticipated deliverance can be portrayed in terms of the seasonal rains which occasion rejoicing. [5] This verse may be a reflection of the ancient pagan habit of weeping at sowing time in keeping with the superstitious belief that such weeping would please the gods and would result in the fertility god being resurrected from the dead. If so, however, the psalmist has transformed the concept into a monotheistic faith. Genuine penitence and fervent petition touch the compassionate heart of God so that he will answer favorably (cf. 86:15-17; Jer. 3:12-14; Ps. 138:3; Isa. 49:8; Jer. 31:15-20). [6] The sheaves here represent the restoration of Israel's fortunes (cf. vs. 4). Peace, prosperity, freedom, and tranquility may be included in this concept.

Psalm 127: Unity in the Home

Some have seen a wide disparity between the sentiment of verses 1-2 and that of verses 3-5, and have concluded that this psalm is composed of two different psalms pieced together by some editor. However, if the two stanzas are at such great variance, it is difficult to understand why an editor would have combined them. It seems more likely that the psalmist either originated or borrowed the first stanza to delineate a general principle by which unity in the family can be illustrated. It is not clear why Solomon's name has been attached to this psalm.

Need for God's blessings (vss. 1-2). This stanza emphasizes that nothing worthwhile can be accomplished by human effort alone. Unless our efforts are complemented with God's blessings, we labor in vain. [1] House is not preceded by the definite article in Hebrew. Any house, whatever house, is under consideration. **House** (Heb. *ba-yith*) can refer to a literal dwelling house (Gen. 19:10), a household (Gen. 7:1), the temple, or the king's palace (1 Kings 9:1), or the nation as a whole (Amos 3:1, 13; 7:10), as well as some other minor connotations. The word in a given passage must be interpreted in light of its context. Here, the word **city** provides the clue. This word is also without the definite article in this passage. By synecdoche, **house** or **city** could stand for the nation. **[2]** No amount of **anxious toil** or long hours of labor can insure that our labors will be crowned with success, unless we labor so as to receive the Lord's blessings.

The blessing of a good family (vss. 3-5). This stanza is better understood in light of Israel's rural, suburban society than in our day of population explosion. Nevertheless, children are still a blessed heritage from the Lord.

[3] Sons may be understood here of male children only (cf. the NEB), if emphasis is placed on their hunting prowess (vs. 4), or if they are thought of as defenders of the family (vs. 5). However, the parallel phrase, **the fruit of the womb,** suggests that daughters may also be included. In a patriarchal society it is understandable that sons would receive the greater emphasis. **A heritage from the Lord** is explained by the parallel phrase, **a reward.** This likely denotes primarily a divinely given blessing rather than suggesting a meritorious reward. The patriarchs of Israel and their wives recognized that children are gifts from God (Gen. 29:31-35; 30:1-6, 17-23; 1 Sam. 1:5-6, 11, 19-20). How much better our society would be if we recognized as much!

[4] The primary thought of the psalmist is likely that sons would provide sufficient strength to enable the family to defend itself against marauders. However, the simile may be understood to include other kinds of sufficiency as well. **[5]** The larger the family, the greater the defense against the enemy. This is not necessarily true in our highly structured society. The size of a family should be governed by the parent's capability of adequately providing for their material, social, and spiritual needs, and by society's capability of fitting them into its structural institutions.

Psalm 128: The Blessing of Fearing the Lord

In subject matter, this psalm is similar to Psalm 112, although in poetic structure the two are quite different. The psalm is also similar to Psalm 127 in that both praise the divine blessing of a prolific family. The present psalm expresses the conviction that the welfare of society depends upon the virtues characteristic of religious discipline within the family.

To fear the Lord (vss. 1-2). **[1] Who walks in his ways** is in apposition to **one who fears the Lord**, thus the latter phrase (vs. 1b) explains the former (vs. 1a). For a fuller discussion of what it means to fear the Lord, and concerning the gift of a good family life granted to the God-fearing person, see the notes on Psalm 112. **[2]** Not only will the God-fearing person be prosperous, but he will find happiness and enjoyment in his labors (cf. Eccles. 2:24-26).

A prolific family (vss. 3-4). This is the blessing of the man **who fears the Lord** (vs. 4b). **[3] Within your house** is more literally "in the innermost parts of your house" (cf. NEB and NASB margin). "By the sides of" (KJV) is allowable as a definition of the Hebrew, but does not fit the context of the psalm as well. In Oriental societies, the women's quarters were always in the innermost part of the house. **Fruitful vine** and **olive shoots** are fit similes of prolific fruit-bearing.

May the nation be blessed (vss. 5-6). These verses are to be understood as a priestly benediction (cf. 134:3). By synecdoche, the family (vss. 3-4) stands for the city (vs. 5), which in turn stands for the nation (vs. 6). **[5]** May the God-fearing man be blessed **from Zion**, where the Lord symbolically dwells (cf. 14:7; 20:2). May family prosperity be extended to the capital city and may this **prosperity** continue for a lifetime. **[6]** The blessing of seeing one's **children's children** insures that one will live to a ripe old age, a great blessing to the ancients (cf. Gen. 48:11; Prov. 17:6). The fortunes of succeeding generations depend in part on the heritage which we leave them (cf. Exod. 20:4-6; 34:6-7). The psalm closes with a prayer for **peace** to **be upon Israel** (cf. 125:5).

Psalm 129: Resume of Israel's Suffering

In form and content, this psalm is similar to Psalm 124. In both psalms, Israel's suffering through the centuries and God's deliverance of the nation are emphasized. The principle of historical continuity is applied to present circumstances. As God has so characteristically delivered Israel in times past because of his faithfulness to his covenant promises, so he will deliver from the present distress. The psalm could be understood as making immediate reference to preexilic or postexilic circumstances, although the language and style seem to identify it as postexilic.

Thanksgiving and preservation (vss. 1-4). [1-2] Compare the form of 124:1-2. The psalmist is speaking for the nation. National memoirs may be written from the standpoint of achievement and attainment, or from the viewpoint of suffering and survival. While secular nations usually choose the former, it is singular that Israel glorifies God as her protector and preserver. **From my youth** means from the beginning of Israel's national existence at the exodus from Egypt (cf. Exod. 19:3-6; Hos. 11:1; Jer. 2:2; 22:21; Ezek. 23:3). Persistently through the centuries Israel had been assailed by the Canaanites (Judg. 1:33; Ezra 9:1-2), the Arameans (Syrians; 2 Sam. 8:5-6; 1 Kings 20–22; Amos 1:3-5), the Ammonites (1 Sam. 11; 1 Kings 11:1-8; 2 Chron. 27:5-6; Amos 1:13-15), the Edomites (1 Kings 11:14-22; 2 Kings 8:21-24; 2 Chron. 28:16-17; Amos 1:11-12), the Philistines (Josh. 13:1-3; Judg. 3:1-6; 14–16; 1 Sam. 4–6; 16–17; 2 Sam. 21:15-22; 2 Chron. 28:18; Amos 1:6-8), and the Moabites (Judg. 3:15-30; 2 Sam. 8:2; 1 Kings 11:1, 33; 2 Kings 13:20; 24:2), but none prevailed against her. Even the mighty Assyrians and Chaldeans (Babylonians) could not ultimately and utterly prevail against Israel (Isa. 10:12-19; 46–47).

[3] The figure may refer to Israel's captors passing over their backs and gashing them in the process (cf. Isa. 51:23), or more likely, to gashes made in their backs by the whips of their taskmasters. The cognate accusative, **the plowers plowed**, intensifies the thought. **[4]** It is because **the Lord is righteous**, that is, true to his commitment to Israel, that they have survived (cf. Isa. 45:21-25; Dan. 9:3-19). Because of this commitment, **he has cut the cords of the wicked** oppressors. **Cords** may refer to the ropes attached to the yoke of an ox (cf. Job 39:10; Hos. 11:4), or to fetters attached to a prisoner or slave (Judg. 15:13-14; Ezek. 3:25; 4:8). The figure could mean that Israel is spared from the plowing (cf. Hos. 10:11), or that Israel is freed from bondage (Hos. 11:1-4).

Destruction of the enemies (vss. 5-8). The structure of the Hebrew would allow verses 5-8 to be simple futures indicating a prediction, or jussives (as all our standard English versions render) indicating a prayer. The prayer need not be interpreted as personal vengeance wished against their enemies, but rather a prayer for God's righteousness to be vindicated (vs. 4). **[5] Be put to shame and turned backward** means to be defeated in their sinister purpose.

[6] Grass often would sprout up on the mud roofs of the houses, but because the soil had no depth, the plants would soon wither. This fact became a symbol of defeat of human plans by divine intervention (cf. Isa. 37:27). **[7] The reaper** would not attempt to harvest such a crop, for it is not worth it. Nor would **the binder** find enough to tie in a sheaf. **[8]** Of such a puny harvest **those who pass by** would not pronounce the usual benediction, **The blessing of the Lord be upon you.** Nor would the reaper be able to respond, **We bless you in the name of the Lord** (cf. Ruth 2:4).

Psalm 130: Guilt and Forgiveness

This psalm is timeless in applications and could have been written at any period of Israel's psalmody. The themes of the burden of guilt and the blessedness of forgiveness are frequently found in the psalms (cf. Pss. 32, 38, 51, 103).

The penitent's cry (vss. 1-2). [1] Out of the depths makes use of a common metaphor of distress used in the psalms. Flood waters, or **the depths**, may refer to distress brought on by enemies (cf. 68:22; 124:4-5), by illness (cf. 38:3-4a), by despondency (cf. 71:20), or by guilt (130:1). **Depths** can also depict forgiveness of sin (Mic. 7:19). **[2]** The plea of this and the preceding verse obviously arises from a deeply penitent heart. The Hebrew word translated **supplications** (*tachanun*) comes from the same root as those rendered "grace" (*chanen*) and "be gracious" (*chanan*). A supplication is a plea for God to manifest his favor.

God's forgiveness (vss. 3-4). **[3]** No man can stand on his own merit, for all men are sinners (cf. 143:2; Rom. 3:9, 23-26). **[4]** Man's heart is turned toward God in reverence because he recognizes the forgiving love of God (cf. 33:18; 103:8-18).

Waiting for deliverance (vss. 5-6). By means of stairlike parallelism two principal thoughts are emphasized. **I wait, . . . my soul waits, . . . my soul waits** are explained by **in his word I hope.** He waits for God to fulfill his covenant promise. The second point of emphasis is enhanced by the comparative parallelism of **more than watchmen for the morning,** repeated for added emphasis. As the watchman waits for the danger that lurks at night to be ended by the breaking of day, so the psalmist longs for his distress to pass by means of the light of God's truth being brought to bear upon his circumstances. But his danger is not merely anticipatory like that of the watchman; his danger is real and present. Therefore, his longing for relief is more intense than that of the watchman.

Exhortation to Israel (vss. 7-8). **[7]** It has rightly been said that **hope** is a duty (cf. 42:5, 11; 43:5; 131:3). But at the same time it is also a privilege of those who are redeemed (cf. 107:1-3, 43). **[8] Redeem** here means forgiveness of sins (cf. Eph. 1:7).

Psalm 131: Childlike Trust

This personal prayer (vss. 1-2) has a lesson in it that needs to be shared by the nation (vs. 3). The key to understanding the thought of the psalm rests in the stairlike form of verse 2. "Quieted" is an adequate translation of verse 2a, but verse 2bc should read "like a weaned child," indicating a habit conquered (cf. the KJV, NASB). "Clinging"

(NEB) is as misleading as the RSV is inadequate. The lesson of contentment is one which most of us have to learn through experience (cf. Phil. 4:10-13).

Conquered ambition (vs. 1). The thought is not meant to stifle our natural inclination to inquire into the unknown or to conquer the seemingly unconquerable (cf. Gen. 1:28-29), but it is a warning against an arrogant pride which acknowledges no limit to human ingenuity or attainment (cf. Rom. 11:33-36; 2 Thess. 2:3-4).

Return to childlike trust (vs. 2). "Surely" (KJV, NASB) does not fit the context, although it is one possible rendering of the Hebrew idiom. "But rather" is the best way to capture the full meaning of the strong adversative force of the Hebrew. **Calmed** and **quieted** indicates something overcome or conquered. He is now God-centered instead of self-centered (cf. 2 Cor. 3:4-6).

Lesson to be shared (vs. 3). On verse 3a, see 130:7a and the notes. On verse 3b, see the notes on 113:2.

Psalm 132: David's Continuing Dynasty

For the features of royal psalms, see the introduction to Psalm 89. The theme of these two psalms is similar in that they both emphasize the distinction between the conditional and unconditional features of the Davidic covenant. However, the author of Psalm 89 laments Yahweh's apparent breach of covenant, while the poet responsible for Psalm 132 is fully confident that God is faithful to his promise. Very different circumstances produced the two psalms. In Psalm 132, the disturbing condition of a dethroned and imprisoned king which troubled the author of Psalm 89 is absent. Our psalmist here also reveals a keener understanding of the unconditional nature of the Davidic covenant than does the author of Psalm 89. There the psalmist applied the unconditional promise to the continuance of the political dynasty, but here the poet applies it to only one of David's descendants (vs. 11).

The psalm was apparently written to celebrate the ark's being placed in the temple which Solomon had just built (vs. 8). The author reflects upon David's desire to build

God a house (vss. 1-5) and his action of bringing the ark of the covenant to Jerusalem (vss. 6-7). He prays for the success of priests and kings so that Israel may rejoice (vss. 9-10). He expresses confidence in God's acceptance of David's house (vss. 11-12) and of Zion as his own symbolic resting place (vss. 13-14). Therefore, Zion (vs. 15), the priesthood (vs. 16), and the kingdom (vss. 17-18) will be blessed.

Prayer of temple dedication (vss. 1-10). [1-5] David's **hardships** were **endured** because of his intense devotion to God, which caused him to determine to build God a house commensurate with his own (cf. 2 Sam. 7:1-2). **[1] Hardships** may refer to David's troubles with Saul (1 Sam. 22–31), with his perennial pagan enemies (2 Sam. 8), within his own family (2 Sam. 13–19; 1 Kings 1), the troubles encountered in bringing the ark to Jerusalem (2 Sam. 6:1-11), or possibly to all of these. **[2-5]** There is no mention in Kings or Chronicles of any such oath as that stated here, just as there is no oath recorded of God in making his promise to David (cf. 2 Sam. 7:14-16; Ps. 89:3-4, 35-36, see notes). It was not until after David's death that the temple was built by his son Solomon (2 Sam. 7:11b-13; 1 Kings 2–8). The psalmist wants to emphasize David's determination to so honor God by building him a house.

[6-7] This reminiscing is transitional in that it reflects back upon the sentiment of the petition in verses 1-5 and also prepares the way for the petition of verses 8-10.

[6] Ephrathah, sometimes identified with Bethlehem (Gen. 35:16-21; 1 Sam. 17:12; Mic. 5:2), was apparently an ancient district in which Bethlehem was situated. If Bethlehem were at that time known as the city of David (cf. 1 Sam. 16:1, 4; Ruth 4:11, 17; Luke 2:11), the psalmist may be saying by metonymy that David is the one who began the search for the ark (cf. 2 Sam. 6). Or there is another possible explanation. Caleb had a wife named Ephrath **(Ephrathah)** who bore him a son named Hur (1 Chron. 2:19, 50). One of Hur's sons was Shobal, an ancestor of the inhabitants of Kiriath-jearim, where the ark had remained in seclusion (1 Chron. 13:1-6). Thus the term Ephrathite came to stand not only for one from Bethlehem (1 Sam. 17:12; Ruth 1:2), but also for one from the tribe of Ephraim (1 Sam. 1:1; 1 Kings 11:26, KJV and Hebrew). Verse 6 may be saying that the ark was heard to be in **Ephrathah,** that is, Kiriath-jearim, and that is where it was found. At any rate, **Jaar** is the singular of Jearim, and **the fields of Jaar** (meaning the fields of wood) is a play on Kiriath-jearim (meaning the city of woods). **[7]** The purpose in going to Kiriath-jearim was to **worship** at God's **footstool, his dwelling place,** the ark of the covenant. For the meaning of **footstool,** see the comment on Psalm 99:5.

[8-10] Here is the priestly summons for the ark to be placed in the temple. **[8]** God's presence goes with **the ark of** his **might,** and the ark becomes his **resting place,** which in turn provides a resting place for Israel (cf. Num. 10:33-35). Dwelling place (*mishkan*, vs. 7) and **resting place** (*menuchah*, vs. 8) combine the ideas of the divine presence (the Shekinah) and the permanence of God's home (cf. Ruth 1:9; 3:1; Deut. 12:9; Ps. 95:11) among Israel. The priests must be properly sanctified before they can officiate in the presence of God (cf. 1 Chron. 15:12, 14). Because they had not followed the right procedure (i.e., the priests carrying the ark with poles on their shoulders) in the first attempt to bring the ark to Jerusalem, they met with disaster (cf. 1 Chron. 15:13; cf. ch. 13). When the proper procedure was carried out on the second attempt, the venture was characterized by great joy (1 Chron. 15:15-28).

[10] The prayer is for God to accept the Davidic king (Solomon) who has built the temple according to divine promise (cf. 2 Sam. 7:12-14).

The Lord's answer (vss. 11-18). [11-12] These verses elaborate upon the allusion to the Davidic covenant in verse 10. **[11]** In regard to the mention of an **oath,** see the comments on verses 2-5. The second line of the verse shows the purpose of the **oath** to confirm the promise as being unconditional (cf. 110:4; Heb. 6:13-20). The crucial word **one** is not in the Hebrew or Greek OT, or in Acts 2:30. However, the promise (2 Sam. 7:12-15) and its ultimate messianic fulfillment (Heb. 1:5; Acts 2:30) make clear that only **one** son is involved in this unconditional promise. God set Solomon upon the throne irrespective of what his sinful outcome would be, just as he fulfilled his unconditional promise to Abraham to give to his descendants the land of Canaan for an inheritance (Ps. 105:8-11; Gen. 22:16-18) regardless of the outcome of their lives. The ultimate fulfillment of the unconditional promise is in Christ.

[12] The continuance of the political dynasty would depend on the obedience of the kings, just as continued possession of Canaan depended on the faithfulness of the nation (Pss. 105:44-45; 106:34-43).

[13-18] The Lord accepted **Zion** and the house of David. [13-14] There is the same play on words here as in verses 7 and 8. God has accepted **Zion** as **his habitation** (*moshabh*) and **resting place** (*menuchah*) in answer to the petition of verse 8. [15] Moreover, his presence will be attended by abundant blessings so that the land may truly be a resting place for the nation. [16] This verse indicates God's acceptance of the sanctified priesthood (vs. 9a) so that they will be clothed **with salvation** (success) in performing their ritual duty. As a result, the **saints will shout for joy** (vs. 16b) in answer to the petition in verse 9b.

[17] This promise is in answer to the petition of verse 10. **Horn** is a symbol of strength (cf. 89:17) and **lamp** is a symbol of the continuance of the king (cf., 2 Sam. 21:17; 1 Kings 11:36; 15:4). [18] This verse reflects the frequent promises in royal psalms of the success granted the king, including the defeat and consternation of **his enemies**.

Psalm 133: Unity Within the Nation

This brief didactic psalm employs two beautiful similes to illustrate the beauty and value of unity. [1] Verse 1b literally says "the dwelling of brethren, also together." The context suggests that "together" means **in unity**. [2] The anointing **oil** not only had a pleasant odor, but the anointed priest, in premonarchical days in particular, stood as a symbol of unity. The central sanctuary where the ark of the covenant rested was the only bond that bound that loosely joined amphictyony together. During the period of the united monarchy after David brought the ark to Jerusalem, both palace and sanctuary gave Zion first place in the hearts of the people.

[3] Mount **Hermon** in the north at the headwaters of the Jordan is the highest elevation in Palestine. A spur of the Anti-Lebanon mountains, Mount **Hermon** reaches a height of over nine thousand feet. Heavy **dew** is to be found on its slopes early in the summer mornings even during the dry season. Situated more than one hundred air miles from Jerusalem, its **dew** could not literally come down upon **the mountains of Zion**. This simile is another allusion to the unifying effect that Jerusalem has on the nation.

Psalm 134: Bless God and Bless Men

The word "bless," used in each verse of this brief psalm, is the key to understanding the message of the psalm. The first two verses are best understood as an invitation from the worshipers to the priests and Levites who function at the temple. Verse 3 is a priestly benediction pronounced by the priests upon the people. This psalm is a fitting conclusion to the Psalms of Ascents (Pss. 120–134).

Invitation to the priests (vss. 1-2). [1] **Bless**, when applied to man's blessing God, can only mean to praise, thank, and glorify God for his saving acts. It is significant that in the Greek NT one of the very common words for giving thanks is *eucharisteō*, which derives from the same root as *charis*, "grace." To give thanks is to respond favorably in praise to God for his generosity toward man. In one psalm (18:1), the psalmist says *erchamekha*—literally, "I have compassion for you." What he means is: "I am responding in love to your compassion toward me." Man can give back to God only what God has first given to him (cf. Rom. 11:33-36).

Come (cf. the NEB) could also be translated "behold" (KJV, NASB). The Hebrew particle is an interjection used primarily to catch the attention and alert one to what is happening. **Servants** could apply to the whole nation in a different context, but here refers to those officiants **who stand** to minister (cf. Ps. 135:1-2; Deut. 10:8) day and night

(1 Chron. 9:33) at the temple. **By night** is a plural in Hebrew and probably is to be taken in the distributive sense of "night after night" (cf. the NEB). For **the house of the Lord,** see the comments on Psalm 122:1.

[2] For the phrase **lift up your hands,** see Psalms 28:2 and 63:4, and the note on prayer at the end of Psalm 86. **Holy place** translates one Hebrew word which can mean "holiness" or "holy place." The sanctuary seems to be intended here (cf. vs. 1b).

Priestly benediction (vs. 3). Such priestly benedictions are noted in the Pentateuch (Lev. 9:22-23; Num. 6:22-26). Compare Psalm 128:5-6. **From Zion** alludes to the divine presence at the temple (cf. 132:13-18). **He who made heaven and earth** emphasizes the divine providence which is an extension of divine power and benevolence manifested in God's creative activity (cf. 115:15; 121:2; 124:8; 146:6). God can and will bless his creation, especially his faithful people.

Psalm 135: Praise God for His Uniqueness

Psalms 135 and 136, separately or together, are known as The Great Hallel (Praise), not to be confused with the Egyptian Hallel (Pss. 113–118). These psalms might be sung on the occasions of any of the great festivals.

This psalm can best be described as a mosaic of praise. Practically every statement in it is a quotation or paraphrase of other OT passages. Not all of these references will be included in the commentary. The student should consult his cross-reference Bible.

Invitation to praise (vss. 1-4). It is not clear how many groups are here summoned, but the concluding invitation is clear (vss. 19-21). [1] Compare Psalm 113:1, where the phrases are reversed. **Servants** in 113:1 may refer to all Israel, but here, as in 134:1a, refers to the temple officiants (cf. vs. 2). [2] **House** and **courts** are synonymous here (cf. 134:1b). [3] Three reasons for praising God are briefly stated. First, **the Lord is good** in every way (cf. 106:1; 107:1; 118:1, 29; 136:1). The second reason is not clearly stated. The Hebrew of verse 3b is capable of varied interpretations. The RSV gives a possible rendering of the Hebrew text, which reads, "For it [or "he"] is pleasant." This could mean that God's name is pleasant (cf. the NASB "lovely"), or that God is pleasant (cf. the RSV), or that it is pleasant to sing praises to the Lord. The KJV and NEB follow either the first or third interpretation. **[4]** The third reason for praising God is that **the Lord has chosen Jacob. Possession** (cf. the NASB) comes from a strong word in Hebrew (*seghullah*) which means a peculiar or special treasure (cf. the KJV and NEB). Verse 4 employs synonymous parallelism.

Reasons for praising God (vss. 5-18). This section elaborates upon verses 3 and 4. **[5-7]** First, God's greatness is praised. For the phrase **above all gods,** see verses 15-18 and the commentary on 95:3; 96:4-5; 97:7; 115:3-8. **[6]** See the comments on 115:3. **[7]** In verses 6 and 7 God is portrayed as exercising control over nature, a frequent theme in Israel's praise hymns (cf. 104:1-30; 105:16, 26-36, 39-41; 106:9-11, 16-18; etc.). Weather conditions were especially mysterious to the ancients. Where **the clouds** and **the wind** come from was a mystery. How fire (**lightnings**) and water (**rain**) could come out of the same cloud without the one extinguishing the other was a complete mystery. But the psalmist was sure that God made all this possible.

[8-12] God is to be praised as the God of history, as the praise hymns frequently point out. **[8-9]** The plagues of Egypt at the time of the exodus manifested God's power and concern for his covenant people (cf. 78:42-52; 105:26-37). Here only the last and greatest of the plagues is mentioned. **[10-12]** These verses are given in almost identical form in 136:19-22, with a refrain interspersed. The conquering of the territory east of the Jordan, being the first part of the conquest, would be the most difficult (cf. Num. 21). God gave Israel the victory.

[13-14] God is to be praised for his **compassion** on Israel. Historical continuity reveals to Israel that the constancy of God allows them to know what he will do in the future under a given set of circumstances on the basis of what he has done in the past. Synonymous parallelism employs repetition for the sake of emphasis. **O Lord** is in the emphatic position in both lines in the Hebrew text. **Name** and **renown** (or memorial) are synonymous. **For** provides a reason for the declaration of verse 13. The Hebrew word translated **vindicate** is from a root which means to serve as judge or lawyer in a court of law. God will win his case in court! **Have compassion** is better in this context than "repent" (KJV).

[15-18] God is to be praised because he is the only true and living God. See the comments on Psalm 115:3-8 and the excursus on Canaanite Baalism at the end of Psalm 77.

Concluding summons to praise (vss. 19-21). [19-20] Compare 115:9-11, where similar groups are exhorted to trust the Lord, followed by an affirmation of trust (115:12-13), and 118:2-4, where similar groups are exhorted to praise God. See the notes on 115:9-13. **O House of Levi** is an addition here, designating the temple servants who did not officiate at the altar (cf. Num. 4; 1 Chron. 15:1-29; 16:1-6, 37-42). **[21]** Since **Zion** is God's dwelling place, it is **from Zion** that blessings go forth (cf. 132:13-18; 134:3). The psalm ends as it begins with the Hallelujah (cf. 113, 116).

Psalm 136: The Steadfast Love of the Lord

See the opening comment on Psalm 135. This psalm is from postexilic days (see comments on vs. 26), and is composed of three elements interspersed so as to form a beautiful poetic effect. (1) In the introduction (vss. 1-3) and conclusion (vs. 26), phrases descriptive of God's nature emphasize the goodness and greatness of God. (2) The second line of each verse constitutes a refrain which emphasizes the eternal constancy of God's covenant love for Israel. (3) In the main body of the psalm, God's creative acts and his works of providence toward Israel provide the motive for thanksgiving. The acts of creation are traced only through the fourth day, and only partially so at that (vss. 4-9). The acts of providence pertain to the exodus from Egypt and the conquest and settlement of Canaan (vss. 10-24). The concluding verse of the historical retrospect (vs. 25) enlarges upon the greatness and goodness of God by including all flesh as the object of his care.

Invitation to praise (vss. 1-3). **[1]** This verse is lifted from what must have been a common expression used in the liturgy of worship (cf. 106:1; 107:1; 118:1, 29; 2 Chron. 7:3). **[2-3] God of gods** and **Lord of lords** are superlatives used to magnify the divine supremacy of God (cf. Deut. 10:17; 1 Tim. 6:14-16; Rev. 17:14; 19:16).

God's creative power (vss. 4-9). The series of prepositional phrases (infinitive phrases in Hebrew) employed in verses 4-7 emphasizes the close connection between the description of God's nature (vss. 1-3) and divine activity stemming from that nature. Verses 8b and 9b are in apposition to verse 7b. **[4] Great wonders** are those activities which instill awe and admiration in the hearts of men.

[5] By understanding (discernment) God **made the heavens** (cf. 104:24; see notes there). **[6] Spread out** is one of several metaphors used to describe God's creative activity (cf. 104:1-9). The allusion is to the separation of the waters from the dry land on the third day of creation (Gen. 1:9-10). **Upon** might better be translated "above" (cf. the KJV and NASB). **[7] Lights,** in this context, carries the connotation of luminaries. **Great** magnifies their glory and beneficence. **[8-9] Rule,** in the present context, suggests that which controls the intervals of **day** and **night** (cf. Gen. 1:14-19). The allusion is to the fourth day of creation.

Israel's deliverance (vss. 10-22). Infinitive phrases in Hebrew mark the subdivisions (vss. 10, 13, 16, 17).

[10-12] Phraseology from Exodus is employed here and elsewhere to depict the exodus from Egypt. **[10] Smote the first-born of Egypt** refers to the tenth and last plague (cf. Exod. 12:29; Pss. 78:51; 135:8). **[11]** This last plague resulted in the Pharaoh letting Israel go from their midst (cf. Exod. 12:51; Ps. 105:43). **[12]** Metaphors of strength are employed here (cf. Exod. 6:1; 13:9; Ps. 44:3).

[13-15] The miracle at the Red Sea is stated in characteristic poetic form (cf. Exod. 14:21; Ps. 78:13). **[16]** The wilderness journey is summed up with one sweep of the pen. **[17-22]** The conquest of the territory east of the

Jordan magnifies God's power and his care for Israel (cf. 135:8-12).

Summary conclusion (vss. 23-26). [23] God is especially interested in his defenseless people (cf. Pss. 9:12, 18; 10:14, 17-18; 103:14). **[24]** Therefore, he rescues those in distress. **[25]** God's interest extends to all his creatures.

[26] This concluding refrain carries the same force as verses 1-3. This is the only occurrence in the Psalter of God being referred to as **the God of heaven.** The title is found in some of the later OT books (Ezra 1:2; 5:11-12; 6:9-10; 7:12, 21, 23; Neh. 1:4; 2:4; Dan. 2:18, 19, 44; Jonah 1:9) and twice in the NT apocalypse (Rev. 11:13; 16:11). The reference in Jonah might be an exception to the lateness of the expression (cf. Jonah 1:1; 2 Kings 14:25), although the title in Jonah could be an accomodation to the usage of the Assyrians.

Psalm 137: The Memory of Oppression

This community lament must be dated sometime after the beginning of the Babylonian captivity (587 B.C.) and before the destruction of the city of Babylon by Darius I Hystaspes (ca. 520 B.C.; cf. vss. 1-3, 8-9). When the Medo-Persians took over the Babylonian Empire in 539 B.C., Babylon was not destroyed, but a later rebellion caused Darius to destroy the city. Some interpreters believe that the psalm was written shortly after the exiles arrived in Babylon, but others believe it may have been written after the first group of exiles had returned to Jerusalem (538 B.C.) and beheld the city in ruins. The work on the temple was not resumed until 520 B.C. The city wall was not restored until 445 B.C. under Nehemiah's governorship.

The taunting requirement of Judah's captors that the exiles sing the happy songs of Zion only seemed to add to the torment of being separated from the temple services (vss. 1-3). Not only did the exiles refuse to allow their enemies to make a mockery of their songs of Zion, but they vowed their loyalty and love for the holy city (vss. 4-6). Edom is imprecated because of her complicity in the razing of Jerusalem (vs. 7), and Babylon, as the chief devastator of the holy city, is singled out for destruction equal to that which she had administered (vss. 8-9).

Torment in exile (vss. 1-3). **[1] The waters of Babylon** consisted of a series of canals which surrounded the city (cf. Jer. 51:13). The memory of **Zion** and all that she stood for in Israel's covenant relationship to God caused the exiles to weep. **[2] Lyres** are smaller than "harps" (KJV, NASB, NEB), and would much more likely be carried into exile. A relief from Sennacherib's palace in Nineveh portrays three prisoners of war playing lyres before an armed soldier (see Kidner, *Psalms 73–150,* p. 459 and fn 1). **[3]** The mockery of their taunters apparently caused them to refuse to so desecrate their **songs of Zion** as to sing them as amusement for their captors.

Reflection upon Zion (vss. 4-6). **[4]** This may be an allusion to the idea that any land outside Palestine was unclean for an Israelite (cf. Hos. 9:3; Ezek. 4:13).

[5-6] The poetic form adds to the intensity of feeling. The first four lines form an external chiastic (inverted) order, so that lines one and four and two and three correspond. The fifth and sixth lines take on the force of a summary refrain. Since the **right hand** is symbolic of strength, the psalmist is imprecating himself with loss of vitality if he forgets Jerusalem. If he fails to remember Jerusalem in his praises and prayers, may he be so stricken that he cannot speak anything. **Jerusalem** is given preeminence in his thoughts.

Imprecations against Edom and Babylon (vss. 7-9). **[7]** The prophets often cursed Edom for her perpetual anger against Israel, especially in her times of weakness (cf. Isa. 34; Jer. 49:7-11; Amos 1:11-12; Obad.). **[8]** And they cursed **Babylon** for her insatiable greed and oppression (cf. Isa. 13: 46-47; Jer. 51). There are interesting parallels between this verse and Jeremiah 51:56. **You devastator** would better be rendered as "you devastated one." It may be compared with the declaration in Jeremiah that "a destroyer" has come upon Babylon (using the root *shadhadh*). **Who requites you** can be compared with

Jeremiah's "he will surely requite" (using the root *shalam*), and "with the recompense" (using the root *gamal*).

[9] The atrocious act alluded to here was practiced by the Syrians (2 Kings 8:12), the Assyrians (Hos. 10:14; 13:16), the Babylonians (Nah. 3:10), and the Medo-Persians (Isa. 13:16). Doubtless this very general practice had been perpetrated upon Israel (cf. vss. 8-9). The shocking thing is that the psalmist seems to derive so much pleasure from the contemplation of the misery that is in store for **Babylon.** It may well be, however, that he is only desirous that divine justice manifest itself. The sentiment could have been expressed without the apparent gleeful attitude manifested here.

The prophets were God's spokesmen; therefore, they were merely letting God reveal his will through them. Pentateuchal legislation reveals the principle of divine retribution upon the wicked (Exod. 21:23-24; Lev. 24:19-20; Deut. 19:21). However, personal retaliation is forbidden in both the OT (cf. Lev. 19:18; Prov. 24:29; 25:21-22) and the NT (cf. Matt. 5:38-42, 44; Rom. 12:14, 19-21). The psalmist is doubtless employing the covenant lawsuit, in which Israel is the plaintiff and God is the judge and lawyer for the prosecution. God will vindicate his people. The law of *lex talionis* (like for like) is here invoked.

Psalm 138: Thanksgiving for God's Saving Acts

The Greek title places the psalm in the days of Haggai and Zechariah. However, there is nothing in the psalm to reveal the time or specific circumstances which produced it. It sets forth a familiar psalm theme of thanksgiving for God's saving acts, and it inculcates a familiar secondary theme of universalism, that is, that all nations will come to know God through what he has done for Israel. The psalm opens with a declaration of thanksgiving (vss. 1-3), moves on to the expression of faith that all men will profit by God's action toward him (vss. 4-6), and concludes with a declaration of confidence that God will preserve him from his enemies (vss. 7-8).

It is not clear whether this is a personal or community

psalm of thanksgiving. The "**I**" could be used collectively for Israel. the theme lends itself more readily to a community psalm, but if the individual is a corporate personality such as a king, he may well represent the nation's fortunes.

Declaration of thanksgiving (vss. 1-3). **[1]** **O Lord** comes from the Greek; it is omitted in the Hebrew text. **With my whole heart** means with sincerity and full devotion (cf. 111:1). **Gods** (*'elohim*) is translated "angels" in the Greek. However, there is little, if any, clear evidence in the OT for taking the word *'elohim* to mean angels. The Jewish translators of the OT into Greek were influenced by the Hellenistic concept of angels mediating to man the will of a God so transcendently holy that he refused to communicate directly with sinful man. Verse 6 shows that the psalmist did not accept such a viewpoint of God. See the notes on Psalm 82:1. Verse 4 would suggest that **gods** is here used by accommodation for the so-called gods of the heathen. See the notes on 96:4-5; 115:3-8; 135:15-18.

[2-3] **Bow down,** often translated "worship" (cf. the KJV), is frequently used in conjunction with a second word (*kara'*), which means basically to bend the knee (cf. 2 Chron. 7:3; 29:29; Pss. 22:29; 95:6), or with still another term (*qadhadh),* which means basically to bow down in homage (cf. Gen. 24:26, 48; Exod. 34:8). **Steadfast love** (covenant loyalty) and **faithfulness** are two covenant terms commonly used in the psalms. **Faithfulness** better suggests divine activity (cf. vs. 3) than the abstract word "truth" (KJV, NASB). Verse 2 presents a theological problem as it is usually translated. Surely God exalts nothing "above" his name (cf. the RSV note, KJV). "According to" (NASB) is better and is a possible rendering of the Hebrew. The reading "wide as the heavens" (NEB) represents an emendation from the Hebrew term meaning **thy name** (*shimekha*) to that meaning "your heavens" (*shamekha*). The Greek reads, "You have magnified your holy name above everything," omitting the phrase **thy word.** The RSV adds the conjunction **and** before the phrase **thy word. Word** is to be taken in the sense of "promise" (see NEB).

Verse 3 suggests that verse 2 is meant to say that God's **name** (character, nature) is upheld by his keeping his covenant promise to vindicate his faithful ones. The use of the two covenant terms, **steadfast love** and **faithfulness,** also seems to verify this conclusion.

Lesson for the world (vss. 4-6). [4] The Hebrew word rendered **praise** is from the same root rendered **give thanks** (vss. 1, 2). It can also mean "to confess." Grammatically, the verb here could be taken as a future or as a jussive expressing a wish (cf. the NEB). At any rate, the declaration needs to be understood as an expression of hope rather than a direct prophecy. **For** introduces the reason for the nations to give thanks to God; namely, **they have heard the words** of God through communication with Israel, and they have seen the fulfillment of God's promises. This thought frequently provides the motive for petitions in psalms of lament (cf. 9:15-16, 20; 10:17-18; 22:25-31) and for confidence in psalms of thanksgiving or praise (cf. 96:7-13; 98:1-3; 99:1-5). **[5]** Antithetic parallelism contrasts God's intervention on behalf of **the lowly** and against **the haughty. The Lord is high** emphasizes the transcendance (holiness, separateness) of God, and **he regards the lowly** emphasizes his immanence (nearness, interestedness). God is always presented in the Bible as both transcendent and immanent (cf. Isa. 57:15). **Knows** means here to take cognizance of and to act accordingly (cf. Pss. 1:6; 73:11, 18-20, 27).

Confidence in the midst of trouble (vss. 7-8). [7] The psalmist has already been delivered from his recent danger (vs. 3), but he knows that other trials must be faced. Past deliverance gives him confidence for the future. For the expression **thy right hand,** see the notes on 110:1.

[8] The RSV paraphrases the first line which literally reads "will accomplish what concerns me" (NASB; cf. the KJV). The confidence expressed here and the petition in the third line are based on the truth expressed in the second line. Compare the refrain at the end of each verse in Psalm 136. The thought is that God is dependable.

Psalm 139: The God Who Knows Us Perfectly

The Greek title has prefixed the strange phrase "for the end," and the Alexandrinus text has appended the phrase "of Zechariah in the dispersion." Nothing in the text of the psalm gives any insight into the date of composition. There are several Aramaisms in the psalm ("my thoughts," vss. 2, 17; "ascend," vs. 8; "your enemies," vs. 20b, KJV). However, the presence of Aramaisms is not necessarily an indication of a late date of composition.

The psalm is poetically balanced with four paragraphs of six verses each. In the first paragraph (vss. 1-6), the psalmist praises God for his minute knowledge of him, the contemplation of which fills the psalmist with awe (vs. 6). In the second paragraph (vss. 7-12), the psalmist states that God is everywhere the psalmist might go, and God is there to lead and hold him (vs. 10). In the third paragraph (vss. 13-18), the psalmist combines the idea of God's omniscience (vss. 1-6) and omnipresence (vss. 7-12) and applies these divine qualities to God's knowledge of the psalmist's embryonic development (vss. 13-15) and God's planning of the psalmist's life (vss. 16-18). All this contemplation fills the psalmist with a feeling of intimate closeness to God (vs. 18). In the fourth paragraph (vss. 19-24), the psalmist thinks of God as the judge of all the earth and in complete confidence asks God to judge him with a view to his correcting his life so as to please God (vss. 23-24).

There are three key ideas set forth in the psalm. The first is God's intimate knowledge of the psalmist (vss. 1, 2, 4, 6, 14, 23 [twice]). Second, God searches man's ways as a judge scrutinizes evidence which is brought into court (vss. 1, 3, 23-24). It is this perfect judgment of God which gives the psalmist the confidence to entrust his soul to his creator. Third, God is a personal God who is interested in individuals (*passim*). God is not discussed here with academic detachment, but as one who acts on behalf of the psalmist.

God's awesome scrutiny (vss. 1-6). [1] Searched is from a verb which sometimes means to dig for precious metals (cf. Job 28:3). In the context here, it refers to the fact that God discerns the thoughts of man (vs. 2b). The verb is repeated in verse 23, where God is requested to search the heart of the psalmist. In the phrase **and known me,** there is no word for **me** in the Hebrew, although it is found in the Greek. The sense seems to justify it.

[2] **When I sit down** describes man's passive moments or his resting places, and **when I rise up** suggests his active moments or his travels. The two phrases declare that God knows all about the psalmist's day to day activities. **From afar** can mean from God's vantage point in the heavens (cf. 138:6), but here the phrase likely means that God knows our thoughts before we become fully conscious of them.

[3] **Searchest** here is from a word which means to winnow (cf. Ruth 3:2; Isa. 30:24). Sometimes it is used in a negative sense of scattering or dispersing as a chatisement (cf. Jer. 4:11; 15:7; Ps. 44:11), but here it means to trace out carefully. God knows us better than we know ourselves (cf. Amos 4:13). **My path and my lying down** have the same meaning the adverbial clauses "when I sit down and when I rise up" in verse 2. **All my ways** is a literal summary of both verses. Anthropomorphical language is used to communicate the concept of God's constant knowledge of man. God does not have to search out anything to know it any more than he has to look down from heaven to see what we are doing (cf. Pss. 14:2; 80:14; 102:19). [4] This verse might be a protestation of innocence in an effort to vindicate himself before his enemies who have falsely accused him (vss. 19-20), but this is not clear. In all likelihood, the psalmist has a much larger purpose in mind. He is again saying that God knows him better than he knows himself (cf. vs. 2b).

[5] God encompasses (literally "fences in" or "besieges") him and lays his hand upon him in loving care (cf. vs. 10). [6] Contemplation of God's perfect knowledge of him does not frighten the psalmist, but fills him with awe.

God's guiding hand (vss. 7-12). [7] Synonymous parallelism is employed here. In these perfectly balanced lines, **go** and **flee** are to be taken as synonymous, as are **Spirit** and **presence. Spirit** here does not refer to the third person in the godhead and, therefore, should not be capitalized (cf. the KJV and NEB). **Flee** in this passage means no more than **go.** **[8]** This psalm is fond of opposites and these contrasts vivify its salient points (cf. vss. 2a, 3a, 5a, 9, 12). **Heaven** and **Sheol** are spatial opposites here, **heaven** representing the highest heights and **Sheol** the lowest depths of which the psalmist is capable of contemplating (cf. Amos 9:2). The psalmist is aware of God's presence even in **Sheol,** which is an advance upon the thought of most OT writers (cf. Pss. 6:5; 30:9; 88:4-6, 10-12). However, the psalmist does not express any awareness of man's state in **Sheol** beyond that of his contemporaries, and eschatological theological presuppositions based on this passage are unwarranted.

[9] **The wings of the morning** is the spatial opposite of **the uttermost parts of the sea.** The Mediterranean, being to the west of Palestine, came to stand for the direction west. The direction of the sunrise is, of course, east. It is not likely that the psalmist meant to imply any more than this in his phraseology. He may have borrowed mythological language which describes the goddess of the dawn as riding on **the wings of the morning,** as God is said to ride **on the wings of the wind** (cf. 104:3). If such language is intended here, there is no reason to assume that the psalmist accepts the mythological idea in either passage. This would simply be understood as accomodative language employed for the poetic effect of vivid description. It is also possible that the psalmist is reflecting upon the rapidity with which the early morning light reaches from its source in the eastern sky to its destination in the far reaches of the western sky.

[10] This verse shows that the primary intent of verses 8 and 9 is to say that God is everywhere, whether vertical (vs. 8) or horizontal (vs. 9) space be contemplated. God's omnipresence is a source of comfort, not terror.

[11-12] The poet is not trying to hide from God in the darkness. He may have been so accused by his enemies (cf. vss. 4, 19-20), although one should not insist on this interpretation. The psalmist is likely reflecting upon God's presence day and night in order to add a temporal idea to the spatial ideas expressed in verses 8-10.

God's creative power (vss. 13-18). **[13]** **Inward parts** is from a word which means the "reins" (KJV) or kidneys, often used to indicate the lower viscera and the vital organs found there. The reins and heart, in combination, usually translated "heart and mind" in the RSV, refer to the seat of the emotions and the intellect which God examines (cf. Pss. 7:9; 26:2; Jer. 11:20; 17:10; 20:12; Rev. 2:23). Here the word refers to the physical organs. **Knit together** describes the workmanship of a weaver who weaves together a basket or garment (cf. Job 10:11). Here the psalmist describes the intricate handiwork of God.

[14] The Hebrew of verse 14a can be read literally, "I am awesomely wonderful" (Kidner; cf. "wondrously," RSV, Job 37:5). This thought may be paraphrased, "I am fearfully and wonderfully made" (KJV, NASB). The Hebrew of verse 14c literally reads, "And that my soul knows right well" (cf. the KJV and NASB). **[15]** The phrase **intricately wrought** literally means to embroider and adds force to the colorful picture of the handiwork of a skilful weaver (vs. 13b). "Curiously wrought" (KJV) draws its idea from **made in secret. The depths of the earth** is an idiom for the darkness of the womb and does not carry with it here any mythological idea, although the language may stem from a superstitious belief that the fetus was first formed in the earth and then placed in the womb. There is no clear connection here with the forming of the first man from the dust of the earth (Gen. 2:7).

[16] It is not clear whether **every one of them** refers to the various parts of the body which became "formed substance" in contrast to the previously **unformed substance** ("unperfect," KJV, in the sense of incomplete), or **the days that were formed** for the psalmist. "Which in continuance were fashioned" (KJV) and "day by day they were fashioned" (NEB) are unwarranted paraphrases. The Greek here is more confusing than helpful. The Bible clearly teaches that God can, and at least at times does, plan a person's life so as to fulfil the divine purpose (cf. Job

14:5; Jer. 1:5; Acts 9:15; Gal. 1:15-16). However, it is equally clear that man can alter the length of his life by his conduct (cf. Deut. 5:16; Eph. 6:2-3; Prov. 3:1-2, 13-16; 4:10; 9:10-11; 10:27). Also, God may, in answer to prayer, add length of days to one's life (cf. Ps. 21:4; Isa. 38:1-5). The rigid view of fatalism which robs man of responsibility is biblically untenable. That God has a symbolical **book** of remembrance in which he records the deeds of men and other matters is clear (cf. Exod. 32:32-33; Pss. 56:8; 69:28; Mal. 3:16), but that he has there recorded a definitely fixed number of days for each person to live is not clear. The NT speaks of the book of life as a record of those who are God's faithful people (Phil. 4:3; Rev. 3:5; 21:27; etc.; cf. Isa. 4:3).

[17-18] The psalmist breaks forth in exuberant praise as he contemplates the incomprehensibility of God (cf. Job 5:8-9; 26:14; 37:5; Ps. 40:5; Rom. 11:33-36). It is not clear whether verse 18b means to **awake** from sleep or musing (cf. the KJV and NASB; Ps. 17:15; Jer. 31:26), or to "come to an end" (cf. the NEB, RSV note, as from the noun *qets,* "end"). It is not certain that the verb was ever used in biblical Hebrew in the latter sense, although noun forms are used scores of times.

God's just judgments (vss. 19-24). [19-20] These verses seem to imply that the psalmist is presently confronted by such enemies, although this is not absolutely certain. It is not clear whether verse 20b refers to taking God's name in vain (cf. the KJV, NASB, and the present vocalization of the Hebrew text) or to maliciously defying God (RSV, NEB). The Greek translation mistakes the Aramaic word for "your enemies" for the Hebrew word for "your cities," and renders, "They shall take your cities in vain."

[21-22] The **hatred** expressed here need not be taken to mean personal vengeance or malice, but should be understood to mean that one hates the evil and withstands it (cf. Prov. 6:16-19; Hos. 9:15; Rom. 12:9; Heb. 1:9).

[23-24] This sincere petition results from an earnest desire to be right with God, and it expresses complete confidence in the righteousness of God's judgment. The Hebrew word rendered **wicked** means literally "hurtful" or that which causes pain or sorrow (cf. the NASB, NEB, RSV notes). The Hebrew word translated **everlasting** could be rendered "ancient" (NEB), but the rendering of the RSV, which emphasizes the eternal constancy of God's ways, is preferable.

Psalm 140: Prayer for Deliverance

This psalm deals with one of the most familiar themes in the psalms, and for the most part uses familiar metaphors and similes. Wicked men spend their time thinking up ways to ensnare the psalmist (vss. 1-5), but he prays that the day will come when the wicked will be no more (vss. 6-11), and he is fully confident that such a day is coming (vss. 12-13).

Prayer for deliverance (vss. 1-5). [1] Evil men and **violent men** are singular forms in Hebrew (cf. the KJV), but the plural verbs in verses 2 and 3 indicate that these singular forms are used in a collective sense. **[2] Continually** is from a Hebrew phrase which means "all the day," or better here, "every day" (cf. the NEB). **Plan evil things** and **stir up wars** (literally "battles," a plural of intensity) refers here to evil plots to harm the psalmist through slander (cf. vss. 3, 9, 11). **[3]** Mixed similes describe the slanderous **tongue** as being like a sharpened razor or sword (cf. 52:2; 55:21; 57:4; 64:3-4) and like the poison sack of the viper on the back of the lower jaw. The serpent's sharp-pointed tongue is likened to that of the sword or razor. Lying tongues are likened to the stealthily injected venom of a viper or adder (cf. 58:3-4).

[4] Wicked and **violent men** are singular (collective, cf. vs. 1) in Hebrew, but the verb **have planned** is plural. **Guard** and **preserve** are here synonyms. **[5]** This triplet contains three descriptive metaphors. (1) **Trap** ("snare," KJV) and **cords** refer to a trap prepared in the form of a noose hidden in the ground so as to catch the leg (cf. vs. 4c). (2) The **net** was used to catch birds (cf. Prov. 1:17; Hos. 7:12) or sea creatures (Ezek. 32:1-3). It is used figuratively in the case of men (cf. Pss. 9:16; 10:9;

25:15; 31:4; 35:7; 57:6). (3) The **snares** ("gins," KJV) are traps to catch birds (cf. Amos 3:5), or larger animals (cf. Job 40:24), or the word might be used figuratively of the plots of the wicked (cf. Pss. 18:5; 64:5; 69:22; 106:36). Note the similarity to Psalms 141:8-10 and 142:3.

Prayer for destruction of enemies (vss. 6-11). [6] Yahweh (**Lord,** vs. 6a) is the mighty one (**God,** *'elohim*) who can deliver. [7] And as the master (**Lord,** *'adonay)* of the psalmist, he protects him with a helmet **in the day of battle.**

[8] The Hebrew phrase translated **do not further** (cf. the KJV; "promote," NASB) means literally "do not let issue [successfully]" (cf. the NEB). [9] The RSV transposes the last two words in verse 8, putting the *selah* one word earlier, so that verse 9 in Hebrew begins with the words **lift up.** The prayer here is for the principle of *lex talionis* (like for like) to be administered. [10] **Burning coals** (cf. 11:6; 21:9) and **pits** are metaphors of destruction. **No more to rise** refers to death from which there will be no resurrection (cf. 36:12). [11] The second part of the verse refers to the just judgment of God whereby he permits the wicked to destroy themselves (cf. 9:15-16; 34:21).

God will act (vss. 11-13). Faith progresses from simple petition (vss. 1, 4) to bold affirmation (vss. 6-7) to full confidence (vss. 12-13). [12] **Cause** is a word from the law-courts and means a case at law (cf. 9:4; Deut. 17:8) or a principal of conduct under trial (Prov. 29:7; 31:5, translated "rights" in the RSV). **Afflicted** and **needy** are common metaphors used to describe those who trust in the Lord for deliverance in a time of trial. [13] **Righteous** and **upright** are synonymous here, and these words further define the **afflicted** and **needy** of the previous verse. **In thy presence** here refers to God's protecting hand which grants security and serenity (cf. 11:7; 102:28). God's protecting arm gives occasion to the righteous to **give thanks** (cf. 16:11; 17:15; 97:10-12).

Psalm 141: Prayer as Incense

This psalm gives no clue as to its time of composition. The psalmist utters a personal lament begging God to strengthen him so that he will not succumb to the pressures heaped upon him by the wicked to become like them. He prays for the destruction of his enemies as a just retribution from God.

Verses 5-7 contain several textual difficulties which are almost insurmountable. An effort is made in the comments to interpret these verses in harmony with the psalm as a whole, while at the same time emending the text as little as necessary.

Plea for help (vss. 1-2). [1] The cryptic phraseology indicates urgency. The poet pleads with God to hasten to rescue him from present danger. [2] **Incense** was offered at the **evening sacrifice,** as well as at the morning sacrifice, which consisted of the offering of a lamb, a cereal offering, wine, and incense (cf. Exod. 29:38-41; 30:7-8; Num. 28:4-8). **Incense** symbolized the prayers of the saints (Rev. 5:8) and the priestly intercession accompanying their prayers on behalf of the people (cf. Rev. 8:3-4; Exod. 30:10). Solomon understood that acceptable prayers could be offered away from the temple (1 Kings 8:35-36, 37-40, 44-45, 46-53). **Lifting up** the **hands** was a common posture assumed in prayer (cf. 28:2; 134:2).

Prayer for strength (vss. 3-4). [3] **Set a guard** and **keep watch** may well be allusions to the guards and watchmen stationed at the temple (cf. 1 Chron. 15:18, 24; 2 Kings 11:4-8; 2 Chron. 23:1-7). The psalmist desires not to sin in word (cf. 34:13; 39:1; Prov. 13:3; 18:21; 21:23).

[4] He also knows that the **heart** (mind) is the fountain of speech and action; therefore, he prays that he may not succumb to the wickedness about him (cf. Prov. 4:23). To **eat of their dainties** could mean to eat of their delicacies attained through wickedness, or it could suggest the strong temptation to follow the ways of those who used a false hospitality to influence him for evil (cf. Prov. 23:6-8, 20-21; Hos. 7:1-7).

Righteous and wicked influences (vss. 5-7). [5] **Wicked** follows the Greek "sinners" and involves a slight change in Hebrew from *rosh,* "head," to *rasha'.* This makes good sense out of the passage. The rebuke of the **good man**

(literally "righteous man") is more in one's best interest than the flattery of the wicked (cf. Prov. 12:1; 13:18; 20:30; 24:23b-26; 27:6; 28:23; 29:5). Verse 5b is a contrast to verse 5a in our version, which does better than most in rendering the Hebrew. **[6]** The RSV text paraphrases the verse, which reads literally, "when their judges are thrown down by the side of the rock, then they will hear my words, for they are sweet." Apparently this means that when his enemies are being destroyed by being cast against the rocks (cf. 2 Chron. 25:12), they will see the righteousness of the psalmist's prayers. This is what the RSV intends to convey.

[7] Whether the simile refers to cutting wood (cf. the KJV) or to plowing a field, that is, breaking up clods (cf. the NASB), he likens these scattered chips or broken-up clods to "our bones" (MT) being scattered **at the mouth of Sheol.** The RSV reads **their bones** instead of "our bones." The Hebrew can be a reference to the widespread oppression of the righteous. However, since the rest of the psalm deals with personal matters rather than community or national distress, the RSV may have restored the original reading (cf. the NEB).

Seeking refuge in the Lord (vss. 8-10). [8] Yahweh (**Lord**) the mighty **God** (*'elohim*) is an adequate refuge. **Leave me not defenseless** paraphrases the Hebrew (cf. the KJV, NASB, and NEB), which reads, "do not pour out my soul." Apparently this refers to the libation of wine in connection with the evening sacrifice (see vss. 1-2) as a metaphor of the shedding of innocent blood. **[9-10]** For the meaning of these verses, see the notes on 140:4-5, 9.

Psalm 142: The Prayer of the Faint

The title should be compared with that of Psalm 57. It is much more likely that these titles reflect a later analysis of the psalms by pious students than that they are authentic and contemporary with the composition of the psalms. In content, the psalm is similar to the two preceding psalms. Enemies lay a trap for him, but he trusts in God as his refuge.

The God who knows (vss. 1-36). [1] The synonymous

parallelism repeats the phrase **with my voice** to emphasize that he cries aloud. The Hebrew word rendered **supplication** comes from the same root as that translated "grace." The psalmist is begging for God's favor to be manifested toward him in the form of deliverance.

[2] This verse also employs synonymous parallelism. **Complaint** refers to the description of the **trouble.**

[3ab] Perhaps the psalmist means by the word **faint** that he is at his wit's end and does not know how to pray adequately. However, God **knowest** (understands) his **way** (the real intent and desire of his soul; cf. Rom. 8:26-27).

'No man cares for me' (vss. 3c-4). [3cd] See Psalm 140:4-5. [4] If the verbs in the first line be taken as imperatives (cf. the NASB), the psalmist is requesting that someone come to his rescue. The RSV (cf. the KJV and NEB) understands the verbs as infinitive absolutes, "looking" and "watching" used to intensify the force of the verbs. In this case, he is describing his own action. **To the right** suggests the place where a helper would stand (cf. 16:8; 109:31; 110:5; 121:5). No one **takes notice of** him (befriends him, cf. the NEB; Ruth 2:10). **Refuge** here is from a word which means a way of escape (cf. the NASB and NEB). **Cares** is from a word which means to seek after, desire, take interest in.

'God is my refuge' (vss. 5-6b). [5] **Refuge** here means a shelter from storm or danger. **Portion,** here in apposition to **refuge,** means a prized possession or source of great good (cf. 16:5; 73:26). **The land of the living** is the opposite of Sheol, the place of the dead (cf. Pss. 27:13; 52:5 [Hebrew 7]; 116:9). [6] God is compassionate toward those who are **brought very low** (cf. 79:8). The phrase refers to one in a helpless condition.

Prayer for deliverance (vss. 6c-7). [6cd] **They are too strong for me** explicates **I am brought very low** in the preceding line. [7] **Prison** is apparently used metaphorically to indicate trouble from which he cannot extricate himself (cf. Isa. 42:7; Ps. 102:20). **That** indicates a reason for giving thanks, namely, a new saving act, deliverance from prison. **Surround** (cf. the KJV and NASB) fits the context better than "crown" (cf. the NEB). The word can mean to encircle the head with a crown (cf. Esth. 1:11; 2:17; 6:8); here, metaphorically this could refer to the righteous seeing their own triumph in his victory.

Psalm 143: There Is None Righteous

The psalmist makes his plea for deliverance, not on the merit of his own righteousness (vs. 2), but on the basis of God's righteousness (vss. 1, 11). Like Psalms 140–142, this is a personal lament. The psalmist begs God to act on the basis of God's own faithfulness (vs. 1b) and steadfast love (covenant loyalty, vss. 8a, 12a), as well as on the basis of God's compassion toward his suffering servant (vss. 2a, 3-4, 7, 12). God should act for his own name's sake (vs. 11a), and because the psalmist puts his trust in God (vss. 8b, 9b) and prays sincerely to him (vss. 6-7b). The psalmist prays for God to help him do his will (vss. 8cd, 10).

Verses 1-6 contain his complaint, being subdivided into a description of his situation (vss. 1-3) and his reaction to it (vss. 4-6). Verses 7-12 contain his petition, including pleas for deliverance (vss. 7-8b, 9, 11-12), and petitions for spiritual rehabilitation (vss. 8cd, 10).

Plea for mercy (vss. 1-2). **[1]** **Hear** and **give ear** are terms frequently employed in urgent pleas. **Righteousness** is an appositive of **faithfulness,** so that the one word helps to explain the other. The use of **righteousness** with **steadfast love** (covenant loyalty, vss. 11-12) also tempers the meaning of **righteousness** in this context. The word does not mean strict equity or legal justice, for no one could be judged **righteous** (innocent) before God's court (vs. 2). God is faithful to his covenant commitment to his servant (vss. 2a, 12), and he is true to his own **righteousness** (character) in forgiving the penitent sinner. **[2]** "Do not judge me on a legal basis, for I could not come out right." The book of Job also teaches the basic truth that no one is truly or absolutely righteous (Job 4:17; 9:2; 15:14; 25:4). **Righteousness** in the OT often means "salvation," "deliverance," "vindication" (cf. Pss. 51:14; 98:1-3; 103:6; Isa. 45:8; 46:13; 51:5, 8). The OT also teaches that God freely forgives because of his grace (cf. Pss. 32:1-2, 5; 51:1-2; 103:3, 11-13; 130:3-4).

The complaint (vss. 3-4). [3] For connects the following with the preceding and introduces a motive for the above petition. He cannot expect to be delivered from his enemies on his own merit (cf. vs. 11b), but rather appeals to God's loyalty to him. Three metaphors describe the intensity of his suffering. His enemies have relentlessly **pursued** him like an animal in the chase (or this might be taken literally of one pursued in battle), his life is **crushed** like a stone or a clod of dirt broken up (see 141:7), and he is made to **sit in darkness** as if forsaken in Sheol (cf. 88:4-6).

[4] Faints (cf. 77:3; 142:3) is a word which describes one drained of strength and will. **Appalled** describes one numb with pain and unable to function adequately. **Spirit** and **heart** are synonyms for the inner drives and emotions.

Musing on the past (vss. 5-6). [5] The purpose of this reflection is to bolster faith (cf. 42:4-8; 44:1-8). **[6]** Because of this faith he can pray with confidence. Stretching out the hands is symbolic of the soul's upreach to God (cf. Job 11:13; Pss. 44:20; 68:31; 88:9). Thirst is a common metaphor for longing and yearning for God (cf. Pss. 42:1-2; 63:1). **A parched land,** a common sight in Palestine, is a metaphor of a soul whose spiritual thirst is not quenched (cf. 63:1).

Petition for deliverance (vss. 7-8). [7] Make haste is a frequent idiom used to express urgent need for deliverance (cf. 38:22; 40:13; 69:17; 70:1; 71:12). **Hide not thy face** means do not disregard my cause (cf. 27:9; 55:1; 69:17; 89:46; Isa. 1:15). The threat of death is described as going **down to the Pit** (cf. vss. 3, 11a). **[8] In the morning** could be a metaphor for "early" or "soon," or it could be taken literally to mean "let the distress be over by morning" (cf. 30:5; 88:13; 119:147; 130:6). **To thee I lift up my soul** means the same thing as **in thee I put my trust** (cf. 25:1-2). Prayers for God to teach one how to live are not uncommon (cf. vs. 10; 51:6; 119:18, 27, 29, 32, 33, etc.).

'Deliver me and lead me' (vss. 9-10). [9] The second line reads literally "for with thee I have hidden myself," meaning "I have taken refuge in you." [10] God's **good spirit** is his gracious disposition and holy presence with the saints (cf. 51:10-12). The Hebrew phrase translated **level path** means literally "level land" or "upright land" (cf. the KJV). In the first phrase, a land with no obstacles in one's path is indicated. In the second, a land free from defilement is under consideration. Divine leadership to keep him from going astray is intended.

'**Preserve my life**' (vss. 11-12). [11] **For thy name's sake** means for the vindication of your character and **in thy righteousness** means in being true to your commitment. The two expressions are here synonymous. The **trouble** is the danger of death, as the synonymous expression, **preserve my life,** indicates. [12] The second line is synonymous with the first, and the third line assigns a reason for deliverance. **Steadfast love** (covenant loyalty) here indicates God's commitment to his **servant.**

Psalm 144: The King's Praise and Prayer

This psalm is a mosaic of other psalm passages. Apparently it was composed to recount the divine blessings which God had bestowed upon the king (vss. 1-11) and to pray for their continuance (vss. 12-15). It is not clear whether verses 12-15 are a part of the king's prayer or a response by the people.

The king's need of God (vss. 1-4). [1] Compare 18:2, 34 and the notes there. [2] Compare 18:2, 35, 46. These first two verses give God credit for the king's successes.

[3] Compare Psalm 8:4. [4] The brevity of life is variously described in metaphorical language in the Bible (see the notes on 102:3).

Prayer for a theophany (vss. 5-8). In imitation of God's appearance on Sinai, the psalmist presents a poetic description of God's appearing on the scene of battle and bringing victory to the king (cf. 18:7-19). Compare verse 5 with 18:9, verse 6 with 18:14, and verse 7 with 18:16.

[8] For **right hand,** see the notes on Psalm 110:1, 5.

A new song (vss. 9-11). [9] For **new song,** see 96:1; 98:1.

[10] Compare verse 10 with 18:50. [11] Apparently this

reveals that the psalm was composed as a liturgy to be used by a king going out to battle.

Prayer for success (vss. 12-15). [12] The prayer here is for the blessing of human resources, the greatest blessing a king or a nation could possess (cf. 127:3-5; 128:3-4). The metaphors of **plants full grown** and **corner pillars** suggest strength and beauty. **[13]** The blessing of material prosperity is here requested. **Thousands** and **ten thousands** are symbolic numerals used in an ascending scale with greater emphasis on the second numeral. The large numerals used here suggest abundant prosperity. **[14]** This prayer reflects the conditional promises given in Exodus 23:26 and Deuteronomy 28:4. **[15]** This verse reflects the sentiment of 33:12. It is a summary statement reflecting the condition upon which divine blessings would be forthcoming.

Psalm 145: Praise Par Excellence

There is no more beautiful or skilfully structured hymn of praise in the Psalter than this. The alphabetic framework has not appreciably hindered the development of the theme. Each verse begins with the succeeding letter of the Hebrew alphabet. Though the letter *nun* has been omitted in our present Hebrew text, it is included in the Greek and in one Qumran text (11QPs^a). The RSV and NEB include this material in verse 13cd. The added material is identical to verse 17 except for two words: "faithful" (vs. 13c) rather than "just" (vs. 17a), "words" (vs. 13c) rather than "ways" (vs. 17a). "Gracious" (vs. 13d) and "kind" (vs. 17b) come from the same Hebrew word, as do "deeds" (vs. 13d) and "doings" (vs. 17b). It is impossible to know whether the Greek and the Qumran text or the MT represents the original. Other alphabetic psalms are 9–10, 25, 34, 37, 111, 112, 119.

The psalmist borrows statements from several other praise hymns in the Psalter, but they are skilfully woven into the fabric of his theme. The psalm gives the impression of being the product of a studious and pious effort to combine and unify the various praise themes in the Psalter. At any rate, this end result is marvelously achieved. As such, this psalm could well provide a good orientation into the praise themes of the Psalter.

The psalmist skilfully combines praise for God's greatness and goodness in such general and comprehensive terms as to make his psalm applicable to all men of all time. He also returns time and again to a missionary zeal which causes him to want the praise of God to become universal and continual (cf. vss. 4, 6-7, 11-12, 21). The varied gifts and works of God are pointed out in the comments below.

After an opening doxology (vss. 1-3), he praises God for his great works (vss. 4-7) and his great mercies (vss. 8-9). Then he praises God for his universal lordship over men (vss. 10-13b) and for his tender loving care of his creatures (vss. 13c-20). He closes with a reaffirmation of his firm resolve to spread the good news about the marvelous Lord (vs. 21).

The greatness of God (vss. 1-3). [1-2] Extol (exalt, vs. 1a) and **bless** (vs. 1b) are synonymous, as are **bless** (vs. 2a) and **praise** (vs. 2b). The poetic structure defines clearly what it means to **bless** the Lord, namely, to **extol** and **praise** him. **Every day** (vs. 2a) also explains what is meant by **for ever and ever** (vss. 1b, 2b; cf. 34:1; 104:33; 119:44; 146:2).

The Hebrew of verse 1a reads "my God, O King" (cf. the KJV, NASB). The RSV and NEB follow the Greek, which reads "my king," a possible interpretation of the Hebrew idiom. God is referred to as king in the Psalms (and the entire OT) more frequently than by any other figurative connotation. He is most often referred to as king of the universe (cf. 10:16; 29:10; 47:6-7; 95:3-5; 96:10, 13; 97:1, 5, 9; 98:6, 9; 99:1-2). He is infrequently designated Israel's king (cf. Isa. 41:21; 43:15; Zeph. 3:15; Ps. 149:2; possibly Ps. 89:18, but see the notes there). Several times he is designated as the personal king of individual psalmists (cf. 5:2; 44:4; 68:24; 74:12; 84:3). The universal rule of God is the paramount biblical concept. From this it could easily be deduced that in a special way God is king over his covenant people, Israel. And even in a more special way, he is king over those righteous individuals within the cove-

nant nation who willingly and fully surrender to his lordship in obedience.

[3] This verse reflects 48:1 and 96:4. **Unsearchable**
means "unfathomable" (NEB). Man is incapable of fully
comprehending the greatness of God (cf. 40:5; 116:12;
147:5).

God the Mighty One (vss. 4-7). [4] **Mighty acts** should be
compared with "wondrous works" (vs. 5) and "terrible
acts" (vs. 6). The first word refers to those divine acts
which reveal the power of God, the second describes
God's works which cause wonder and amazement in the
minds of men, and the third suggests those acts of God
which cause man to stand in awe of him. Israel was much
concerned that these divine acts should be remembered
generation after generation (cf. 22:30-31; 45:17; 48:12-14;
78:1-8; 79:13; 89:1; 102:18-22).

[5] Verse 5a reads literally "the splendor of the glory of
your majesty." All three terms are royal terms applied to
God's role as king (cf. vs. 12; 21:5; 96:6, 10; 104:1, 31).

[7] **Goodness** and **righteousness** refer to God's faithfulness in keeping his covenant commitments (cf. 31:19-20;
143:1). **Pour forth** is from a word which often refers to
waters flowing from a fountain, and is used here metaphorically of words which flow in abundance from a heart
which is full (cf. Prov. 18:4; Pss. 78:2; 119:171). **Fame** literally means "memorial." God will be remembered in Israel's
praises.

God is compassionate (vss. 8-9). [8] This verse repeats
almost verbatim God's self-revelation to Moses (Exod.
34:6). With slight variations, the Exodus passage is also
reflected in many other passages (cf. Num. 14:18; Neh.
9:17; Pss. 86:15; 103:8; 111:4; 112:4; Joel 2:13; Jon. 4:2).
Meditation upon these passages will reveal how much the
OT, as well as the NT, emphasizes the grace, mercy, and
love of God. (See the excursus at the end of Ps. 86.)

[9] God's goodness is not only equated with his righteousness (vs. 7), but also with his compassion. The universal interest of God in his creatures is a common theme
in the psalms (cf. 100:5; 104:27-28; 136:25).

God the eternal King (vss. 10-13b). **[10]** **Give thanks** and **bless** are synonymous here (cf. vss. 1-2). **All thy works** is from the same Hebrew phrase as "all that he has made" (vs. 9b), with the exception of the pronouns. In this context, the word **saints,** apparently synonymous with **works,** seems to limit the meaning to rational beings.

[11-12] Terms similar to those used in verses 4-7 are here applied to God's ruling as king. **[13]** This verse is reflected in Daniel 4:3 [3:33 in Aramaic]. In all likelihood, Daniel couches Nebuchadnezzar's confession in words familiar to Israel. It seems likely that the psalmist borrows from Daniel as he also borrows from other OT passages. Those who insist on Davidic authorship of the psalm will of necessity conclude that Daniel borrowed from the psalm. The full force of Daniel's teaching (as well as that of the Psalms) concerning the **everlasting kingdom** was not felt until after the OT canon was closed. Intertestamental writings (e.g., First Enoch) developed the idea, but the teaching of Christ and the apostles brought the concept to fruition. The concept of the after-life went through the same developmental stages.

God the universal Provider (vss. 13c-20). **[13cd]** See the introduction concerning this addition. This strophe says nothing uncommon about God. It employs synonymous parallelism and can serve as a general introduction to the paragraph. **[14]** All four verbal forms are participles in Hebrew. **Upholds** and **raises up,** as participles, emphasize the continuance of the action in present time. **Falling** and **bowed down** probably should be taken as potential participles setting forth the conditions which give rise to the divine activity. The word for **bowed down** can be used of a reed or rush which is bent over to the ground (cf. Isa. 58:5). The word-picture is of a fallen, stooped person who needs someone to raise him up and support him along the way. Metaphorically, the words describe those in desperate need of help. **[15-16]** These verses reflect 104:27-28. The verbal forms in verse 16 are participles in Hebrew. The participles emphasize the continuance of the action and possibly also modify or explicate the thought of verse 15.

The NEB catches this nuance beautifully with the paraphrase "with open and bountiful hand."

[17] **Just** (righteous, *tsaddiq*) and **kind** (gracious, *chasidh*) are synonyms here. The first term technically means what is right, just, and fair. The second term refers to one who is faithfully keeping covenant. The NEB catches the thought of the second term with the word "unchanging." It is the same word as in verse 13d. The only other time it is applied to God in the OT is in Jeremiah 3:12. Many times the word is used of Israel as God's covenant people.

[18] **Near** is an adjective which in Hebrew means friendly toward or interested in another, sympathetic, entering into the very midst of the situation. **In truth** means genuinely, sincerely. Here it refers to that which is genuine prayer rather than a mechanical, heartless performance.

[19-20] **All who fear him** (vs. 19a) is to be equated with **all who love him** (vs. 20a; cf. 33:8, 18). Reverence and devotion are the two essential ingredients of acceptable worship. Fear of the Lord involves obedience (cf. 103:17-18). This thought explicates verse 20b. **The wicked** refuse to honor and obey the Lord. God's righteousness and holiness demand that the impenitent wicked be punished (cf. Isa. 5:15-16; 32:16-17).

Reaffirmation of praise (vs. 21). The psalmist desires that his firm resolve to **speak the praise of the Lord** be shared by **all flesh. Praise** and **bless** are synonymous (cf. vss. 1-2, 10). **All flesh** means here all rational beings (cf. vs. 10).

Psalm 146: God, the Only Sufficient Help

Each of the last five psalms in the Psalter begins and ends with the imperative exclamation "Praise the Lord (Heb. *hallelujah*)!" These psalms, like Psalms 113–118 (the Egyptian Hallel) and 135–136 (The Great Hallel), are known as Hallel (Praise) Psalms.

Psalm 146 is like 144 and 145 in that it borrows freely from other psalms. It would appear that the last five psalms were meant to summarize the composite elements of Israel's praises, and, as such, they serve as a beautiful conclusion to a wonderful collection of songs.

The psalm begins with a firm resolve to praise God continually (vss. 1-2) and closes with an affirmation of God's eternal reign (vs. 10). The insufficiency of man's help (vss. 3-4) is contrasted with the sufficient (vss. 5-7b) and kind (vss. 7c-9) help of the Lord.

Resolve to praise (vss. 1-2). The progression of thought in these two verses is emphasized by the structure of the psalm. **[1] Praise the Lord!** (vs. 1a), a plural imperative in Hebrew, is addressed to the community of worshipers. The second **Praise the Lord!** (vs. 1a), a singular imperative, is addressed to himself as an exhortation (cf. 103:1; 104:1).

[2] Next, in his resolve he changes to an imperfect (future) singular, **I will praise** (vs. 2a). All these expressions involve the same Hebrew word for **praise**. He reaches a grand climax with the phrase **I will sing praises** (vs. 2b), emphasizing the method of praising God by employing a different word. For the thought of verse 2, see 63:4 and 104:33.

Man's insufficient help (vss. 3-4). This paragraph, by contrast, enhances the next by setting forth the subject of trust from a negative standpoint, whereas the following paragraph sets forth hope in God from a positive standpoint.

[3] Princes is from a word which means conspicuous or influential ones, and may refer to leaders or rulers in various functions. Psalm 82 presents the case of wicked princes who were failing to provide justice (cf. 146:7ab). Here the psalmist seems to be reflecting upon human limitations rather than the wickedness of men. **No help** means no sufficient or perfect help. The comparative parallelism of 118:8-9 shows that limited help might be received from man or from princes, but that it is better to put one's trust in God who is unlimited in power and goodness. **A son of man** (not "the son of man," KJV) indicates man in his weakness or earthiness (cf. "mortal man," NASB). **[4] His earth** is very expressive and involves a wordplay in Hebrew. The Hebrew word for **man** (vs. 3b) is *'adham,* and the word for **earth,** *'adhamah.* Genesis 3:19, in pronouncing the divine curse on man for his sin, equates **man** (*'adham*) with the **dust** (*'aphar*). Man (*'adham*) made in the image of God is a glorious creation (cf. Gen. 1:26-31; Ps. 8:3-8), but man in his sin and subject to death is somewhat less glorious by comparison. How very much less glorious is he than his Creator! The earth is **his** [man's] **earth** because he was taken from it and returns to it. **His plans** [or "purposes"] **perish** or come to an end at his death; therefore, man's help at best is temporal.

God's all-sufficient help (vss. 5-7b). [5] This is the last of the twenty-six beatitudes in the Psalter, sometimes translated **happy is** and sometimes rendered "blessed is." In the Psalter, blessings are pronounced upon the righteous and obedient (1:1; 89:15; 106:3; 119:1, 2), on those forgiven (32:1, 2), on those whose God is the Lord (33:12; 144:15b; 146:5), on those who take refuge in the Lord (2:12; 34:8) and trust him (40:4; 84:12), who recognize that their strength is in the Lord (84:5), who accept God's chastening and instruction (94:12), who fear the Lord (112:1; 128:1, 2), and who consider the needs of the poor (41:1). In a special way, those are blessed who have been chosen to minister at the temple (65:4; 84:4), and those who have large families (127:5). God often blesses man with prosperity (144:15a). In an imprecation, a blessing is pronounced upon the devastator of Babylon (137:8, 9). **Hope** (vs. 5b) and "trust" (vs. 3a) are synonymous in this context (cf. Heb. 11:1). Verse 5 is in contrast to verse 3.

[6-7] The Hebrew participles (relative clauses in English) employed here are in the emphatic position, placing stress on the divine action and its continuance. The God **who made heaven and earth, the sea, and all that is in them** can surely bless his creatures (cf. 115:15; Matt. 6:25-34). That God **keeps faith** (better than "truth," KJV) **for ever** means that he is always reliable. God helps the defenseless because they cannot help themselves.

The Lord is kind (vss. 7c-9). The phrase **the Lord** begins each of the five clauses in verses 7c-9a, thus laying stress on the fact that it is God who provides these things.

[7c] Sets the prisoners free might be taken literally of God's setting free the innocent person wrongly imprisoned (cf. Gen. 41:14; Ps. 105:16-22; Acts 5:17-20; 16:25-34), or metaphorically of those delivered from captivity (Isa. 42:7; 61:1-2) or set free from their sins (Luke 4:18-19). **[8] Opens the eyes of the blind** could be taken either literally (cf. John 9:1-7) or figuratively (cf. John 9:39-41). However, since no miracle of healing the physically blind is recorded in the OT, it is likely that the psalmist is thinking in metaphorical terms (cf. Isa. 6:10-12; 32:1-3; 35:5-7; 42:16, 18-25). For the clause **The Lord lifts up those who are bowed down,** see 145:14. **The Lord loves the righteous** reveals the fact that if the afflicted would be blessed of God, they must be willing to humble themselves in obedience (cf. Isa. 9:17).

[9ab] Sojourners, the widow, and **the fatherless** are often grouped together in Deuteronomy as objects of God's special care, and Israel is enjoined to be generous toward them, remembering the deliverance which God had granted the nation in her helpless state in Egypt (cf. Deut. 10:18-19; 14:28-29; 16:9-12, 13-15; 24:17-18, 19-22; 26:12-13; 27:19).

[9c] See the notes on 145:20b and compare 147:6.

God's eternal reign (vs. 10). Since **the Lord will reign for ever** (vs. 10a), men should praise him always (vs. 2). The concept of the eternal reign of God was first enunciated by Miriam as she led the women of Israel in a triumphant victory song (Exod. 15:18). The idea is repeated frequently (cf. Pss. 10:16; 29:10; 45:6=Heb. 1:8-9; 66:7; 145:13; Isa. 9:6-7; Dan. 2:44; 4:34 [31 in Aramaic]; 7:13-14; Mic. 4:7; Luke 1:33; 2 Pet. 1:11; Rev. 11:15; 22:5). **Zion** here, by metonymy, stands for the nation, Israel. The psalm ends, as it began, with the Hallelujah!

Psalm 147: God, the Builder of Israel

For the beginning and ending, see the introduction to Psalm 146. This psalm focuses attention on three works of God which make him praiseworthy. First, he is the builder of Jerusalem (vss. 1-6). Second, he is the sustainer of the universe (vss. 7-11). Third, he is the God of Zion (vss. 12-20). Verses 19-20 indicate that the security of Jerusalem, by synecdoche, stands for the security of the nation (cf. 48:11). The threefold summons to praise or thanksgiving (vss. 1, 7, 12) reveals the structure of the psalm.

The poetic structure in Hebrew is both striking and informative. Practically all the verb forms, with the exception of verse 20a and possibly verse 13, need to be translated by the English present tense. The psalmist is vividly describing action taking place at the very time he writes. In verses 3, 6, and 8, each line begins with a participle which lays stress on the continuance of the action. In verses 11 and 19, the one participle is related to both lines. In verses 2, 4, 9, 14, 15, 16, and 17, a participle begins the first line and an imperfect ends the second line (except that in vs. 15b the verb is next to the last word). The inverted form in which the word order is reversed in the two lines lays stress on both the action and objects of the verbs. The imperfect, preceded by a participle, is to be taken as a frequentative imperfect and translated by the English present tense. The two imperfects in verses 10 and 18 should also be rendered as present tense, in light of the context. No verbs are written in verses 1 and 5, but the context suggests that the present tense be supplied. The two perfects of verse 13 might be taken as indicating completed action (KJV, NASB), but again, in light of the context, are probably perfects of certainty and thus are to be translated in present tense. The summonses to praise the Lord in verses 1, 7, and 12, and at the end of the psalm are imperatives indicating an exhortation in each case. The perfect tense of verse 20a is used in the sense of a Greek perfect indicating action of the past with results continuing to the present. The perfect of verse 20b is a stative and, as such, should be translated in present tense.

The rebuilding of Jerusalem (vss. 1-6). [1] This introductory verse shows why it is appropriate to praise God. For **gracious,** see 135:3. The first **for** may assign a reason, although the Hebrew particle could also be translated "surely" (NASB). The second **for** definitely assigns a reason for what is said in the preceding line. **Seemly** ("becoming," NASB) is from a word which basically means desire. Though usually used in a bad sense of lust (cf. 10:3), it is occasionally used in a good sense of God's desire (cf. 132:13-14) or man's (cf. 10:17; 38:9). **[2] Builds up,** a participle, and **he gathers,** an imperfect, suggest that the rebuilding of the city was in progress when the psalm was written (cf. Ezra 1–2 and Neh. 6–7). The word for **builds up** can mean either "build" or "rebuild" (cf. 51:18-19; 102:13-17). **Outcasts,** in the emphatic position in Hebrew, refers here to those who had been in captivity (cf. Isa. 56:8). **[3] Brokenhearted** describes these exiles as having been in a state of dejection (cf. Isa. 61:1; Ps. 137:1-6). **Their wounds** probably refers metaphorically to healing the sin-sick people (cf. Isa. 1:5-6; Jer. 30:12-13; Hos. 5:13-14; Mic. 1:9; Jer. 30:17). **Heals** and **binds up** are Hebrew participles indicating continuing action.

[4] The psalmist here enlarges his thoughts to show God's control of the vast universe. **Determines** is a Hebrew participle indicating continuing action. Though man cannot number the stars (cf. Gen. 15:5), God knows their number, for he created them. **He gives** (literally "he calls") is a Hebrew imperfect which, following a participle, is to be rendered in present tense. The psalmist may be alluding to the original creation in part, but he is not content to leave the matter there. God continues to control and utilize his creation to serve his purpose. Notice the same shifting from past creative acts to continuing divine control in 104:1-23. **Determines the number** and **gives . . . their names** here means that God determines the function of each star. The Hebrew word for **name** includes the idea of character or function (cf. Gen. 2:19-23).

[5] The works of God which are enumerated above prove that he is **great** and **abundant in power. His understanding,** or wisdom, by which he created and sustains the universe, **is beyond measure** (cf. 104:24; 136:5; Job 28:12-28). **[6]** The paragraph closes with a return to God's acts of kindness (cf. vss. 2b, 3). **The downtrodden** can refer to the afflicted and the humble. **Lifts up** is another participle indicating continuing action, as is **he casts.** For the contrast between the righteous and the wicked, see 145:20 and 146:9. Antithetic parallelism stresses the contrast between God's treatment of the righteous and the wicked. **He casts to the ground** is the opposite of **lifts up.**

God sustains his creation (vss. 7-11). [7] The Hebrew text shows the synonymous parallelism by using the same preposition in both lines. The verse reflects the thought of 98:4-6. [8-9] The verbs in verses 8-9a are participles indicating continuing action and that in verse 9b is an imperfect used with the force of a present tense. God, the Creator, cares for his creation (cf. 104:10-15; 145:15-15).

[10-11] These two verses employ external antithetic parallelism. The two lines of verse 10 are synonymous, as are the two lines of verse 11. Thus each verse contains a single thought. The thought of verse 11 is in contrast to that of verse 10. **The legs of man** suggests strength as in the parallel phrase, **the strength of the horse. Delight** and **pleasure** are synonymous. **Those who fear him** (reverence him) are **those who hope in his steadfast love** (covenant loyalty; cf. 33:8, 18; 145:19-20). God does not **delight** in (Hebrew "glory in") any manifestation of the strength of his creatures, but rather in the voluntary loving devotion of those who thus glorify God.

The God of Zion (vss. 12-20). [12] Synonymous parallelism again employs repetition for emphasis (cf. vs. 7). **Jerusalem** and **Zion** are metonyms for the people.

[13-14a] The result obtained in the building and fortifying of Jerusalem (cf. vs. 2) is that the parents feel that their children are secure. Verse 14a in Hebrew is much more expressive than our English versions. It reads, "He makes your borders peace." **Peace** *(shalom)* is doubtless a play on the word **Jerusalem,** the latter part of which comes from the same Hebrew word (cf. 76:1-6; 122:6-9).

[14b-18] God brings on the **snow** and **ice** of winter and the thawing in the springtime. Only in the area of Mount Hermon would people in Palestine be accustomed to seeing much **snow** and **ice.** The unusual nature of these phenomena around Jerusalem may have caused the psalmist to refer to these items as things which would arrest the attention of people there. **His ice** and **his cold** (vs. 17) and **his word** and **his wind** (vs. 18) lay stress on the fact that God causes both the freezing and the thawing.

[19-20] **Word** here refers to God's **statutes and ordinances**

which revealed his will for **Israel,** here called **Jacob.** In this respect, Israel was a favored nation, for God had not given any such detailed revelation of himself to **any other nation.** Israel often forgot the responsibilities which went with that privilege (cf. Amos 3:1-2).

Psalm 148: A Chorus of Praise Enjoined

The last five psalms in the Psalter give evidence, by their comprehensiveness, of having been composed or placed here to serve as a conclusion to the Psalter. In Psalm 148 the whole creation, animate and inanimate, is called upon to praise God.

The psalm is naturally divided into two parts by the poetic structure. First, the summons goes out to **praise the Lord from the heavens** (vs. 1) and then **from the earth** (vs. 7). Next, in each section certain persons and things which inhabit **the heavens** (vss. 1b-4) and **the earth** (vss. 7b-12) are addressed in the second person and exhorted to praise God. Finally, in each section a partial refrain is uttered in the third person in which reasons for praising God are stated (vss. 5-6, 13-14). The psalmist moves from conscious (vs. 2) to unconscious (vss. 3-4) praise and then from unconscious (vss. 7b-10) to conscious praise (vss. 11-12). The climax is reached in verse 14 where there is an apparent allusion to restoration from exile.

Praise from the heavens (vss. 1-6). For the beginning and ending, see the introduction to Psalm 146. **[1] Heavens** and **heights** are synonyms used here to indicate the dwelling place of the **angels** (vs. 2) and the heavenly bodies (vs. 3).

[2] Angels and "host" are here synonymous. The word **host** can refer to the heavenly bodies (cf. Deut. 4:19), but the parallel structure here suggests that it refers to **angels** (cf. Josh. 5:14-15; 1 Kings 22:19). **[3] Sun and moon,** the most prominent heavenly bodies to the eye, are mentioned first, followed by the innumerable **stars** (cf. 147:4, see notes). **[4]** The Hebrew expression rendered **highest heavens** literally means "heavens of heavens," a Hebrew superlative which could have a spatial or qualitative connotation (cf. Pss. 8:1; 113:4). Solomon knew that even the highest heaven cannot contain God (1 Kings 8:27). **Highest heavens** is parallel with the **waters above the heavens,** referring to the Genesis creation account (Gen. 1:6-8).

[5] The reason that these inanimate things of the heavens should praise God is that God by his mere command called them into being (cf. Gen 1:3, 6; Ps. 33:6, 9).

[6] **Bounds** can refer to the boundaries of things or to laws given to man. The Hebrew phrase translated **be passed** literally means "pass over" or "transgress." Here a passive rendering better fits the context, which refers to inanimate creation. The word **bounds** may refer literally to that which God made for the seas (cf. Jer. 5:22; Prov. 8:29; Job 38:10; cf. Ps. 104:9, where a different Hebrew word is used). The thought is that God controls the universe which he created. This is the meaning of **he established them** (literally "caused them to stand"). Jeremiah (31:35-36; 33:25) thinks of these "ordinances" as being tantamount to a covenant between God and his creation.

Praise from the earth (vss. 7-14). [7] **Sea monsters** (cf. Gen. 1:21) and the **deeps** suggest the lowest parts of the earth. [8] In an ascending scale, he thinks of that which fills the atmosphere, **fire** (lightning) and **hail,** etc. **Fulfilling his command** emphasizes that God controls weather conditions. [9] The majesty of **mountains** and **hills** and the beneficient value of **fruit trees** and **cedars** glorify God. [10] Animals are the creatures closest in nature to man, so this verse prepares us for what follows.

[11-12] People of all classes, high and low, young and old, should praise God.

[13] In this verse a reason for mankind to praise God is given. **His name** refers to God's character and reputation manifested in his creative and saving acts. **Above** here means greater than. [14] This is the grand climax. **His people, his saints** (loyal ones), and **the people of Israel** are all synonymous here. **Raised up a horn** means that God has provided strength for his people in the form of deliverance (cf. Deut. 33:17; 1 Sam. 2:1; Pss. 89:17; 132:17). **Are near to him** literally reads "are of his nearness" in the Hebrew.

God's condescending love which brought him near to his covenant people is in mind (cf. 119:151; Isa. 55:6).

Psalm 149: Let Israel Praise the Lord

This psalm takes up the thought of verse 14 in the preceding psalm and elaborates upon what God has done for Israel. It doubtless pertains to the period of restoration following the return from Babylonian captivity. Verses 6-9 might be taken in a historico-eschatological sense, looking to complete victory on the Day of the Lord. See the excursus on imprecations in the Psalms at the end of Psalm 79.

Praise for victory received (vss. 1-4). [1] For the significance of the **new song,** see on 96:1-2; 98:1-3; 144:9-10, where the idea of a victory song is in the forefront. However, any fresh act of kindness from God should occasion new songs of praise (cf. 33:3; 40:1-3). Three times in the psalm **the faithful** (*chasidim*) are mentioned (vss. 1, 5, 9). Since these are the loyal, pious ones, it is not appropriate to think of them as bloodthirsty men who hold hatred in their hearts toward their enemies (cf. vss. 6-9). The song is to be sung **in the assembly** so that all can benefit by it.

[2] **His Maker** is plural in Hebrew, a plural of intensity or majesty. Israel was created as a nation by God (cf. 95:6; Isa. 45:5, 11; 51:12-13; 54:5; Hos. 8:14). Though Israel had forsaken her **Maker** and had been disciplined through exile, when she repented, God took her back to himself and restored her. For **their king,** see on 145:1. **Sons of Zion** is parallel to **Israel.** By metonymy, the phrase stands for the people of Israel.

[3] The religious dance was especially appropriate in a time of victory and great jubilation (cf. Exod. 15:20; Judg. 11:34; 1 Sam. 18:6; 2 Sam. 6:14; Jer. 31:4). [4] For **takes pleasure in,** see 147:11. **The humble,** parallel to **his people,** may refer to those afflicted because of their sins (cf. 107:17; 119:67, 71, 75) or to those who humble their hearts in the meekness of obedience (cf. 25:9-10; 37:10-11; 147:6). Probably both ideas are in the present passage. The humiliation of exile led them to a state of penitence. The Hebrew

word translated **victory** means literally "salvation," but the context justifies the translation.

Praise for victory anticipated (vss. 5-9). [5] For the faithful, see verse 1. **Glory** doubtless here refers to the restoration of Israel's honor after the return from captivity (cf. Isa. 43:4; 49:5). **Couches** were places for relaxation and meditation, but in times of distress became a further reminder of the people's grief (cf. 4:4; 6:6). To be able to **sing for joy on their couches** would indicate a state of tranquility.

[6-8] These verses may refer to a ritual celebration of victory at the temple. [7] **Vengeance** is equated with **chastisement,** and, therefore, refers to the just judgment of God rather than a feeling of personal hatred on the part of the people. God had promised to take vengeance on Israel's enemies (cf. Isa. 61:1-4; 63:4-6). The Day of the Lord which the preexilic prophets declared was coming upon the covenant people, Israel, to discipline them (cf. Amos 5:18-20; Joel 1:15; 2:1-2, 11; Zeph. 1:1–2:4) would eventually be turned into a day of judgment against their enemies and a day of deliverance for Israel (cf. Isa. 34:8-17; Joel 2:31-32; ch. 3; Zeph. 3:8-20). Because of the universalistic language used in these redemption passages, these promises in time took on an eschatological interpretation, looking to the day when God would banish Israel's enemies from her presence for ever. In the NT the thought is applied to the final victory of the saints and the eternal destruction of the wicked (1 Thess. 5:1-11; 2 Thess. 1:5-10; 2:1-12). How much of this idea the psalmist understood is impossible to determine, but it is not at all likely that he is here speaking of the concept of final judgment.

[9] **The judgment written** may be the sentence kept in store in God's book of records (cf. Isa. 65:6-7; Dan. 7:10), or that recorded in the Law and the Prophets (cf. Deut. 32:40-43; Isa. 45:14; 49:7, 23). The NT sets forth the idea of the final judgment of men on the basis of what is written (Rev. 20:12).

Psalm 150: A Swelling Chorus of Praise

This psalm is a most wonderful conclusion to the book of

Psalms, which in Hebrew carries the title "Praises." The psalm is obviously liturgical and alludes to the various performances of the priests and Levites and possibly the people in the worship assemblies. The psalm answers four basic questions about praise: Where (vs. 1)? Why (vs. 2)? How (vss. 3-5)? Who (vs. 6)?

Where should God be praised (vs. 1)? The verse employs synonymous parallelism, which means that **his sanctuary** and **his mighty firmament** are the same. **Firmament** is a synonym of heaven (Gen. 1:6-8). The psalmists often picture God as symbolically dwelling in the earthly **sanctuary** in Jerusalem (cf. 20:2; 63:2; 68:24; 78:68-69; 80:1; 99:1; 132:13-14), but they also recognize that he dwells in the heavens (cf. 2:4; 14:2; 20:6; 33:13; 80:14; 85:11; 102:19; 103:19; 115:3; 123:1). It is not clear whether it is angels (cf. 148:1-2) or men who are here exhorted to praise God, who dwells in the heavenly sanctuary. The latter understanding seems preferable.

Why should God be praised (vs. 2)? The Hebrew word translated **for** (Heb. *be*, not *ki*) might also be rendered "in," meaning "in keeping with" or "according to," to correspond with the second line which uses a different particle (*ke*). In any case, both lines seem to assign reasons for praising God. For **mighty deeds**, see 106:2; 145:5, 12. For **greatness**, see 145:3.

How should God be praised (vss. 3-5)? The most complete list of musical instruments used in Israel's worship to be found anywhere in the OT is given here. Perhaps each group began to play upon their instruments at the time they were announced, so that the effect would be an ever-increasing chorus of praise. The **trumpet** here is the Hebrew *shophar,* the ram's horn or goat's horn, not to be confused with the silver trumpet (Num. 10:2). The *shophar* might be used for giving signals (cf. Judg. 3:27; 1 Kings 1:34, 39; Isa. 18:3), but was also employed in worship (cf. 47:5-7; 98:6). The silver trumpets were blown by the priests in the worship assemblies (cf. Num. 10:10; 1 Chron. 15:24; 16:6, 42; 2 Chron. 5:12; 29:26). The *shophar* was apparently generally not used in conjunction with other instruments except to increase their noise (1 Chron. 15:28; 2 Chron. 15:14). Apparently the *shophar* was not generally blown by laymen (but see 2 Kings 11:14; 2 Chron. 23:13).

The **lute** ("psaltery," KJV) is a stringed instrument made of wood, with gut strings which were plucked with the hand, or an instrument of ivory or metal. **Harp** (*kinnor*, usually translated "lyre" in the RSV, is a small stringed instrument, which was portable (cf. 137:2). The **timbrel** is a percussion instrument usually played by women (cf. Exod. 15:20; Judg. 11:34; Ps. 68:25). For the religious **dance,** see 149:3. **Strings** seems to be a generic term which might be applied to a variety of instruments. **Pipe** ("organs," KJV) refers to a wind instrument used on very happy occasions (cf. Job 21:12; 30:31). **Sounding cymbals** were apparently made of brass and had a low-pitched sound (cf. 1 Chron. 15:19; 16:5); **clashing cymbals** had a shrill sound. The Levites played the harps (*nebhalim*), lyres, and cymbals (1 Chron. 15:16; 2 Chron. 29:25). Whether the other instruments were restricted to priests and Levites is not clear.

Who should praise the Lord (vs. 6)? Everything that breathes could include animals (cf. 148:7, 10), but it is not certain that they are intended to be included here (see on 145:21). Some have thought that this psalm provides a doxology to Book V of the Psalter (cf. 41:13; 72:18-19; 89:52; 106:48). It could easily serve as a doxology not only to the last section but to the entire book.